DANCING IN THE DARK

Youth, Popular Culture, and the Electronic Media

---

by

Quentin J. Schultze—Project Coordinator
Roy M. Anker—Project Editor

James D. Bratt
William D. Romanowski
John William Worst
Lambert Zuidervaart

Calvin Center for Christian Scholarship

WILLIAM B. EERDMANS PUBLISHING COMPANY
GRAND RAPIDS, MICHIGAN

Copyright © 1991 by Wm. B. Eerdmans Publishing Co.
255 Jefferson Ave. S.E., Grand Rapids, Mich. 49503

Printed in the United States of America

Reprinted, February 1991

Library of Congress Cataloging-in-Publication Data

Dancing in the dark: youth, popular culture, and the electronic media /
    by Quentin J. Schultze . . . [et al.].
        p.   cm.
    Includes bibliographical references and index.
    ISBN 0-8028-0530-2 (paper)
    1. Mass media and youth—United States.   2. United States—Popular
culture.   I. Schultze, Quentin J. (Quentin James), 1952-   .
HQ799.2.M35D36   1990
305.23'083—dc20   90-45977
                                                           CIP

The authors and publisher gratefully acknowledge permission to reprint
copyrighted material granted by the publishers listed on p. 348.

28758
n/92

Contents

CONTRIBUTORS   vii

PREFACE   ix

1. The Big Chill:
   Adults, Youth, and Popular Culture   1

2. From Revivalism to Rock and Roll:
   Youth and Media Historically Considered   14

3. Lost in Time and Space:
   Youth in an Electronic Culture   46

4. Risky Business:
   Youth and the Entertainment Industry   76

5. Consuming Visions:
   Popular Art in Consumer Capitalism   111

6. The Heart of Rock and Roll:
   The Landscape of a Musical Style   146

7. Rocking to Images:
   The Music Television Revolution   178

8. Looking at Teen Films:
   History, Market, and Meaning   211

9. Chasing the Grail:
    Youth in a Culture of Leisure   250

10. Zappa Meets Gore:
    Evaluating Popular Art   278

    SELECTED BIBLIOGRAPHY   310

    INDEX   342

    ACKNOWLEDGMENTS   348

Contributors

ROY M. ANKER is Professor of English at Calvin College, where he teaches literature and film. Long a student of popular culture and a gifted writer, Anker has authored many essays and reviews on the religious dimensions of film. Currently he is preparing a book on the self-help tradition in American popular culture.

JAMES D. BRATT is Professor of History at Calvin College. His book, *Dutch Calvinism in Modern America: A History of a Conservative Subculture* (Eerdmans, 1984), was a case study of the intersection of religious ideas and social development. He lectures regularly on the history of American Protestantism, especially fundamentalism and evangelicalism. Currently he is researching the religious patterns in American popular culture.

WILLIAM D. ROMANOWSKI is a teacher, performer, raconteur, and critic. As Assistant Professor of Communication Arts and Sciences at Calvin College, he teaches courses on the media, popular culture, and the entertainment industry. Romanowski co-authored *Risky Business: Rock in Film* (Transaction Press, 1991) and has written numerous other book chapters, journal essays, and popular articles. He is currently working on a book on the popular music industry.

QUENTIN J. SCHULTZE is Professor of Communication Arts and Sciences at Calvin College. His books include *Television: Manna from Hollywood?* (Zondervan, 1986), *American Evangelicals and the Mass Media* (Zondervan/Academie, 1990), and *Televangelism and American Culture: The Business of Popular Religion* (Baker Book House, 1991). Schultze has also worked in radio and television as a copywriter, an advertising salesperson, a scriptwriter, and a media critic.

JOHN W. WORST is a teacher of music as well as a composer, collector, and critic of music. As Professor of Music at Calvin College, he has developed innovative approaches to the study of traditional and contemporary American music, from jazz to rock. Worst contributes musical reviews and essays to periodicals, and also collects African music and instruments.

LAMBERT ZUIDERVAART is Professor of Philosophy at Calvin College and an adjunct faculty member at the Institute for Christian Studies in Toronto. The author of *Adorno's Aesthetic Theory* (MIT Press, forthcoming), he is currently writing a book on postmodernism and the idea of artistic truth in German aesthetics. Zuidervaart has led conferences on the arts and aesthetics for artists, educators, and church workers, and he has worked as a radio announcer, a high-school music teacher, and a church musician.

Preface

In the fall of 1988, we took up residence together at the Calvin Center for Christian Scholarship at Calvin College in Grand Rapids, Michigan. Considering the normal demands of full-time teaching, the situation at the Calvin Center was close to idyllic: we worked in a suite of offices overlooking pine trees on a beautiful campus, we were assisted by superb secretaries, we were provided with excellent computer facilities, we had access to a marvelous library and an excellent library staff, and (most incredibly) each of us had to teach only one course each semester. Such are surely the things of academic heaven.

For eleven months we struggled excitedly but often frustratingly with the topic "Youth, Popular Culture, and the Electronic Media." Our mandate as a team was to write a book that would make sense out of what was happening in North American society and culture. If it were not for our Calvinist bent, which provided ample intellectual space for God's grace amid human depravity, we probably would have given up the project.

For one thing, it was not easy to separate the topic from the reality of our own lives. Most of us could easily recall how it felt to be a high school or college student (five of the six of us were under forty years of age). For another thing, each of us was dealing with the reality of either raising our own children or working closely with college students, advising them on personal as well as academic matters. Finally, we tried in various ways to immerse ourselves in the youth culture, attending youth-oriented events (including ear-splitting hard rock concerts) and even conducting in-depth interviews with students from private and public high schools in the area. The interviews were not meant to be scientifically precise studies of a random sample of North American youth. Rather, under the direction of John Worst, they provided specific data for the Center team's sometimes obtuse discussions of adolescent development and cultural theory.

From the beginning, our goal was first to understand and then to evaluate. We had no axes to grind or agendas to advance. If such axes or agendas emerged during our many discussions, we quickly found that they were readily and incisively challenged. The final manuscript was truly a collective product, one that survived many group meetings and revisions.

We wish to admit up front that the book probably suffers from two biases, one basically good and the other basically bad. The good bias, from our perspective, is the Reformed Christian commitment of all the authors. Although we have written this book for a general audience, we are hardly representative of the religious pluralism of North America: all of us embrace that portion of the historic Protestant faith represented in the Reformed tradition. For us this means, among other things, that the world belongs to God, that God created humankind, that humankind's purpose in life is to magnify the Creator, and that Christians should not only save souls but also transform society and culture for the good of all people. The Reformed tradition especially demonstrates a passionate interest in caring for the whole of creation and culture as an expressive arena for the loving, redemptive action of God. Today that arena includes popular culture, especially the popular entertainment distributed through the mass media.

Practically speaking, we tried to write a book that was informed by this common faith but that also would be of interest to anyone concerned about the fate of contemporary America. We hope that theists and skeptics alike will listen to the voices speaking on the following pages. In the rhetorical style of Robert Bellah & Company's *Habits of the Heart*, this book seeks to engage the North American public in conversation on crucial cultural questions that affect residents of North America and, increasingly, the world. Youth everywhere increasingly share the same cultural boat, bouyed by the electronic media and steered more and more by large corporations run by adults. For us, this situation necessitates dialogue not just among Christians but across the social landscape. Therefore, we invite all travelers to consider the implications of our arguments for their own journeys.

The bad bias grows out of the fact that we are a homogeneous group of white, middle-aged, North American males. Although several of us come from working-class families, we all share the sensibilities, values, and tastes that accompany a rather homogeneous background. In order to eliminate some of the blind spots resulting from our homogeneity, we sought advice and criticism from outside of the team. Three students—two white females and one black male—participated in our research and contributed to the formulation of our ideas. We thank Keri

Bruggink, Joy DeVries, and David Whettstone for their willingness to enter the den of academic pretention with fresh ideas and humble convictions. At times we felt that they should be writing the book for us.

We also solicited the advice of many people who we thought could contribute significantly to our project. Among them were Jack Balswick of Fuller Seminary, Tony Cox, John Dodge of Calvin, Martin Medhurst of Texas A&M, Margaret Koch of Bethel College, and Tom Willett of Word/Epic Records. We benefited considerably from academic and professional meetings where we presented tentative findings and audiences responded insightfully if not always supportively. At Fuller Seminary we met one day with scholars from the Los Angeles area, and on another day with youth workers and clergy. We offer our deepest gratitude to Richard Mouw, Fuller's provost, and Steve Murray, a youth minister from the area, for organizing those successful meetings. At the Institute for Christian Studies in Toronto, we met with a lively group of Canadian scholars. Brian Walsh and Bob VanderVennen deserve our deep appreciation for making the meeting possible and for creating a cordial environment for discussion and fellowship.

The most difficult facet of our research lay in locating professionals within the entertainment industry who would talk candidly about their work and their perceptions of the role played by the media in the lives of young people. Thanks again to Richard Mouw at Fuller, we were able to meet in Los Angeles with numerous producers, writers, directors, and the like. We also toured Hollywood, sat in on program tapings, and met privately with interested professionals. This trip was made possible in part by a grant provided by Mr. C. Davis Weyerhaeuser, a man who has repeatedly demonstrated heartfelt concern for American youth.

We received substantial on-campus support, both from Dean Rodger Rice, who personally oversaw the Calvin Center during our research year, and from the Calvin Center Board, chaired by Dr. Susan Gallagher of the English Department. The board gave us a great deal of freedom to pursue our ideas and showed its enthusiastic support on many occasions.

In our ongoing work at the Center, we were blessed by two gifted individuals who were far more than secretaries. Kate Miller and Donna Romanowski not only did most of the word processing for the manuscript. They also did much of the bibliographic work, compiled the index, helped organize meetings, and generally kept the Center running while the team walked around with its heads in academic fog. To them we offer our deep gratitude for a job done carefully and joyfully.

A project such as this invariably squeezes more work out of

some individuals than others. Quentin Schultze ably and gracefully coordinated and directed the labors of the team. In addition, he undertook extensive liaison work both on campus and off. His service was invaluable. During the post-residency period, someone had to revise and edit the manuscript. That burden fell upon Roy Anker, who did much to clean up abundant obfuscation and awkward or poorly organized writing. Mary Hietbrink of Eerdmans shored up the team with her able copyediting, while Eerdmans' editor in chief, Jon Pott, encouraged the team from the beginning. We're grateful for Eerdmans' willingness not only to publish the manuscript but also to give it special care and attention.

The Calvin Center is a special place of academic hope and grace, even when it deals with a sometimes depressing or unwieldy topic. So we thank the Creator for fashioning the Center amid a fallen (academic) world. And we pray that this book will help restore the Creator's world.

Roy Anker
James Bratt
William Romanowski
Quentin Schultze
John Worst
Lambert Zuidervaart
Summer 1990

1. The Big Chill:
Adults, Youth, and Popular Culture

When I was a boy of fourteen, my father was so ignorant I could hardly stand to have him around. But when I got to be twenty-one, I was astonished at how much he had learned in seven years.

Mark Twain

The denunciation of the young is a necessary part of the hygiene of older people.

Logan Pearsall Smith

Youth is the trustee of posterity.

Benjamin Disraeli

One of the signs of maturity among North American adults is a recurring sense that not all is right with youth. Adults often think disparagingly about teenagers in general, not just their own offspring. Probably every parent and teacher—not to mention every pastor and police officer— has muttered about the peculiar attitudes or misguided actions of youth. Part of this reaction undoubtedly results from personal experience. All adults know what *they* were like in the years between kidhood and adulthood. Hindsight should breed patience, but it rarely does. And patience is certainly valuable in dealings with teens, since it seems that youth is a step toward maturity that cannot be rushed.

Everywhere one looks in North American culture, two sides of youth—immaturity and energy—clash like discordant cymbals. In the eyes of many adults, rock-music concerts and MTV videos offer the clearest examples of this conflict. If only the young would direct their restlessness toward something worthwhile. If only they would take life more seriously. If only they would work instead of play. Alas, if only they would stop being, well, young.

Adults' love-hate relationship with youth says much about the "problem with kids" in North America. For one thing, adults often unfairly criticize youth. As we shall argue repeatedly in this book, youth are who they are in no small measure because of how adults view them; adolescence is implicitly defined by adult-run media, churches, and schools. And adults in their perplexity with youth turn to these kinds of institutions for assistance—ironically, the very institutions that place youth in their own subculture where they have little to do but expend energy on looking good and entertaining themselves.

Moreover, what many adults think is so admirable about youth—namely, their beauty and energy—is not always worth celebrating. In a consumerist culture, beauty is often not in the eye of the beholder but is "applied" via the tricks of the merchandiser, and energy can often be plain frenzy—a sign of anxiety and discontent. Parents complain about clothing prices and competitive dressing, but they nevertheless buy their teenagers the kinds of clothes that will insure attention from their peers. And when teens are antsy, parents often give them money for rock-concert tickets or some other exploit that will help them let off steam; the parents rationalize that it's worth it to get the kids out of their hair. In short, youth's beauty and energy run in many directions, using adult-abetted means to achieve a wide variety of adult-approved ends. Not all of those ends are worthwhile. Unfortunately, many parents spend little or no energy looking for alternatives for their children. It is simply so much easier to grumblingly give youth what they want than to listen to them, explore other options, or show them what they should have.

In this introductory chapter we ask our adult readers to take a brief and, we hope, revealing journey into the world of the North American youth culture. Although the tour guides are hardly young in age, they are in spirit both young and sympathetic. We like young people. And we believe that most adults have not really considered how they themselves have conspired among themselves, with the electronic media, and with various social institutions to make life increasingly difficult for youth. This short trip will not be an impassioned denunciation of modern youth, their music, or their language. Rather, this particular tour is conducted by six sympathetic souls who like much about the youth culture and who believe that adults can learn much from youth.

The purpose of this tour is to prod the imagination of adult readers, to arouse their interest, and to prepare them for the rest of the adventure of this book. Be warned, however, that this might be a cool journey; there is a chill in the air. Relations between youth and adults are not marked by warmth and peace. Not only that, but there are some adults who like it that way; they profit from the hardships that so many families, churches, schools, and neighborhoods face these days. Warmer relations require empathy and insight. In this tour we will try to view the situation with both.

First Site: Generations

"In our generation," said the frustrated senior citizen, "things were a lot different." Perhaps they were. Certainly clothing and speech have changed in the last twenty to thirty years, the traditional length of a generation. But what that is fundamental has really changed? And what has not?

One of the great myths of contemporary life is that youth today have little in common with youth of the past. The truth is that youth have been a "problem" for hundreds, probably thousands, of years. Every adult reading this book was very likely part of a generation that criticized and was criticized by its elders. Generational conflict stretches far back into recorded history. As we show in the second chapter, even some of today's most popular debaucheries—alcohol, drugs, provocative dance, and promiscuous sex—are merely variations on long-standing themes of behavior that have channeled and expressed youthful energy and excitement.

Contemporary society merely exacerbates the patterns of generational conflict begun long ago. To put it more strongly and more critically, more and more adults are very much in the business of giving youth the means to show how different they are from older people. In the past, youth typically had to "generate" their own values, beliefs, and practices. Now, however, corporate North America has found that encouraging relatively distinct generational groups helps the proverbial bottom line. Since youth like to be different, these corporations have decided to heighten that sense of distinctiveness. Why not sell them their "own" music, clothing, films, TV shows, radio stations—whatever subgroup product the youth market will buy? After all, modern marketing rests on the dual premise of giving people what they supposedly want and creating needs they don't yet realize they have. Everywhere North Americans look these days, corporate business manufactures a plethora of products for teenagers.

This kind of generational marketing has accelerated the speed and complexity of cultural change beyond what most adults can comprehend. Musical styles, for instance, shift decisively every couple of years. Hairstyles and clothing styles seem to have an even more rapid and chaotic pattern of change. Even the most popular films generally last only a month or two in the theaters. Popular music recordings and rock videos change every week. Two siblings, though born only three years apart and raised by the same parents, can sometimes feel like they grew up in very different worlds, depending on what cultural products were available to them. The days of pass-along clothing have nearly disappeared, unless some lucky parents catch fads on their second time around.

Electronic technologies feed this seemingly insatiable appetite for new cultural expressions and experiences. Today's electronic media are far more market-sensitive to generational change than any media of the past. Given the speed afforded them by modern technology, merchandisers can quickly shift gears with the latest apparent fads or rapidly test-market a new product. If a product does not catch fire almost immediately, it dies quickly, and is replaced by another potential success story. Youth often prove fickle consumers at the cultural trough, and if they do not like this product or tire of that one, they will soon scramble to sample another.

This kind of cultural pace makes it increasingly difficult for anyone to maintain some sort of generational continuity. Clergy, for example, are in deep trouble these days. How can they make traditional religion relevant to youth? One answer, of course, is for churches to hire youth pastors whose age, energy, and style supposedly will "speak" to young people. Then the main or "old" pastor is free to be pleasantly outdated and blissfully irrelevant to the "youth group." Not surprisingly, churches go through youth pastors like fast-food restaurants go through cashiers and cooks. Trying to remain relevant and "make a difference" in young lives, youth pastors simply burn themselves out. Worse than that, they burn out to the tune of adult criticism. Faced with their own irrelevance, parents increasingly look to other adults, especially teachers and youth workers, to do what they should be doing but do not feel equipped to do—that is, raise their children. But parents are seldom satisfied with the nurturing other adults do.

Consider the plight of high-school teachers. Is there any doubt about the extreme difficulty of teaching in schools that many students regard as either playgrounds or prisons? Many adults see discipline as the only answer. In most cases, however, discipline only fortifies the generational barriers between youth and adults; the prison-and-punishment strategy does not work. To many youth, adult discipline offers yet another sign that adults live in an alien world that values neither spontaneity nor fun. Not surprisingly, a growing number of youth-oriented films, musical recordings, and TV shows are popular because they poke fun of the disciplined culture imposed by adult authority. In this way, the products of the electronic media help youth express their frustration with the generational conflict.

Parents undoubtedly bear some blame for this great generational divide. Instead of creatively involving youth in adult tasks and responsibilities, parents often find it much easier and less time-consuming to turn their children loose in adolescent culture. After all, middle-class and upper-middle-class parents have their own hopes and dreams to pursue, such as more and/or bigger homes, cottages, and cars, and more—and more extravagant—leisure activities. This leaves them little time or energy for nurturing. Thus it is far easier, for example, to buy teenagers their own TV sets and VCRs than to watch programs with them and discuss what is worth viewing. In effect, parental attitudes have usually aided the corporations, especially those involving the electronic media, that market products to adolescents. Parents' actions suggest that they would rather have Hollywood raise their children than handle the task themselves. The long-term effect creates a distinct chill in relations between parents and children.

Second Site: Planned Immaturity

Despite what many adults believe, North American culture does not really promote the maturation of youth. Adults can recite all the standard lines about "growing up," but the culture says something very different. Everywhere adults look—if they will merely open their eyes—lies evidence that our culture rewards youthfulness and criticizes maturity. Young people, remember, are admired primarily for their beauty and relative energy and immaturity. Deep down, most adults covet such characteristics, which leave youth largely free to explore life, to take chances, and simply to have fun without the encumbrance of adult obligation. To some extent, North American parents want their teenage offspring to grow up not because they so highly value maturity but because they want, eventually, to lighten their own load: once their children are out of the nest, their lives as parents become a lot easier.

It used to be relatively accurate to equate "teenagers" with "youth." Today the signs and symbols of the youth culture pervade the whole of society. Forty-year-old men and women try to dress like their teenage children; some of them even undergo surgery to make their faces and bodies look younger. Meanwhile, teenagers dress like the mature-looking fashion models in upscale magazines. But relatively little of the adult culture is embraced by youth, and this pattern can now extend well into what is, by chronological standards, adulthood. Indeed, some thirty-year-olds refuse to adopt their parents' life patterns, refusing to marry, purchase a house, or buy a "family" car. (This explains Oldsmobile's latest slogan: "This is not your father's Oldsmobile—this is the new generation of Olds.") These adult "adolescents" hope to prolong their youth as long as they can. In their eyes, maturity steals the joy and fun from life.

While these kinds of cultural shifts happen on the surface of everyday life, they do reflect deep crises in North American culture. As psychologists have found, the postponement of maturity is an attempt to hang on to youthfulness as long as possible. Unfortunately, such delayed maturity extends the identity and intimacy crises faced by so many North American teenagers. More and more adults breeze through one cultural fad after another in search of their real "self," as if they can find it by constantly changing their look or speech or car. Similarly, more and more adults handle romantic relationships in an adolescent fashion, trying out one person after another in hopes of finally finding the ideal mate.

Amid all of this, the electronic media have become major purveyors of these crises and of supposed solutions to them. As we shall see in later chapters, MTV and teen films are heavily geared toward providing visions of identity and intimate relationships, visions that often function like panaceas. As long as families, schools, neighborhoods, churches, and the like do not help provide more inviting, healthy, and personal ways of meeting these psycho-relational needs, the media will play an overbearing role in determining what youth deem worthwhile and significant. Currently the media have an ambiguous effect on youth's attempts to find themselves amid a cacophony of disparate voices offering stability and hope. On the one hand, the media's images and stories can and do offer hope, joy, and consolation to perplexed youth; on the other hand, the media sometimes exacerbate teen confusion by trivializing the depth and poignancy of adolescent quests.

Third Site: Buying Happiness

Contemporary North American youth grow up in a society that finds much meaning in buying and displaying products. Their parents, teachers, counselors, and clergy typically consume the latest technology, styles, and services. Their peers are probably similarly immersed in the purchase of everything from shoes to CDs. Is it really surprising, then, that so many adolescents find their sense of community at the local shopping mall?

Over and over again, night and day, North Americans find temporary solace and at least fleeting happiness at the cash register. We are bombarded by consumerist messages that preach consumption as a cure-all. If you're depressed, buy some new clothes. If you're bored, take in a movie or rent a video. If you're hungry, head for a restaurant. And so it goes—more and more people and families buy something to change a mood or to "create" a social event. Real joy is purchasing the latest product or catching the most recent entertainment, especially if it bestows status. The pattern for finding identity and intimacy is increasingly clear: reach out and touch some*thing*—your wallet at the store.

Those with limited time to spend on the pursuit of consumer products can do many kinds of shopping at home via telephone. Pizza, drinks, and a video can be delivered to one's home. The well-to-do can use catalog services to deliver designer clothes, even cars. And everyone can purchase products any time of day from the comfort of his own living room: cable TV home-shopping channels push their wares around the clock. In short, there abound ever faster and more efficient ways of purchasing an ever wider range of products and services. Today only the worst kind of inertia would keep someone from the marketplace. It has never been easier to buy.

In this kind of cultural setting, identity and intimacy turn into marketable commodities, like clothes that consumers try on for fit and look. Put simply, probably the most important trend in youth entertainment is the marketing of happiness (which has much to do with identity and intimacy) through products and services. From MTV to films and recordings, different sectors of this youth-oriented entertainment industry often conspire to peddle alluring visions of identity and intimacy. MTV's "veejays," the video equivalent of deejays, create the illusion of intimacy between themselves and the individual viewer, all the while hawking recordings, concert tours, new movies, and every other imaginable teen-oriented product. Rock videos equate physical intimacy with emotional intimacy as they create visually pleasing images. Rock stars recline in intimate settings while the camera repeatedly returns to their faces to fabricate a sense of closeness between them and the viewer.

Much entertainment, then, is not really intended just for fun or pleasure. Its purpose is frequently to develop dedicated customers by offering what few seem to have—the keys to knowing oneself and becoming popular with other people, especially peers. The electronic media in particular have established their own place in the youth culture as an important source of information that functions like a kind of alternative high school on life. Young people often turn to these media for guidance in developing meaningful identities and satisfying needs for intimacy. Indeed, the media think of themselves as quasi-parents who help youth find their way in a rapidly changing society. Of course, such advice can come at a personal price, particularly if the media do not really care about the emotional or physical health of individual consumers. Youth-oriented commercial appeals to intimacy and identity are most often made in the name of mass marketing. On the other hand, it is not fair to ask entertainment corporations to become *de facto* parents, school boards, and church leaders as traditional sources of nurture lose their confidence and resolve. What responsibility we can rightly expect makers of electronic entertainment to assume remains very much open to question.

The rise of the entertainment industry, then, parallels the decline of local sources of authority and modes of communication. Youth's eyes and ears attend less and less to the suasive powers of local institutions and increasingly to the messages from anonymous, distant media from Hollywood, New York, or some other industrial capital. Adolescents often care far more about the content and style of media made thousands of miles away than about what takes place in their own neighborhoods and even in their own families. Indeed, they frequently shape the important stuff of their lives from the cues marketed by corporations rather than from those offered by parents, pastors, teachers, and community leaders. So it is not surprising that as youth face west to Los Angeles, sometimes genuflecting, many adults shudder, feeling a chill set in.

Fourth Site: Adult Compliance

All of this would not be so disturbing if it were not for the fact that adults conspire to put youth into the very predicament about which they so constantly complain. Adults' responses to youth's problems typically make the situation worse. Because adults do not recognize their own complicity, they only fight fire with fire. Again and again, to the point of ridiculousness, adults succeed only in giving youth the equipment they need to further enmesh themselves in cultural discontent.

How do adults manage to defeat themselves and youth in this way? First, they misguidedly try to solve the "youth problem" by plunging young people deeper into the sea of teen-defined media. It seems that every troubled social institution—from the home to the school to the church—supports organizations that produce more and more youth-oriented media. Church denominations, for example, have adult writers and editors who publish youth magazines. In the quest for relevance, they try to appeal to youth with visual and literary "hipness." Not surprisingly, most of these periodicals prove woefully unsuccessful. Youth see them as tools of indoctrination that use the external symbols of the youth culture—how things look and how youth speak. In a controlled setting like that of a church-sponsored youth group, the magazine might get some attention. At home, however, it quickly ends up in the trash.

The church youth movement reflects the second misguided solution to the youth problem: adults isolate youth from the adult community and virtually the entire adult world. Given the fact that generational discontinuity is a major part of the "youth problem," the creation of all kinds of youth-specific institutions cannot be seen as any solution. In fact, youth organizations, even those sponsored by churches, largely serve corporate North America by accentuating the various trends of the teen culture and thereby increasing market segmentation.

How are youth going to mature except by contact with adults? In the long run, isolation and market segmentation stall or retard maturity because they separate youth from the broader society, especially from the real world of adults. Some churches have learned this and have consequently devised new forms of interaction between youth and adults. For example, church members of all ages work together on community projects such as renovating older homes for resale to lower-income residents. Or adults and youth travel together during vacation periods to assist in rural redevelopment projects. In such interaction youth learn from adults and adults learn from youth; both groups come to better understandings of themselves, each other, and the society they both inhabit. Such production-oriented exchange between youth and adults has proven far more effective than adult-produced "church" media for teen consumption.

A third factor exacerbating the problem is that North American adults have fueled the storm of consumerism by seeking answers to the youth problem in consumption itself. For every problem there is product after product promising to take care of it. In the contemporary Christian music industry, for example, promoters have hawked religious rock and roll as the answer to the "problem" of rock music. In other words, many have tried to sell an idea of what youth should listen to and purchase. Unfortunately, much "Christian rock" amounts only to an artistically inferior "cleaned-up" version of secular rock. Further, the notion that youth should or can get their answers to life's problems from a mass-produced recording is far too simplistic. Although the Christianized lyrics might be less offensive, they are still part of an anonymous economic transaction instead of a relationship between people who care about each other. Certainly there are good and bad products, including musical recordings, but no products should substitute for interpersonal relational nurture. As things now stand, both the entertainment industry *and* many local authority figures treat youth as mere objects or receptors to be molded by good or bad consumption.

Part of the chill in relations between adults and youth results from the belief that consumption can solve personal and collective difficulties. While we affirm a free marketplace, we must caution adults that responsibility must be shouldered by both the entertainment industry and those adults who shape homes, churches, schools, and other local and regional social institutions. As we shall argue at length, the answer to the youth crisis does not lie in increased consumption.

Fifth Site: Passive Entertainment

Finally, we suggest that contemporary young people struggle within North America's pervasive cultural confusion over whether life should be leisure or work. As we see it, the tensions between work and leisure reflect North Americans' larger obsession with the self. Old and young people alike increasingly believe that entertainment-oriented leisure provides the basic reason for living. Happiness consists of having a quiver full of electronic gadgets that give sensate pleasure during all non-working hours. Work amounts to no more than a means of generating sufficient income to make leisure more exciting. To be sure, youth learn this from adults. Adults in turn learn this from youth, who in their energy strive continually to achieve the ultimate entertainment experience.

In no sense do we oppose leisure or even the electronic media. The media have enormous social potential as entertainers, informers, and nurturers. Nor are we rabid Calvinists who see sin in the nooks and crannies of every idle moment. We firmly believe that leisure is one of the great gifts and purposes of a God whose people have inherited the creation. Our concern is that an industrial world, saturated with electronic sounds and images, has distorted leisure so that more and more provides less joy and intimacy. Instead of imparting delight in the good gifts of human life, the land of instantaneously accessible, mass-produced pleasure distracts humankind from its high calling to relish and revere both work and leisure within the creation.

North American youth frequently grow up with little or no sense of the value of work or play. Having accomplished little with their own hands, hearts, and minds, their self-esteem is low and their dependence upon the products produced by others is very high. Indeed, many youth do not have a single "product" that they can call their own and display to others. Many young people discard schoolwork soon after arriving home. They see mowing lawns and trimming hedges as mere drudgery, not a means of beautifying or celebrating the creation. If they play musical instruments, they try to imitate the "professional" music on recordings but rarely make "personal noise" to express themselves or the joy of communal leisure.

Our point here is that youth, popular culture, and the electronic media, largely under adult supervision, have interacted in such a way that young people have been reduced to passive consumers of culture. Most youth do not significantly shape the culture around them because they are too busy consuming the prefabricated electronic visions from Vancouver or Hollywood. In this situation we cannot reasonably expect youth to contribute much to the wider society—they neither know how nor are inspired by personal experience. Imagine, by contrast, a home or school or church that genuinely encourages young people to interact with adults to determine what media products they will listen to and watch. To put the matter more directly, consider how young people might mature if they acted in and on the world rather than simply consumed it. Some adults might think this a rather chilling suggestion. Potentially at least, it threatens the alleged sanctity of adult society. However, once we concede the fallenness and limitations of adults, what is at stake becomes still clearer. And so does an important lesson: youth must have freedom as well as resources and support in order to contribute meaningfully and lastingly to North American culture.

Symbiosis and Beyond

The aforementioned journey taken in this book is based primarily on the theory that the electronic media and youth are in a *symbiotic* relationship. In short, our thesis is that youth and the electronic media today are dependent upon each other. The media need the youth market, as it is called, for their own economic survival. Youth, in turn, need the media for guidance and nurture in a society where other social institutions, such as the family and the school, do not shape the youth culture as powerfully as they once did.

According to this thesis, the electronic media do not have complete freedom to influence youth in whatever way they please. Since the media must sell their products to youth in North America (by which we mean Canada and the United States), they must pay attention to what youth want and sometimes even to what youth might need. Although some media bashers would like to say that the media create the needs that youth have, including their needs for identity and intimacy, this claim seems only partly true at best. Intimacy and identity are basic human needs, not media-fabricated ones. The media simply offer their own versions of how youth can fulfill these needs, along the way changing the roles of other nurturing groups in North America. As homes, churches, schools, and the like have become ineffective nurturing institutions, the media have moved in to fill the gap, in the process widening the gap between youth and traditional nurture. In the following chapters we offer perspectives on how the media entered into this symbiotic relationship with youth. We also evaluate that relationship.

Chapter Two shows that the "youth problem" is hardly a new one; it has roots in early American culture. Moreover, this chapter describes how generation after generation of adults have tried to keep youth in line by using the latest innovations in media. Chapter Three looks at how communications technologies have affected the cultural and social environment, especially the relationship between generations and the rise of a distinct youth culture in North America. Today's youth grow to adulthood amid an incredible supermarket of media technologies, from portable stereos to cable television, VCRs, and satellite delivery systems. The next two chapters examine the business side of the youth-media symbiosis. Chapter Four develops the theme of symbiosis by examining the rise of the contemporary youth culture in the 1950s and 1960s. Those decades were the heyday of Top 40 radio stations and drive-in movies, among other youth-oriented media. Chapter Five traces the ethos of consumption that increasingly pervades media marketing and the youth culture. At present, the latest media technologies foster expanding global communications systems controlled by a small number of high-finance corporate players.

The next three chapters offer portraits of particular youth media. Chapter Six focuses on rock music, probably the most hotly contested and widely misunderstood form of youth entertainment. Chapter Seven takes rock music to its obvious conclusion in the era of the image—rock videos and music television. The chapter reports on what the creators of the MTV cable channel had in mind when they began pursuing the increasingly valuable youth market. Chapter Eight looks at teenage films, especially horror movies and teen initiation films, both of which have fetched enormous profits.

The last two chapters analyze important aspects of the youth-media symbiosis in an attempt to offer some guidelines for redeeming North America's complex and frustrating predicament. Chapter Nine strives to offer a balanced approach to the proper role of leisure in contemporary culture—an important topic, since North America largely lacks the sort of daily labor that dominates most other cultures. Indeed, attitudes toward work and play in no small measure explain the huge infusion of electronic entertainment into Canada and the United States since World War II. Finally, Chapter Ten offers guidelines for evaluating both the quality and the appropriateness of popular art for youth and adults. Most critics of popular entertainment narrowly evaluate popular-art products merely in terms of their morality or their marketability. The discussion will expand the vision of the producers as well as the consumers of popular art.

In 1988 the biggest exporter in the United States was the aerospace industry; the second-largest exporter was the entertainment industry. It would not be hard to argue that the latter will soon become the more influential of the two, if the world does not face another major war. If that happens, we wonder how today's young people would fare in a battle waged on foreign soil. The cultural war at home would likely affect any military war in a distant place. Indeed, it might be that in these days of talk about de-militarization, arms accords, and peace, North Americans should increasingly consider the battles that still rage at home. Surely the decline in education, the spread of drugs, and the breakdown of the family are as important as international politics. Perhaps the rise of the youth-oriented entertainment industry, which is increasing its global influence, is also equally important.

We offer no simple solutions for any of these problems. We do believe, however, that the future of youth is necessarily part of the future of the entire society. Furthermore, we are convinced that the "problems of youth" cannot be understood or solved apart from an investigation of how youth, the electronic media, and popular culture interact in contemporary society. This introduction has provided a quick tour of the sites that we shall visit at length in the following pages. We hope that each chapter will enhance the reader's understanding of the contemporary predicament and will encourage all to take up the reconstructive task with renewed energy and fresh perspectives.

2. From Revivalism to Rock and Roll: Youth and Media Historically Considered

Kids!
You can talk and talk 'til your face is blue
Kids!
But they still do just what they want to do
Why can't they be like we were—perfect in every way?
What's the matter with kids today?

Kids!
They are just impossible to control
Kids!
With their awful clothes and their rock and roll
Why can't they dance like we did—what's wrong with
   Sammy Kaye?
What's the matter with kids today?

"Kids," from the musical Bye-Bye Birdie

The twentieth-century American pattern for youth is one of prolonged struggle. Contemporary life creates domestic war zones that pit parents against adolescent alliances of teenagers and their peers. But if this pattern did not always exist, when and how did it emerge? An answer lies in several key junctures in American history, times when an old set of norms gave way to a new one. Significantly, for the broader purposes of this book, these changes paralleled the emergence of new communications media, and these new media invariably featured major, even explosive innovations in popular culture and entertainment. The contemporary youth crisis is only the latest variation on centuries-old problems.

This conjunction between restless youth, new media, and new entertainment is more than coincidental, because all these share a common origin in the broader course of American social development, specifically the process known as modernization.[1] Since early eighteenth-century America, powerful forces have fostered an economic development that has regularly triggered profound social and cultural changes. Modernization has (1) moved economic exchange from local, face-to-face encounters into a larger impersonal market; (2) constantly advanced technologically; (3) multiplied social institutions; and (4) complicated interpersonal relations. To be sure, this process did not occur steadily or with unanimous approval; in fact, some of the most interesting social movements in American history struggled to combat it. But wherever it spread, the modernizing process became a (perhaps *the*) force to reckon with. Modernization set the agenda.

To win their cause, the sponsors of economic modernization attacked the power of tradition; in particular, individual mobility and profit-seeking challenged the norms of community and social hierarchy. In response, every social institution changed. Some disappeared, like the local militia, and some prospered, like business corporations. Still others—especially the church, the family, and the school—have at once seemed imperiled and strengthened. In fact, regardless of intentions, the modernizing process has challenged *every* set of social rules and has muddied the future. To be sure, the prophets of modernization assured skeptics that the future would necessarily turn out brighter, better, richer, and happier than the past. But even they could not predict the exact shape modernization would take or how all would live in it. Instead, the burden of these questions has fallen heavily on youth, those who would have to find their way in a rapidly changing world.

Of course, "troubled youth" are never just isolated malcontents in a happy society but betoken larger cultural disturbances. In addressing these troubled youth, American cultural leaders have felt great responsibility and faced great dilemmas. Their duty demanded they take up the most obvious task of any society: perpetuating itself by affording its young an identity and by preparing them occupationally, politically, sexually, and so on for adulthood. Their dilemmas arose from their own adult confusion, ambivalence, and hesitancy about the vast changes

---

1. Classic accounts with an American focus are Richard D. Brown, *Modernization: The Transformation of American Life, 1600-1865* (New York: Hill & Wang, 1976), and James A. Henretta and Gregory H. Nobles, *Evolution and Revolution: American Society, 1600-1820* (Lexington, Mass.: D. C. Heath, 1987). In *The Homeless Mind: Modernization and Consciousness* (New York: Random House, 1973), Peter Berger et al. explore the paradoxical cultural consequences of the process.

happening all around them. Their options were limited. They might lash out against a disturbing future, or they might try to adapt to a new order, no matter how threatening it seemed. Underlying this perplexity was another. Adults surely wished to help their young, but just as surely, if not as consciously, they wished to control them. By the same token, youth wished to emulate their mentors—but also to get loose from them. The circumstance was complex, and the motives and solutions were not clear and simple.

Amid very real human dilemmas, new means of communication could sometimes play a decisive role. New media (promising salvation) emerge from the very economic innovations that have complicated the social situation, and they readily attract a displaced, youthful audience. If the message of traditional nurture has not "spoken" to some youth, they will seek lessons in a new tongue, and the new media will provide the language. In such circumstances, the mentors of society must decide whether to use the new media in an attempt to regain guidance and control. Although conservatives typically protest the new communications, adoption usually wins out—with keen irony the result. In American history, every new communications technique—from Benjamin Franklin's lending libraries and Samuel Morse's telegraph to radio and television—has been hailed for its potential to "save the young" from crime, sin, ignorance, or moral chaos. In the long run, this optimism has served only to adapt the young—and the leaders also—to the very socio-economic system that fostered the new communications and that seemed so troubling in the first place. In other words, the supposed cure for the symptoms has come from the disease itself. Cultural leaders always intend to use new media to convey and even revive old values, but the new media usually end up obscuring, weakening, or triumphing precisely over those conservative values.

Popular entertainment enters here because it is often the chief cargo the new media carry. The media instruct, but ideally they will also entertain. Better yet, their promoters promise, they will instruct—painlessly, enticingly—by *means* of entertaining. A little sugar coating helps the pill go down. For many observers, however, that promise is quickly dashed by a surprising development, part of an ironic drama persistently repeated on the American cultural stage. Act I: a youth-targeted, youth-championed form of entertainment emerges, drawing sharp parental suspicion. (The recent adult alarm over heavy-metal music is the latest instance, but the same objections greeted the popular pastimes we will treat subsequently: irregular preaching in the 1740s, women's novels a century later, football in the 1890s, movies and jazz in the 1920s, comic books and rock and roll in the 1950s.) Act II: the new format's promoters proclaim its "health" and "safety" and its "educational value" or some other legitimate end. Act III: that defense invites attempts to harness the new form to the ends of order and control, specifically of reviving threatened values. Act IV: success in Act III generates efforts to recover the format's original ideal, to push it toward more extreme expressions, or to seize upon a still newer medium, which begins the drama all over again.

In sum, youth-oriented popular entertainment constitutes regularly contested ground—contested between generations and contested internally. On the one hand, new media promise freedom, but on the other hand, they contain their own covert system of control that helps to conform youth to a new socio-economic system. This cycle provides a fitting summary of all the familiar layers of the youth struggle—the struggle for identity, trustworthy intimacy, and meaningful futures; the struggle to win recognition *as* adults *from* adults while avoiding the drudgery, routine, and compromise in which adults seem to be mired. Young people battle to find a voice all their own but one that will at the same time win adults' respect and response. These two desires cannot both be met, however. For once heeded and shared, the voice no longer belongs exclusively to the sender. In all their struggles the young act in tandem with adults, not independently of them. "Youth" itself cannot be defined except in terms of the life stage that preceded it and (especially) the "adult" stage that will follow it. As much as the youth culture in its struggle for independence wishes to set its own agenda, the terms of that agenda can emerge only from an adult-dominated culture.

Youth and Revival Discipline: 1740-1790

As we have suggested, the drama of youth, media, and popular entertainment plays on a stage set, spun, and re-set by the process of economic modernization.[2] That movement itself has proceeded through distinct epochs. For our purposes, the first significant "act" spanned the centu-

---

2. Obviously, the history of American youth could take us into the history of all American society and culture. To make our present task more manageable, we will concentrate not just on key moments of transition but also on those sectors of the American population most directly touched by the modernizing process. The recent boom in scholarly studies on American youth has revealed enormous variations in their experiences according to differences of region, class, ethnicity, and gender. To focus as we will upon the "core culture" of the northeastern, white, upper and middle classes is not to imply their superiority but to recognize their power to shape public life, the policies, structures, and expectations that impinge upon other populations as well.

ry-long "commercial revolution" that began in New England in the 1730s and climaxed in upstate New York in the 1830s. Although it moved gradually, this revolution wrought complex and far-reaching changes. Faster transportation and quicker means of exchange (credit and brokerage) created larger markets that in turn encouraged larger-scale production, technological innovation, greater profits, greater employment, and population growth. Slowly but inexorably, the usual expectations and traditional norms by which people found their place, did their work, and anticipated their future gave way to the pressures of change. Significantly, both the place where this transformation began and the place where it ended were notorious for religious explosions. American revivalism was virtually invented in New England in the 1730s-1740s (the Great Awakening) and reached its wildest crescendo along the Erie Canal in the 1830s (the "burned-over district" of the Second Great Awakening). In both cases youth were the revival's special target, new communications its special tool, and a mixture of protest and accommodation its overall social function. In short, in the great century of commercialization, evangelical revivalism played a leading role in the larger cultural transactions of modernization.

For a hundred years before the first Awakening (that is, since the founding of the Massachusetts Bay colony in 1630), New England had tried to order itself by means of a tight, thoroughgoing, patriarchal communalism. While the young might find themselves farmed out or apprenticed at a tender age, they remained under their parents' authority for (by our standards) an exceedingly long time. The marks of adulthood—marriage, full church membership, and inheritance—often did not come to men before their thirties, though to women somewhat earlier. In New England, inheritance or patrimony was the key to maturity. As long as young men could only look forward to a viable craft or tract of land from their parents, "children" they would remain, dependent upon and under the sway of their parents.[3]

By the 1730s that arrangement began to break down. A population explosion took over more and more of the land reserves, making property more expensive, and drove many young people to move to the frontier or to cities. Otherwise, as many others did, they could stay at home and rebel. Deliberately or otherwise, their new leisure pastimes

3. Steven Mintz and Susan Kellogg, *Domestic Revolutions: A Social History of American Family Life* (New York: Free Press, 1988), pp. 1-23; Edmund S. Morgan, *The Puritan Family: Religion and Domestic Relations in 17th-Century New England* (New York: Harper & Row, 1966); Philip J. Greven, *Four Generations: Population, Land, and Family in Colonial Andover, Massachusetts* (Ithaca, N.Y.: Cornell University Press, 1970).

looked a lot like rebellion. "Night-walking" and "company-keeping," also known as "revels," helped produce some of the highest premarital pregnancy rates in American history. For instance, in this era fully 30 percent of first births to women in Hingham, Massachusetts, came within the first eight months of marriage.[4] These circumstances forced parents, sometimes grudgingly, to grant land, independence, and adulthood at an earlier age. Analogous disruptions reverberated through the rest of society: political factionalism, regional animosities, and disputes over currency and trade—all forbidden by traditional norms—rose sharply. The well-ordered rural commune had begun to come apart under the demands of the marketplace.[5]

Seen in this light, the Great Awakening served to restore social order for youth by supplying a new discipline to take the place of the old. The New England revival began, in fact, with Jonathan Edwards' pointed sermons to the "night-walkers" in his own congregation—sermons, he was glad to report, that turned revelers into saints. Over the next decade, Edwards' converts and thousands like them learned to separate themselves psychologically from "the world" in order to bond intensively with each other, to guard their lives by strict conscience, and to watch fellow believers. Thus, their reordered souls and the spiritual bonds of fellowship created for many youth a new identity that enabled them to steer a clear path through the maze of a fragmenting world.

The Awakening attracted the youth of the day (people in their twenties), and the whole movement seemed to emphasize youthfulness. The foremost revivalists themselves—George Whitefield, Gilbert Tennent, James Davenport—were praised (or disdained) as "striplings." Those revived—not just on the rural and urban frontiers but even in the heartland—were youthful too. The average age of conversion dropped as a whole generation of younger people joined the church. In Andover, Massachusetts, for instance, the average conversion age for males dropped from 36 to 27; for females, from 27 to 22.[6] This gave the revival

4. Henretta and Nobles, *Evolution and Revolution,* p. 108; Daniel Scott Smith, "Parental Power and Marriage Patterns: An Analysis of Historical Trends in Hingham, Massachusetts," in *Growing Up in America: Historical Experiences,* ed. Harvey J. Graff (Detroit: Wayne State University Press, 1987), pp. 156-69; Daniel Scott Smith and Michael Hindus, "Premarital Pregnancy in America, 1640-1971: An Overview and an Interpretation," *Journal of Interdisciplinary History* 5 (Spring 1975): 537-70.

5. Richard L. Bushman, *From Puritan to Yankee: Character and the Social Order in Connecticut, 1690-1765* (Cambridge, Mass.: Harvard University Press, 1967); Patricia U. Bonomi, *Under the Cope of Heaven: Religion, Society and Politics in Colonial America* (New York: Oxford University Press, 1986).

6. Philip J. Greven, "Youth, Maturity, and Religious Conversion: A Note on the Ages of Converts in Andover, Massachusetts, 1711-1749," in *Growing Up in America,*

its strongest vindication, for the ministers of the old order had fretted for decades about the spiritual recalcitrance of the young. By tapping the spirit of protest, the revival worked to tame moral rebellion and restore New England's virtuous order. This result, claimed its adherents, provided ample justification for the Awakening's unusual means of persuasion.

The most controversial of these means was a new communications strategy, a new style of exhortation. Traditionally ministers preached very much to their congregation's heads; repentance of the heart was to come later, in the privacy of home. These standard sermons were in fact written texts delivered orally in formal settings and bearing the authority of tradition. In contrast, revivalists held weekday meetings in any convenient street or field and traveled widely among parishes ("itineracy") instead of being settled in one. They spoke spontaneously (without written text) and to the heart, which was precisely how their hearers were supposed to respond—immediately and with the heart. And many did, with great exuberance and in full public view. Altogether the revivalists gave an *oral* performance that skirted the accepted grounds of authority. Just as the revivalists' style reflected the psychological and social upheaval of their converts, the format also gave rise to a new type of community—a voluntary association led by charismatic force and bound by mutually "edifying *conversation.*"[7]

The revival made use as well of nontraditional print media (i.e., besides books). The colonies' few newspapers reported the words and deeds of revivals elsewhere, serving in effect as advance publicity and priming for later "spontaneous" outbursts. The infant publishing industry got a boost as ministers dashed off pamphlets to praise or defame the movement. Revival leaders even set up early correspondence committees to coordinate their movement along the whole American seaboard and even across the Atlantic.

Inadvertently, half-consciously, the Awakening crystallized and spread a new form of entertainment. New Englanders typically had found recreation in activities that served "serious" purposes and meshed with the normal round of life. Hunting and fishing allowed a break from routine work but also put food on the table. The Sabbath demarcated the week; the town meeting and Thanksgiving the year; weddings and

---

pp. 144-55. On the Awakening as a whole, Bonomi in *Under the Cope of Heaven* provides the broadest context, and J. M. Bumsted and John E. Van de Wetering in *What Must I Do To Be Saved? The Great Awakening in Colonial America* (Hinsdale, Ill.: Dryden Press, 1976) provide a close and thorough analysis.

7. Harry S. Stout, "Religion, Communications, and the Ideological Origins of the American Revolution," *William and Mary Quarterly* (third series) 34 (Oct. 1977): 519-41.

funerals the course of life. With the "worldliness" of the eighteenth century, more worrisome activities proceeded from grog shops and seasonal fairs.[8] Revivals crossed and blended these two tracks wonderfully, mixing the lure of "extraordinary" excitements with the serious purposes of religion and community. Revivalists knew their audience and knew how to meet them. As popular-culture theory would put it, the itinerant preachers repackaged pieces of folk sentiment (traditional denominational religion) into a new, broader-reaching "pitch" that defied established limits. And their performances clearly had entertainment values: commonplace idiom, dramatic force, and theatrical flair. George Whitefield, the greatest itinerant, matched twentieth-century rock stars in celebrity and (self-)promotion. His critics sensed the point in their litany of rebuke. The revival was "wild" and "extravagant," luring the innocent from their "plain duty" (i.e., work) to an orgy of "enthusiasm." The orgies of spirit proved fleshly as well. Because of the revival, one critic complained, "our presses are teeming with books and our women with bastards."[9]

As with other fads, the trappings of revivalism disappeared from New England almost as fast as they had come. But the evangelical movement lived on in its own institutional and theological framework, and it continued to help many youth secure a place in society. For society as a whole, however, the Awakening inserted but one more element of discord amid the forces of modernization. Its oral charisma worked only for particular groups that heeded a particular voice. Increasingly thereafter, politics came to supplant religion as the ground of social unity. Instead of seeing the devil lurking in the woods, New Englanders began to see the devil first in French and then in British designs on North America. New communications strategies from the revival fit the political cause well. Committees of correspondence, polemical pamphleteering, and especially spontaneous mass meetings of fervid oratory helped trigger the American Revolution. In addition, another strain from revivalism, a youthful, anti-patriarchal idiom, colored the rhetoric of revolution.[10] Unlike that of the revival, however, the zeal of rebellion

8. David Freeman Hawke, *Everyday Life in Early America* (New York: Harper & Row, 1988), pp. 88-100, 143-56, 174-77.

9. Timothy Cutler, quoted in Cedric B. Cowing, "Sex and Preaching in the Great Awakening," *American Quarterly* 20 (1968): 624.

10. Nathan O. Hatch, "The Origins of Civil Millennialism in America: New England Clergymen, the War with France, and the Revolution," *William and Mary Quarterly* (third series) 31 (1974): 407-30; Stout, "Religion, Communications, and the Ideological Origins of the American Revolution"; Jay Fliegelman, *Prodigals and Pilgrims: The American Revolution against Patriarchal Authority, 1750-1800* (New York: Cambridge University Press, 1982).

Whitefield: The Boy George of the Eighteenth Century

A low-born boy in a provincial English town, fatherless, idles away his hours dreaming of glory on the stage. He scores some early successes, locally, then in London, dazzling crowds with his charisma, raw talent, and sheer youthfulness. But he senses greater things across the Atlantic, although his fans will barely let him go: "I was nearly half-an-hour going out the door. . . . They would run and stop me in the alleys, hug me in their arms, and follow me with wishful looks." His tour of America is a pure triumph, attracting unprecedented crowds, media coverage, and hot word-of-mouth. He hits city after city, with increasing thousands turning out each time. The young men wave their arms, the young ladies scream and faint, and the gate receipts pile up.

Thus went the "British Invasion" of the mid-1960s and numerous British onslaughts since—but also George Whitefield's evangelistic crusade of 1740. In ten weeks Whitefield traveled 800 miles (at the time, a 50-mile trip was arduous), gave 130 sermons, and gathered crowds upward of 50 percent of a city's population, sometimes exceeding that number. Collections for his orphanage in Georgia equaled the life earnings of a working man.

Whitefield's tour rode a cascade of publicity fueled by its novelty, its cult of numbers (of those addressed, of those converted, of funds donated), and its star's appearance ("almost angelical—a young, slim, slender youth . . . with a bold undaunted countenance"). His theatrical practice served him well. David Garrick, London's best actor at the time, deemed the revivalist's ability to say "Oh!" worth a hundred guineas, and swore he could move a crowd to tears simply by the way he pronounced "Mesopotamia." The more calculating Ben Franklin noted that Whitefield's small stock of sermons "was so improved by frequent repetitions that every accent, every emphasis, every modulation of voice was so perfectly well turned and well placed, that without being interested in the subject, one could not help being pleased with the discourse, a pleasure of much the same kind with that received from an excellent piece of music. This is an advantage itinerant preachers have over those who are stationary: as the latter cannot well improve their delivery of a sermon by so many rehearsals."

Whitefield also thrived on, while earnestly bewailing, controversy. The diary of his first American tour was quickly published, complete with insults to various parties who therefore protested his next visit, which redoubled his followers' show of support—and which kept him in the spotlight. So on he went his whole life, fondly recalled in his fans' devotion; fondly recalling their tears, their embraces, their numbers; ever preparing for one more tour. Whitefield died on crusade, his fifth, in Newburyport, Massachusetts, at age 56. A few years later American Revolutionary troops raided his tomb for bits of clothing, which they passed around the ranks before battle. (Elvis lives!)

Student Revolts

Student riots around the turn of the century included boycotting classes, barricading college buildings, breaking windows, trashing the commons and/or chapel, setting fires around or to college buildings, beating faculty members, and whipping the president or trustees. Riots broke out in the following years at the following schools:

1798 at Brown
1799 at the University of North Carolina
1800 at Princeton
1802 at Williams, Yale, William & Mary, Union, and Princeton
1805 at the University of North Carolina
1807 at Harvard and Princeton
1809 at Union and Dartmouth
1811 at Columbia

Thereafter, "almost without exception there was a wave of disorders every four or five years. . . . Student revolt became a tradition. A college education was incomplete without one confrontation."

In response, college authorities encouraged religious revivals, which in New England alone burst forth repeatedly at several schools:

at Yale in 1802, 1808, 1811-12, 1815
at Middlebury in 1805-06, 1809, 1811
at Williams in 1805-06, 1812, 1816
at Dartmouth in 1805, 1815

—From Steven J. Novak, *The Rights of Youth: American Colleges and Student Revolt, 1798-1815* (Cambridge, Mass.: Harvard University Press, 1977), pp. 17-25, 129.

proved harder to contain, and it did not simply disappear once the British fleet left. In the first decades after Independence, authority of all sorts came under challenge on grounds political, religious, and generational, separately and in combination. Ironically, the fruits of the Awakening, its churches and colleges (Princeton, Brown, Dartmouth), were now the targets, set upon with riots by none other than young students.[11]

11. Steven J. Novak, *The Rights of Youth: American Colleges and Student Revolt, 1790-1865* (New York: Cambridge University Press, 1981). In *The Democratization of American Christianity* (New Haven: Yale University Press, 1989), Nathan O. Hatch shows how renegade young evangelicals attacked more established evangelical churches under the inspiration of the American Revolution.

In this climate, the president of Yale and grandson of Jonathan Edwards, Timothy Dwight, began a conversion campaign among students that heralded the second Awakening. The solution to the disorders that had for three generations fed and followed upon revival dynamics would be . . . well, more revival.

Revival Discipline in the Young Republic: 1790-1840

Rekindling revivalism made sense in that the same forces the first Awakening had addressed were again pressing very hard, only now on a much wider front. In the fifty years after the Revolution, Americans flooded westward from the Atlantic seaboard to the Mississippi River. Perhaps more important, in the northern states began the epochal shift from the countryside to towns and cities, from farming to commerce and manufacturing. In the 1730s-1740s the young had wanted early entry into full adulthood, especially the economic privilege that would allow for marriage. The youth of the 1830s confronted a whole new way of life. Young women faced the greatest challenge. The enormous demographic shift had pushed them out of farm households into textile factories, school-teaching, hired domestic service—even into prostitution. But young men were troubling because they kept to an *established* pattern, leaving home for much of the year to work for wages, to apprentice at a craft, to attend school. The classroom mixed all ages from the early teens through the early twenties. The shop mixed boys with men for wages that were supposed to go home. A given year combined home and boarding house, dependency and autonomy, in random proportions; and the passing years did not build these into a natural developmental process.[12]

Flux, irregularity, and wild oscillation thus characterized the young man's life, just as they did the boom-bust economy as a whole. Cultural leaders did not miss the coincidence, nor could they overlook the opportunity that the open countryside and the red-lighted city gave youth to escape at will from their past and their parents. Males could now achieve virtual independence by their late teens, and they commonly moved two or three times a year. The young roaming en masse haunted the fledgling republic with questions of order and virtue. The

---

12. Joseph F. Kett, *Rites of Passage: Adolescence in America, 1790 to the Present* (New York: Basic Books, 1977), pp. 11-108; Mintz and Kellogg, *Domestic Revolutions,* pp. 43-65; Nancy F. Cott, *The Bonds of Womanhood: "Woman's Sphere" in New England, 1790-1835* (New Haven: Yale University Press, 1977).

young were haunted too, but by questions of freedom and identity. If kin, sponsors, and village mores no longer shaped behavior, neither did they any longer offer shelter from mistakes or accidents. Freedom from home came at the cost of submitting to the harshness of the marketplace and of life in general. The city offered bold freedoms and temptations but exacted puzzling punishments. Autonomy came in anonymity, but anonymity also meant impersonality and insignificance. How might the young know themselves, if others did not know them and they did not know others? Where was the web of roles and rules in which the self could find identity?

From Yale to the Erie Canal, from the frontier to Broadway, wherever mobility and flux prevailed, revivalists arose to once again turn personal and social confusion to order. In technique they borrowed colonial examples but made them conscious and calculated. Charles Finney, the champion revivalist of upstate New York, led the way theologically by dumping the first Awakening's Calvinism for an explicit doctrine of free will. People themselves had to choose their salvation, and the revivalists' task was to catalyze that choice. Finney even wrote a manual showing exactly how. The free-will theology of the new revivalism thus fit perfectly with the free agency of the mobile young, and the revival as a whole promised to solve all the problems of a baffling world.[13] Overloaded with free choices, youth could make the one big choice that would settle basic issues of identity and life purpose and supply a standard with which to work out the rest. Anonymous and lonely, the urban young entered the intimate bonds of a religious surrogate family that bestowed identity and community. Amid flux they found anchorage; amid temptation, a strict and, as it proved (and as revivalists themselves would point out), an economically profitable discipline. Campus converts at Williams and Amherst, at Oberlin and Lane Seminary in Cincinnati, found in religious crusading a career that at once offered humble service and grand ambition, pious fame and social power.[14] It is little wonder, then, that revivalists enthused about a

13. Fine overviews of the Second Great Awakening are Whitney R. Cross, *The Burned-Over District: The Social and Intellectual History of Enthusiastic Religion in Western New York, 1800-1850* (Ithaca, N.Y.: Cornell University Press, 1950); Percy Miller, *The Life of the Mind in America: From the Revolution to the Civil War* (New York: Harcourt, Brace, 1965), pp. 3-95; William L. McLoughlin, *Revivals, Awakenings, and Reform* (Chicago: University of Chicago Press, 1978), pp. 98-140. Key contrary interpretations are provided by Paul E. Johnson, *A Shopkeeper's Millennium: Society and Revivals in Rochester, New York, 1815-1837* (New York: Hill & Wang, 1978); and Timothy L. Smith, "Righteousness and Hope: Christian Holiness and the Millennial Vision in America, 1800-1900," *American Quarterly* 31 (Spring 1979): 21-45.

14. Lois W. Banner, "Religion and Reform in the Early Republic: The Role of Youth," *American Quarterly* 23 (1971): 677-95; and John Demos, "The Rise and Fall of

future when all the nation, all the world, would be made over in their new image: boom economy and strict morality, intimate piety in a mass market, righteousness and productivity embracing, bringing heaven on earth.

The answer was not quite so simple, however. In this larger, more open scene, theological novelties multiplied, each with its own proselytizers and organization. "Revival" in fact did not end choice but multiplied it. Moreover, salvation gained by individual decision could be lost the same way. Salvation also required stricter behavior than ever, for if people could freely choose salvation, they were free as well—perhaps obligated—to perform righteously in every act. Finney's free-will theology quickly developed obligations to achieve perfect holiness, complete sanctification in all of life, in this moment, now. Free will was hounded on every side, called to titanic exertions—again, like the free enterpriser in the free market.[15]

To bolster willpower for moral and spiritual struggle, an army of exhorters flooded the field, enlisting new communication and transportation technologies to sell freedom through discipline. If we adjust for different messages and media, upstate New York would resemble contemporary California or today's landscape of TV commercials. On the canal boats and railroads traveled not just revivalists but savants of self-help, practitioners of innumerable medical, mystical, educational, and political nostrums—and all virtually without credentials beyond the bearer's charisma. One town might host Emerson extolling the virtue(s) of "culture," the next a reformer promising the millennium through phrenology, teetotaling, new diet, or new schools. National leagues for every sort of reform organized to use print to disseminate their program systematically. "Self-reliance" required a lot of help, and the new print technology made a free-lance, advice-giving career possible for the first time.

Not to be outdone by religionists, "secular" advisors too urged ever more heroic discipline: not just moderation but abstention from alcohol, not a negotiated but an "immediate" end to slavery. Medical "authorities" whipped up a veritable orgy of restraint against indulging the physical appetites. They might demean Sylvester Graham—Presbyterian minister turned temperance lecturer turned dietary reformer—as

---

Adolescence," in *Past, Present and Personal: The Family and Life Course in American History* (New York: Oxford University Press, 1986), pp. 100-103.

15. The competitive and marketing processes among revivalists are dramatically presented in Nathan O. Hatch, *The Democratization of American Christianity*. On Finney's perfectionism, see Smith, "Righteousness and Hope," pp. 32-42.

a quack, but probably duplicated much of his advice (the regimen of the all-bran "graham" cracker excepted). Alcohol and tobacco were proscribed; coffee and tea were suspect. Some lists went on to eliminate meat and spices; many advocated infrequent sex even within marriage; and very many absolutely prohibited masturbation. On this last score, Graham was but a small figure in one of the age's most remarkable crusades. The footloose young clerks of the new cities were pointedly and repeatedly warned that "wasteful expenditure" of one's finite "seed" would so debilitate the "abuser" in mind and business that any progeny he might one day manage to sire would live (and soon die) puny and poor.[16]

Whether young people heeded all this advice or not, they were clearly entertained by the advice-givers. The latter intended their wisdom to supplant the dangerous recreations of the cities. They promoted their cause with flamboyant advance publicity, bold claims, and pointed challenges to skeptics to debate and risk conversion. Such flamboyant tactics often compromised the very message of discipline they were meant to convey: style was at odds with substance. Sometimes the challenges worked, but at other times they prompted raucous heckling or riots, such as those that greeted Theodore Weld and other anti-slavery lecturers. And whatever works of the revivalists the young might buy, they also bought large quantities of salacious literature. In fact, the Davy Crockett almanacs, really nineteenth-century comic books, simply reversed the revivalists' terms, ridiculing fathers, flaunting sexually voracious women, and cultivating an ethic of violence, excess, and animal spirits. This was male free will with a vengeance, hugely entertaining and hugely profitable.

Youth and Victorian Nurture, 1840-1890

By 1840 it had become obvious that leaders had asked too much of individual willpower to overcome a wide-open world with overabundant temptation. In response, a few weary radicals removed themselves

---

16. Ronald G. Walters' *American Reformers, 1815-1860* (New York: Hill & Wang, 1978) is the best account of the general syndrome treated in these two paragraphs. For specific bodily regulations, see pp. 145-56. For closer analysis, see Ben Barker-Benfield, "The Spermatic Economy: A Nineteenth-Century View of Sexuality," in *The American Family in Social-Historical Perspective,* ed. Michael Gordon (New York: St. Martin's Press, 1973), pp. 336-72; and R. P. Neuman, "Masturbation, Madness, and the Modern Concepts of Childhood and Adolescence," *Journal of Social History* 8 (Spring 1975): 1-27.

Antebellum Comic Books: The Davy Crockett Almanacs

On father: "The old gentleman passed by, puffing and blowing as though his steam was high enough to burst his boiler."

The ideal woman: "[She] wore a bearskin petticoat, an alligator's hide for an overcoat, an eagle's nest for a hat with a wild cat's tail for a feather . . . [and] sucked forty rattlesnake's eggs . . . to give her sweet breath the night she was married."

On racist cannibalism: "I smashed number one [of two Indians he was fighting] into injun gravy with my foot, and spread it over number two, and made a dinner for me and my dog. It was superlicious."

On sexual thrills in the backwoods: "I went to a tree about two feet threw and not a limb on it for thirty feet, and would climb up to the limbs and then locking my arms and legs together around it, . . . slide down to the bottom again. This would make the inside of my legs and arms feel mighty warm and good." ·

—Quoted in Carroll Smith-Rosenberg, *Disorderly Conduct: Visions of Gender in Victorian America* (New York: Alfred A. Knopf, 1985), pp. 94, 103, 98, 105. Summarizing, Smith-Rosenberg states, "Allusions to themes of buggery, *vagina dentata* exhibition, and male homosexuality occur in virtually every Crockett almanac" (p. 318).

---

to wilderness communes or joined apocalyptic sects. The bulk of the middle class favored a more moderate refuge—the home. In fact, the home seemed to promise solutions for all the problems of the urban-commercial world, and that hopeful, if sentimental, image reigned over bourgeois life for the rest of the century. "Domesticity's" primary strategies involved (1) regathering youth into the home for an extended stay during which (2) they would be sheltered from a wicked world and (3) intensively nurtured in good habits and character. The home was to reduce the strains of choice from without and within.[17]

The new perspective also assumed a new model of work. In farming and traditional crafts, the home had also been the workplace. In an industrial age, "gainful employment" shifted to the office, the factory, or the store, and men moved with it. By middle-class norms the home

---

17. Kett, *Rites of Passage,* pp. 111-43; Cott, *The Bonds of Womanhood,* pp. 65-91; Mary P. Ryan, *Cradle of the Middle Class: The Family in Oneida County, New York, 1790-1865* (New York: Cambridge University Press, 1981); Colleen McDannell, *The Christian Home in Victorian America, 1840-1900* (Bloomington: Indiana University Press, 1986).

was left without an economic function—as were the women who stayed there. Busy though they might be, women in the home were not "working." Rather, they adopted the new vocation of homemaking, nurturing the family as a narrower yet deeper institution. So also, children stayed at home much longer. The days of footloose teenagers, seasonal comings and goings, and laboring and living away from home under another adult's roof were disappearing. Even working-class youth, the ultimate wanderers, began to stay longer with their parents, handing their wages directly to them.[18]

Victorian concern focused most strongly upon younger children (pre-teens). Compared with their country counterparts, who could attend "infant schools" from age three onward, city children started school later, stayed in it longer, and passed through a far more thoroughly "graded" (i.e., both age-segregated and performance-evaluated) program. The new training was "regular" (rule-based and routinized) instead of "haphazard." Thus, children at once received more maternal tenderness (at home) and closer training for the business world (at school).[19] The same ideal took hold in religion. Revivalism too seemed haphazard when compared with the regularities of the new "Christian nurture." As codified by Hartford pastor-theologian Horace Bushnell and dispensed in countless advice columns and church magazines, the program of nurture called upon the home to provide such thorough conditioning in "moral influences" that children might grow to maturity never knowing a time when they had not been Christian.[20] The developmental psychology of Charles Finney was reversed: conditioning replaced catalyzing; children replaced young adults; growth supplanted crisis; and maturation displaced decision. If the revival had tried to end anxiety, Victorian nurture proposed to ban anxiety altogether. The new scheme still focused on the will, but hoped to shape it from the ground up to turn it into a strength of "character" that would prove immune to moods and temptation.

In this grand plan of nurture, "woman" held the key. She had

18. Michael Katz and Ian E. Davey, "Youth and Early Industrialization in a Canadian City," in *Turning Points: Historical and Sociological Essays on the Family,* ed. John Demos and Sarane Boocock (Chicago: University of Chicago Press, 1978), pp. 81-119; Glen H. Elder, Jr., "Adolescence in Historical Perspective," in *Growing Up in America,* pp. 30-32; Kett, *Rites of Passage,* p. 171.

19. Kett, *Rites of Passage,* pp. 122-32; Carl F. Kaestle and Maris A. Vinovskis, "From Apron Strings to ABC's: Parents, Children, and Schooling in Nineteenth-Century Massachusetts," in *Turning Points,* pp. 39-80.

20. Kett, *Rites of Passage,* pp. 111-21; E. Brooks Holifield, *A History of Pastoral Care in America* (Nashville: Abingdon Press, 1983), pp. 114-31, 150-58.

daily to resuscitate her husband, nurture her children, and make the home a combination of church, school, and refuge, which is what domestic ideology demanded. The demands were indeed high, as were the stakes. Without her care the ethos of business would corrupt everyone; more than anyone else, she had to preserve the virtue of the republic and proffer the consolations of religion. Both democracy and faith would wither without her help. And she had to accomplish all these tasks with arguably less economic and political power than before.[21] To carry on, women seized upon a new communications medium for themselves. By 1840 innovations in printing, distribution, and business made it possible "to turn out books as rapidly and efficiently as shirts, nails, or matches." The ensuing torrent of print constituted the first mass-produced cultural artifacts in American history. There were "ladies" magazines and gift books, children's stories, advice manuals, and above all novels, mostly written by and for women. Traditionally, cultural leaders had proscribed fiction as false and seductive, especially for young ladies, but by 1850 only a few held out against the tidal wave of popularity. Once again the "dangerous" was to be turned into the educational and uplifting, into the very salvation of society.[22]

On the surface these stories told a familiar enough tale. A young woman suddenly loses all external supports (family, wealth, or prospects) and is cast into a threatening world. Through chaos and temptation she learns to know herself and to develop the judgment and character that will ensure her place in the world. Crucially, she learns to subdue all passion and resist those men who appeal to it. She can accept only the suitor who is trustworthy and dependable enough to provide for *her* future dependency as wife and mother. But the stories also took bolder aim. They set forth a domestic ethic of "love, support, and mutual responsibility" to displace and discredit the male market world "governed purely by mercenary and exploitive considerations." Women

21. Barbara Welter's "The Cult of True Womanhood, 1820-1860," *American Quarterly* 18 (1966): 151-74, is a classic sketch of the syndrome; in *Catharine Beecher: A Study in American Domesticity* (New Haven: Yale University Press, 1973), Kathryn Kish Sklar profiles one of its chief promoters. In *The Feminization of American Culture* (New York: Alfred A. Knopf, 1977), Ann Douglas brilliantly interprets the syndrome's underpinnings and consequences. As Nancy Cott shows in *The Bonds of Womanhood*, the commercial revolution all along had increased the complexity and openness of women's future much more than their power to control it. Now they were to do unto youth as had been done unto them.

22. Russel Nye, *The Unembarrassed Muse: The Popular Arts in America* (New York: Dial Press, 1970), pp. 23-28. On fiction's growing acceptability, see Nina Baym, *Novels, Readers, and Reviewers: Responses to Fiction in Antebellum America* (Ithaca, N.Y.: Cornell University Press, 1984), pp. 32-33. See also Nina Baym, *Women's Fiction: A Guide to Novels by and about Women in America, 1820-1870* (Ithaca, N.Y.: Cornell University Press, 1978).

The Emergence of a Publishing Industry

By 1840 book publishing had become "a separate, professionalized business"

    —relying on 400 paper mills (up from 150 in 1830)
    —using the new electroplating technology (1841) and cylindrical
     presses (1830s)
    —producing the new format of the paperbound book
    —dominated by large enterprises like the House of Harper.

—Russel Nye, *The Unembarrassed Muse: The Popular Arts in America* (New York: Dial Press, 1970), p. 24.

     The American Bible Society was printing 1,000,000 Bibles every year; the American Tract Society 6,000,000 tracts; the Adventists 1,000,000 tracts per year for four years, predicting the imminent end of the world.

—Nathan Hatch, *The Democratization of American Christianity* (New Haven: Yale University Press, 1989), pp. 141-42.

     The British Museum by 1859 had collected 27,000 novels published since Sir Walter Scott's *Waverly* (1814).

—Nina Baym, *Novels, Readers, and Reviewers* (Ithaca, N.Y.: Cornell University Press, 1984), p. 27.

faced, these stories intimated, a historic opportunity to "master not only themselves but the world."[23]

    But below that surface loomed still other tales. The homes portrayed in the bestsellers ranged from the monotonous to the abusive, with desperate unhappiness the norm. Story after story focused on the process of female self-discovery and self-control and rarely on the marriage on which the domestic counterculture would be built. A "good marriage" was the seal of good character, but paradoxically marriage would demand the sacrifice of the very independence that contributed to strong character. Even if independence had to submit to mutual dependency, the terms of exchange—male material sustenance for female moral influence—held difficulties. Since moral influence derived from internal character, women were eternally thrown back into cultivating and exhibiting their own interiors; "serving others" could in actuality promote self-absorption and self-display. Novel-reading itself

23. Baym, *Women's Fiction*, pp. 20, 27, 278. On the story type, see pp. 11-30.

became a ritual mechanism of this irony. The flip side of such narcissism was rage, rage at male defiance of "influence," rage "almost homicidal in its intensity" against male power, male brutality, male responsibility for the sins of the world.[24]

The medium of story-telling and story-reading compounded these problems still further. Denouncing the commercial ethos proved big business; novels celebrating love sold for cash to a mass audience. Women authors prided themselves on their professionalism, measuring success by copies sold, measuring their "moral influence" by their celebrity. Like their male counterparts, young female readers were buying advice that taught *self*-formation, *self*-education, and *self*-reliance, and they were buying it in such quantity that observers could liken novel-reading only to "dram-drinking" for its addictive appeal and narcotic effect. If the novels proclaimed mutuality, novel-reading itself was a "solitary and self-centered activity" indulging the individualism it decried. Finally, a book's popularity rose directly with its "energy" or ability to "excite." That in itself contradicted the lesson of rational self-control, and over time the search for sales pushed the genre to exhibit ever more the emotionalism and vivid temptations it was preaching against.[25]

A number of limitations, then, beset Victorian domestic fiction. More debilitating than its often criticized "low" artistic merit was the political bargain it accepted. Professing contentment with the male monopoly on economic power, women novelists berated that power and tried to array against it the vaunted moral force of domesticity, all the while fearing that that very force would prove ineffectual. They could not relish even the nurture that was their prize in the bargain. To succeed in the world, sons needed lessons opposite from those their mothers taught. Instead, young men sought counsel in another, male-written flood of mass-produced literature whose sheer scale betrayed "the irrelevance . . . of the mother's educational function."[26]

As pioneers of popular culture, women writers fell into a difficulty that has great significance for this study. By entering the mass market, they ventured into a system that contradicted their exalted "home" values. Impersonal commerce had caused the corruption and chaos from which they wanted to save themselves and the young, but their books and huge readership were possible only in that world of

24. Douglas, *The Feminization of American Culture,* p. 273. The dynamics described in this paragraph form a chief thesis of Douglas's book.
25. Baym, *Novels, Readers, and Reviewers,* pp. 50-59; Baym, *Women's Fiction,* pp. 30-35.
26. Barker-Benfield, "The Spermatic Economy," p. 337.

money, sales, and success. They hung, then, in the same paradox as the revivalists who had gone before them. Like the women writers, the revivalists had ironically seized the media of a new socio-economic system to cure the problems caused precisely by that system, problems which ran wild among youth. They *did* manage thereby to give some youth a coherent life-pattern. But the consequence was to acclimate the young and their would-be saviors alike to a system and to values that had proved so disturbing in the first place. From that irony the players might have noticed another. Just as the domestic system arose out of the shortcomings of revivalism, so domesticity would provoke and empower the young enough to prod them to construct a new system in their own time. That time came at the end of the century.

The 1890s

The twentieth century has been the heyday of youth, and it dawned with the 1890s. In that decade a great public outcry erupted over the problems of youth. A bevy of reform efforts tried to resolve these, and an intellectual enterprise struggled to redefine what "youth" was—or ought to be. That concept was labeled "adolescence" and has prevailed ever since.

Before we analyze the concept per se, we should look at the social world of its birth. Most youth-targeted activities in the 1890s grew from worries about the opposing extremes of the social spectrum. On the one end, the children of the slums seemed too clever, too "physical," too numerous, and altogether immune to the regime of the Victorian home. Social missionaries and legislation poured into the inner cities to provide surrogates: "real" homes via adoption or relocation, "settlement *houses*" to keep street urchins from committing crime, "juvenile" or "detention *homes*" to reform them when they did.[27] Still, the elite and middle-class reformers also felt some ambivalent attraction to slum life. The vitality and spontaneity of the streets, the self-rule of its boy gangs were precisely the traits missing in the children of privilege.

For on the opposite end of the social spectrum raged an epidemic of "neurasthenia" or the "collapse of nervous energy." The condition left its victims prostrate for months, even years at a time. Ap-

---

27. Kett, *Rites of Passage*, pp. 173-228; Leroy Ashby, *Saving the Waifs: Reformers and Dependent Children, 1890-1917* (Philadelphia: Temple University Press, 1984); Anthony Platt, *The Child Savers: The Invention of Delinquency* (Chicago: University of Chicago Press, 1969).

1890s Headnote

"The twentieth century was to put a special premium on youth . . . and it was in a college setting about the end of the nineteenth century that the model of a youth culture came into being. Invented by a pulp magazine writer in 1896, [Frank] Merriwell, the carefree champion of every sport at Yale, was the first great hero of American popular culture whose exploits took place on a college playing field."

—John Higham, *Writing American History* (Bloomington: Indiana University Press, 1979), p. 77.

---

parently, the Victorian home had taken all too well, overwhelming youth with the father's strict conscience and strenuous career and the mother's smothering sentimental tenderness. These children needed release from their stuffy cloisters into the free space of nature (provided by the newly founded Boy Scouts with their hiking and camping excursions), into vigorous body-building (provided by the gyms of the remodeled YMCA), into the combat of football (made into a national cult in the 1890s by elite "Ivy League" colleges).[28] The new youth prescriptions, in short, were following an old formula. What the "dangerous" classes had, the "better sorts" needed, would redeem, and then use to revitalize the nation. Wall Street and the White House could use a tough boys gang to set them right.

The new notion of adolescence gave all these trends theoretical sanction. It was proclaimed in 1904 by G. Stanley Hall, research psychologist and sometime president of Clark University. Hall's influence showed a broad shift in elite cultural authority. Whereas the revivalists and motherly nurturers had linked their ideas more or less closely to religion, the chief sponsors of "adolescence" were largely secular colleges and universities, their research coming out of the social sciences. This very shift in cultural authority had troubled Hall during his own youth and doubtless shaped his interest in and conception of adolescence. Hall had first set out to be a theologian and then a philosopher, before finally settling into psychology. He then justified the switch by

---

28. John Higham, "The Reorientation of American Culture in the 1890's," in *Writing American History* (Bloomington: Indiana University Press, 1979), pp. 73-102. A broad and insightful treatment of the neurasthenic crisis is T. Jackson Lears' *No Place of Grace: Antimodernism and the Transformation of American Culture, 1880-1920* (New York: Pantheon, 1981), especially pp. 47-58.

Defining the Adolescent

"The key contribution of the 1900-1920 period was not the discovery of adolescence . . . [but] the invention of the adolescent, the youth whose social definition—indeed, whose whole being—was determined by a biological process of maturation.

". . . adolescence was essentially a conception of behavior imposed on youth, rather than an empirical assessment of the way in which young people actually behaved."

—Joseph F. Kett, *Rites of Passage: Adolescence in America, 1790 to the Present* (New York: Basic Books, 1977), p. 243.

---

investing social science with messianic potential. Psychology was to be "a new theology," and Clark University the new model seminary of laboratory experimentation. And like his New England forebears, Hall determined to save the young first. The theory of adolescence was thus literally a new gospel—and a new law.[29]

Its premises came from Darwinian recapitulation theory: the individual life-course replicated the evolutionary progress of the entire race. Adolescence was a distinct "stage" through which each person passed on the way from childhood (the "primitive" stage) to adulthood (the "civilized" stage). Adolescence therefore was transitional but essential, its traits dangerous but its labor vital for attaining maturity. Squelching it was just as bad as giving it free rein. The "civilized" elite had tried the first, the "brutish" laborers the second; the new theory provided a better way. It required two steps. First, youth were to be removed as much as possible from adult concerns and contacts, especially of the casual sort, and sequestered in their own institutions. Second, in those institutions they were to perform the vital "work" of adolescence, developing sociability and physical capacity in preparation for adulthood.[30]

These two principles justified the new treatment of youth in the earlier twentieth century. The problem with lower-class youth, experts agreed, was their direct and unsupervised immersion in the world of adults. There they were exposed to crime, dulling their moral sense; there

29. Kett, *Rites of Passage*, pp. 204-21. The best biographical analysis of Hall is Dorothy Ross's *G. Stanley Hall: The Psychologist as Prophet* (Chicago: University of Chicago Press, 1972).

30. Kett, *Rites of Passage*, pp. 217-28.

they prematurely fell into wage labor, foreshortening their maturation; thence their doom to perpetual primitiveness. Reform measures would correct this by prohibiting child labor, requiring longer schooling, and setting aside (i.e., separate from adult activity) the special space of parks and playgrounds where youth could go about their task of socializing play. Adult contacts would be supervisory, and these adults would be from the "better sorts" of people. On the elite end of the social spectrum, the listlessness of youth was taken as evidence of premature exposure to adult worries about career, moral obligation, and metaphysical certainty. But solving this problem required a special twist.

On the one hand, prolonged schooling would keep the young out of the world of work and with each other. Accordingly, the often private, nineteenth-century "academy" gave way to the new public "high school," and the enrollment of fourteen- to seventeen-year-olds began its great twentieth-century leap upward.[31] Similarly, church-related agencies (the Epworth League, Christian Endeavor, the YMCA, the Boy Scouts) multiplied to absorb the spare time of youth's after-school hours. On the other hand, since intellectual and religious concerns had supposedly triggered the neurasthenic crisis, school and church had to be reoriented to new purposes. Christianity in this era turned "muscular" and connoted moral vigor; that translated for adolescents into physical vigor. Camping, hiking, and competitive games became both the lure and the end of church youth group.[32] High schools expanded from their classical intellectual curriculum to offer commercial, vocational, and general education courses (which in fact accounted for most of the expanded enrollments). But for all its students, the pre-collegiate included, the high school mandated "social education"—that is, training for "leisure, home life, and citizenship." Specific courses might do this, but a well-supervised system of student activities could do it better, and athletics could do it best of all.[33]

If the house of adolescence was designed by psychology, it was the economy that would build it and bring it to every corner of the country. Technological innovations late in the nineteenth century deci-

---

31. Ibid., pp. 183-89, 234-44. See also Selwyn Troen, "The Discovery of the Adolescent by American Education Reformers, 1900-1920: An Economic Perspective," in *Growing Up in America,* pp. 414-25.

32. David I. MacLeod, *Building Character in the American Boy: The Boy Scouts, YMCA, and Their Forerunners, 1870-1920* (Madison: University of Wisconsin Press, 1983); Kett, *Rites of Passage,* pp. 173-98. In *A History of Pastoral Care in America* (pp. 167-75), Holifield describes the larger tide of "muscular Christianity" of which these practices were a part.

33. Troen, "The Discovery of the Adolescent," p. 421. On athletics, see Joel H. Spring, "Mass Culture and School Sports," *History of Education Quarterly* 14 (Winter 1974): 483-98.

Table of High-School Enrollment, 1890-1980

Percentage of American children 14-17 years old in school:

1890	6	1940	70
1900	10	1950	75
1910	16	1960	85
1920	30	1970	90
1930	50	1980	90

—Glen Elder, Jr., "Adolescence in Historical Perspective," in *Growing Up in America: Historical Experiences*, ed. Harvey J. Graff (Detroit: Wayne State University Press, 1987), p. 15.

mated the youth labor market by rendering obsolete all sorts of jobs that mid- to late-teens had filled in shops, stores, or factories: set-up and clean-up tasks, delivering cash and telegrams, apprenticeships in a skilled trade, and so on. Increasingly, job training would shift from the work site to the high school, as the latter's new curriculum indicated. For many, the diploma became the passport beyond the "dead-end job."[34] For the more ambitious, success required a different set of traits than it had before: the corporate world did not want the heroic creation of new enterprises so much as the more effective organization and promotion of existing ones. In this light the neurasthenia epidemic signaled a crisis at work as well as at home, and it struck most among the children of the elite. They had been taught "character"—to be decisive, unbudging, and self-reliant, as befit the doughty entrepreneurial past. Suddenly they had to learn "personality"—to be flexible, progressive, oriented to others, fit for a sleek managerial future.[35] For some the shift was too jolting, leaving them paralyzed or confused. Others were successfully retrained by socialization and play.

In sum, the new practice of adolescence rejected some parts of earlier systems while expanding upon others. If ambivalent toward the Victorian home, it accentuated the Victorian removal of youth from "premature" adult contacts. Twentieth-century youth would have to stay in school even longer, would enter the job market even later, and would be far less likely than the youth of 1820 to work or live with adults outside their family. Like those earlier youth, they would associate with

34. Troen, "The Discovery of the Adolescent"; Kett, *Rites of Passage,* pp. 144-62.
35. Lears, *No Place of Grace,* pp. 47-58; Warren Susman, *Culture as History* (New York: Pantheon, 1984), pp. 271-85; Kett, *Rites of Passage,* pp. 232-34.

peers but only in special youth institutions managed by adult professionals. Athletics, student activities, and casual play were to fit into
an adult-regulated system that would discourage spontaneity, autonomy, and self-formation.[36]

Finally, adolescence forbade not just adult contacts but also adult
concerns: issues of religion, vocation, and intellectual life. This was a step
beyond any previous regimen—in fact, an abrupt about-face from what
had been expected of youth before. In the twentieth century, adolescence
became less a time to prepare for adulthood than an attempt to delay or
prevent it; it created "a self-contained world in which prolonged immaturity could sustain itself."[37] But a self-contained world can become self-
educated as well, shaping its own culture and mores. Here the strategy
of separation for adult control ran into a wall. The new ideology of
adolescence made possible a new youth community with a powerful
influence that could surpass any outside influence on its members' lives.
The creation of that community remains one of the 1890s' profound
legacies to American life. The same decade forged new transportation and
communications technologies, producing the automobile, the radio, and
moving pictures. And the 1920s would bring the new community and the
new technologies together in volatile combination.

The 1920s

The 1920s evoke congeries of images: Wall Street boom and corporate
derring-do, the hyper-advertising of ballyhoo, the national craze for
sports, the psychology of "self-realization" and "adjustment," and, of
course, "flaming youth." Disparate as these seem, they together spelled
the arrival (1) of the managerial economy for broad ranges of the middle
class and (2) of that phenomenon which is this book's primary concern—the symbiosis between a self-standing youth culture and a self-
conscious entertainment industry.

The new economic system revolved around huge, impersonal,
sleekly coordinated firms. Success *for* the firm required both controlled
competition against other firms and a proliferation of managers who
could work reliably together as a team. Success *within* the firm required
"personality": on the one hand, a distinctive "self-realized" personality

36. Spring, "Mass Culture and School Sports," pp. 483-98; Kett, *Rites of Passage*,
pp. 243-44.
37. Kett, *Rites of Passage*, p. 210.

College Football, 1900

Athletics seemed a fine cure, real and symbolic, for the neurasthenia sweeping elite households late in the century, so it was elite colleges that developed athletics most deliberately and successfully. Of all sports, football was favored as best exemplifying vitality and virility. Harvard built the nation's first concrete stadium (in 1903), and Yale dominated the field of play. From 1876 to 1909, Yale won 95 percent of its games, losing only 14 during the entire period. One year, 1888, it outscored its opponents 698 to 0.

Much of Yale's success stemmed from the presence all these years of Walter Camp—first as player, then as coach, then as advisor. A New Haven corporate executive and the brother-in-law of William Graham Sumner, America's leading social Darwinist, Camp epitomized the meaning and purpose of football for his time and class. If hard physical combat made for manliness, systematic discipline brought victory. Camp introduced rule changes—yard markings, downs, point differentials—that defined American football as a distinctive sport; he invented the All-American team that set national standards of success. Together, these systematized and regularized football and demanded " 'work' efficiency on the 'play' field. . . . Yale had the smoothest running football machine, emphasizing team cooperation rather than individual effort." Thus the physical vitality that was supposed to rescue youth from mechanical and social routine was itself routinized.

The lesson carried far beyond Camp's elite circle thanks to the publishing boom that made 1890-1915 the first golden age of American juvenile sports fiction. Its two greatest heroes were cast as Yale football stars, Frank Merriwell and Dink Stover, exemplars of the Camp ethic and of what fame and glory would mean to a whole generation of American boys.

—Ronald A. Smith, *Sports and Freedom: The Rise of Big-Time College Athletics* (New York: Oxford University Press, 1988), pp. 84-88.

—Walter Evans, "The All-American Boys," *Journal of Popular Culture* 6 (Summer 1972): 104-21.

for identity within the faceless ranks; on the other, an "adjusted" personality to insure cooperation with others. Success *within* and *for* the corporation required advertising: the display of an attractive self to gain promotion, and the display of the firm's products or services to promote their sale. To a large extent, the world of sports exemplified and ritualized the duality of competition and teamwork; an expanded higher education and its own hot youth culture gave lessons in personality; and the entertainment industry showed how to exhibit personality via leisure-time pursuits and the consumption of products. Sports, school, and entertainment alike fit into the advertising complex as subjects, targets, and methods. Altogether, the flaming youth of the twenties were simply the middle-class settlers who had followed the trail blazed by the elite pioneers of the 1890s. They simply (1) shifted physical culture from sexual repression to sexual expression; (2) poured into high schools and colleges in such numbers as to realize the potential for self-socialization; and (3) found the tools of their trade in the new communications media, which turned around to advertise the results to an attentive nation.

The whole syndrome depended on a historic expansion of higher education, and that expansion hinged on the twenties. By the end of the decade, half of those of eligible age were enrolled in high school, three times the proportion of 1910. One-sixth of the relevant age group were in college, over half of them in liberal arts institutions—again a 300 percent increase over 1910. On both levels the largest growth in absolute numbers came in the twenties.[38]

Yet the life of the mind did not fare as well. If campus newspapers of the time do not exaggerate, professors hardly mattered and courses deserved little work and encouraged a good bit of cheating. "Schools had become centers of youth life and youth activities which had little to do with the basic aims of education as they had been heretofore understood."[39] Rather, they had become camps for socialization, present pleasure, and future rewards. For women, school was the stage for courtship, a whirl of engagements that would lead to engagement. For men the campus social round, not academics, provided what was necessary for business success: contacts, "style," "leadership experience." In school and business alike, peer relations and peer molding stood supreme. The most dramatic triumph of youth came in seizing control of courtship, for in the twenties the peer-regulated system of dating replaced the parentally controlled mode of home visiting. More broadly, the peer group became the way one passed from the intimacy of the affectionate family into an impersonal, rationalized society. From the peer group the young learned "the demands of social roles."[40]

Those demands were, first, to "become an individual"— that is,

---

38. Ibid., p. 245. See also Elder, "Adolescence in Historical Perspective," pp. 15-18; Paula S. Fass, *The Damned and the Beautiful: American Youth in the 1920s* (New York: Oxford University Press, 1979), pp. 122-24, 211, 407, 438.

39. Fass, *The Damned and the Beautiful*, pp. 46-47. Fass's volume gives the overall argument presented in these paragraphs. See also Helen Lefkowitz Horowitz, *Campus Life: Undergraduate Cultures from the End of the Eighteenth Century to the Present* (New York: Alfred A. Knopf, 1987), pp. 118-50.

40. Fass, *The Damned and the Beautiful*, pp. 121-22. On dating, see John Modell, "Dating Becomes the Way of American Youth," in *Growing Up in America*, pp. 452-77; and Beth L. Bailey, *From Front Porch to Back Seat: Courtship in 20th Century America* (Baltimore: Johns Hopkins University Press, 1988).

Table of College Enrollment, 1880-1970

Percentage of American youth 18-21 years old attending college:

1880	2	1940	16
1890	3	1950	30
1900	4	1970	48
1920	8		

—Helen Lefkowitz Horowitz, *Campus Life* (New York: Alfred A. Knopf, 1987), pp. 5, 6.

---

to leave behind family, ethnic, and religious identity; and second, to conform to the ways of the group. The system of peer conformity on the college campus was "dazzling in its complexity and elegant in its basic simplicity."[41] Its *structure* (rules, enforcement, and stratification) came from fraternities, which grew as never before in the twenties. They determined a student's status, and they determined campus leadership. The system's *dynamics* came from conspicuous consumption. The right clothes made the person; the right destination, partner, and activity made the dating couple; and money made it all possible. Expense became the norm because style turned over rapidly with passing fads. Indeed, the twenties campus remains legendary for faddishness. The latest behavior, apparel, quirk, routine, or slang provided an excellent vehicle for breaking with past identity, for cementing a new one, and for ranking individuals within a conformist system. Leaders led the fads; losers followed.

Naturally, business advertising sprang upon this market as a gold mine. But they also spread collegiate styles well beyond campus. High-school students, working youth, and older adults all picked up the latest fashion from college. That required still faster change on campus in order for the real collegians to distinguish themselves, but merchandisers managed to keep up with the demand. "Youth" therefore became not only a market for sales but also an object—an image commodity—for sale, and college became a prime mode of advertising. In this respect, its real educational mission was to acculturate large portions of the middle class to high-scale, rapid-turnover consumption as a way of life.

As with earlier youth transitions, the new communications media figured centrally in this process. If youth were on their own, they also needed "national agencies like movies, magazines, and advertising"

---

41. Fass, *The Damned and the Beautiful,* pp. 121-29.

to tell them who they were. " 'Modern youth' as a national phenomenon was thus a byproduct of the means of long-range communication and large-scale distribution of goods as well as the more intimate associations of youth groups."[42] The hot technologies of the twenties each played a role. Movies and glossy magazines broadcast collegiate styles to the outside world. Cars provided an ideal combination of mobility and intimacy for dating. Radio and records fed jazz dancing, "unquestionably the most popular pastime" on campus and a rich lode for fads.[43] Altogether these spelled SEX—more precisely, the open display of sexuality, particularly by women. Nowhere did youth assert their liberation more graphically or elders react more fearfully. Nor was this just talk. The average age of sexual initiation dropped, albeit slightly, to 17 for males, 18 for females, and the discovery and refinement of varieties of noncoital contact constituted a boom industry.[44] But even here controls were manifest. Sex was freer but still absolutely marriage-oriented. Coeds tried to regulate the market by shaming more men into the dating pool and shaming "fast girls" out of it. Everything depended on one's "reputation," which was established by peer gossip and calibrated by peer standards.

The kings (and plums) in this market were the BMOC—Big Men on Campus. The title fell on fraternity leaders and athletes for epitomizing campus values. If students invested the extra-curriculum "with a kind of religious devotion," the fraternity chiefs were the high priests of the cult, the regulators of conformity.[45] Athletes were the gods themselves, the embodiment of competition and physicality. Around these two poles—"competition within conformity and conformity in the service of competition"—revolved all campus life.[46] By that token college *did* prepare students for life, for the same principles governed the corporate economy: standardized goods were promoted to a mass society via a fierce competition of images that magnified trivial differences and mandated the consumption of products as such.

Athletics had the extra advantage of connecting these games to childhood nostalgia and of ritualizing them in entertainment for a broader audience. The twenties' college students had inherited the mythology of the first golden age of juvenile sports fiction (1890–World War I). Since the collegiate level accounted for most of the decade's sharp

---

42. Ibid., pp. 126, 128.
43. Ibid., pp. 227-34, 241, 300. See also Horowitz, *Campus Life*, pp. 123-28.
44. Fass, *The Damned and the Beautiful*, p. 276; Horowitz, *Campus Life*, pp. 203-11.
45. Fass, *The Damned and the Beautiful*, pp. 141-47.
46. Ibid., p. 226.

College Football in the 1920s

	1921	1929
Attendance	1,504,319	3,617,421
Gate	$2,696,160	$9,032,160

—Joel H. Spring, "Mass Culture and School Sports," *History of Education Quarterly* 14 (Winter 1974): 495.

increase in spectator sports, more than students were watching college teams play. Already defined by pre–World War I fiction, the sports mythos valued individual heroics less than group loyalty, disciplined combat, and the eradication of peculiarity. And contrary to the hopes of the original sports visionaries, spectatorship tended to decrease actual participation and so also the promised physical fitness. Other hopes were realized, however. Athletics became the leading form of self-advertisement for universities, just as athletic "personalities" became pitchmen for all sorts of goods. And spectators learned to pay admission to the ritual display of their daily life.[47]

How far the new system triumphed showed in the inability of traditionalists to find institutional leverage against it. Universities obviously were part of the problem, not the solution. While middle-class parents might wish their children to slow down sexually, those same parents held few scruples, to judge from their role in the twenties' economy, about those "lusts of the flesh" that were speculative and consumerist. The Protestant churches in the twenties were too busy conducting theological civil war to do much more than scold youth from the sidelines. In the 1930s, with that war over, the mainline denominations took up a "peace of mind" theology that gave the notions of adjusted personality and manipulable image a vaguely Christian sanction. The Fundamentalist losers of the war renounced modern culture altogether but did so by means of the latest communications technologies—using the radio to rally an anonymous, scattered clientele, and the automobile to ride the faith-healing circuit. Radio and movies as national networks seem to have penetrated traditional ethnic and working-class communities at the same time. The values or media of the system seemed to implicate everyone.

47. Spring, "Mass Culture and School Sports," pp. 494-98; Fass, *The Damned and the Beautiful,* pp. 238, 255. On juvenile sports fiction, see Walter Evans, "The All-American Boys," *Journal of Popular Culture* 6 (Summer 1972): 104-21.

Conclusion

The rest of this book will examine the interrelationships among the economy, the media, and youth entertainment in our own time. For now, we can conclude that these connections are at once heir to historical patterns and challengers of them. Put another way, if the momentum holds, twentieth-century patterns of youth management might be following their success to the point of self-obliteration.

Since the 1890s, "youth" seem to reappear on the national stage as a "problem" about every thirty years, a problem signaled by their "dangerous" forms of entertainment. In fact, these intervals chart the immersion of new groups in the twentieth-century corporate-managerial economy. That economy requires youth to stay in school longer in order to learn assorted skills and to keep down unemployment rates. If the 1890s marked the entry point for the elite and the 1920s for the broader middle class, the 1950s brought the turn of the South, of blacks, and of the white working class. Nicely, just these three contributed the elements which blended together to form the fifties' badge of youth identity, rock and roll music. As adolescence expanded beyond the middle class to embrace all youth, it had to extend education for all too—first high school, the youth hot spot of the fifties, then college, the site of the sixties.

The political explosion on the sixties campuses pointed out the perplexities built into adolescence as a system.[48] The structures and concepts of adolescence flattered, protected, and indulged youth—but they also ordered and segregated them from wide ranges of power and activity. Youth were, in short, sequestered and disenfranchised. Their discovering this triggered the campus revolt, a revolt which showed more boldly than ever that the instruments adults intended for control, youth could turn to liberty. On the other hand, in the long run the liberties won in the sixties yielded less fundamental political change than a richer smorgasbord of lifestyles, themselves marketable by the same media system that took over youth socialization in the fifties and co-opted political protest in the sixties.

48. Background for the summary in this paragraph and the next is available in the following: Christopher Lasch, *The Culture of Narcissism: American Life in an Age of Diminishing Expectations* (New York: W. W. Norton, 1978); David Elkind, *All Grown Up and No Place to Go: Teenagers in Crisis* (Reading, Mass.: Addison-Wesley, 1984); Joshua Meyrowitz, "The Adultlike Child and the Childlike Adult: Socialization in an Electronic Age," *Daedalus* 113 (1984): 19-48; Susan Littwin, *The Postponed Generation: Why America's Grown-Up Kids Are Growing Up Later* (New York: William Morrow, 1986); and Barbara Ehrenreich, *The Hearts of Men: American Dreams and the Flight from Commitment* (Garden City, N.Y.: Doubleday, 1983).

The "liberated lifestyle" of the sixties campus spread through the general culture over the next two decades. Thus the last thirty-year benchmark, the 1980s, showed a scale of confusion that portends future dramatic change. Confusion arose because the "youth" values of the fifties and sixties seemed to become the regnant *adult* values of 1980, namely, the pursuit of perpetual personal freedom, of material plenty, of romance that will never have to settle down—all symbolized by games afield and abed. Since "lifestyle" has come to define not just *doing* but their very *being*, adults have now become dependent on the very psychological experts who wove the web of adolescence in the first place. The classic youth tasks of "growth," "finding oneself," and preparing for one's life-work have *become* the American life-work, even into "the golden years" of retirement. As subsequent chapters will detail, paying for all this help and play takes a lot of money, which requires a lot of work, which diminishes leisure, which requires that play be more intense and entertainment ever more enthralling. To keep up with the activities that adolescence as a system prescribes for them, teenagers have had to enter the "adult" preserve of work—just as they have, for other reasons, the domain of sex—as virtual peers of their parents. In short, just as adults have become eternal youths, or (to parody Karl Marx) as "youth" has become all, so youth are early enmeshed in adulthood and adolescence threatens to "wither away" as a distinct life stage. How the young, and adults too, will find their bearings in the emerging system remains unknown. We can certainly expect the answer to emerge via another struggle between the ages, mixing freedom and control. In that contest, communications technology will again constitute a chief medium of exchange.

3. Lost in Time and Space: Youth in an Electronic Culture

Enormous improvements in communication have made under-standing more difficult.

Harold Innis, Canadian economist

Our heroes change as quickly as TV shows and the news.

A teenager

[Young] people everywhere have a kind of experience that none of the elders ever have had or will have. Conversely, the older generation will never see repeated in the lives of young people their own unprecedented experience of sequentially emerging change.

Margaret Mead, anthropologist

In a small midwestern city, a teenage girl turns on her favorite rock video channel. In the privacy of her bedroom, she watches and listens to the latest "hot" rock singer or movie celebrity. Although alone, she has instantaneously joined the shared culture of several million other video devotees. From coast to coast, even from continent to continent, and from disparate ethnic, racial, and religious backgrounds, tens of millions of teenagers share the same visual and aural medium. Later that same day, the same young woman enters her favorite music store to buy a best-selling tape by a new rock group featured on the video channel. She listens to the cassette on her car stereo headphones while driving home, and again in her bedroom on a 50-watt stereo system replete with CD and cassette players. That night she goes to an early movie and then to a dance club with friends; the film soundtrack and the dance music echo the same sounds she has heard throughout her day. The following morning a clock radio will awaken her to the local radio station playing the same recordings. In short, the marvels of modern communications technology have allowed this teenager to participate in the same entertainment rituals as millions of other teens, even though she is separated from them by geography and cultural tradition. In the process, she and these countless others have become citizens in a new, commercially prescribed electronic culture.

Day in and day out, contemporary youth live simultaneously in the world of their parents and in a separate generational enclave created by the electronic media. Of course, they have daily contact with nearby friends and relatives, but electronic communications technologies tie them to millions of other young people whom they will never know personally. Indeed, it is hard to underestimate the dramatic extent to which radio, television, cable, satellites, and the VCR have changed the ways that youth relate to each other and to other generations. New communications media do much more than enable masses of young people to absorb the same entertainment simultaneously. They also isolate youth from the more traditional worlds of previous generations, including the daily lives of their own parents.

In this chapter we will examine the "bias" of communications media, especially modern electronic media. Specifically, we will contend that all media invariably emphasize either spatial or temporal relationships. The electronic media, for example, disseminate messages quickly and cheaply over great geographic distances. They enable people to communicate instantaneously with millions of others in distant places, a consequence that can yield untold social good. At the same time, however, these same media work in subtle ways to disconnect audiences from local communities and traditional ways of life. In fact, some of the most avid consumers of the electronic media have little or no sense of how they relate to the broader culture or to previous generations. By means of this spatial "bias," the electronic media have produced an actual "generation gap." Like the fictional teenager whose "media day" we sketched, many young people are anchored in a specialized media world, a youth subculture, that gives their lives meaning but at the same time distances them from their own family life. Often all that really remains of strong personal relationships is the peer group, which is immersed in the same electronic environment.

As we shall see, the media policies and practices of North American business and government contribute to the inherent bias of electronic media. As a result, the United States—which historian Daniel Boorstin calls the "republic of technology"—has increasingly favored communication by the electronic media over face-to-face and printed communication. With remarkable facility, North Americans have established communications systems that send messages across the continent in seconds. These messages do indeed conquer enormous geographic space, but they do so at a considerable price. Their means of transmission have disrupted the flow or "handing on" of culture from one generation to the next. Mass communication effortlessly, magically sails across space but fails to tie the continent together in trans-generational time; it hinders the transmission of historical culture. Its spatial orientation has given rise to—among other things—a relatively distinct youth culture whose unsteady center promotes the production and consumption of mass-media entertainment. This inherent spatial "bias" is only encouraged by the commercial hunger and optimism of media producers and regulators. In its great love affair with electronic dazzle, North American culture has reached a point where it must seriously consider whether "bigger is better" and "quicker is slicker." Too often the electronic media allow for horizontal spatial connection between people but discourage vertical temporal connection between generations.

Community and Communication

To the typical consumer, the media appear to be little more than sources of information and entertainment frequently interrupted by the incessant siren of advertisers. Most of the time audiences take in the offerings of the electronic media casually, giving almost no thought to their origin or impact. However, among youth and adults alike—particularly youth—the media provide far more than mere entertainment or background "noise" in their public and private lives. If only because of their sheer pervasiveness and constancy—they are everywhere all the time—the media have generated for young people *shared* understandings and feelings about the world in which they live. From news to sports, music, and drama, the media create for youth emotional and intellectual portraits of themselves, the wider society, and their place in it. In short, mass communication enables young people to transcend local and personal isolation to participate in one large, national and increasingly international youth community. Already in 1985, youth in the United States—

regardless of their gender, ethnicity, economic status, or grade level in school[1]—had equal access to VCRs. Mass communication has become a great equalizer that puts youth in the same cultural arena regardless of their individual personalities or social backgrounds.

Of course, the "mass" media are not modern culture's only vehicles for sharing lives and building community. Long before people are able to read and write, they relate to each other through the spoken word and through nonverbal communication, including the intimacy of touch and the assurance of a smile. Even in schools and churches, which greatly value the written word, oral communication is the foundation for face-to-face, interpersonal relationships. Among teens, the peer group also plays an important role in forming their picture of the world and helping them establish healthy relationships. In fact, youth often select their friends from among peers on the basis of common tastes in entertainment. Increasingly, peer groups and the media are two sides of the same set of cultural values. For example, even youth from conserva-tive religious backgrounds learn more about sex from their peers and from films than they do from their parents.[2]

Nevertheless, a quick survey of contemporary youth culture shows how powerfully the electronic media shape the quality and quantity of relationships among individuals and groups. The electronic media have linked youth together into new kinds of specialized commu-nities that exist partly in and through audio and video recordings, films, and radio and TV shows. The electronic media began developing their current influence over youth in the 1950s, which saw the birth of rock and roll and the popular Top 40 radio formats as well as Dick Clark's *American Bandstand* TV show. Soon came special teen films with plots built on youth-oriented leisure (e.g., beach parties) or on the fictional romantic escapades of a rock star like Elvis Presley. The 1960s saw the proliferation of new rock-music formats, especially on the FM band. In the 1970s, the stereo-radio boom exploded as up to a third of all FM stations geared themselves to the rock-music tastes of youth. The 1980s provided MTV and hundreds of other video shows.

For all of these media, formats, and genres, there emerged an ever-increasing young audience that formed an ever-expanding national youth subculture. Through the last three decades, youth have shared teen films, rock music, and rock videos, some of the most important

1. Bradley S. Greenberg and Carrie Heeter, "VCRs and Young People," *American Behavioral Scientist* 30 (May/June 1987): 509-21.
2. Josh McDowell Ministry, "Teen Sex Survey in the Evangelical Church" (Dallas: Josh McDowell Ministry, 1987).

International Youth—American Style

Europe, the most significant foreign audience for American television, is speeding toward radical technological change. Meanwhile, squeezed by growing competition domestically, American television executives are courting European governments and viewers, especially youth. During the next decade European youth will probably look, sound, and think more like American counterparts.

By the end of 1992, twelve European nations will become a single trading zone—a market of some 320 million consumers, almost as large as Japan and the United States combined. According to the Single European Act, these nations will become an economic environment similar to the one in the United States. There will be a free flow of goods, services, and currency. And there will probably be an explosion in American-produced mass communication.

Not all Europeans are happy about these prospects. Some of them have suggested publicly that there ought to be limits on the import of "foreign"—meaning "American"—television programming and films. Canada has been swamped by the American popular-culture blitz emanating from media across the border, and Europeans worry that they might lose some of their cultural distinctiveness.

But Europeans will have a difficult time stopping the American onslaught for two big reasons. First, the technologies needed to launch the onslaught—primarily cable and satellites—are already in place. Second, European youth and many European adults like American programming. As Europe privatizes its mass communications media, encouraging market-driven systems, audience demand will convince native media moguls to forego cultural autonomy in favor of financial success.

As a result, we should expect the Americanization of European youth, who will be intensively exposed to programming from across the pond. Over time, these young people will look, sound, and think more and more like their Western media cousins. Technology will provide the web. Marketing will feed the spider.

cultural "artifacts" of each teen generation. The media and groups of peers sharing media tastes have increasingly defined the youth culture.

Together, interpersonal and mass communication establish the tone and shape of the youth culture in North America. As youth have interacted with each other, with the broader culture, and with the entertainment industry, they have formed their own attitudes toward schooling, dating, parenting, and the like. From the 1950s to the present, the electronic media have shaped the youth culture by changing adolescents' patterns of communication and redefining their community life.

North American youth increasingly live in their own generationally defined, media-maintained communities.

Creating a National Youth Culture

As we have suggested in previous chapters, young people's sense that they belong to a distinct national subculture is relatively recent. In fact, without the electronic media there would not be a youth culture as we now know it. "It was technology," says cultural analyst James Curtis, "in the form of a complex system of recording studios, radio stations, radio receivers, and record players that linked the performers to a huge national and international audience." By this technological linking, new varieties of music were able "to create a new subculture with a language and identity of its own."[3] These media, along with the automobile, changed the shape and texture of daily life for most white youth in the 1950s. The new electronic and transportation linkages drove a whole generation of middle-class and working-class teenagers to develop common tastes in fashion, language, habits, and mores. Rock music in particular "changed the audience . . . by gradually creating a self-conscious teen generation. Remember that before 1955 there was no music which spoke clearly to the interests and needs of teen-agers. Rock changed that. It defined the correct behavior of a 'teen queen,' outlined the 'fast stud,' and 'bad-good' male ideal, reveled in the joy and agonies of puppy love, noted the irrelevance of school routines as compared with the reality of fast cars, surfing, and the exhilaration of dancing. Throughout rock lyrics there were pointed contrasts between the teen way of life and the behavioral norms imposed by adults."[4]

From the 1950s to the present, the media have continuously reformulated the youth culture according to the latest trends in clothing, language, leisure activities, technology, and especially electronic media consumption, which has added to its own influence. The entertainment industry has attempted to read the tea leaves of social and cultural change in order to capitalize on the hungers and discontents of youth. Its sense of nascent trends has dictated its investment in a potential box-office smash, a promising radio format, a likely high-rated broadcast

3. Curtis, "Toward a Sociotechnological Interpretation of Popular Music in the Electronic Age," *Technology & Culture* 25 (Jan. 1984): 92.

4. R. A. Peterson and D. G. Berger, "Three Eras in the Manufacture of Popular Music Lyrics," in *The Sounds of Social Change*, ed. R. S. Denisoff and R. A. Peterson (Chicago: Rand McNally, 1972), p. 296.

Youth and Cable TV: To Consume or Not to Consume

The promise of cable TV has always been twofold: better-quality reception and a wider variety of programming. In both cases cable has triumphed or failed, depending on how one looks at the situation.

In both rural and urban areas, cable TV has greatly improved reception for many viewers. The technology has eliminated shadows, "snow," and fading caused by buildings, airplanes, atmospheric changes, and the like. Cable also increased the variety of programming available to viewers. Systems installed in the early 1970s have as few as 12 channels; the latest ones offer about 100 channels. (If fiber optics replaces coaxial cable, the number of channels could reach into the thousands, although the marketplace would not support that many.)

Most cable channels specialize in one area of programming: sports, news, financial information, children's shows, religious programs, and so forth. Teenagers tend to watch the music-video channels, reruns of old programs, and movies. Contemporary movies are offered by "pay" channels such as HBO and Showtime, which require special subscription. Not surprisingly, nearly all of the movie-oriented pay channels attract many teenage viewers.

As the teenage market grows in the United States, there will likely be more and more channels aimed at young people. There will be more teenage comedy, more teenage drama, more teenage game shows, and even more teenage movies. Like an enormous web, cable TV will increasingly tie young people across the continent into a common youth culture. Most importantly, every new channel and program will probably give youth only one major choice: to consume or not to consume.

or cable-TV show, and a probable gold recording. In the dynamic interplay between the entertainment industry and youth, the media have learned how to appeal to young consumers, and in turn, American youth have learned how to live a hyped-up, Hollywood version of teen life.

As a result, today's youth are not as interested in local or traditional ways of life as they are in the newest national and international fads and trends—"what's hot and what's not." Nor are they as moved by the calls of the past and of tradition as by their desire for novelty—the latest musical recording, the "hottest" new group, the "in" movie. With the incessant prodding of these media, youth gravitate away from localism and traditionalism and toward broader national trends and movements—to new dance styles, to spring vacation spots, and even to well-known universities.

As Kinsley Widmer has observed, post–World-War-II youth

built a culture of their own upon notions of identity and community that came in part from the national media. "The electronic hooking-up brought not only feelings of sophistication, however spurious at times, but of relationship, of a larger movement in style autonomy and behavior variation."[5] The electronic media did present youth with more and broader cultural options in dress, hairstyles, fashion, and speech and behavior patterns. At the same time, however, they clearly helped cut youth off from local communities and traditional ways of life.[6] Fostered by media, this new world of youth was not the same as the one their parents had experienced. Ironically, while the new media gave the appearance of providing broad personal choice and freedom from the world of parental restrictions, it in fact only tied adolescents to the latest fads and to some of the most trivial cultural expressions, from hairdos to dance styles. While teenagers thought and felt as if they were breaking free from the binding localism of parents, they merely exchanged one sort of coercive conformity for another. Despite their frequent shallowness, the new youth-oriented media successfully promoted a specialized national culture that diminished the influence of previously esteemed local culture. While this was not altogether bad, the current emphasis on national cultures overwhelms most efforts to sustain the vital ways and connections of local life.

Compared with localism and traditionalism, then, the electronic media offered young people membership in a broader and seemingly more important, significant, and exciting national community. Frustrated by the often staid conservatism or parochialism of parents, pastors, and teachers, teens ran eagerly to the record stores and movie theaters to grab a piece of a new and liberating identity. Before long, the entertainment media began to "pitch" just about everything to youth according to the industry's image of the needs and wants of youth. The media began to tailor their presentation of national events and personalities to the interests and mood of youth—from rock-group tours to record releases, from movies to news about their favorite entertainment celebrities. Even local radio stations played to a larger youth community with a "corporate" identity by announcing the latest "national" youth events, including rock concerts and Hollywood gossip.

By the 1980s a national video channel like MTV[7] could look back

5. Widmer, cited by R. Serge Denisoff in *Inside MTV* (New Brunswick: Transaction Books, 1988), p. 347.

6. Joshua Meyrowitz, *No Sense of Place: The Impact of Electronic Media on Social Behavior* (New York: Oxford University Press, 1985), p. 134.

7. In the 1980s hundreds of local rock-video channels attempted to compete with

on thirty years of youth media as the test market for its own hopeful vision. Today MTV offers a complete audiovisual smorgasbord in a format aimed at the more prosperous and undiscerning white, middle-class viewer: bulletins about upcoming rock-music tours and live broadcasts from various youth "events"; friendly on-air personalities; back-to-back contests and other promotions; lots of sex and plenty of romantic suggestion; entertaining commercials; and even quiz shows. Magazines such as *Rolling Stone* and *Tiger Beat* reinforce the general sense that teenagers form a broad cultural and economic movement. In short, the mass media enable North American youth to transcend what they perceive to be the limiting provincialism of their own neighborhoods, schools, and families. And in breaking free of these, teenagers believe they join a relatively distinct and more sophisticated culture of leisure and consumption. These new media, then, become a primary cultural force, offering youth a special world whose ties and associations supplant or at least "compete with those formed through live interaction in specific location."[8]

Given this scenario, it is not surprising that teenagers are usually the first to adopt the latest electronic communications technologies. Historian Robert Snow recalls how quickly teenagers adopted the transistor radio: "By the late 1950s, transistor technology enabled teenagers to 'take the sound' to the beach, the park, dance parties, drive-in movies, burger stands, and even to bed at night. To be without radio during normal leisure time periods was frustrating, and to have a car without a radio was just plain stupid. In those days, kids would rather cruise the streets in a Desoto with a radio than a Ford without one. My father said that the only thing on my old Plymouth that always worked well was the radio. He was right."[9]

Youth believe that new media open doors to potentially exciting communities, and they embrace these media en masse. In the 1960s, for example, the market for FM-stereo systems exploded as high-school and especially college students began purchasing their own equipment. Until then the FM band offered a lot of "easy listening" music and some "elite" programming for jazz and classical-music buffs. But soon after teenagers entered the FM market, FM rock stations sprang up in cities

---

MTV. By 1987 it was clear that none of them could successfully take on the slicker, more sophisticated fare of New York City. In many cases, appropriately enough, local video channels were replaced with home-shopping channels (Denisoff, *Inside MTV,* p. 225).

8. Meyrowitz, *No Sense of Place,* p. 147.

9. Snow, "Youth, Rock 'n' Roll, and Electronic Media," *Youth & Society* 18 (June 1987): 329-30.

across the country. Similarly, in the 1980s youth adopted the VCR en masse, believing that watching and emulating the characters in the numerous teen films being produced could open the door to their success as "real-life" teens. In 1989 teenagers viewed twice as many videotapes as their parents did; almost 75 percent of them rent at least one videotape a week.[10] Similarly, car audio systems and portable stereos were quickly adopted throughout North American youth culture. The market potential of teen-directed electronics and programming is illustrated by MTV, which is one of the great success stories of cable television in the United States. The network began in 1981 in 2.5 million homes.[11] In the next eight years MTV increased its viewership nearly twentyfold, reaching 47 million homes.[12]

Generational Discontinuity and the Crisis of Authority

With the media-inspired national youth culture comes generational discontinuity and crises of authority. Traditionally parents have raised their children, but now the electronic media accomplish much of the socialization of youth, if only because of their sheer pervasiveness in North American culture. And very often youth seem to turn intentionally to the media for the guidance and support that they fail to receive at home. The media connect the disconnected to other youth and to a handful of adults who seem to care about them personally. Television and film celebrities, rock stars and disc jockeys can become important surrogates or mentors in the lives of adolescents. These figures fast become the "elders" of the new youth community, the fathers and mothers of the national teen "family." Although they are usually barely older than their young audience, these personalities often have greater authority than parents, ministers, or teachers.[13] Invariably, media personalities of every sort now have more power and appeal than anyone in the "local tribe."

Renowned anthropologist Margaret Mead decades ago claimed that the mass media fueled generational discontinuity in Euro-American societies. She worried that youth would have less and less in common

---

10. Kirsten A. Conover, "Teen 'Video Culture' Grows," *Christian Science Monitor*, 18 Apr. 1989, p. 14.

11. Jay Cocks, "Sing a Song of Seeing," *Time*, 26 Dec. 1983, p. 56.

12. Bob Wisehart, "MTV Is Growing Up and Changing Format as Audience Matures," *Grand Rapids Press*, 23 July 1989, pp. H-1, H-6.

13. Jack Balswick and Bron Ingoldsby, "Heroes and Heroines among American Adolescents," *Sex Roles* 8 (1982).

with their parents and other older members of society. Mead concluded that the twentieth century has created "cofigurative" cultures in which young people learn more about life from their peers than from their elders: "The nuclear family was established, a close relationship to the grandparents no longer was expected of grandchildren, and parents, as they lost their position of dominance, handed over to children the task of setting their own standards. By 1920, style setting was beginning to pass to the mass media in the name of each successive adolescent group, and parental discipline was passing to an increasingly unsympathetic and embattled community."[14] In the new cofigurative society, messages flow horizontally within generations rather than vertically across generations—in other words, this society follows the communication pattern used by the media, a pattern that isolates as it connects. Even though adults often produced teen-oriented media messages, adults did not, as a rule, share in youth's consumption of them. Already in 1968, adolescents used the media very differently than their parents did[15]—a difference in consumption still evident today. Instead of watching TV with their families, teens generally watch it alone or in peer groups and talk little to their parents about their viewing.[16]

While it is impossible to assess exact degrees of influence, the electronic media have undoubtedly contributed to the general crisis of authority in Western societies. Many traditional social institutions now compete with the media for control and influence over young people. This is a relatively new phenomenon. Even as late as 1950, most white, middle-class American adolescents located authority in three places: home, peer group, and local organizations such as school, synagogue, church, scouts, and 4-H clubs. These groupings generally guided and inspired youth, providing images of "the good life," elevating particular personality traits over others, and establishing moral sensitivities as well as civic virtues. Before long, however, the entertainment industry had forged a privileged alliance with the peer group and set about challenging the authority of parents, churches, and civic organizations.[17] Media

14. Mead, *Culture and Commitment: A Study of the Generation Gap* (Garden City, N.Y.: Doubleday–Natural History Press, 1970), p. 45.

15. Steven H. Chaffee, Jack M. McLeod, and Charles Atkin, "Parental Influences on Adolescent Media Use," *American Behavioral Scientist* 14 (Jan.-Feb. 1971): 330.

16. Walter Gantz and James B. Weaver III, "Parent-Child Communication about Television: A View from the Parent's Perspective," paper presented to the Theory and Methodology Division of the Association for Education in Journalism and Mass Communication at their annual convention in Gainesville, Florida, Aug. 1984.

17. Robert Gussner, "Youth: Deauthorization and the New Individualism," *Youth & Society* 4 (Sept. 1972), pp. 106-8.

Youth and Sex: No Place for Elders

According to numerous studies of teenage sexuality, American youth increasingly believe that sexual behavior is merely a matter of personal choice. Rather than looking to adult values and mores, youth look to the media and their peers for appropriate sexual practices. As one sociologist puts it, young people consider it "their right" to engage in sexual relations. Youth believe they are entitled to have sex, and popular culture seems to support their beliefs.

—Lena Williams, "Teen-Age Sex: New Codes Amid the Old Anxiety," *New York Times*, 27 Feb. 1989, pp. 1, 12.

---

analyst Conrad Lodziak attributes to the rise of television the decline of the family as the major socializing agent. He claims that TV helped to undermine the "authority of the father" and the "protective will of the mother," resulting in "social fragmentation" rather than "decentralization."[18] For adolescents, TV viewing came to compete—successfully— with such away-from-home activities as school clubs, church fellowships, and civic groups.[19] Moreover, adolescents who watched more TV spent less time socializing with friends outside the neighborhood.[20]

Far more than other forms of mass communication, the electronic media supply appealing alternative mentors and "friends" when the adult world seems unattractive. Furthermore, they fill the cultural void caused by the declining appeal and authority of local institutions other than the peer group. Traditional authority has experienced marked erosion, and the electronic media regularly challenge its lingering vestiges of influence by offering youth non-traditional values, attitudes, and behaviors. As a result, many adolescents feel sharply torn between local influence and mores and the media world. In many homes, parents and teens argue about teen media. Parents seek to exert some control over this area while their children demand freedom to watch their "own" films and listen to their "own" music.

Indeed, teen-oriented music and films launched the electroni-

---

18. Lodziak, *The Power of Television: A Critical Appraisal* (New York: St. Martin's Press, 1986), pp. 150, 159.

19. Gary W. Selnow and Hal Reynolds, "Some Opportunity Costs of Television Viewing," *Journal of Broadcasting* 28 (Summer 1984): 321.

20. James W. Tankard and Murray Harris, "A Discriminate Analysis of Television, Viewers and Nonviewers," paper presented to the Association for Education in Journalism and Mass Communication at their annual meeting in Houston, Texas, 5-9 Aug. 1979.

cally maintained youth culture, openly distinguishing the teenage world from the world of adults on the one hand and the world of kids on the other. In contemporary mainstream culture, adults have generally lost their role as conduits for transmitting the meaning and purpose of life. Most traditional institutions now seem to have at best slight relevance for youth, who find little value in history, maturity, or wisdom. This is true across ethnic and social groups. For example, in the Mexican-American communities of the southwest United States, teens' "media habits" resemble those of Anglo-American youth and clearly distinguish them from their own ethnic elders. Like these Hispanic teenagers, each new generation either affirms its past or establishes new sources of authority. The "increasing cultural gap between parent and child" that we see today has a great deal to do with differences in the amount and kind of media that parent and child consume.[21] Lately the realm of popular culture—culture disseminated widely through the mass media—has supplied numerous figures for baptism and devotion. Indeed, as this book argues, the entertainment industry has readily taken up—and in many ways taken over—the task of socializing young people with its own unique set of values, beliefs, and attitudes. Only the peer group offers an alternate locus of meaning for young people, but usually in strong alliance with the media.

Nor is this crisis of authority helped by the inherently transient quality of what the electronic media produce. By their very nature, these media can show little respect for the cumulative wisdom of previous generations. They communicate many messages quickly over vast spaces, allowing little time for either absorption or reflection. The quantity and speed of their messages do not allow for sustained gazes into the depths of history or into the richness of particular ethnic, racial, or religious traditions. Consequently, they impede cross-generational communication and cultural continuity through time. The vast array of youth-oriented media are loaded with messages that saturate the youth market, but their brief life span, lasting no longer than last year's ad campaign, offers little hope for a stable culture. To a great extent, the success of the media depends on ongoing crises in social authority. It is within an unstable social climate of this sort, one to which the media themselves contribute, that more people turn to the media for authority and diversion.

Not only the nature of the electronic media but also the rapidity of change in their format and content fragments intergenerational com-

---

21. Bradley Greenberg and Carrie Heeter, "Mass Media Orientations among Hispanic Youth," *Hispanic Journal of Behavioral Sciences* 5 (Sept. 1983): 320-21.

munication and cohesion. From the beginning, the content of the electronic media has changed even more rapidly than seasonal shifts in fashionable clothing. Every week the radio and video charts list the new hits in response to sales and taste. Some teen films last only a few weeks in theaters before they are consigned to the home video and cable TV markets. Yesterday's box-office hits normally hold their value only for the people whose generation made them. A few "classic" songs and films are played and replayed, but even on radio, every new "oldies" format attracts primarily the generation that first heard the music. The plethora of contemporary radio formats and cable TV channels reflects the generational discontinuity that pervades American mainstream culture. Each successive generation seems more isolated than the last in its own special niche of experience and style. In 1985, pollster George Gallup, Jr., concluded that "in the seven years since the Gallup Youth Survey was started, it has become apparent that the current generation of teenagers bears little resemblance to previous generations."[22] Gallup's point is well taken, for in the popular-culture industry there is much offered to specifically targeted groups but very little offered to the general audience. Prime-time TV sitcoms offer the only remaining examples of general-interest popular culture in the United States.

Electronic Intimacy

The success of the electronic media in providing social authority depends heavily on their capacity for creating special "relationships" with youth, bonds which then establish allegiance. Unlike the printed word, and more like the spoken word, electronic mass communication naturally creates a feeling of closeness, sometimes bordering on intimacy, between media celebrities and individual viewers and listeners. Radio and television inherently convey a sense of "immediacy"—that the programming is taking place here and now when in fact much programming is pre-recorded and transmitted from far away. Disc jockeys and video announcers are often trained to create this sense of intimate contact with listeners and viewers. As we shall see in the chapter on MTV, its founders designed the network to create a sense of live, personal communication, as if the viewer and the "veejay" were together watching videos in the veejay's rec room. Such electronic inti-

---

22. Gallup, quoted in *America's Youth: 1977-1988,* ed. Robert Bezilla (Princeton, N.J.: Gallup Organization, 1988), p. 11.

macy can rival the spontaneous atmosphere and personal communication of a live concert, where the surrounding audience and the distance
between performer and audience often diminish the feeling of a one-
to-one relationship between a performer and an individual audience
member.

Youth in particular inhabit a developmental phase of life in
which they quite naturally seek meaningful intimate relationships in the
process of building their identities and preparing for adulthood.[23] Traditionally this demand for intimacy has been fulfilled by peers or parents,
teachers, counselors, or other adults. In the shift of social authority to the
media, however, young people have established new patterns of significant intimacy with people they have never met—rock and movie stars,
radio personalities, sports heroes, and so on. Even more than young
males, young females integrate these electronic creations into their personal surroundings and dreams, not only decorating their bedrooms
with posters and memorabilia but often purchasing gossip magazines,
biographies, and other "intimate" materials.

The entertainment industry capitalizes, quite literally, on this
desire for intimacy by using stars to promote its products, whether they
be movies or songs or colognes. This has been true from the days of Elvis
Presley and Pat Boone. In the case of rock stars, young people often
fantasize about a solo act or a particular band member, usually a lead
singer or a guitarist. The extent to which this pattern of mass-mediated
intimacy holds sway is indicated by social research among ethnic groups
in Canada. Adolescents in these groups tend to select heroes and heroines not from their own heritage but from the "dominant culture" of the
popular entertainment industry.[24] Social scientist Joan Tierney has concluded that adolescents choose to "imitate the dress, speech, activities
and social behavior patterns of TV heroes and heroines to strengthen
membership in the peer group at school."[25] In other words, the electronic
media depict the prevailing cultural values and habits that ethnic youth
wish to assimilate.

Due to advances in audio and video quality, the electronic media
seem to get better and better at fostering this sense of intimacy. Perpetual
technological advancements produce ever "fuller representations of

23. Barbara M. Newman and Philip R. Newman, *Development through Life: A
Psychosocial Approach* (Evanston: Northwestern University Press, 1985).
24. Joan D. Tierney, "Parents, Adolescents and Television, Part III: Defining
Ethnicity through Measurement Constructs: A Cultural Perspective according to Harold A.
Innis," research report prepared for the Canadian Radio-Television Commission, Ottawa,
Ontario, 1979.
25. Ibid., p. 14.

face-to-face sensory experience."[26] This is of crucial importance because the power of mass communication depends upon the electronic media's capacity for creating the *illusion and feeling* of interpersonal relationships, not their capacity for actually supplying such relationships. Viewers and listeners may feel like they "know" their favorite stars, especially in the case of soap-opera characters, but they in fact know only the public personas created with the help of public-relations wizardry and vividly projected by the media in a quasi-personal form that in fact reaches millions of viewers and listeners simultaneously. Videotape, far more than film, creates the impression of spontaneous, live, intimate communication, so it is now the primary vehicle for recording sitcoms, soap operas, and even the veejay spots on the rock video channels—wherever a sense of immediacy is required to achieve viewer response.

In addition, technological improvements in the size and portability of electronic communications equipment and their lower cost have notably enhanced the illusion of intimacy. Most teenagers have their own radios if not stereo systems in the most private and intimate setting—their bedroom. Growing numbers of them have their own TV sets and VCRs as well. They generally do not have to enter the more public space of the family room or the movie theater to commune with their favorite stars; they can do so while lying on their beds alone or with one or two close friends. The portable private world created by headphone stereos, which teens (and adults) use while jogging, studying, or traveling, further enhances feelings of interpersonal relationship while simultaneously shutting out the "real" world. In film, video, and audio, the clear trend is toward deeper and more pervasive fabrications of intimacy.

For Westerners generally but Western youth especially, the quest for intimacy is defined on the one hand by traditional interpersonal communication and on the other hand by mass-mediated electronic communication. The latter seemingly reduces loneliness and isolation, but that is accomplished by creating illusory relationships, which to some feel more real than life itself. Increasingly, as sociologists have observed, "face-to-face interaction is no longer the only determinant of personal and intimate interaction."[27] To a great extent, the electronic media have filled the void created by the erosion of authority and relationship within the family and between the family and local institutions. For example, conflicts between teenagers and parents, teachers, and other adults occur over youth's need for intimacy and their elders'

26. Meyrowitz, *No Sense of Place*, p. 121.
27. Ibid., p. 122.

desire for authority and control. Parents often exert authority without developing intimacy: they tell their children what to do, but they work too hard making a living and building for the future to invest time and energy in establishing close relationships with their children. Adolescents frequently "complain that parents have no time to spend with them, no interest in what interests them, or no desire to 'talk' to them. . . . This was confirmed by refusals [or reluctant agreement] of so many parents to watch favorite TV shows of their children."[28]

Teachers, another traditional source of local authority, struggle with large classes and a host of disciplinary problems as well as with diminished authority. A study of education majors at a Canadian university dramatizes the challenge of the mass media to the intellectual authority of educators. Researchers determined that these future teachers believed that the mass media, especially television, provided more "reliable and trustworthy sources of information and ideas" than professors and books.[29] Like educators in classrooms, clergy in churches are often frantically trying to extinguish dozens of emotional and moral fires. But clergy—and parents—must compete with the media in their attempts to guide youth: in 1982 "religious" adolescents watched an average of three or more hours of TV daily, about which they had "little or no conversation with parents."[30] The unfortunate truth is that in many communities and family settings, youth no longer look to traditional authority sources for intimate relationships. They turn to peers and the media, the only two groups that always seem to be there with open arms. As anthropologist Margaret Mead has suggested, local communities are indeed "embattled."

If peers and electronic communication remain the only two viable sources of intimacy for teens, one would think that the "one-way" nature of most electronic communication would tip the balance toward peers. Why would youth turn to TV, radio, and film, which cannot really interact with the individual viewer-listener? Part of the answer may lie in the fact that genuine intimate relationships contain much risk and potential for hurt. Rock stars and disc jockeys, on the other hand, accept individual young people as they are, with few requirements for mem-

28. Joan D. Tierney, "Parents, Adolescents and Television: Culture, Learning, Influence: A Report to the Public," summary of findings of a report prepared for the Canadian Radio-Television Commission, May 1978.

29. Leroy D. Travis and Claudio Violate, "Mass Media Use, Credulity and Beliefs about Youth: A Survey of Canadian Education Students," *Journal of Educational Research* 27 (Mar. 1981): 31.

30. Peter L. Benson, Phillip K. Wood, and Arthur L. Johnson, "Highlights from the National Study," *Momentum* 15 (Feb. 1984): 10.

bership in their mass-mediated communities. Over the years, Wolfman Jack, Dick Clark, and thousands of local deejays have seemed like friends to teens. Such media celebrities are infinitely accepting and affirming, never judging their followers or embarrassing them among their peers. Clearly this is not true of the local peer group, which constantly changes, adapts, and evolves. Teenagers will undoubtedly find greater intimacy by engaging in interpersonal dialogue than by absorbing media monologues, but the emotional and psychological risks of peer intimacy often push teenagers to the media instead. As local cultural life erodes, mass-media intimacy plays an increasingly major role in the lives of just about everyone but especially in the lives of young people.

Locality and Identity

As we have observed, the electronic media often define youth's sense of time and space by their continuous influence on and substitution for the prevailing mix of local, regional, and national institutions. These media promote national intra-generational communication at the same time that they isolate teenagers from the adult world of their own parents, neighbors, teachers, and clergy. For a variety of reasons, bonds with traditional sources of authority lose out to the promise of intimacy with celebrities whose public identities are carefully fashioned by the entertainment industry. Thus youth have moved away from local adult groups and toward a national smorgasbord of media-produced images and sounds. This development has increased the distance between locality and nationality as sources of identity. Put simply, youth feel more at home absorbed in the airwaves of national media than they do in their parents' house.

This predicament has, of course, been aggravated by the problematic relationship in North America between geographic space and personal identity. Historically, one of the most compelling promises to immigrants to North America was the continent's vast, largely untrammeled land. The United States especially has been a remarkably mobile nation, and throughout the twentieth century families have moved frequently in search of better jobs, more property, different lifestyles, closer friends, new experiences, and better climates. In fact, in the world of business, personal "success" has often depended upon the willingness to be geographically mobile. In this fluid national context, localism and ethnicity have appealed far less than new "American" sources of identity.

Among young people, the electronic media have provided the appearance of cultural continuity amid high rates of geographic and social mobility. As families move from one place to another, dislocated youth bring along their portable, media-made intimacies and identities. Although friends change with geography, media culture remains amazingly uniform. All across the continent, teenagers view the same videos, watch the same films, and listen to the same music. More often than not, uprooted youth seek new friends among those who share their tastes in entertainment; these tastes and electronic gadgets tend to shape peer groups and activities. Common entertainment will generally create peer groups with common slang, dress, dating habits, and attitudes toward drugs. One study found that teens with VCRs are "more likely to be dating, to have a special friend, more likely to use the VCR with their special friend, and less likely to be able to talk about their dating with their parent(s)."[31]

Like other self-contained generational subcultures, however, the youth culture nourished by the electronic media generates relatively superficial and temporary groupings. This contrasts with relationships in local inter-generational communities anchored in race, ethnicity, or religion. The unstable groupings of the youth culture grow out of the instability of the media the culture feeds on. By themselves, these media cannot sustain a stable culture; that requires oral, face-to-face communication. Lacking this personal dialogic communication and inherently unable to provide it, the electronic media invariably move identity formation from a relatively stable locality to the wildly dynamic, boundaryless arena of mass communication.

According to North American mainstream culture, an identity crisis characterizes the transition from youth to adulthood. Not ready for full-fledged adulthood and its attendant responsibilities, yet beyond the innocence of childhood, youth do not know when and how to find a place among adults. The challenge is double-edged, both social and personal: young people must "find themselves" amid a fluid and multivocal culture. Unable to simply declare an identity—"Today I am this or that"—young people look to "significant others" for guidance and affirmation. As a result, youth invariably forge their personal identities by interacting with the world around them. In the past that world was highly local and relatively stable. Routes were settled and few. In today's electric environment, however, that world has become increasingly nonlocal and unstable.

The crisis of identity is worsened by the electronic media's

31. Greenberg and Heeter, "VCRs and Young People," p. 520.

tendency to prolong adolescence by delaying the formation of stable, mature identities. The content of the electronic entertainment media only compounds the destructive potential of its inherent uprooting "bias." Despite the enormous quantity of programs in every medium, there is nothing particularly "adult" in the content of any of those media directed toward youth. On the contrary, they are largely in the business of providing markedly immature views of life. Programmers reduce love to romance and raw sex; rock music concerns itself with little else. On MTV pseudo-adult veejays and rock performers mouth the latest "hip" talk and display quasi-rebellious clothes and hairstyles. Recent teen films feature outlandish plots about boys trying to trick girls into helping them reach "full manhood" by having sex with them. Indeed, much popular art for youth obsessively equates adulthood with some simple act of sex. There is rarely any glimpse of self-sacrifice or long-term commitment, marital or otherwise. In the domain of romance, teenagers are far more likely to find mature relational models in the local community, where commitments deepen over time. Whether founded on civic virtue or racial or ethnic tradition, strong local communities deflect some of the identity-forming power of the electronic media. Weak localities, on the other hand, relinquish their authority to peer groups and the entertainment industry.

In multiple ways, then, like a "double whammy," electronic media frustrate both the maintenance of local communities and the formation of adult identities. Indeed, it is easy to argue that the electronic media effectively impede if not altogether reverse the development of maturity. A veritable "cult of youth" encourages everyone, including adults and young children, to think and act like adolescents. As the media increasingly blur the many lines between youth and adults, adolescence and adulthood no longer seem nearly so distinct and identifiable.[32] Evidence of this cult of youth abounds. In the 1980s, middle-aged rock stars and disc jockeys dressed and acted more like teenagers than they did in their heyday in the 1960s. And MTV's veejays, all well into their twenties, "look like kids you know from high school or college."[33] Media celebrities of all kinds, from George Burns to Johnny Carson, endlessly flaunt their youthfulness, including all the appropriate appetites. Even pre-teens dress more and more like adolescents and consume large quantities of teen entertainment. While not all of

32. Joshua Meyrowitz, "The Adultlike Child and the Childlike Adult: Socialization in an Electronic Age," *Daedalus* 113 (1984); and Neil Postman, *Amusing Ourselves to Death* (New York: Viking Press, 1985).
33. Snow, "Youth, Rock 'n' Roll, and Electronic Media," pp. 331-32.

these trends may be socially or personally problematic, they do reflect a deep, potentially troubling fact: mainstream as well as youth-oriented electronic media view life as a perpetual unsolvable identity crisis. They portray human existence as an unending process of adapting to the latest adolescent consumer fads in clothes, cars, music, and other "hot" items. Their credo and rallying cry glamorize the search for personal happiness in and through material and interpersonal consumerism. The electronic media offer few reference points outside the ethos of white, consumer-oriented middle-class and upper-class North American youth. MTV, for example, at first refused to play music by blacks, primarily because the network's target market (it was far more a market than an audience) was middle-class white teenagers with expendable income. This exclusion extends to other significant groups and influences: by rarely referring to traditional forms of community and ways of life except in occasional TV sitcoms, the youth-oriented media in effect deny their very existence.

The effect of this media-sponsored psychological homogeniza-tion of different life stages falls under the heading of "youthification." The natural instability of youth, once viewed as simply a *stage in life,* is now projected upon much of adult society, presented as a normative *attitude toward life.* Few purely "adult" norms or expectations distinguish generations, separate children from teenagers or teenagers from adults. Both youth and adults live estranged from community life and im-mersed in a "hot" media world. Their worlds are different, but their problems are essentially the same. MTV Networks, Inc., began VH-1 as a pop-music channel but within a few years reformulated programming for a nostalgic baby-boom generation. "Their bodies may be in the 30s or 40s or older," said the channel's vice president about the new audi-ence, "but their minds are still young."[34] In other words, age no longer denotes personal stability and maturity. Increasing years seem to breed not acceptance of mortality or the pursuit of wisdom but a deep yearning to return to the bliss and innocence of youth. This state of arrested development appears most clearly in rapidly changing patterns of adult consumption, lifestyles, and leisure activities, all pursued in the hope of recovering adolescent bliss. The VH-1 channel showed how central product consumption was to the "older" audience. Said one observer, "Hollywood, TV and the music industry are all addressing the Boomers now. . . . And that's where VH-1 fits—as a center of entertainment, lifestyles and related information."[35]

---

34. Quoted by Jim Pettigrew in "MTV Networks Strives to Broaden Video Base," *Electronic Media,* 22 May 1989 (Special Report), p. 12.
35. Ibid.

Even though conventional wisdom rightly has youth and adults consuming different media and pursuing different lifestyles, the two groups in fact follow essentially the same route, and that is consumption. This underlying pattern appears in shared emphases on clothing style, leisure, youthful looks, and recurring identity crises. While increasingly disconnected generationally, young and old alike engage in individual searches for identity, and a good number of these searches are mediated by the mass media, cultural entities whose primary focus is consumption. Within this climate, leisure activities become influential barometers of personal identity, while work is reduced to a mechanism for attaining greater levels of consumption. As Conrad Lodziak puts it, "Socialization through television, play groups, pop culture and youth sub-cultures would seem to be preparing the young for a leisure-time use which at one and the same time is an extension of their socialization into adulthood, and reproduces the dominant patterns of leisure-time currently in evidence."[36] In other words, the culture of the electronic media prescribes perpetual adolescence and consumption as developmental ideals. Indeed, perpetual adolescence and consumption constitute the twin-pronged gospel of these media. Youthful faces and bodies flood the TV screen, pitching everything from diet cola to pantyhose to cars. The media emphasize novelty and glamour, endlessly reciting the magic incantations for youthfulness—which in many ways is preserved, according to media preachers, by trendy consumption.

Unfortunately, while promising to satisfy deep longings for identity and meaning, the electronic media both aggravate and frustrate. Without a specific anchor in geographic space and another in cultural time, they will necessarily foil committed searchers of any age. To the extent that American society has surrendered parenting, schooling, and socialization to the electronic media, the nation will suffer renewed fractures and fissures between generations and new crises in authority. The quest for youthfulness mobilizes just about everyone to consume media, and their appetite mobilizes the media to stress youthfulness, but neither provides stable, intergenerational ideals and mores.

The commercial impetus for most electronic media dictates this emphasis on youthfulness. Stable, local social institutions are not nearly so ripe for commercial picking as are the unstable, consumptive lifestyles of youth. "Even for products aimed at the middle-aged consumers," write marketing consultants, "companies choose models in their early twenties." People of all ages want "to be vigorous and energetic—and, naturally, they identify these characteristics with young people. . . .

36. Lodziak, *The Power of Television*, p. 153.

What's hot among young people today can often become the rage for all America tomorrow—from fashions to fast foods, from music to movies."[37] Clearly, there is no end to the search for youthfulness in this kind of mass-mediated culture. Adults, like adolescents, attempt to find individuality through the conventional formulas provided by the mass media. Meanwhile, everyone gets older, responsibilities invariably mount, and the quest for adolescent fulfillment seems ever more unattainable—and more desperate. The only hope lies in living vicariously through the fictional lives portrayed by the electronic media. And there the emphasis is relentlessly on youth. Dick Clark was able to host *American Bandstand* for three decades, but he was a rarity. On MTV, the "aging" veejays were dumped from the show after five years in order to maintain the channel's adolescent image. Even on MTV, make-up and fashion can go only so far toward the manufacture of youth.

Whither Public Policy?

Presently the electronic media freely traverse geographic space at the expense of cultural continuity and cohesion. Lacking a coherent public policy for the communications industry, North America has decided to let the marketplace establish the cultural landscape of adolescent life. In neither Canada nor the United States is there much public sensitivity to the relationships between local community life, traditional social institutions, and the national entertainment industries. Ethnic, racial, religious, and women's organizations frequently complain about stereotyping, immorality, and bias in media content. Rarely does anyone address the broader questions of locality and cultural pluralism. Only public education, because of local control of funding and curriculum, has remained somewhat sensitive to these issues. The electronic media are so taken for granted and so national and commercial in character that their effect on cultural stability seldom enters public discussion. That this is the case is a great misfortune. As sociologist Joan Tierney found in her study of ethnic Canadian families, available programming partly determines the influence of national and local cultures.[38] In a national, commercial system of communication, the dominant media culture tends to overwhelm local ethnic culture. The effects of TV as a socializing

37. Lawrence Graham and Lawrence Hamdan, *Youthtrends: Capturing the $200 Billion Youth Market* (New York: St. Martin's Press, 1987), pp. 5-6.
38. Tierney, "Defining Ethnicity through Measurement Constructs," p. 12.

agent can be offset by alternative media but are intensified by "complementary" media.[39] In other words, public policy inevitably influences both the variety of media and the cultural, social, and economic impact of those media. National technologies, especially satellites, favor national cultures. Local technologies, if they are adequately funded, can protect local cultures.

Since the 1930s, the U.S. government has supposedly regulated all broadcasting to serve the "public interest, convenience and necessity." When that creed was developed it meant, among other things, that stations were to provide diverse programming for the needs and interests of the local community. As first radio and then television reached for ever larger audiences, that regulatory concept proved increasingly meaningless. Many stations met the demand for "diversified" programming by offering various public-affairs programs late at night or on weekend mornings. Few stations found it commercially viable to direct their programming to traditional or local groups. (Those that did were almost all religious.) Moreover, until the rise of cable TV, none of the national networks seriously oriented programming toward pluralism or traditional racial, ethnic, or religious groups (though even cable's diverse programming has been offered primarily for marketing purposes). Simply put, broadcast policy has not dealt with how the electronic media could protect cultural continuity amid the increasing influence of the entertainment industry.

In a democratic society, of course, it is extremely difficult for the government to determine which groups and purposes should shape the public sphere. In the case of the electronic media, the principal question is this: Who shall determine the nature, purpose, and extent of mass entertainment? So far the most consistent approach has been to "let the marketplace decide." In this open arena, the media have been largely free to pursue their own commercial interests in all program domains. Few electronic media have come forth on their own to speak for local and traditional groups. For most broadcasters, the primary purpose of commercial broadcasting has been to attract audiences for advertisers.

Solutions to complex and pervasive cultural conditions are not simple, but that certain steps should be taken is obvious. For one, given the biases of the electronic media, there should be considerably more public discussion of the role of the electronic media in preserving and extending cultural continuity. While there is nothing inherently wrong

39. Michael Morgan and Nancy Rothschild, "Impact of the New Television Technology: Cable TV, Peers, and Sex-Role Cultivation in the Electronic Environment," *Youth & Society* 15 (Sept. 1973): 48.

with youth-oriented media, societies cannot long sustain the intergenerational conflict and large-scale cultural discontinuity that such media foster. The issue can also be gotten at with a simple question: Which institutions in society should assume the primary role of raising youth and integrating them into adult life? Parents, teachers, clergy, and civic leaders may deserve criticism for relinquishing many of their responsibilities to the media, but the problem today is much deeper and more complex than is suggested by a simple call for better education and family life.

Throughout this and earlier chapters we have argued that the electronic media and youth are now locked together in a national system for creating and satisfying youth's needs for intimacy and identity. It is not possible, nor would it be advisable, for modern culture to renounce the electronic media or to smash them in a flurry of anger and violence. The media and popular art are not inherently evil or invariably destructive of the fabric of culture. Those shaping public policy must assess the current state of affairs in order to establish workable standards that will serve the "public interest, convenience, and necessity." That poses a reasonable goal for a democratic society, and its implications are important if not crucial for North American culture. In keeping with that goal, we offer the following suggestions.

First, media content must be truly pluralistic. The changes in and proliferation of technologies have not accomplished this. Social scientists Michael Morgan and Nancy Rothschild have concluded that even in the fundamental area of sex roles, "the new electronic environment will not ensure diversity, but, like its predecessors, will monopolize message systems by further standardization and homogenization of this culture's most common myths."[40] Currently, television is the narrowest medium: even cable TV is terribly homogenous ethnically, religiously, and racially. Film and music are significantly more pluralistic, but many of their products do not find adequate means for broader distribution. We believe that the electronic media, if left to their own devices, will not promote any so-called minority views of life or any other less than mainstream viewpoints. Instead, the media will continue to promote— because it is in their interest—the dominant, consumption-oriented world of leisure and entertainment; this approach fills their coffers. New technologies like cable TV and video cassettes will not by themselves produce pluralism. Even the VCR, once naively touted as the answer to network oligopolies, is only as useful in promoting diversity as the available videotapes permit. The news on this front is not good. Increas-

40. Ibid.

ingly, the distribution of tapes lies in the hands of a few major retail chains. Furthermore, the public's taste for videotapes is dictated by both national promotion and local availability. Because of the VCR, teens see many more films in the privacy of their own homes (six per year in 1984 compared with twenty-seven per year in 1987), but generally these are the same kinds of films they would view in theaters.[41]

Second, the electronic media should work as hard for cultural preservation as for national market penetration. Clearly, this goal requires greater emphasis on locally and regionally produced popular culture. Local TV and radio stations rarely reflect the composition or address the specific needs of their local communities. They are too busy attracting broader audiences for advertisers. Local TV is especially deficient because so much of its programming comes from national networks. Even public TV produces very little local programming, although because of its philosophy it offers much more diverse programming than commercial stations and networks do. This deficiency demands that indigenous local groups acquire the resources and abilities necessary to make effective use of the media and give themselves a voice in the media world. Traditional subcultures cannot survive the ascendancy of national media unless they are producers as well as consumers of programming.

The present symbiosis between the youth culture and the entertainment industry should shift some of its emphasis to developing an awareness of more traditional local institutions. Not all popular and folk art has to be turned into commodities. When a society puts a market price on all its entertainment, some forms of cultural expression will win out over others. The losers might have great cultural value but little market potential. The desire to preserve such cultural expressions is one reason why the public broadcasting system was established in the United States. While not panaceas, traditional social institutions can offer much to youth by orienting them in space and time. Cultural resources like popular art are more than commodities for barter.

Mediating Structures

At this stage in the so-called communications revolution, North American culture needs more than anything else healthy mediating structures between audiences and the entertainment industry. It is vital that the

41. *America's Youth: 1977-1988*, p. 230.

electronic media do not further weaken and thus dominate oral communication and the rich cultures that depend upon face-to-face interaction. Youth peer groups, organized around the media and leisure, are not adequate. At the same time, print communication deserves encouragement, especially in the face of its erosion in schools, religious organizations, and public life in general. A possible solution lies not only in regulation but also in the development of local mediating structures. Various kinds of community groups might well provide cultural "space" for the nurture of strong identities and intimate relationships.

In the case of American youth, it is increasingly clear that the entertainment industry has contributed significantly to weakened schools, churches, and ethnic identities. Televised national sports events, for example, now compete seriously with local events for the attention, energy, and time of youth (and their parents). Although some think that responsibility for nearly all social problems rests with the family, this is an oversimplification; a multi-institutional response will more fully consider local and regional differences. Civic groups might help in some communities, religious groups in others. Most often the sponsor of these mediating structures is less important than the very existence of such structures. This continent's enormous variety of lifestyles and traditions suggests that successful mediating structures will not likely emerge from mandates by federal or regional governments. Rather, they must emerge from the desire of local communities for a fuller and richer public and private life.

Clearly, there need to be more checks on and alternatives to the profound influence that the electronic media currently have on young people. Ironically, youth in some highly "protected" local environments today, specifically the family, are often those most influenced by the media. In ages past, parents rightly assumed that the home and the family created a haven for the adolescent amid a cruel and uncaring world. However, in the age of electronic communication, such "havens" have become major consumption outlets for the entertainment factories. Already in the 1970s, adolescents from protective homes spent far more time viewing TV than any other adolescent group. Indeed, when parents value protection above all, "obedience and social harmony are valued and there is little concern with conceptual matters." Uncritical about what they absorb, these protected youth are "highly susceptible to influence from external persuasion," especially the mass media.[42] View-

42. Jack McLeod and Jane Delano Brown, "The Family Environment and Adolescent Television Use," in *Children and Television*, ed. Ray Brown (Beverly Hills: Sage Publications, 1976), p. 274.

ing in the home does not prevent the erosive effects of national media, especially if adolescents do not share and discuss the media products with their parents. Ample social research shows that youth deeply desire to share their lives—ideas, feelings, hopes—with elders, including their parents. They interpret a lack of parental interest in *their* interests as an indication that parents do not really care.[43]

A sensible offensive strategy must bring generations together for communication and shared leisure. This demands far more than a knee-jerk defense that seeks only to protect youth from the outside world. For example, when home and school together teach critical media consumption, youth treat TV viewing as a cultural exercise and watch programs selectively. Home supervision that reinforces school-taught messages about the media can result in "television viewing habits that are educationally productive" for youth. Problems result when there is insufficient "parental intervention" in the home[44]—problems that can be exacerbated by what is *not* taught in school. "Unless educators view leisure education as an integral part of the school curriculum," says one educator, "they may indeed be preparing a generation of spectators whose discretionary time is spent passively in front of a television set and/or expect other persons to provide them entertainment."[45]

Mindless or empty traditionalism does not provide an answer to the current problems of media consumption. Too often a multi-ethnic North America has found its past turned into mere nostalgia. Such sentiment imagines that answers to social problems lie in a return to some glorious past. No matter how we may wish we could turn back time, there is no way we can return to an earlier age of peace and harmony before the "pernicious" influence of mass entertainment. Besides, there really is no such point in time; as we argued in Chapter Two, youth have always been a "problem." Instead of invoking a supposedly idyllic past, North Americans must deal with present realities. This means, among other things, that local and traditional institutions must adopt fresh strategies that will foster identity and intimacy. Ethnic and racial organizations, churches, schools, and families must either influence the new media environment or be co-opted by it. If they fail to realize the important stake they have in the electronic media, and it in them, they will slowly lose their social roles and influence. The most

43. Tierney, "Parents, Adolescents and Television, Part III," p. 5.
44. Lloyd P. Campbell and Betty Roether, "Suggested Guidelines for Television Viewing for Children and Adolescents," *Contemporary Education* 55 (Summer 1984): 220.
45. Mary F. Compton, "Television Viewing Habits of Early Adolescents," *Clearing House* 57 (Oct. 1983): 61.

difficult challenge for traditional groups lies in determining how to use the media without adopting its beguiling consumerist ways of life. Hollywood is especially notorious for its ability to turn high-minded artists into profit-mongering hacks with little social conscience. And more than one TV critic has concluded that the affluent world depicted on the tube directly reflects the lifestyles and values of TV producers, writers, and directors.

Many adults hold on to a strong but ill-directed hope that the new age of electronic communication makes new mediating structures unnecessary. Media apologists argue that technical innovations—the abundance of cable-TV channels, the pervasiveness of the VCR, and the advent of low-power television—allow every family and community to tailor its media consumption to its own tastes and interests. As history has shown, such thinking occurs in response to rapid technological innovations.[46] History also shows that such optimism is naive, for decentralization and proliferation of means of communication are soon transformed into greater centralization and control. North Americans now see this in the national economic trend toward takeovers, buyouts, and conglomerates. Each "mega-company" will have the capability to produce, distribute, air, publish, and promote its own products. (In the next chapter we will look at that process in depth.) Some critics even predict that within a decade, or two decades at most, less than ten major entertainment corporations will dominate communications worldwide. This may increase the number of films, recordings, and video channels available, but they will nearly all be under the control of a few large companies. Only with strong traditional local structures will a new generation of media producers create entertainment as representatives of the public rather than as hacks for a consumerist industry.

Conclusion

This chapter has argued that electronic technology cannot by itself solve the youth "problem"; history shows us that advances in communications technologies have not solved major social problems of the past. Ironically, new electronic communications technologies have often fostered, not cured, certain crises in authority and generational discontinu-

---

46. James W. Carey, *Communication as Culture: Essays on Media and Society* (Boston: Unwin Hyman, 1989); and Daniel J. Czitrom, *Media and the American Mind: From Morse to McLuhan* (Chapel Hill, N.C.: University of North Carolina Press, 1982).

ity that plague families, schools, ethnic groups, religious organizations, racial neighborhoods, and the like. In some ways new media technologies and strategies have supplemented traditional social institutions, but in other ways they have supplanted these institutions. While the new media are impressive and powerful, how they are used will determine whether they will be a cultural bane or blessing. Increasingly it seems that the North American ideals of "bigger is better" and "quicker is slicker" are no longer relevant. Instead, the time has come to look beyond the volume and speed of mass communications to gauge the impact of the entertainment industry on North American youth.

4. Risky Business: Youth and the Entertainment Industry

The adolescent is dumped into a society of his peers, a society whose habitats are the halls and classrooms of their schools, the teen-age canteens, the corner drugstore, the automobile, and numerous other gathering places.

James Coleman, sociologist

It's getting so show business is just one big puberty rite.

Hollywood executive

The life of a rock & roll band will last as long as you look down into the audience and can see yourself, and your audience looks up at you and can see themselves—and as long as those reflections are human, realistic ones.

Bruce Springsteen, rock artist

Movies, records, radio, and television occupy a huge place in the lives of teenagers. They spend an extraordinary amount of time and energy selecting and consuming their art diet ("devouring" might be a more accurate word). A recent Gallup survey showed that teenagers' favorite pastimes are going out with friends, watching television, and going to movies.[1] Entertainment impresarios know well this teen devotion to popular art—mass-produced entertainment disseminated through the

---

1. See *America's Youth: 1977-1988*, ed. Robert Bezilla (Princeton, N.J.: Gallup Organization, 1988), p. 206.

media—and work hard to expand pop art's already major role in youth culture. To do so, the industry directs its attention to adolescents' primary psychological needs for identity, intimacy, and meaning. For example, the pioneering executives of MTV sought to appeal to a host of adolescent longings and susceptibilities. Shortly after its beginning in the early 1980s, one MTV executive boasted of the channel's appeal to insecurities about identity and social acceptance, claiming that a teen would have to "be a social outcast not to watch it."[2] Such comments say much about the nature of youth-oriented entertainment, the role of the entertainment industry, and its problematic relationship to marketing strategy.

The popular entertainment industry sees youth as a prime market—a distinct, ever-renewing demographic group possessed of ample leisure and money to make sales soar. Further, adolescents have shown themselves, because of their particular stage of life, to be especially susceptible to the marketing wiles of the entertainment industry. This industry is adept at perpetually recycling timeless adolescent anxieties and hopes into easily adaptable formulaic fads and fashions. In doing so, entertainment does more than provide diverting amusement for bored teenagers, although it surely does this as well. To a surprising extent, young people rely on the industry's products to learn about life and society. Popular music, films, and television form an appealing and lively cultural reservoir from which young people draw in their struggle to understand themselves and the larger world. Adolescents want guidance through the maze of modern teen life, and the entertainment industry obligingly supplies them with "maps of reality"—popular artifacts that metaphorically explain life and society and suggest ways of understanding and responding to dilemmas and perplexities.

In the decades since World War II, these two groups have forged an extremely close relationship based on mutually beneficial interdependence. Indeed, at the current pass in American culture, it is not overstatement to claim that the world of adolescence and the electronic entertainment industry need each other in order to survive—that they have developed a symbiotic relationship. The result of this symbiosis is a powerful cultural world whose influence effectively rivals and often surpasses the influence of traditional sources of adolescent nurture such as family, church, and school.

This chapter seeks to trace the emergence of the North American youth culture and to explain its workings and its cultural significance.

2. Quoted by Christian Williams in "MTV Is Rock around the Clock," *The Philadelphia Inquirer*, 3 Nov. 1982, p. D-1.

As we have seen in Chapter Two, American youth seem historically to have been especially receptive and adaptable to new communications media and technological gadgets. We pick up this historical analysis in the 1950s, when youth and the entertainment industry began to shape a stronger and broader symbiotic relation than they had in the past. Some precedent for this more powerful tie flourished briefly among college youth in the 1920s, but that courtship never achieved the breadth and durability of the relationship that developed after World War II. At present, North American youth and the entertainment media together form a separate quasi-educational culture—a culture that is about youth and for youth *and* for profit. The entertainment industry makes money from the symbiosis, while youth acquire the maps that help them steer their way through the troubled and confusing waters of teenage life.

"Dumped" into a Society of Peers

Contemporary youth culture flowered after World War II. To be sure, it did not emerge full-blown overnight but developed gradually from a large number of changing conditions in mid-century American culture. By the 1960s, however, a large, powerful, and autonomous commercial and sociopolitical entity had emerged. To a large extent, adolescents had come to live in a world whose content and shape derived from other adolescents and increasingly influential commercial entertainments and diversions.

Perhaps the most decisive of the changes following World War II was the amazing economic prosperity whose fruits fell upon the white baby-boom generation (blacks and other racial minorities were largely excluded from this prosperity). The children of the boom grew up in an era of unprecedented affluence, rapid technological advance, and educational innovation. The progressive income tax and union wage demands brought a level of income only dreamed about by workers in the 1930s. Blue-collar families could for the first time enjoy the security and afford the pleasures previously confined to the middle class. By the mid-fifties more than half of the suburban population (where almost all of the decade's population growth occurred) consisted of working-class families. Specifically, the new suburban lifestyle meant improved housing, more leisure, and "a better place to raise kids." The thriving postwar economy turned the luxuries of the past into everyday necessities. More than ever prosperity defined the very pulse and purpose of American life and held forth the promise of resolving all social problems. So great was the economic miracle that the mood of the culture itself began to shift. In a reverse of the Protestant work ethic, leisure and enjoyment became the order of the day. The masses now lived as the elite once did, with money and time to spare. A great unending flow of new goods and services fueled a climate of instant gratification. From the end of World War II to Vietnam, economic growth soared.

The chief benefactors of this economic upswing and slow change of national mood were teenagers. Unscarred by the traumas of the Depression and World War II, the children of the baby-boom generation had a very different orientation toward life than their parents. They experienced few of the problems of earlier generations. If in the past young people were labor assets for a family, this was the first generation of student consumers. The effect—a major one—was to make teens more independent from their parents. The percentage of teenage boys with after-school jobs doubled between 1944 and 1956. Between after-school jobs and allowance, the weekly income for teenagers jumped from $2.50 in 1944 to about $10.00 in 1958. During the 1950s teenagers spent $9.5 million annually (a figure that doesn't include what their parents bought for them). By the mid-1960s, even though the number of teenagers grew at only three times the rate of the general population, their consumption had skyrocketed to about $12 *billion*. Business entrepreneurs quickly recognized teenagers as the new and possibly final "merchandising frontier."[3] Advertising once directed at parents now targeted teenagers. In a 1965 cover story on "Today's Teenagers," *Time* estimated that young people spent $570 million on toiletries, $3.6 billion on women's clothes, and $1.5 billion on entertainment each year.[4] Fifty-three percent of all movie tickets and 43 percent of all records were bought by teenagers.

Along with their own and their parents' money came leisure, a commodity that teens as well as their parents wished to pursue. For teenagers, that meant free time and, more than anything else, cars, the ideal way to use that time and "show off" the newfound affluence. In the United States, the number of cars in use doubled between 1940 and 1955 and again between 1950 and 1965. A symbol of maturity and status, the automobile held a central place in the social world of the high school. Having "wheels" also meant unchaperoned transportation, especially

3. Dwight MacDonald, "Profiles: A Caste, a Culture, a Market-1," *New Yorker*, 22 Nov. 1958, p. 58.

4. See "Today's Teenagers," *Time*, 29 Jan. 1965, p. 57; and Landon Y. Jones, *Great Expectations: America and the Baby Boom Generation* (New York: Ballantine Books, 1980), pp. 84-85.

Cashing in on a Good Thing

One of the first and most successful companies established to do market research among teenagers was Gil-bert Teen Age Services. While still in high school in the 1940s, founder Eugene Gilbert recognized "that his contemporaries had a style of life that was fast becoming *sui generis,* and that manufacturers and merchants, practically all of whom labored under the disadvantage of being adults, were losing sales because they were ignorant of this special world." In a stroke of genius, Gilbert used teenagers to interview their peers. He found a host of clients who were extremely interested in the information he gathered, including Esso gas, Borden's milk, *Seventeen* magazine, Simplicity (maker of dress patterns), Mars candy, Hires soft drinks, Van Heusen shirts, and even the United States Army. By the mid-1950s, Gilbert was writing a weekly column for the Associated Press called "What Young People Think" and earning a gross annual income estimated to be between $500,000 and $1 million.

—Dwight MacDonald, "Profiles: A Caste, a Culture, a Market-1," *New Yorker,* 22 Nov. 1958, pp. 57-94.

for dates. The combination of cars and teens spawned the drive-in restaurant, car hops, and the "junk food generation," phenomena that paved the way for the fast food industry. Cars and teens also gave rise to the drive-in movie theater, whose number in the U.S. went from 480 in 1948 to a peak of 4,000 in 1958. These "passion pits with pix," as *Variety* called them, were an important part of teenage sociality, especially between the sexes. Writer Lisa Alther caught the interaction in her novel *Kinflicks:* "Mixed with the dialogue were the various sighs and gasps and sucking sounds from the front seats and blasts from car horns throughout the parking area as . . . couples signaled that they'd gone all the way."[5]

If money, time, and cars gave youth new levels of freedom and autonomy, the educational system increased the growing separation between adults and teenagers. Education, for the first time widely available to the children of the working and lower classes, was heralded as the ticket to the "abundant life." By the 1960s, ninety-five percent of teenagers between the ages of fourteen and seventeen were in school, and over half of all high school students continued their education in college. Honors courses, team teaching, language labs, the new math, and curriculum reform promised "a golden era in education." With

5. Alther, *Kinflicks* (New York: Alfred A. Knopf, 1976), p. 61.

curriculum change came new technology for the classroom. Most parents were glad to support such change, since it promised better futures for their offspring. But high expectations and rapid change in education further isolated adolescents from adults and increased generational discontinuity. The same effect appeared in the 1980s with the widespread use of the computer and video games. Children acquired new skills, terminology, and knowledge that mystified parents, making the "old people" appear all the more out of touch with contemporary life.

As prosperity, consumption, leisure, and education leapt forward, so did technology, especially in electronics. An electronics explosion made media consumption far more pervasive, varied, and individualized than ever before. Transistor technology swept the radio industry; the medium became inescapable. Ultimately, this too created a separate sphere, like cars and school, in which teenagers could "live" and create a culture of their own. They listened to the Top 40 hits at home and work, at the beach and local hangouts, and while cruising in cars. Before long the radio meshed with the automobile to create a mobile teenage heaven (later depicted in the film *American Graffiti* [1973]). The number of cars with radios went from nine million in 1946 to 50 million in 1963. By the end of the 1970s nearly all cars had radios. The 1950s brought another revolution in electronics, the 45-rpm record. At home, a friend's house, or the sock hop, teens played 45s on new hi-fi stereos, sometimes dancing to the driving beat of the new rock-and-roll music. And then came television, which fast became "a passion, a craze, a social event, and a new focus for family life."[6] The sale of television sets grew at an annual rate of 500 percent until by the end of the fifties 87 percent of American households owned one. While primarily a family entertainment medium, viewing periods on the fringe of prime-time periods—late afternoon on weekdays and Saturdays—were geared toward young people. On Saturday afternoons teens learned new dances and watched favorite pop idols lip-synch their hits on Dick Clark's *American Bandstand*.

The dramatic and sweeping change that began in the 1950s greatly altered the cultural alignments of North American society. A collection of economic, social, educational, technological, and artistic forces gradually and firmly reshaped institutions of nurture. With the advent of progressive secondary education, parents were relieved of the burden of supplying occupational training for their children. Parents gratefully yielded this responsibility; it seemed that prosperity and the high school could do far more than they ever could. In a new era of

6. Geoffrey Perrett, *A Dream of Greatness: The American People, 1945-1963* (New York: Coward, McCann & Geoghegan, 1979), p. 229.

"'Til Her Daddy Took the T-Bird Away"

The new teenage culture was baffling to parents, educators, and public officials. Youth seemed to have gone berserk. It was difficult for the adult community to pinpoint the source of the problem, though many tried blaming everything from rock and roll to the Communists. In 1959, *Newsweek* did a special report on "a subject of nationwide concern"—the growing teen car culture. Reckless "auto" pranks, wild joyrides, and speeding rattled parents, police, and insurance companies. Just as disturbing was the possibility "that teen-agers roaming around in cars, unsupervised and unchaperoned, can fall into early sex experiences." Reportedly, the automobile was also having a negative impact on the social and intellectual development of the young, who were dropping out of high-school sports and ignoring their education as they became "addicted to cars." *Newsweek* cited a study done at a high school in Idaho that tried to make a causal connection between academic performance and car ownership. The survey "showed that no straight-A student had owned a car. Of the B students, 15 per cent owned cars. But 41 per cent of the C students, 71 per cent of the D's, and 83 per cent of the F's were car owners."

—William J. Brink, "Crazy Kids with Cars," *Newsweek*, 2 Mar. 1959, pp. 26, 28, 30.

democracy and progress, optimism about the fate of youth was abundant, at least for a while. In 1967 *Time* lauded the new adolescent as the Man of the Year, proclaiming loudly the blessings and hopes *of* and *for* the baby-boom generation:

> Reared in a prolonged period of world peace, he has a unique sense of control over his own destiny. . . . Science and the knowledge explosion have armed him with more tools to choose his life pattern than he can always use: physical and intellectual mobility, personal and financial opportunity, a vista of change accelerating in every direction.
>
> Untold adventure awaits him. He is the man who will land on the moon, cure cancer and the common cold, lay out blight-proof, smog-free cities, enrich the underdeveloped world and, no doubt, write finis to poverty and war.[7]

A photograph accompanying the story showed those heralded baby boomers sunbathing on Florida beaches. And there came the rub. The teens were off by themselves in pleasure land, not busily studying or accomplishing their elders' hopes.

7. "The Under-25 Generation," *Time*, 6 Jan. 1967, p. 18.

Quite another scenario had already displaced *Time*'s glowing profile and optimistic prophecy. In countless ways, youth seemed to be going their own way—not the well-designed path of success and public service their elders had envisioned. For the host of reasons just recited, parents, teachers, and civic leaders found themselves rather suddenly out of touch with the new age-segregated teen society that looked elsewhere for help in facing the larger challenges of life: identity formation, social development, religious meaning, and morality. Parents and teachers awakened to the presence of a powerful, self-contained youth ghetto whose citizens turned to one another and, most importantly, to the entertainment media for solutions to the common psychological and social struggles of adolescence. The circumstances pushed teen society and adult culture into a new alignment of influence and formative social bonds. And it became a precarious and continuing predicament, full of mutual distrust and acrimony. Contemplating the brash and prominent force of the youth culture, adults wondered who would train the young and what they would learn. Could the high school and its hallways, teen hangouts, friends, cruising, deejays and rock music, and teen movies supplant the nurture traditionally supplied by home and church?

The questions were real and enormous. For the first time in history, the majority of teenagers from all classes and racial groups were brought together in high schools; they were bound together in a recognizable social class. "Teenager" no longer referred just to a chronological period or developmental phase on the way to adulthood but to a whole subculture. Still more, it meant the steady and fundamental questioning of traditional adult authority in everything from musical taste to sexual morality. The prime location for this rebellious retraining was the culture of the high school, not the classrooms but the halls, lunch rooms, and parking lots—wherever teenagers gathered to listen to their music, drive their cars, pursue romance, and generally have "fun."

The School of Popular Entertainment

In the culture of the high school, what would teenagers learn and from whom? Part of the answer to what they would learn would come from their stage of life—adolescence. One social analyst, Joseph Kett, has defined contemporary adolescence as "the period after puberty during which a young person is institutionally segregated from casual contacts with a broad range of adults."[8] Two points of this definition warrant emphasis. First, adolescence is in part biological, "the period after puberty," when young people are supposedly psychologically and sexually vulnerable because of the hormonal blitz they experience in the process of maturation. Physically capable of having sex and sometimes eager to do so, yet strongly admonished by their elders to abstain, most teenagers both enjoy and suffer from an intense preoccupation with sex. It is not surprising, then, that teen activities often revolve around the mating ritual called dating, which involves clothing, cosmetics, social hangouts, concerts, movies, and so on.

The second key feature of adolescence which Kett emphasizes is more social than biological—the teen's institutional segregation from "casual contacts with a broad range of adults." This feature is easily explained. Rapid technological change and economic specialization require longer periods of training outside the family. Public secondary schools have become the accepted means of imparting the necessary social and vocational preparation. The current structure of this educational system dictates that youth stay largely isolated—save for their teachers and parents—from the rest of society. As a result, adolescents form most of their significant social bonds with peers, who in many ways fill the role of substitute parent. To be sure, those peers are as exacting as any parent. The teenager must fashion a self and a future amid a maze of locker-lined hallways, shopping mall corridors, teen hangouts, and new fads and fashions. Lest we doubt it, surveys reveal that teenagers do suffer intense peer pressure to date at an early age, have sex, and use alcohol and drugs.[9]

Maneuvering through this world is no easy task. The desire for acceptance looms large, and teenagers often take great emotional and social risks in their attempts to gain acceptance. In any case, every teen must chart a path through new and challenging domains. This predicament largely dictates youth's educational agenda; they are driven by what they must learn to survive and thrive in the struggle for identity, acceptance, and meaning. For the postwar youth culture, the prime teacher and supplier of curriculum has been popular entertainment, especially of the electronic variety. Indeed, it is hard to underestimate its effect.

For members of the youth culture, popular entertainment has played this role for a long time. As early as 1929, just after sound came to motion pictures, an extensive research project investigated the impact

8. Kett, *Rites of Passage: Adolescence in America, 1790 to the Present* (New York: Basic Books, 1977), p. 36.
9. See *America's Youth: 1977-1988*, p. 22.

of movies on young people.[10] Interviews revealed that adolescents learned how to dress, put on perfume and make-up, and practice rules of etiquette from watching movies. They discovered ways of attracting the opposite sex and techniques in the art of love. "As far as I can remember, almost all of my knowledge of sex came from the movies," explained a male college freshman. "There was no other place where I could have gotten it. Ideas about kissing definitely came from the movies. This is absolutely true; the first time I ever kissed a girl was after I saw Greta Garbo and John Gilbert."[11] Teens testified that after seeing movies they felt dissatisfied with many things about their own lives— their social environment, parental restraints, work, clothing, and lack of freedom. Similarly, they absorbed the movies' numerous racial and ethnic stereotypes. The comment of one writer remains as apt today as it was sixty years ago: "What the screen becomes is a gigantic educational system with an instruction possibly more successful than the present text-book variety."[12] Indeed, current research amply confirms that adolescents continue to rely on popular entertainment—music, movies, and TV—for information about everything from manners to religion. Despite today's enlightened sex education, teens still learn more about dating and sex from popular entertainment than from parents, teachers, and youth workers.[13]

Just as popular entertainment provides American youth with a kind of transitional bridge into adulthood, historically it has eased the assimilation into North American culture of immigrants and youth from a host of different ethnic and racial minorities. For the tens of millions of immigrants who entered America and Canada in the early twentieth century, the cinema offered a "passport to the American Dream . . . a crash course in their adoptive country's history, behavior, values, ideals and follies."[14] In 1934, one education journal noted the effect of movies

10. The pro-censorship bias was only one of several weaknesses that blunted the value of the studies for enhancing an understanding of the impact of movies. However, the results of the Payne Fund studies remain convincing regarding the pedagogical aspect of films for youth. See Robert Sklar, *Movie-Made America: A Social History of American Movies* (New York: Random House, 1975), pp. 135-40.

11. Quoted by Henry James Foreman in *Our Movie-Made Children* (New York: Macmillan, 1933), p. 166.

12. Foreman, *Our Movie-Made Children,* pp. 64-65.

13. Josh McDowell Ministry, "Teen Sex Survey in the Evangelical Church" (Dallas: Josh McDowell Ministry, 1987). See also Elizabeth F. Brown and William R. Hendee, "Adolescents and Their Music: Insights into the Health of Adolescents," *Journal of the American Medical Association* 262 (22-29 Sept. 1989): 1659.

14. Richard Corliss, "Magic Shadows from a Melting Pot," *Time,* 8 July 1985, p. 92.

on American-born children of immigrant parents: "Especially where the other agencies and institutions in a young person's life do not adapt themselves adequately to his psychological and cultural situation, the cinema may very well be, and, in fact, often is, the refuge to which the individual goes to discover that which he considers really 'American.' "[15] More recently, one young refugee from Saigon explained that television was a primer on American culture. "We all loved *Happy Days*. All kids watched, and the next day, everybody talked about it. . . . I didn't know anything about American history or the '50's. TV gave me an idea what Americans thought. I watched and I assimilated. Now, I realize that view is narrow, one-dimensional. But television introduced me to America."[16] Popular entertainment helped immigrant families to shed their own traditions and ethnicity and adapt to the peculiarities of American culture.

While influenced by media, today's teenagers are by no means naive, and they are sophisticated enough to know that movies, songs, and TV shows are not reality. They do not mistake dramatic realism for truth or swallow whatever stars say. Nonetheless, they are susceptible to a kind of realism that affirms common social and emotional experiences and longings. This kind of realism sometimes shapes the low-budget "sex-ploitation" film that pictures adolescence as a long party in the waiting room to adulthood. And it clearly figures in John Hughes's zestful dream of adolescent freedom in *Ferris Bueller's Day Off*. The pull of this theme can come through many avenues—an actor, a character, a theme, a catchy soundtrack. Something grabs the teenager, and he or she enters the world the film has created. By such means, popular entertainment helps adolescents size up their world, organize and interpret experience, and develop strategies to deal with the challenges they face.

Through movies, music, and television programming, young people can identify with dramatic counterparts who are struggling to survive not only in the youth culture but also in the larger society. Teenagers relate to pop singers who capture, and sometimes encourage, the full spectrum of adolescent emotional tumult—heartbreak, insecurity, joy, sexual fantasies, and infatuation. Or they connect with a TV series that speaks to their problems or dreams. Familiar characters, resolved conflicts, and happy endings in TV series can provide security and comfort, hope and triumph. Movies can dramatize teenage fear,

15. Paul G. Cressey, "The Motion Picture as Informal Education," *Journal of Educational Sociology* 7 (1934): 513.

16. Quoted by Susan Littwin in "How TV Americanizes Immigrants . . . for Better or Worse," *TV Guide*, 9 Apr. 1988, p. 10.

embarrassment, or desire, something the films of John Hughes have done successfully.

Heroes and heroines supply ways for teenagers to check the adequacy of their own reactions—and to learn, sometimes by watching but not imitating. After four months of research on youth in the mid-eighties, one Hollywood marketing executive observed, "Young people like to go to movies they think will be emotionally daring but they are not there as sexual voyeurs. . . . They'd rather see a film that is passionately involving. The kids want to go through a passionate experience vicariously so that they can walk out of the theater feeling they've had the experience without having to undergo any of the dangers and without having violated their own ethical or moral standards."[17] Popular entertainment provides a free imaginative realm in which young people can explore the world and life without fear of danger or failure. Alone or with peers, teens watch movies and television and listen to music. Adults do not intrude or "butt in" with their wisdom or advice. Although the purpose of "entertaining" is usually seen as mere amusement or just moneymaking, its real purpose is education. The teenager goes to the school of adolescence with entertainment as the friend and teacher.

In Search of the Magic Market

By such means, however inadvertent, youth ended up in a culture of their own, one to which parents, like the editors of *Time*, at first gave their hopeful blessing. Amid the prosperity, optimism, and good faith (naive trust) of the fifties, those blessed teenagers were handed freedom, innocence, "youth," leisure, mobility, and disposable cash. What they perhaps did not have, and were eager for, was an appealing mentor who would show them what to do with their multiple blessings. The authority of traditional figures of wisdom, like parents and teachers, seemed notably less appealing than the stars of popular entertainment. The teen rebel pictures of the fifties cast those traditional sources of nurture in a dubious light. In *Rebel without a Cause*, parents seemed incompetent, indifferent, or harshly repressive. *Blackboard Jungle* portrayed teachers as cynical, bumbling, elitist, or tyrannical; the committed teacher was the exception. In any case, postwar teenagers did not find an attractive

---

17. Quoted by Dora Albert in "Youth May Be Wasted on Young But Its Appeal Is Showbiz Asset If You Understand What It Is," *Variety*, 16 Jan. 1985, p. 92.

traditional mentor who spoke sympathetically about their pleasures, worries, and hopes. Whether adults abdicated their authority or powerful competitive voices rose to usurp their traditional roles, adult nurture of youth eroded. What took its place or at least became a powerful competitor was a mentor most eager to address in drama and song youth's central concerns about identity, intimacy, and meaning. Through the entertainment media, youth talked to youth about youth. For fun and profit—but mostly profit—the electronic entertainment media supplied an attractive alternative voice for youth.

Fortunately for the entertainment industry, the separation of youth from adult culture came at the right time—amid hard times for pop music and movies. In fact, Hollywood, New York, and Nashville could not have asked for a more favorable turn of events than the birth of a huge demographic mass for which they would supply a sense of definition and direction. Producers eagerly embraced the youth market, incessantly and profitably reworking its language, fads, fashions, mores, values, ideals, and dreams. The industry exalted its own significance by promoting constant media consumption, consumerism, and, paradoxically, perpetual adolescence as the best ways to maturity. It was a perfect match; each got what they most wanted. Youth got a beguiling companion, lively and understanding. And the industry, well, it got customers—in droves.

The youth culture, then, proved salvific for the entertainment industry. The adolescence of the baby boom was not simply another market but economic salvation. From 1945 to 1955, radio, film, and recording industries had suffered dwindling audiences and revenues. Most of this decline resulted from the arrival of the new player on the block—television, which usurped the family audience the other media had traditionally relied on. On the lookout for a new source of revenue, record and film companies as well as radio programmers undertook market research on the burgeoning youth population. Based on these findings, production and advertising soon struggled to appeal to teenagers. This proved so lucrative that in 1965 one Hollywood executive complained, "Teenage tastes are exerting a tyranny over our industry. . . . It's getting so show business is just one big puberty rite."[18]

The first to feel the full effect of television and to recognize the potential of the youth market was radio. Television had rapidly replaced radio as the provider of comedy and variety entertainment, which left radio stations with the task of filling hours of vacant, unpurchased air

18. Quoted by Peter Bart in "Hollywood Finds Gold on Beaches," *New York Times*, 22 June 1965, p. 25.

time. An easy resort was popular music, particularly the new rock and roll. How this music was played was given a new twist by radio magnate Todd Storz. He noticed that bar patrons often chose the same songs over and over on the jukebox. Recognizing a desire for musical repetition and familiarity, Storz developed a new radio format to satisfy it. In 1955 in Omaha, Storz introduced on KDWH what soon came to be known as Top 40 radio (after the 40 selections contained in most jukeboxes at the time). With more radio stations playing more recorded music, a new type of radio personality, the disc jockey, rose to celebrity status. By 1958 there were some three thousand disc jockeys spinning rock-and-roll records. Virtually overnight, the combination of the new music format and the portability of the transistor radio made rock an ever-present part of life. The rise of Top 40 radio represented a gigantic technological change that gave recorded music broad exposure. A technological shift of something of the same magnitude would happen again in 1981 with the advent of MTV—music television.

At virtually the same time, the recording industry was undergoing a technological challenge of its own, one that would have a profound effect on marketing. In the late 1940s, the recording industry had introduced two new formats for recorded music. In 1948 Columbia introduced a 12-inch, 33 1/3 rpm long-playing vinyl disc; soon after, RCA countered with the 6-inch, 45 rpm disc. The ensuing "battle of the speeds" established 45s as the medium of the single pop song and 33s as the format for album-oriented popular music, various artist compilations, and classical and Broadway scores. Between 1948 and 1955, with the new formats in use, the four major recording companies (Columbia, RCA, Decca, and Capitol) dominated the charts of Billboard magazine (the major trade publication of the recording industry) with over 75 percent of the listings.

Before long, however, the new music of rock and roll used one of those formats to revolutionize the industry. The new music reached the public not through the major companies but through the "indies," the small, independent record companies, for whom the 45 was the ideal economic format—it was short so it could be quickly and cheaply produced. Neither the indies nor their fledgling sock-hop artists would have been able to gather enough original material for a full-blown album, but they could scrape together enough material (and money) to release a 45 (usually two songs). The indies taste for the new music and format coincided nicely with radio's need to fill air time: the flood of independent 45 releases provided an abundant pool of "quick-listen" music to choose from. The music, the format, and the broadcaster seemed the ideal trio. Prior to the technological explosion in the recording industry in the late 1940s, radio stations had relied quite heavily on studio bands and live performances of the popular music of the day. But with the advent of the new 45 rpm record and improved playback equipment, playing pop music became far less complicated and expensive. The revolution in technology, music, and market radically changed *Billboard* statistics: by 1958 the major recording companies' share of best-selling records had shrunk to 36 percent. Although the major companies eventually signed early rock legends like Chuck Berry and Elvis Presley, their quick rise to fame occurred when they were recording with Chess and Sun Records, two small independents.

Most spectacular of all, though, was the rise of the music itself, a new form that seemed ideally suited to chronicle and express the privileged restiveness of youth. All the technological innovation and business savvy would not have amounted to much if it had not been for the music itself. It was a siren song, a new pied piper for teenagers searching for identity. Suddenly, it seemed, the loud jiving and thumping alchemy of rock and roll appeared out of nowhere, grabbing the hearts and moving the feet of teenagers everywhere. It came, in fact, from everywhere, a mélange of three popular music traditions. The first was Tin Pan Alley music, which had emerged from nineteenth-century Anglo-American high culture. Full of melodic sounds and sentimental lyrics, the music seemed determined not to offend the domestic sensibility of Victorian America. Considerably less tame was the second tradition—the largely African-American music of the deep South: blues, rhythm and blues, jazz, and gospel. The third tradition came mainly from the middle South and the Southern uplands, the music of rural Southern whites that falls under the general heading of "country music"—blues, gospel, honky-tonk, and bluegrass (another outgrowth of this tradition became contemporary country and western). The second of these, black music, exerted a growing influence on American popular music after World War II, and the merging of the second and third traditions gave birth to rock and roll. For those caught up in the great postwar influx to urban centers in the North, rock and roll was the "sound of the city" hammered out of the musical styles loved by countless disenfranchised blacks and whites. As rock penetrated the white mainstream market, elements of style and form from Tin Pan Alley were adopted in the process of commercialization.

With such a lineage, it is no wonder that rock and roll provided some excitement for young people in the bland suburbs, filling their leisure hours with a driving backbeat that was good to dance to. Rock's first inroad came in 1951. A Cleveland record-store owner alerted disc jockey Alan Freed to the popularity of R&B records among white teenagers. Freed in turn introduced the white teenage radio audience to black rhythm-and-blues artists by programming R&B on WJW's "Moondog's Rock and Roll Party." From there the ambitious Freed went on to arrange for live shows by black artists for predominantly white audiences. In hindsight, this connection between a minority's music and white teenagers makes some sense. At least in part, rock did for white suburban teenagers what R&B did for urban blacks who sought relief from grueling industrial labor or unemployed "leisure." In adopting the vernacular of African-American culture, rock and roll brought to the white teenage audience the language, attitudes, and feelings of a distinctive and alien oppressed minority. The embrace of a black sense of distinctiveness and alienation had the effect, and perhaps the intention, of announcing the distance separating white young people from the ethos of adult society. Indeed, the more adults were agitated by the music, the more teens relished it as an expression of their dissatisfaction with traditional social mores. Whatever the case, rock was produced for and marketed to a white teenage audience, and they en masse claimed it as their own. For radio and the recording industry, it meant that the slump of the late forties and early fifties ended. Radio became an indispensable means of exposure for rock music. Between 1954 and 1960 record sales tripled as rock and roll dominated the charts.

Hollywood also fell on hard times with the emergence of television. In the early fifties film attendance dropped spectacularly. Faced with a dwindling audience, film companies began to examine the youth market as a potential source of new revenues. A 1958 study by the Motion Picture Association of America (MPAA) showed that over half the moviegoing audience was under twenty. The percentage of people attending theaters was inversely proportionate to age. Sixty-eight percent of the tickets were purchased by people under twenty-five, while only 19 percent were purchased by those over forty-five.[19] Despite such obvious indicators, the major Hollywood studios were surprisingly slow to react to the changing audience. The major studios did produce the "restless youth" films in the mid-fifties—*Blackboard Jungle, Rebel without a Cause,* and *The Wild One*—but most of the youth exploitation fare came from independent producers and film companies. Sam Katzman and Alan Freed capitalized on the rock-and-roll explosion by producing B-grade films that showcased rock singers. American International Pictures made a fortune on movies designed for the teenage drive-in crowd. AIP made the cult classic *I Was a Teenage Werewolf* for under $125,000, and the movie caused traffic jams at drive-in theaters, eventually grossing over two million dollars—a proportionately big take in the 1950s

19. MacDonald, "Profiles," p. 82.

movie market. On a roll, AIP followed with a profitable series of low-budget beach party films featuring buxom ex-Mouseketeer Annette Funicello and rock swoon Frankie Avalon. In the late sixties the company exploited countercultural themes in pictures dealing with drugs, West Coast hippies, motorcycle gangs, and student rebellion. At about the same time, the major studios acquiesced to the youth market and began treating similar themes in their productions, a subject to be discussed more fully in Chapter Eight.

In the odd alchemy of society and culture, the commercial impetus for radio, records, and movies fostered an unforeseeable entity—a distinct and vigorous subcultural ethos. Together rock music and teen films told teenagers of the 1950s who they were, emphasizing that they were a separate social group. For them, the stories, symbols, and "feel" of popular entertainment provided a kind of interpretive glass and glue that made their experience, ideas, and emotions clear and cohesive—they were that new species called "teenager." For example, the movie *Blackboard Jungle* (1955) associated teens not only with rock music but also with rebellion and juvenile delinquency. The soundtrack featured Bill Haley's driving "Rock around the Clock" as an anthem for bitter and violent teenagers. Although the virtues of Americanism won out over the teenage rebels, the young audience latched onto the film's depiction of teenage identity and discontent. Avant-garde rock musician Frank Zappa remembered, "I didn't care if Bill Haley was white or sincere . . . he was playing the Teenage National Anthem and it was so LOUD I was jumping up and down. *Blackboard Jungle* . . . represented a strange sort of 'endorsement' of the teenage cause: 'They made a movie about us, therefore, we exist.' "[20]

Indeed, for an increasingly segregated teen society, rock music and teen films clarified and affirmed ordinary experience and expectations. These media functioned as a kind of mirror in which young people saw their own lives, their own conflicts and longings. Popular entertainment at once displayed, suggested, and exalted who and what teenagers were and wanted to be. In objectifying and making public such themes, popular entertainment furnished a means by which teenagers could share themselves with each other. For postwar youth, rock and roll was a shared enterprise, everybody's music, collectively owned, so deep was the emotional investment in and identification with the music. Rock was made for them, and artists and producers courted teenage tastes. It is no exaggeration to say that the music became a soundtrack for their lives. Teenagers listened to the Top 40 hits everywhere—at home, at work, at the beach, at local hangouts, in their cars. They bought the records and

20. Zappa, "The Oracle Has It All Psyched Out," *Life,* 28 June 1968, p. 85.

played them on phonographs at home and danced to the driving beat at parties.

The clout of rock and roll became clear in the early debates over its social message and value. On the one hand, as *Billboard* reported in 1956, a significant number of radio stations had started to play more rock and roll largely in response to pleas from teenagers. On the other hand, many station managers were reluctant to make this change. "We do not consider rock and roll [to be] music," said one. Another thought rock was "the worst influence to ever hit the music business—a disgrace." Aware of adult hostility to the music, many station owners felt forced to resist rock in one way or another "for the good of the youngsters." In response to the fuss, *Billboard* correctly surmised who would be the eventual victors and why: "When consumers buy rock and roll at the record store and slip coins into juke boxes to hear it in quantity, it is bound to get its due from radio stations."[21]

Television networks and record companies felt the same tension. For a time in 1956, ABC attempted to tame teenagers with a new style of music—"polkas played with a pop feeling, and pop tunes played with a polka beat."[22] Inspired by the success of Lawrence Welk and numerous local polka bands, ABC launched nationally the *Polka Time Show*, and ABC–Paramount Records released a series of dance albums by the band featured on the show. But the scheme failed completely while the spectacular success of Presley and others continued unabated. The major labels realized that rock was here to stay, at least for awhile. Survival meant incorporating the new music, so major labels added sanitized versions of Elvis to their rosters. The change was rapid: in 1956 ABC–Paramount was releasing polka albums; in 1957 they signed teen idol Paul Anka.

By 1964 the gulf separating youth culture and adult culture had reached the magnitude of a "generation gap," and American teenagers were ripe for the British Invasion, the onslaught of British pop stars on American pop charts, a charge led primarily by the Rolling Stones and the Beatles. A writer in the *New York Times Magazine* rightly identified the crucial ingredients that made for the new phenomenon: national Beatlemania was "ultimately the product of an affluent society which, for the first time in history, has made possible a leisure class of professional teenagers."[23] The vitality and profitability of the youth culture

21. Gary Kramer, "R. & R. a Teen-Age Must," *Billboard,* 10 Nov. 1956, p. 21.

22. See "Polka Rhythm Push Aimed at Teen-Ager," *Billboard,* 7 July 1956, p. 19.

23. David Dempsey, "Why the Girls Scream, Weep, Flip," *New York Times Magazine,* 23 Feb. 1964, p. 70.

continued to thrive through the 1970s. Rock music completely dominated the recording industry and sold well despite a sluggish economy.

While the major movie studios were much slower to "develop"
the young baby-boom audience, their heyday began in the late 1960s
with the first increase in box-office attendance since the end of World
War II. Three films responsible for this rise—*Bonnie and Clyde* (1967), *The
Graduate* (1967), and *Easy Rider* (1969)—were different in manner and
mood than other films of the day and were about and for young people,
especially the later two. The mild economic surge generated in the
seventies by emphasis on youth finally exploded in 1977-78 with *Saturday Night Fever* and *Grease*. Each film earned Paramount over $100
million. The two soundtracks together sold over 42 million units worldwide; *Saturday Night Fever* became the largest-selling LP in history.

The surge of economic success in the entertainment industries
faltered in the early eighties when, as all things do, the baby boomers
aged. "Where is the Woodstock generation," all those who flocked to
outdoor rock festivals and bought the music? One executive mourned
that they had all grown "old and bald."[24] In following years, the entertainment industry reeled from the economic recession, escalating production and marketing costs, cutbacks, and new competition from cable
television and the VCR. Recording sales and box-office figures fell
drastically. Already in 1980 an executive at Warner Records worried that
"there's more than a recession going on right now in the record business.
There's a transition to something that we're not sure what it is."[25] In
retrospect, it is clear that a transition was being made from the aging
baby boomers, the majority of whom were past twenty-five and no
longer so easily lured into record stores and theaters, to the upcoming
youth market. The sensibilities of those who protested during the sixties
and disco-danced in the seventies did not gel or resonate with the mood
of the youth of the eighties. Again, new communications media, advanced technology, and an improved economy had a dramatic impact
on youth, as did a new factor: the conservative mood of the Reagan era.

A new day dawned for the entertainment industry with the
advent of MTV in 1981. The rock-video cable channel, on the air around
the clock, revolutionized the industry by providing a new avenue for the
promotion of both music and movies. The audience for this "new thing"
was the same audience that bought most of the records and went most
often to the movies—a new generation of youth from ages twelve to

24. Quoted by Jay Cocks in "Sing a Song of Seeing," *Time*, 26 Dec. 1983, p. 63.
25. Quoted by Jean Callahan in "WB's Cornyn Tells Tribunal of Cost Fears,"
Billboard, 12 July 1980, p. 4.

twenty-five. The first performer to take full advantage of the new audio-visual medium and to show its remarkable profitability was Michael Jackson. Dubbed the "Fred Astaire of video," Jackson mesmerized the MTV audience with his sequinned glove and dramatic androgynous looks and wowed them with his ability to dance. *Thriller*, the album he released in 1983, became the largest-selling album of all time, with over 40 million copies sold internationally. One of the primary "hooks" that sold the album was Jackson's video of the cover song, which was a mini horror movie.

As Chapter Seven will show, MTV's great marketing contribution was its infusion into the industry of a new presentational style for both entertainment and advertising. Fast and unpredictable, full of noise and sexual allure, it pushed the limits of conventional narrative and of conventionality itself. Whatever its aesthetic merits, it paid for and set the direction for further marketing in the industry. The director of the movie *Flashdance*, a 1983 Columbia/CBS Records collaboration with a thin plot line about an aspiring young dancer, admitted to "deliberately exploiting video imagery because that's the state-of-the-art look for dance."[26] Critics panned the film because it looked like a feature-length video, but that was precisely its ploy and what made it such a hit. The movie cost only $8 million to produce but grossed over $100 million. The soundtrack sold over five million copies. Observers agreed that the chart-topping single releases "Flashdance (What a Feeling)" and "Maniac" contributed greatly to the success of the film. Both songs were coupled with energetic dance scenes from the movie and featured on MTV. "Paramount didn't know what they had, but they knew where to sell it," a rival marketing executive observed. "The MTV buys allowed them to shot-gun directly at their target, instead of scattering buckshot through a general TV approach."[27] With this trend established, a flood of profitable films with rock soundtracks spanned the decade, from *Footloose* in 1984 to *Batman* in 1989.

Indeed, the entertainment industry witnessed a dramatic turn-about in the 1980s, finding alternate if not entirely new ways of providing maps of reality for young people. *Washington Post* film critic Tom Shales dubbed the eighties the "ReDecade," observing that popular culture was simply a replay of the past several decades.[28] Adolescent formulas were again adapted to new fads and fashions reflecting the

26. Quoted by Richard M. Levine in "Life after *Flashdance*," *Esquire*, Jan. 1984, p. 86.

27. Quoted by Gregg Kilday in "Ninth Annual Grosses Gloss," *Film Comment*, Mar.-Apr. 1984, p. 63.

28. Shales, "The ReDecade," *Esquire*, Mar. 1986, pp. 67-72.

The 1980s: The "ReDecade"

In 1986 *Washington Post* film critic Tom Shales dubbed the Reagan era the "ReDecade." A by-product of the new communications technology—especially the VCR—American culture became a "replay, recycle, recall, retrieve, reprocess, and rerun" of every previous decade of the past, he suggested. "In the ReDecade, old legends never die," wrote Shales. "They just come back as new legends." Rock superstar Madonna was just a remake of Marilyn Monroe, " 'Diamonds Are a Girl's Best Friend' all dressed down with somewhere to go." Sylvester Stallone's Rambo was a 1980s version of John Wayne's World War II movie heroes. Lucille Ball times Janis Joplin equaled Cyndi Lauper.

By the 1980s "youth" had become a reliable marketing formula. New names and faces simply replaced previous pop idols who aged and were retired; steady-selling products were given a facelift.

Generations may come and generations may go, but the youth culture remains the same. The quest for business entrepreneurs is to package the universal fears, dreams, and desires of adolescence in the latest fashions and trends of the day. So Pepsi became "the choice of a new generation."

—Tom Shales, "The ReDecade," *Esquire,* Mar. 1986, pp. 67-70, 72.

cultural climate. Pepsi became "the choice of a new generation," the new youth culture.

By this time precedents had been set for the entertainment industry's targeting of youth as a major market. Although the postwar baby boomers had been displaced by "a new generation," the symbiotic relationship that had developed between the industry and youth in the fifties continued to flourish in the eighties.

The Entertainment Industry: Doing Its Job

The celebrated, or infamous, bottom line in the popular entertainment industry is financial profit. The business world produces cultural commodities such as movies, records, and TV shows for consumption by a mass audience. The high production costs of technology-dependent commodities—higher than production costs of, say, novels or paintings—mean such commodities demand a larger audience in order to turn a profit on the initial investment. Technology-dependent entertainment is a capital-intensive business, and an enormous response is necessary to retrieve production costs. Just how large that response must be sometimes surprises those outside the industry. To rank as a "hit," a TV show must capture almost 20 percent of the country's TV-viewing households. If a singer has an album that goes platinum—sells a million copies—the recording industry celebrates, but the artist is granted superstar status only if the album goes "multi-platinum." In the late 1980s the average movie cost about $19 million to produce, and distribution and promotion costs were as high as the production figure, which meant the film had to earn more than twice that amount just to break even. In today's marketplace a huge hit tops $100 million. Big-time producer-directors like Steven Spielberg have brought in well over a billion dollars in tickets.

Needless to say, the creative process is tempered by the investors' gamble on what the audience wants to see or hear and how to keep that audience coming back for more. Distributors and exhibitors also enter the calculation. Artists often emphasize aesthetics and art rather than commodity production, but they too recognize that to continue making art they must bring in profits. Consequently, artists as well as executives have one eye on the market potential of any project. Screenwriter and director Paul Schrader (*Taxi Driver, American Gigolo, Raging Bull*) captures the artist-audience symbiosis in his explanation of the creative process for commercial screenwriters. They find "a rip in the social fabric and create a film metaphor which deals with that tear, that is as good a way as any to be commercial." Screenwriters choose topics by keeping a finger on the pulse of ordinary people, Schrader explains. "Look around you. Read the newspaper, watch people on the street, listen to conversations; you can see the problems people are trying to deal with. If you can confront those needs with film metaphors, the want will be there."[29]

Popular entertainment, if it is to be popular *and* profitable, must take due note of marketability—how much audiences out there want to *pay* attention to the art piece, which is also a commodity up for sale. The romantic notion of the pure-hearted integrity of the starving artist in the freezing garret doing art for art's or truth's sake has little to do with popular art or, for that matter, elite art. In highly technological art forms such as film and television, art pieces must pay for their production and thus fast become commodities. The consideration of what audiences want to see or hear will shape the product. According to Paul Schrader, "Sex and violence are all-encompassing fantasies that permeate every

29. Schrader, quoted by John Brady in *The Craft of the Screenwriter: Interviews with Six Celebrated Screenwriters* (New York: Simon & Schuster, 1981), pp. 290-91.

Medicine and Rock and Roll

Even the American Medical Association has gotten into the discussion of rock music. "Traditionally the role of physicians has been to conquer disease and promote health," an essay in the *Journal of the American Medical Association* began. "For physicians who treat adolescents, this role has become increasingly challenging. . . . Frequently the tragic health problems of teenagers, such as unplanned teen pregnancies, accidents, and violence, have strong roots in the psychosocial environment." As young people gain independence from their parents, the report continued, "they turn to music as an information source about sexuality and alternative lifestyles, subjects that are largely taboo in both home and school." To gain a better appreciation and understanding of the adolescent environment, the writers of the essay suggested that physicians should be aware of the important role which rock music plays in the lives of teenagers and "use music preferences as clues to the emotional and mental health of adolescents."

—Elizabeth F. Brown, M.D., and William R. Hendee, Ph.D., "Adolescents and Their Music: Insights into the Health of Adolescents," *Journal of the American Medical Association* 262 (22-29 Sept. 1989): 1659-63.

---

possible market. Screenwriting needs them more than the other forms of media—because the numbers have to be bigger."[30] Thus film scripts often repeat past plot formulas or genres or tailor a story to a certain bankable actor or actress who has been cast. Sometimes the production company films several endings and experiments with them with "test audiences" to find the most popular one for general release. When the producers of *Fatal Attraction* discovered that test audiences disliked the film's original somber ending, it willingly reversed the meaning of the film by switching to an ending that left audiences cheering. Similarly, TV shows often target the issues and lifestyle of a certain segment of the viewing audience, thereby delivering a "demographic" for anxious advertisers. Most albums are "producer-oriented," geared to molding an artist's compositions into imitations of tracks that have cracked the Top 10. As a result, rock artists treat *ad nauseam* the emotional, social, and physical tensions of their adolescent market.

Popular art does not emerge in a cultural vacuum but usually results from a negotiated interaction between artists, profit-minded producers, and an eager and interested but unpredictable mass of people

30. Ibid., p. 280.

known as clientele, an audience, or a market. This is not to say that all artists and executives work daily with this symbiotic relationship in the forefront of their minds. Most simply do their jobs. They read the tea leaves of probable audience interest as best they can. More often than anyone will admit, however, many hits come as a great surprise to creators and marketers.

Popular Art as Maps of Reality

Of course, for all these entertainment media to be as popular as they are, especially among youth, they must supply something of value to their audiences. Great debates have raged about the value of the commodities they offer, however. The relation of the American automobile industry to American culture provides a helpful analogy. The industry supplies particular products that serve different functions of greater and lesser importance: cars can provide transportation, status, entertainment, diversion, investment, and the focus for a hobby. Entertainment products serve a somewhat parallel list of functions in the lives of American youth.

Of major importance among the cultural functions of popular entertainment is its capacity to serve as an ongoing source of *maps of reality*, especially for youth. Just as a map is not a territory itself but an abstract representation of its roads and rivers, so popular artifacts provide stories, metaphors, and symbols that explain life and suggest responses to its quandaries and mysteries. Cultural maps depict and chart meanings, values, assumptions, attitudes, behavioral norms, and social and gender roles. The versions of reality supplied by movies, TV, and music provide, in the words of literary theorist Kenneth Burke, "equipment for living" in both the youth culture and the larger world.[31] As such, popular entertainment works on a number of levels that can be diagrammed as a series of concentric circles representing a psycho-emotional core, the youth culture, the larger society, and a prevailing mythos.

31. Burke, "Literature as Equipment for Living," in *The Philosophy of Literary Form: Studies in Symbolic Form,* 3rd ed. (Berkeley: University of California Press, 1973), pp. 293-304. The idea of popular art as a means of cultural mapping is drawn from several sources. See Clifford Geertz, *The Interpretation of Cultures* (New York: Basic Books, 1973), p. 220; Fredric Jameson, "Cognitive Mapping," in *Marxism and the Interpretation of Culture,* ed. Cary Nelson and Lawrence Grossberg (Urbana: University of Illinois Press, 1988), pp. 347-60; Robert Darnton, *The Great Cat Massacre and Other Episodes in French Cultural History* (New York: Vintage Books, 1985); Dick Hebdige, *Subculture: The Meaning of Style* (New York: Methuen, 1979), p. 17.

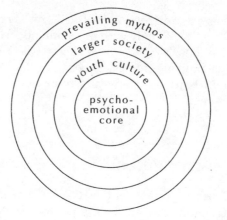

A powerful illustration of the complex interplay of myth, audience, psychology, and popular entertainment appears in the phenomenal success of Bruce Springsteen, a major rock figure of the mid-eighties. "I generally try to write songs that are about real life, not fantasy material," says the New Jersey rock artist: "I try to reflect people's lives back to them in some fashion. And if the show is really good, your life should flash before your eyes in some way . . . I think on a night when we're really good you can come and hopefully you can see your relationships with your parents, brothers, sisters, your town, your country, your friends, everything—sexual, political, the whole social thing. It should be a combination of a circus, a political thing and a spiritual event."[32]

Like Springsteen's live concert performances, his record-breaking album of 1984, *Born in the U.S.A.,* blends personal, societal, and spiritual dimensions in lyrics and music. Although Springsteen recorded much of the material for *Born in the U.S.A.* in 1982, the same year he recorded his *Nebraska* LP, which was notable for its dark emotional landscape, *Born* has a much different sound and mood. This album blends Springsteen's stories with the sounds of 1980s mainstream rock, including synthesizers and an aerobics beat. A more significant change lies in the optimism of the album, which one reviewer explains incisively: In *Nebraska* "the characters are dying of longing for some sort of payoff from the American Dream," but in *Born* "Springsteen's exuberant voice and the swell of the music clues you that they haven't given up."[33]

---

32. Springsteen, quoted by Kurt Loder in "Bruce!" *Rolling Stone,* 28 Feb. 1985, p. 23.

33. Debby Miller, "Bruce Springsteen Gives the Little Guy Something to Cheer About," *Rolling Stone,* 19 July/2 Aug. 1984, p. 102.

His lyrics and music—sober ballads and hard-driving rock—fuse together into a realistic but hopeful portrait of the frustrations and grand dreams of American life. Springsteen is a troubadour of American populism who has been described as "a Huck Finn whose raft is a 1969 Chevy or a Pink Cadillac."[34]

The gap between expectations and reality is an overriding theme in Springsteen's music, but it is frequently tempered by a defiant hope. In a faithless world filled with disappointments and fears where nothing seems to make sense, music can impart passion for living in the here and now. In fact, Springsteen's albums and especially his concerts have functioned like worship services for young people, enabling them to go back to their worlds with renewed strength. Springsteen himself has noted that his songs are imbued with religious searching, hopefulness, and faith in the human spirit. His songs dramatize fears, exploitation, the hunger for relationships, broken families, unemployment, deferred dreams, unanswered prayers, and so on. Numerous images of rivers, cars, streets, and highways suggest, says Springsteen, "people in transition. They've left and they haven't arrived anywhere."[35] The rock singer openly proclaims his affection for home, family, and those who struggle to endure. For him and apparently for his fans, a secret to survival lies in finding new dreams to replace those that have suffered damage or been lost; a recurrent theme in his music is the refusal to surrender to disillusionment. In his weaving of passion and hope into stories of ordinary people, Springsteen's work deftly ties together the personal, the social, and the mythic.

The incisiveness and poignancy of Springsteen's portraits go a long way toward explaining his popularity. In *Born in the U.S.A.*, a self-conscious teenager is "Dancing in the Dark" ("I check my look in the mirror / I wanna change my clothes, my hair, my face") to the aerobic beat of a rock song. "No Surrender" tells about growing up in the youth culture and the promise two friends made to each other to follow their dreams. To do that, the song suggests, they need to rebel: "We busted out of class had to get away from those fools / We learned more from a three-minute record than we ever learned in school." In another cut two wild boys drive from New York to "Darlington County" in search of work. Along the way they meet two pretty girls and feed them lines: "Our pa's each own one of the World Trade Centers / For a kiss and a smile I'll give mine all to you." Old friends gather at a bar to talk about nostalgic yearnings for those "Glory Days" back in high school.

34. Brian D. Johnson, "The Boss," *Maclean's*, 2 Sept. 1985, p. 26.
35. Springsteen, quoted by Johnson, "The Boss," p. 26.

The Young and the Restless

Message keeps getting clearer
Radio's on and I'm moving 'round the place
I check my look in the mirror
I wanna change my clothes, my hair, my face
Man, I ain't getting nowhere
Just living in a dump like this
There's something happening somewhere
Baby I just know that there is

You can't start a fire
You can't start a fire without a spark
This gun's for hire
Even if we're just dancing in the dark

—Bruce Springsteen, "Dancing in the Dark"

"Downbound Train" exposes the personal despair of losing a job. A pounding rock sound fuses with the hurt of betrayed patriotism in the lyrics of the title song, "Born in the U.S.A." "My Hometown" deals sensitively with the effects of racial conflict.

Although Springsteen had been an important figure in rock music since the mid-seventies, with *Born in the U.S.A.* he achieved superstar status. The 1984 release sold more than 10 million copies in the United States alone and over 18 million worldwide, thereby becoming Columbia Records' all-time best-selling album. An international tour in support of the album reportedly grossed between $80 and $90 million in ticket sales (the sale of T-shirts and other paraphernalia upped the earnings). Such success can be explained in part by his broad appeal: both adults who grew up on his music and today's teenagers from across the social and economic spectrum have felt a strong bond to his music, his persona, and the ideals he sings about.

In this regard Springsteen is no doubt something of an exception. Few rock artists enjoy the kind of broad success and devotion that he has elicited. In the last few years his popularity has faded. For awhile, however, "the Boss," rock music's loving folk hero from New Jersey's blue-collar ethnic neighborhood, seemed to epitomize in a larger-than-life way everything that a rock-and-roll star could mean to vast numbers of people: he was minstrel, troubadour, son or older brother, priest, prophet, friend, and the guy down the block. He got his audience where they lived, even if they didn't know it until he sang it. What Springsteen saw, felt, and displayed in his songs—which he performed with a paradoxical mix of abandon and precision—resonated with deep feelings in his audiences: hurt, joy, fear, hope, despair, claustrophobia, lust, nostalgia, and so on. When Springsteen sang it and showed it, it became true, or at least understandable; he made the world and its experiences clear and, on occasion, showed the way amid life's confusion. As a cultural icon, Springsteen performed numerous cultural functions of mapping and mentoring that usually fall to a wide assortment of media figures—this rock band or that movie star—who cumulatively construct teendom's portrait of life and how to get along in it. And he was "the Boss" in more ways than one: he made a lot of money for Columbia Records, and he made himself a rich man.

The Symbiosis at Work

The constant and decisive factor in the world of entertainment is the ongoing interplay between audience desire and industry concern for profit. It is this dynamic exchange, what we have labeled symbiosis, that continues to shape the content of contemporary entertainment for better or for worse. Executives, producers, agents, business imperatives, aesthetic considerations (style and content), audience, cultural context— these factors work insistently and incessantly in symbiotic relation. How central and crucial this interaction has been is illustrated by the following sketches of pivotal developments in entertainment that have both embodied their time and promoted accepted (or changing) ideas, mores, and art forms. These developments, which seem to have set trends of understanding or interpretation and style both in particular media and in American culture, would spawn hosts of imitators. We look first at two instances of the financially profitable ability of art to fathom the public mood.

From *Sgt. Pepper* to *Saturday Night Fever*

The Beatles were the most innovative and most popular rock group of the 1960s. By some uncanny intuition or foresight, their themes and styles led their audience and anticipated what it wanted to hear. In the beginning the Beatles wrote simple love songs ("I Want to Hold Your Hand"), but over the course of a decade their lyrics became more poetic and covered an increasingly broad range of topics. Their 1967 album,

Sgt. Pepper's Lonely Hearts Club Band, proved a watershed in rock history because of the way it integrated a wide variety of musical styles and sounds—Indian raga to European classical—into a single organic concept that treated the major issues of the time. A sitar wailed on a track about Eastern mysticism. Psychedelic imagery alluded to drug experiences. Lyrics exposed the absurdity of everyday life, poked fun at growing old, and left the listener weeping for a runaway girl whose parents thought love was giving her everything money could buy. In short, *Sgt. Pepper* expressed the social and emotional turmoil of life in the late 1960s. One Beatles' fan explained that "their songs are about the things I think about—the world, love, drugs, the way things are." A hippie runaway loved the songs because the Beatles were "saying all the things I always wanted to say to my parents and their freaky friends."[36]

At least part of their enormous success in the United States grew out of the emerging international counterculture. What was true of the Beatles' experience in London had ready parallels in America. Just after the Beatles finished *Sgt. Pepper,* Paul McCartney visited the Haight-Ashbury district in San Francisco, legendary home of the West Coast hippies. Biographers have noted his comparison of American hippies and the Swinging London set: "It was curious that they both blended under the same, global, peace-flowers-LSD umbrella. It was even more curious how well the Beatles' already-finished album [*Sgt. Pepper*] . . . complemented all of this."[37] In the United States the album topped the *Billboard* charts for 15 weeks and sold a whopping 2.5 million copies; global sales eventually reached 30 million copies.

A similar success, another rage, occurred a decade later. The movie *Saturday Night Fever* (1977) turned the dying disco culture into an overnight sensation. Suddenly John Travolta's polyester shirts and three-piece white suit became the rage at the 20,000 discos that sprang up across the country. Some two hundred radio stations switched to all-disco formats. In 1978, 20 percent of *Billboard's* Top 100 were disco songs. The two-disc soundtrack of the movie sold an astounding 25 million copies and became the largest-selling album in history. The film earned Paramount $74 million in domestic rentals.

Travolta and screenwriter Norman Wexler did on-site research, and much of the script and Travolta's role were drawn from what they learned about Brooklyn discos, their regular customers, and their fami-

---

36. Quoted in "The Beatles: Their New Incarnation," *Time,* 22 Sept. 1967, pp. 61-62.

37. Peter Brown and Steven Gaines, *The Love You Make: An Insider's Story of the Beatles* (New York: McGraw-Hill, 1983), p. 241.

lies. "A lot of what I put on the screen came from guys I met," Travolta explained. "They were extreme in their personalities. I'd see where their values were—where women and dancing stood in their lives. They all had one thing in common—they wanted to get out of Brooklyn."[38]

In a particularly arresting way, *Saturday Night Fever* captured the spirit of the "culture of narcissism," the label that sociologist Christopher Lasch gave American culture in the late 1970s. The film's characters knew little of the angry social upheaval of the previous decade. Representing a clear retreat from politics and an assimilation of American middle-class values, the movie celebrated an ethic of self-preservation and the passion of the moment, making a hero out of an everyday man. The movie and the Bee Gees' music struck a chord in disco patrons across the country. "*Saturday Night Fever* is my life," explained a student who had just graduated from a Washington, D.C., high school in 1978. "It says that if you dance well and look great, you're on top, even if you work pumping gas." A regular at a southern California disco admitted, "That movie really talked to me. It told the truth about boring jobs and what the club means to us."[39] The movie and music combined to picture young adults in post-counterculture, post-Vietnam, post-Watergate America. Amid feelings of despair and uncertainty, disco life offered a thrilling escape from the darkness of everyday living in an age of diminishing expectations.

From *Gunsmoke* to *M*A*S*H*

When Robert D. Wood became president of the CBS network in 1969, he was aware that although CBS was number one in the overall ratings, in the large metropolitan markets the network's share ranked second or even third. The unchallenged success of the network rested on variety shows and staid programs about rural life—almost all comedies— whose audience was mostly over fifty. The 1969-70 season featured *Gunsmoke* (ranked #2), *Mayberry R.F.D.* (ranked #4), *The Red Skelton Hour* (ranked #7), *The Beverly Hillbillies* (ranked #18), *The Glen Campbell Goodtime Hour* (ranked #20), and *Hee Haw* (ranked #21). Also on the schedule were standbys *Green Acres* and *Petticoat Junction*. Wood also realized that advertisers directed only one-third of every advertising dollar to the

---

38. Travolta, quoted by Maureen Orth in "From Sweathog to Disco King," *Newsweek,* 19 Dec. 1977, p. 63.

39. See Frank Rich, "The Year of John Travolta," *Seventeen,* Nov. 1978, p. 113; and Susan Cheever Cowley, "The Travolta Hustle," *Newsweek,* 29 May 1978, p. 97.

over-fifty age group. When the Nielsen ratings began, advertisers had wanted to know only the number of households viewing a particular program. CBS's competitors soon argued that the precise demographic composition of households mattered more than the total number of households. Advertisers had long been aware of this but had not done much about it. When trailing NBC offered advertisers more potential buyers for the dollar, CBS rethought its position.

Wood decided to change the clientele of the network by cultivating a young urban market with "realistic" and "relevant" programming. At the risk of losing the network's top rating, he undertook a complete revamping of the program schedule. By the fall of 1971, Wood had cancelled all the old hits except *The Glen Campbell Goodtime Hour*, which was given one more season but made to undergo substantial changes. Clearly, Wood's gamble rested on economic necessity. Perhaps Wood saw more clearly than his counterparts the vast cultural shifts taking place in North America. "Remember . . . that in '69, '70, '71, this country was undergoing considerable sociological changes and points of view," he later said, referring to the student revolution, the antiwar movement, and the counterculture.[40] Wood kept his eye on other media, polls, and network research, which indicated that most young people, though not out protesting, supported the goals of the student movement. Todd Gitlin, from whom much of this illustration is drawn, has argued that Wood's achievement lay in distilling "a marketing strategy from a cultural shift" and finding "the right programs to make it stick."[41]

After two failures, Wood launched three new programs that captured the young professional baby boomers' anxieties and idealism: *All in the Family*, *The Mary Tyler Moore Show*, and *M*A*S*H*. All three shows were extremely well-written, cast with talented actors, and run during prime time. *The Mary Tyler Moore Show* benefited particularly from the following Moore had developed while starring in *The Dick Van Dyke Show*; *M*A*S*H* traded on the success of the Twentieth Century-Fox film of the same title. With unusual timeliness these series both stretched and adapted the dramatic mainstay of the traditional sitcom, the family. In *The Mary Tyler Moore Show* the newsroom staff became a quasi-family, and in *M*A*S*H* an army surgical unit served as the family far from home. Both series redefined the notion of a family when "shifting middle-class mores were making it harder for Hollywood writers to imagine—and probably harder for mass audiences to accept—the nu-

40. Wood, quoted by Todd Gitlin in *Inside Prime Time* (New York: Pantheon Books, 1983), p. 210.
41. Ibid.

clear family as an arena for weekly excitement."[42] *All in the Family* blatantly capitalized on these shifting mores in its ongoing feud between gung-ho patriot and chauvinist Archie Bunker and his liberal-minded son-in-law Mike Stivic. Both liberals and conservatives among the viewing audience felt that their own convictions were confirmed.

Equally pertinent but more subtle was the portrayal of women on *The Mary Tyler Moore Show*. In a major shift in focus for television, a female figure, Mary Richards (Moore), primarily pursued her career, not a man; her emotional and social conflicts occurred chiefly on the job and not at home. In a stroke of marketing genius, CBS had picked up on the emerging struggle over changing sex roles and the feminization of work in America. In a similar fashion, *M*A*S*H* rode the wave of anti-Vietnam war sentiment. Todd Gitlin explains what made these new shows work:

> Far from depicting active, concerted rebellion, *All in the Family, The Mary Tyler Moore Show,* and *M*A*S*H* depicted younger people bearing "sixties values"—anti-authoritarianism and the desire for the authentic—while trying to get on with their lives under rules imposed by arbitrary authority. This had long been a theme in American culture, but television had usually said that when push came to shove Father rather than Mother, Son, or Daughter knew best. Now less soluble generational conflicts moved to the center of the show and comedy made them bearable. But what really made these comedies work was their gift for making light of the quandaries of young humanists and elder authorities alike.[43]

These three series were all commercially successful, and the network maintained its dominance until 1975. The CBS programming coup proved a forerunner to narrowcasting, the targeting of a specific demographic segment, as opposed to broadcasting, the reaching of the widest possible audience. These three shows exerted a profound impact on television and American culture. *All in the Family* ranked first for five of its twelve years. It spawned two spin-offs, *Maude* and *The Jeffersons,* which became the longest-running TV series about a black family. *The Mary Tyler Moore Show* ran for seven years, begetting *Rhoda, Phyllis,* and the topically controversial *Lou Grant*. It also initiated the trend toward productions charged with realism—*Hill Street Blues, St. Elsewhere* (both from Moore's MTM Enterprises), and *L.A. Law* (from the producer of *Hill Street*). *M*A*S*H* remained near the top of the ratings for eleven seasons and continues to thrive in reruns as one of the most widely syndicated series in television history.

42. Ibid., p. 215.
43. Gitlin, *Inside Prime Time*, p. 211.

Robert Wood's genius was to recognize that "television success often comes from finding the main fault lines of value conflict in the society, and bridging them. The successful shows found ways to enshrine, confirm, finally to soothe even acute psychological conflicts: the ones that inhabit the same breast."[44] In short, Wood read the tea leaves of cultural flux and, businessman that he was, made himself a cultural guru—and a very rich man.

"In a galaxy far, far away"

In Hollywood, George Lucas and Steven Spielberg share the title "Mr. Blockbuster," and well they should, for their impact on the film industry has been enormous, both artistically and commercially. To develop plots and themes for the 1980s, the two moviemakers mined comic books and Saturday-matinee westerns and adventure movies from their own childhood. They updated the old genres with the latest technology, special effects, and modern and/or futuristic settings. Like the Beatles, Robert Wood, and the other media notables who successfully read the times, Lucas and Spielberg showed unusual sensitivity to national moods and longings, especially among kids.

For that, Lucas's early academic training suited him well. Having studied anthropology and the social sciences, Lucas began "looking at a culture as a living organism, why it does what it does." In the mid-1970s, Lucas described the sober mood that gave rise to the *Star Wars* saga: "I thought: we all know what a terrible mess we have made of the world, we all know how wrong we were in Vietnam. We also know, as every movie made in the last ten years points out, how terrible we are, how we have ruined the world and what schmucks we are and how rotten everything is. And I said, what we need is something more positive."[45] In addition, fan mail that Lucas received following *American Graffiti*, the 1973 film Lucas had made about young love and hot cars and big dreams, convinced him that kids in the mid-1970s missed having a fantasy life inspired by the cinema. Gone were the John Wayne westerns and Errol Flynn pirate films of Lucas's own generation. So he developed *Star Wars* as a classic western adventure fable set in the new frontier of space. The major film studios were not interested. Finally, Twentieth Century-Fox agreed to finance the project based on the success of *Amer-*

---

44. Ibid., p. 218.
45. Lucas, quoted in "The Force behind George Lucas," *Rolling Stone*, 25 Aug. 1977, p. 43.

ican Graffiti. The relatively small production budget of $7 million showed the studio's lack of confidence in Lucas's project.

Lucas's imaginative film vision included metaphysical-moral conflict, unforgettable characters, and a dazzling array of special effects. The movie capitalized on the advent of personal computers and video games with the "droids" R2D2 and C3PO, who were truly user-friendly (they were also modeled after Dorothy's friends in *The Wizard of Oz*). Amid the pessimism and confusion of the time, the film fashioned a future of hope where humans and technological wonders lived in harmony and good triumphed over evil. In its overwhelming success—the film almost achieved cult status—*Star Wars* set a pattern for future blockbusters that sought to draw in young audiences for repeated viewings. The film soon ranked second on *Variety*'s list of All-Time Film Rental Champions, followed by the two sequels in the series, *Return of the Jedi* and *The Empire Strikes Back*. The *Star Wars* series eventually grossed a staggering $524 million. "Besides making money," one critic pointed out, "the *Star Wars* pictures changed the way moviemakers look at film and created a new vision of ancient mythological themes that has deeply affected a whole generation of children."[46]

Entertainment and Witch Doctors: Whither Goes the Industry?

The symbiosis between the youth culture and the entertainment industry has had a profound impact on American culture—one which we can hardly gauge as youth identify with this pop lyric or that movie theme and model themselves after this rock star or that film idol. So much entertainment geared directly and persuasively toward youth has effectively redefined the roles of traditional institutions in the nurture of youth. Amid the powerful presence of popular entertainment, the influence of family, school, and church in the instruction of successive generations has declined dramatically. In fact, at a ground-breaking ceremony for a $14 million cinema-television school at the University of Southern California, George Lucas exhorted others in the business to treat their trade with high seriousness because of entertainment's power as a cultural force:

> Film and visual entertainment are a pervasively important part of our culture, an extremely significant influence on the way our society

46. Gerald Clarke, " 'I've Got to Get My Life Back Again,' " *Time*, 23 May 1983, p. 66.

operates. People in the film industry don't want to accept the responsibility that they had a hand in the way the world is loused up. But, for better or worse, the influence of the church, which used to be all-powerful, has been usurped by film. Films and television tell us the way we conduct our lives, what is right and wrong. It's important that the people who make films have ethics classes, philosophy classes, history classes. Otherwise, we're witch doctors.[47]

Entertainment impresarios have indeed become in some ways the popular revivalists of the late twentieth century. Worse still, despite Lucas's strict demands for responsible story-telling, most of those on the stage and behind the cameras are just what he doesn't want them to be—witch doctors. The Springsteens and Lucases are few and far between. While they are seen as gurus, gods, and prophets by the young, most artists are in the profit-minded bottom-line business of entertainment—the show must go on, and make money in the process. As Lucas argues, providers of entertainment too often perform like high-priest hucksters manipulating the assorted challenges of adolescence. Most executives and artists, themselves products of the entertainment-youth symbiosis, show little sense of responsibility for the cultural impact of their work on the well-being of American youth.

---

47. Lucas, quoted by Aljean Harmetz in "U.S.C. Breaks Ground For a Film-TV School," *New York Times*, 25 Nov. 1981, p. C-16.

5. Consuming Visions: Popular Art in Consumer Capitalism

Beauty has always paid better than any other commodity, and always will.

> Daniel H. Burnham (1907)
> Architect and chief designer of the Columbian Exposition,
> speaking to the Chicago Commercial Club

Movies and radio need no longer pretend to be art. The truth that they are just business is made into an ideology in order to justify the rubbish they deliberately produce.

> Max Horkheimer and Theodor W. Adorno (1947)
> Philosophers and social critics

Today the future occupation of all moppets is to be skilled consumers.

> David Riesman (1950)
> Sociologist and social historian

Imagine a crowded subway train on a snowy night in Toronto. It carries high-brow folks who have just attended a symphony concert at Roy Thompson Hall. Their dress is elegant, their conversation subdued. At the Maple Leaf Gardens stop, the train is invaded by a noisy wave of teenage rock fans who have just come from a heavy-metal concert. Their dress is wild, their banter loud. As the train leaves the station, the two groups eye each other with suspicion and disdain.

The train passengers symbolize a tension played out daily in the families, schools, and religious and ethnic communities of North America. Although the sites of conflict shift—concerts, movie theaters, and record stores—the war between teenagers and adults over popular art continues with no sign of a truce. Between young heavy-metal fans and middle-aged classical-music devotees there is little love lost.

Nor is the battle a new one. Youth and their elders—parents, ministers, and teachers—have fought on this ground for generations, and the conflict between popular art and high art is at least as old as the mid-nineteenth century.[1] But a new and powerful element has entered the struggle: the symbiosis between the popular entertainment industry and the distinctive youth culture described in Chapter Four. To put the matter plainly, new electronic media have dramatically altered the role that traditional social institutions play in the nurture of North American adolescents. Increasingly, the products of the entertainment industry guide young people through the turbulent teenage years, portraying the industry's version of life and society and suggesting responses. Unsure of their changed role, most parents, educators, and civic leaders typically ignore or lament the predicament. Stymied and frustrated, few offer fresh or informed approaches for understanding—much less resolving—the conflict.

A basic condition of contemporary life in North America is that teenagers and adults live within one culture, just as the two subway groups ride one train. For all its seeming divergence, the world of youth is largely shaped, sustained, and strained by the broad and aggressive consumer culture that envelops North America. In spite of youth's posture of autonomy and defiance, young people in fact rely upon the adults who create and distribute the very products and ethos by which youth define their distance from the adult world. However astute in reading the "teen mind" and in targeting the youth market, the entertainment industry remains an adult enterprise. Regardless of how different from the adult culture the youth culture may be in form and texture, the dreams and values of youth-oriented popular art reflect the dominant consumerism of North American society. Despite the supposed differences between the two realms of youth and adults, they are in fact in their inmost character co-extensive. The world of teenagers is but a different version of the adult world's consumerist quest; the "wisdom" that the entertainment industry gives youth is consumerism.

This chapter suggests that disputes about the style or content of popular art amount to mere skirmishes in a larger battle between con-

---

1. Lawrence W. Levine, *Highbrow/Lowbrow: The Emergence of Cultural Hierarchy in America* (Cambridge, Mass.: Harvard University Press, 1988).

sumerist values and other values in North American life. Usually the supposed disputes occur between different versions of the same consumerism. After proposing a perspective for understanding the place of popular art in contemporary society, this chapter explores the central and indispensable role of consumerism in the North American economy. An examination of its effect in the entertainment industry illustrates the means by which the industry's popular art strives to induct North American adolescents into the ethos and practices of consumerism. Despite the pervasive power of the consumer ethos, many—both adults and adolescents—recognize its limitations and its dangers. The conflicts surrounding popular art should encourage adults and youth to band together to find creative ways to share and enjoy the same subway car.

Popular Art and Symbiosis

It is certainly easier to enjoy art than to understand its nature and effects. Indeed, a certain degree of "fuzz" has always characterized definitions of art. This historical imprecision or elusiveness is only compounded by the effort to draw clear distinctions between high and low art, elite and popular art, an effort that is of fairly recent vintage. As a result, both scholars and consumers spend much time and energy trying to figure out what art is and setting forth criteria with which to distinguish its varieties and its limits. Equally difficult is the vital task of tracing the influence of popular art in North American society and culture. The aesthetic dimensions and moral consequences of art, especially of popular art, pose a host of hard questions.

A set of equally difficult questions surrounds the relationship of popular art to specific socio-economic structures and systems. Two questions in particular undergo constant analysis by journalists and scholars.[2] One question asks if an economic system determines the kind of popular art we will make and enjoy, or if a given culture, including its popular art, determines its economic system. With symbiosis as an explanatory model, Chapter Four suggested that neither culture nor economics wholly determines the other. Instead, the two sides interact and push each other along. A second major question, similar to the first, examines the relationship between the production and the consumption

2. For an interesting attempt to distinguish and relate these two questions in a single sociological model, see Paul DiMaggio, "Classification in Art," *American Sociological Review* 52 (Aug. 1987): 440-55.

of popular art. Do companies headquartered in Hollywood and New York dictate consumers' taste, or does the "market" force companies to make saleable art? Again, the model of symbiosis suggests that neither producer nor consumer wholly sets the agenda for the other. Instead, the production and consumption of popular art involve a complex process of exchange and negotiation in which each side contributes its share of influence and demand. Consumers buy what companies make, while companies try to make what consumers will buy.

The assertion that symbiotic relationships exist between art and economic systems and popular-art producers and audiences takes issue with much prevailing wisdom on media and entertainment. The notion of symbiosis allows for a fuller portrait of the complexity of influence in the cultural transactions of modern media-driven societies. Its pertinence readily appears in its response to Western Marxist philosopher Theodor W. Adorno, whose critique of "the culture industry" has won a large following among scholars and media analysts.[3] Democratic in intention but elitist in tone, Adorno argues that the pop-art products of the American entertainment industry are neither popular nor artistic. The industry's movies and music are not authentically popular, Adorno contends, because they do not arise directly from the lives of their consumers. Instead, "popular art" is created and dispensed by huge profit-minded businesses that try to calculate what will bring in the most money. Nor are the products of the entertainment industry artistic, because they are mass-produced and distributed, just like cars, radios, and blue jeans. Amid intense economic competition, mass production and mass marketing diminish aesthetic quality and preclude personal expression.

According to Adorno, good or real art meets deep psychological, social, and intellectual needs. Popular art, Adorno argues, may not

---

3. Adorno's most important general statement of this critique is "The Culture Industry: Enlightenment as Mass Deception," in Max Horkheimer and Theodor Adorno, *Dialectic of Enlightenment*, trans. John Cumming (New York: Seabury Press, 1972), pp. 120-67. Other statements, in chronological order, include the following: "On the Fetish-Character in Music and the Regression of Listening" (1938), in *The Essential Frankfurt School Reader*, ed. Andrew Arato and Eike Gebhardt (New York: Continuum, 1982), pp. 270-99; "On Popular Music," with the assistance of George Simpson, *Studies in Philosophy and Social Science* 9 (1941): 17-48; "Perennial Fashion—Jazz" (1953), in *Prisms*, trans. Samuel and Shierry Weber (Cambridge, Mass.: MIT Press, 1981), pp. 119-32; "How to Look at Television," *Quarterly of Film, Radio and Television* 8 (Spring 1954): 213-35, reprinted as "Television and the Patterns of Mass Culture" in the anthology *Mass Culture: The Popular Arts in America*, ed. Bernard Rosenberg and David Manning White (Glencoe, Ill.: Free Press, 1957), pp. 474-87; "Popular Music" (1962), in *Introduction to the Sociology of Music*, trans. E. B. Ashton (New York: Seabury Press, 1976), pp. 21-38; and "Culture Industry Reconsidered" (1963), *New German Critique* 6 (Fall 1975): 12-19.

provide anything more than momentary diversion from life's troubles, longings, and perplexities. Adorno does not dismiss the need for popular entertainment but claims that the entertainment industry fails to provide genuine entertainment. In short, as Adorno summarizes, "the culture industry perpetually cheats its consumers of what it perpetually promises."[4] Defenders of the industry reply that it simply delivers what audiences want. Adorno in turn rejects this line of argument, contending that audiences have lost the opportunity to make free choices because the media offer so few alternatives. A narrow range of available entertainment and clever marketing leave few real options or decisions for the consumer.

For anyone who enjoys a night out at the movies, Adorno's criticisms seem unduly harsh. For one, he overlooks the legitimate functions of popular art in everyday life. Instead, he fastens on the role of popular art in a highly unified social system where economic power prevails. Unfortunately, his portrait of cultural-economic hegemony precludes the possibility of social transformation. If the social system is as binding as Adorno argues, and if the products of the culture's industry support that system, then there seems to be little hope for fundamental change. Adorno's criticisms begin to lose their point—which, after all, is that both the entertainment industry and the social system must change. The idea of symbiosis avoids this apparent impasse. With this concept as guide, this chapter highlights the ties and conflicts between the economic system and popular art in the youth culture. Subsequent chapters will examine at length the numerous functions of popular art in young people's lives.

Popular Art and the Economic System

The current prominent role of popular art in North America is best understood as part of the modernization discussed in Chapter Two. That has resulted in a society divided into two competing but interdependent levels, systemic and cultural, that pressure every person and institution.[5]

On the one hand, the politico-economic system consists of a centralized network of economic and political institutions, including

4. Adorno, "The Culture Industry," p. 139.
5. See Jürgen Habermas, *The Theory of Communicative Action*, 2 vols., trans. Thomas McCarthy (Boston: Beacon Press, 1984, 1987).

everything from the courts to the Securities and Exchange Commission. Over the years, this gargantuan creature has received different labels, such as "the new industrial state" (Galbraith) and "the military-industrial complex" (Eisenhower). By whatever name we call it, we might usefully compare this politico-economic system in its collective workings and power to the cyclops of Homer's *Odyssey*—a huge, single-eyed, narrow-visioned creature of extra-human power that devours people to feed its insatiable appetite. Whether the creature intends to be cruel or is just hungry, the effect is the same. The creature subtly forces all people and organizations to adapt to its pursuit of power and money, regardless of what they might wish to be or do. For instance, schools presently feel enormous pressure from business and government to prepare students for careers in a highly competitive global marketplace. This is only one example among many of the ways in which politico-economic institutions play a leading role in shaping North American society.

On the other hand, there is the competitor of this politico-economic system, the world of culture. In this context, culture refers not simply to fine art but to a pluralistic array of worldviews, tastes, and lifestyles, including a plethora of ethnic, racial, religious, and age-segmented subcultures. This "life world" encourages every facet of society to serve fundamental human needs and desires for identity, intimacy, and delight. Because these needs and wants often defy the demands of money and power, the politico-economic system faces repeated challenges to its authority, despite its vaunted resilience, power, and prominence. The clearest recent challenges of the life world to the politico-economic behemoth came from the civil rights and countercultural movements of the 1960s and 1970s. And this is as it should be, for politico-economic structures should serve human beings rather than their own impersonal appetites, whether those be for social order, corporate profit, or market share. In short, challenges from the life world often arise because prevailing politico-economic structures fail to meet genuine human longings for physical welfare, communal purpose, individual meaning and identity, and so on.

According to our model, then, North American society operates on two interdependent levels that continually chafe against if not collide with one another. Clearly, the politico-economic system inordinately influences the cultural life world, smothering and distorting its best impulses. However, the life world also at times resists domination by the politico-economic cyclops. Indeed, the politico-economic system cannot sustain itself without the interest and support of the cultural life world, and the life world cannot thrive in isolation from the politico-economic system. Writers and artists need money to buy paper and paint.

Society according to *Batman*

Culture: A society's fabric of meaning which helps human beings interpret their experience and which guides their actions. Example: The movie *Batman* is a part of recent North American culture that helps people interpret the conflict between good and evil in their lives.

Social Structure: A society's network of social relations arising from human actions and interactions. Example: The people who watch *Batman* are members of certain families, citizens of certain countries, and adherents of various religions. They are not simply consumers; they participate in a complex social structure.

Politico-Economic System: A centralized network of political and economic institutions in North American society. Example: *Batman* portrays the corruption of a society where manipulative governments and greedy businesses call the shots, but this film is produced and distributed in a society with just such a politico-economic system.

Cultural Life World: A pluralistic array of worldviews, tastes, and lifestyles in North America. This array includes various ethnic, racial, religious, and age-segmented subcultures. Example: Whereas *Batman* lumps all of Gotham's citizens together as mindless, greedy consumers, Spike Lee's *Do the Right Thing* highlights tensions among ethnic and racial groups in New York City. Through their differing perspectives, both films comment on the North American life world.

Consumer Capitalism: The current stage of the North American economy, in which the necessity of maintaining high levels of consumption strongly colors competition for private profit in the production, distribution, and consumption of goods and services. Example: *Batman* criticizes the consumerist way of life, but it fails to indicate that consumerism is essential for maintaining economic growth in North America.

In its own mysterious way, art occupies a middle ground, serving as a conduit between the worlds of politico-economic power and of ordinary life and culture. As such, art partakes of both worlds—at once a product of a politico-economic system and an expression of the needs and wants of a pluralistic society. Adorno's criticism of popular art emphasizes its politico-economic character by exaggerating its ill effects on the cultural life world. In his lopsided critique, Adorno ignores the fact that high art also operates and thrives in the same system, and he overlooks the legitimate functions of popular art in cultural life, functions discussed in Chapter Ten. In contemporary North American society, little if any difference in economic or cultural function appears between "high art" and "popular art." The most esoteric work of high art and the most familiar piece of popular art are both bought and sold as economic commodities and legal possessions. Both the symphony concert at Roy Thompson Hall and the rock concert at Maple Leaf Gardens provide enjoyment and social interaction. How much either art form questions or ennobles rather than simply endorses the values of the world of which it is a part is difficult to determine.

However, Adorno is right in his observation that popular art now occupies a vastly different role than it once did. Traditionally, popular art was made and consumed by the same relatively few people; today most popular art is mass entertainment, the product of a large, complex, and highly technical industry. For both economic and technological reasons, commercial radio, network television, movies, and musical recordings are all twentieth-century creations. Economically and structurally, the entertainment industry requires a politico-economic system of large corporations and government agencies that control entire sectors of the economy. If these vehicles were not in place, the industry could not mass-produce and mass-market its products. Technologically, the popular entertainment industry requires sophisticated electronic media for dissemination and consumption of entertainment. Because of the favorable economic and technological conditions in the United States, the popular entertainment industry has come to thrive there more than anywhere else.

The remarkable success and prosperity of mass-market radio, television, movies, and recordings has come in part from a profound structural shift in the North American economy. The driving force of the economy is no longer simple competition for private profit or for market share. Although these objectives have not disappeared, the economy's chief economic goal—and necessity—has been to keep levels of consumption high enough to sustain steady economic growth —in short, to keep people buying. In the attempt to attain this goal, the popular art of the mass entertainment industry has assumed a role that it did not occupy prior to the twentieth century. It now fosters wants and needs and lifestyles, the stuff of ordinary cultural life, that keep levels of consumption high enough to sustain the politico-economic system. The label given to this new economic system is "consumer capitalism," and many of the problems afflicting contemporary youth culture proceed directly from the central goal of the system—perpetual consumption. The full extent of the changes wrought by consumer capitalism, especially in relation to the entertainment industry, becomes clear only when placed within the history of capitalism as an evolving economic system.

Capitalism and Cultural Crisis

A standard definition of capitalism casts it as a complex economic system in which competition for private profit governs the production, distribution, and consumption of goods and services. While this definition aptly characterizes the essence of capitalism, the system has undergone different stages of development and emphasis, as economic historian Ernest Mandel has suggested.[6] Mandel asserts that three different stages have occurred in the period since the Industrial Revolution of the late eighteenth and early nineteenth century. These stages correlate nicely with the changing patterns of adolescent nurture and the revolutions in technology, which were discussed in Chapter Two.

The first stage—freely competitive capitalism—began in the 1840s and lasted until the 1890s. The survey in Chapter Two of the history of youth in the United States described these years as the era of Victorian nurture. During this stage, the first technological revolution turned machine-made steam engines into the predominant sources of energy, and railways and the print media transformed the patterns of distribution and consumption. The second stage—monopoly capitalism—began in the 1890s and lasted for about fifty years. It corresponded to the emergence of the notion of adolescence during a thirty-year period from the 1890s to the 1920s. During this stage, a second technological revolution made electric and combustion engines common in all branches of industry and confirmed the average consumer's confidence in material progress by putting a car in every garage and a radio in every living room. The third and current stage—late capitalism—began in the 1940s, and it corresponds to the flourishing of an entertainment-youth symbiosis. In this third stage, electronics and automation become common in industry, air travel dominates in transportation, and television broadcasting flourishes in communications. What Mandel labels late capitalism we call consumer capitalism.

An outburst of productivity in all branches of industry occurred during World War II. Soon after the war the average rate of profit dramatically increased, and the market for consumer goods exploded. The extent and character of this remarkable expansion did much to prepare the way for the commercial-cultural nexus that has shaped

6. Mandel, *Late Capitalism*, trans. Joris De Bres (Atlantic Highlands, N.J.: Humanities Press, 1975). For a path-breaking attempt to uncover correlations between Mandel's stages of industrial capitalism and various periods of cultural history, see Fredric Jameson, "Postmodernism, or the Cultural Logic of Late Capitalism," *New Left Review* 146 (July-Aug. 1984): 53-92. Jameson's approach is debated in *Postmodernism/Jameson/Critique*, ed. Douglas Kellner (Washington: Maisonneuve Press, 1989).

contemporary entertainment. The most conspicuous cause of this preparatory growth lay in the simple fact that huge numbers of young people, married women, and ethnic minority workers entered the urban labor force and the consuming public. Equally important was the fact that industry became far more technologically dependent. To compete and earn profits, companies were forced to increase the pace of technological innovation. This pressure to improvise technologically first appeared in the rapid turn to automation following World War II. This process accelerated after 1954, when electronic data-processing entered the private sector. Non-automated companies quickly lost out. A correlary movement appeared in the pressure from consumers for new and innovative consumer goods. Nowhere is this clearer than in the rapid innovation in recording and playback formats in audio equipment—from simple monaural phonographs (1950) to elaborate stereo systems (1960) to cassette players (1970) to portable personal stereos and CD players (1980) to, most recently, digital audio tape recorders (1990).

With increased rates of change the organization of business became ever more centralized, resulting from efforts at systematic planning and global control. Because rapid innovation carried high levels of risk and uncertainty, companies introduced systematic long-range planning in an attempt to offset the perils of rushing headlong into an unpredictable future. To reduce risks and increase profit, companies tightened control over all elements of production, distribution, and marketing. Although their size slowed their response to unforeseen market changes, larger companies enjoyed an edge. They possessed the economic resources to make full use of product research and development, market research and analysis, advertising, customer services, and the concept of planned obsolescence. The shift toward innovation and centralization tended to favor larger corporations that could afford and efficiently use highly organized product research and thorough market analysis.

It is not surprising, then, that multinational corporations now dominate production and distribution. It is commonplace to find U.S. clothing products "made in Taiwan," Japanese cars sold in Canada, and European investment in North American multinational corporations. Mergers and acquisitions steadily reduce the number of major corporations but increase their size. As we shall see later, the entertainment industry has followed suit, forming international conglomerates designed to control the production and distribution of popular art worldwide. Every major Hollywood studio emphasizes systematic planning at all levels, and now, in the 1990s, the entire industry is scrambling to form global entertainment conglomerates.

It is useful to think of the rise of the entertainment industry as the result of a complex chain of events in economic development. At the same time, it is clear that the electronic entertainment industry has been a prime promoter of technological change, prosperity, and consumerism. Each has helped the other along. Both the rate of change and the effort to plan and control have appeared as strategies to enhance consumption, and in this the entertainment industry has become a major player. In the freely competitive stage of capitalism, large investors concentrated on production, and in capitalism's monopolistic phase, the major emphasis fell upon finance. In consumer capitalism, economic activity concentrates on determining the location and means of sales and consumption. Because of this focus, the entertainment industry, with its close links to advertising and sales, now attracts major international investors such as Rupert Murdoch, who has purchased Twentieth Century-Fox and is investing heavily in Sky Television, a four-channel satellite service for Britain and Western Europe.[7] In 1989 the American consulting firm of McKinsey and Co. ranked entertainment and media as "second only to the super-safe aircraft manufacturing on the best-investment table."[8] As the service sector of the economy has expanded dramatically, large companies have sought new ways to make money from new service-sector wage earners who seek new ways to save time and effort. The increasing importance of the entertainment industry for the service sector is indicated by the discussion it receives in *The Wall Street Journal* and the business pages of *The New York Times*.

In summary, then, over the past forty years of consumer capitalism, the pace, organization, and focus of economic activity have greatly aided the current prominence of the entertainment industry in North America.[9] Accelerated innovation, centralized organization, and high consumption have made the North American economy highly productive. However, this economic growth has come at a significant cultural cost. With expanding consumption has come ever-increasing pressure to purchase additional goods and services. The economic system exerts pressure on wage earners in numerous ways. For example, there is the practical economic necessity to own a car in order to drive to work. But

---

7. Steve Lohr, "Murdoch's Big Bet on Sky Television," *New York Times*, 11 Sept. 1989, pp. 23, 32.

8. Don Groves, "There's No Business Like Show Business, More Banks Say; Investments Lucrative," *Variety*, 14-20 June 1989, p. 16.

9. Our discussion of consumer capitalism is highly selective and ignores several important features such as the formation of neo-colonial relations with foreign countries and the entrenchment of permanent inflation in the domestic economy. In addition, we are speaking simply of *tendencies*, to which one can find some obvious exceptions.

Stages of Capitalism

Dates	1840s-1890s	1890s-1940s	1940s-1990s
Stage	Freely competitive capitalism	Monopoly capitalism	Consumer capitalism
Dominant Sector	Production	Finance	Service
Technological Revolution	Machine-made steam engines	Electric and combustion engines	Electronics and automation

added to this is the social demand to drive a chic car equipped with the fanciest options, which indicate status. Indeed, the desire to indicate social status often takes precedence over considerations of inflated prices, environmental damage, faddishness, and poor workmanship. According to Mandel, this new cultural ethos exacerbates consumer capitalism's inherent contradiction between the economy's seemingly unlimited capacity to produce and its members' limited ability to consume. In this tension lie both the promise and the peril of consumer capitalism. On the one hand, expansion in production and consumption can meet countless human needs. On the other hand, a constant and risky pursuit of profit wastes natural resources, favors economic mobility and acquisition, and obscures demands for social justice. One dramatic example: the damage to the environment and local community wrought by the Exxon *Valdez* oil spill in 1989.

In light of its enormous potential for meeting human needs, consumer capitalism seems inherently wasteful, even more so than earlier stages of capitalism. In spite of, and perhaps because of, a fantastic gross national product, consumer capitalism continues to foster great environmental exploitation and pollution, urban war zones and "rust-bucket" economies, and Third World poverty. The wastefulness of consumer capitalism has led to demands that all levels of government impose more stringent regulations on many sectors of the economy. Unfortunately, the liberal economic democracies contribute to this very wastefulness not by accident but as a matter of policy. Consumer capitalism is a political as well as an economic system. It cannot operate without extensive government intervention, crisis management, and investment. The $500 billion bailout of the savings and loan industry in the late eighties and early nineties and the 1989 debate over funding the half-billion dollar cost of a Stealth bomber illustrate the federal government's prominent role in fostering economic growth in the United States.

This government-supported economy exacts a toll as well on other institutions and cultural traditions. In this connection, philosopher Jürgen Habermas speaks of an impending sociocultural crisis.[10] Such crises generally occur when a society's organization does not permit resolutions to problems that undermine social institutions or cultural authority and motivation. In the United States, such a crisis can grow out of the government's role as administrator of the economy, which may force it to intervene in new areas of life. This intrusion mandates increased mass loyalty and compliance at a time when these responses may have weakened, and it can create a backlash effect. Heavier government involvement in family planning, for example, might prompt resistance rather than cooperation. On countless other issues, from industrial pollution to the lyrics of rock songs, people might tire of merely tending to their careers and their leisure while leaving active politics to the experts. Consider, for example, the pro-choice and pro-life movements. At the same time, discontent over the government's hands-off approach toward highly profitable industries might lead to more frequent boycotts of companies like Proctor and Gamble, which in response to grassroots complaints pulled its advertising from the controversial television series *Married . . . with Children,* and to more intense lobbying for the protection of consumers and American corporations in the wake of foreign takeovers such as Sony's purchase of Columbia Pictures.

Sociocultural crisis, however, requires that something undermine North American cultural traditions—such quasi-sacred notions as the idea that social rewards match individual achievement or that economic competition benefits everyone. In the early 1970s Habermas thought that current structural changes in schooling and family life and a disenchantment among youth with "achievement ideology" and "possessive individualism" foreshadowed massive cultural shifts. Regardless of the accuracy of Habermas's prediction, his approach suggests a perspective for understanding the entertainment industry. Through its popular-art products, the entertainment industry may provide an arena

10. Jürgen Habermas, *Legitimation Crisis,* trans. Thomas McCarthy (Boston: Beacon Press, 1975). McCarthy gives a useful summary and evaluation of this book in *The Critical Theory of Jürgen Habermas* (Cambridge, Mass.: MIT Press, 1978), pp. 358-86. For discussions of this crisis that focus on the United States, see Daniel Bell, *The Cultural Contradictions of Capitalism* (New York: Basic Books, 1976); Michael Harrington, *Decade of Decision: The Crisis of the American System* (New York: Simon & Schuster, 1980); and Robert N. Bellah et al., *Habits of the Heart: Individualism and Commitment in American Life* (Berkeley: University of California Press, 1985).

for expressing and detecting conflicts about consumption between the economic system and the cultural life world. We will explore this possibility by viewing the entertainment industry as an economic and cultural hot spot—as a volatile laboratory for testing consumer capitalist strategies and as a well-lit stage that publicly dramatizes the cultural motivations and effects of these strategies. Although this is only one perspective on the entertainment industry, it is a crucial one for understanding how youth-oriented popular art promotes consumerism at the expense of other ways of life.

Style and Neomania

Within consumer capitalism, the electronic media have been the epoch-making innovation that has reshaped the entire pattern of the economy. Railroads accomplished this during the stage of freely competitive capitalism, cars during the stage of monopoly capitalism. Both of these earlier innovations transformed the location of economic activity, stimulated the production of new goods and services, and enlarged the market for industrial products.[11] These transportation technologies eventually gave way to the new electronic communications technologies, which became the most efficient means of linking buyers and sellers. The electronic media have been an epoch-making innovation because they relocated economic activity and dramatically expanded production and distribution of new goods and services.

In consumer capitalism, businesses compete not so much in prices or product quality as in the status, appeal, or faddishness of their products. Manufacturers unleash a steady torrent of "new" and "improved" products in the hope of increasing their share of the market. Usually the products have a new look and feel but continue to function much like the passé or obsolescent products they are designed to replace. This "production of veneers" is vividly illustrated by the automotive industry. In the 1920s General Motors introduced a strategy of constant stylistic novelty in a deliberate effort to increase sales. For decades, and to some extent still, American automakers annually produced noticeably restyled models, advertising major and sometimes minor surface changes. Usually new features went no farther than styling—design and appearance. Structure, function, and performance were rarely im-

---

11. Paul A. Baran and Paul M. Sweezy, *Monopoly Capital: An Essay on the American Economic and Social Order* (Harmondsworth, Middlesex: Penguin Books, 1966), p. 216.

proved; in engines, suspensions, overall safety, and interior comfort, cars changed little. Detroit's aversion to substantive technological progress led to the Big Three's collusion in the 1940s in undercutting the production of the radically advanced Tucker automobile (the subject of Francis Ford Coppola's 1988 film *Tucker*). Because this emphasis on style influenced the way cars were made and sold, revamping of production sheet-metal presses became essential and routine. For example, the introduction of a "sleek" look not only necessitated annual retooling of automotive plants but influenced machine design, labor relations, and the timing of workers' yearly vacations. Substantive technological change was prompted when the energy crisis and the invasion of efficient, high-quality Japanese and European cars reshaped American taste. Elsewhere in the economy, especially in home electronics, constant consumer pressure for new styles and features accelerated the rate of technological innovation, and this continual industrial and product innovation in turn increased the demand for marketable "new" products. The fast-revolving cycle of industrial innovation, marketing, and consumerist demand reveal a self-perpetuating mechanism at the heart of consumer capitalism.

In this "feedback loop" between technology and style, as we might call it, the electronic media in the hands of the entertainment industry have played a vital if not indispensable role. Specifically, the entertainment industry has exploited and encouraged this link between style and production. For many decades, the entertainment media have provided a means for producers to promote and assess the appeal of "style" changes. Indeed, the industry has fostered this feedback loop by itself experimenting with changes in style, often before they become common in other goods and services. This early test market, a unique mechanism in entertainment, has functioned since the earliest days of the Hollywood movie industry, especially in the glamour of stardom. In countless ways the fashions, lifestyles, homes, and habits of entertainment celebrities have served as trial balloons to gauge what consumers will desire and accept. The clearest examples in recent years include an entire network, MTV, and TV shows like *Miami Vice* and *Dynasty*. Recently, even the making of entertainment has become directly linked to massive marketing campaigns for new consumer goods. Much of the estimated $60 million that Jack Nicholson earned from the movie *Batman*, for example, came from licensing fees for products featuring the Joker, from lunchboxes to T-shirts. Fads and trendiness prevail, wrapped in chic and status, and the entertainment media offer means to foster the appetite for them.

Of course, not all of the taste for change and style can be assigned to consumer capitalism. The desire for novelty is probably as old as the human race. Some would call it a human need, nearly as basic to our well-being as food, shelter, and clothing. Nevertheless, while the entertainment industry does not create the desire for novelty, it clearly does channel it in the direction of perpetual stylistic changes. Stuart Ewen claims that the current American obsession with style dates from the 1920s, when "advertising, industrial design, and the fashion industry all began to draw upon the futuristic imagery of the modern art movement"—thus the lean geometry of women's fashions, the sharp clarity of shop windows, and the functional angularity of offices and factories. This resulted in a quiet but compelling "grammar of suggestion" that linked popular aspirations and consumer goods. This new "machine aesthetic" turned into the smooth and "lubricated" look of 1940s streamlining and the standardized eclecticism of 1950s populuxe, whose hybrid shapes, colors, and textures connoted modern luxuries for the middle class. By giving consumer goods a glossy modern surface with slick sex appeal, such styling directed the desire for novelty toward the appearance of innovation. "Appearance" must be emphasized, for the aerodynamic shape of a 1940s radio and the rocket fins and ballistic chrome "breasts" of a two-tone 1950s automobile had little connection with the products' function and primary use.[12] Such products created an ethos of style that transformed the ordinary human taste for novelty into an obsession with fancy surface innovation that often turned out to be gaudy, expensive, and ephemeral.

The entertainment industry encourages and plays upon a constant desire for new appearances through the images it projects and the means it uses to project them. Among these means, advertising is probably the most conspicuous but not always the most effective method. Indeed, the industry itself relies upon widespread consumer desire in order to survive, and it works hard to constantly whet consumers' appetites for what's new. Perhaps this becomes clearest in the record business. Simon Frith argues that much of the record business "involves persuading consumers to buy a record at the moment of its release, to get bored with it after a few weeks, and to discard it for a yet newer release, and so on."[13] With Top 40 countdowns, untold promotional hype, and "new" sounds, the popular music industry fuels consumers' quest for the newest and the slickest. Similarly, network television

---

12. Ewen, *All Consuming Images: The Politics of Style in Contemporary Culture* (New York: Basic Books, 1988), pp. 143-49, 230-32.
13. Frith, *Sound Effects: Youth, Leisure, and the Politics of Rock 'n' Roll* (New York: Pantheon Books, 1981), p. 8.

constantly primes viewers for the hottest program, the next episode, and the new season, and the movie industry entices audiences with perpetual promises of novelty—better special effects, new sounds, more graphic sex and violence. At the same time, none of the media can be too innovative or they risk losing their audience, who, despite their desire for novelty, like predictability and sameness. To a large extent, concern for "market share" restricts the depth and scope of innovation, particularly thematic or narrative innovation. This conservative tendency toward low-risk ventures helps explain the popularity of movie sequels, at least among film magnates if not among movie patrons. Nevertheless, the entertainment industry must—while maintaining a comfortable level of familiarity—encourage the desire for new appearances.

This ethos of style is precisely what other industries require, especially the producers of consumer goods and services. The feedback loop of stylistic change supports an economic strategy of planned obsolescence. Products do not so much wear out or break down as they become dated, distant from "what is happening now." The key to this is obsolescence of style, a strategy employed by many large corporations since the 1950s. Even when previously purchased consumer goods remain reliable and adequate, they must be made to *appear* worn-out and obsolete. When both producers and consumers commonly assume the desirability of ever-new appearances, culture becomes pervaded by what Roland Barthes calls "neomania," a madness for perpetual and purchasable novelty.[14] If cultures obsessed with consumer goods can be called materialist, then perhaps a neomanic culture should be called hyper-materialist, obsessed with transitory appearances, ever ready at the drop of an advertiser's hat to discard one consumer "good" for another.

The constant desire for new appearances can self-destruct. The pursuit of perpetual and purchasable novelty has its own jading effect, which sometimes leads to numbness or a sated appetite for newness. In fact, parts of North American culture resist neomania. Powerful and perplexing expressions of this resistance sometimes occur within entertainment considered highly innovative. There is, for example, the paradox of the *Star Wars* trilogy. Writer-producer George Lucas describes his space epic as a combination of "classic themes told in an innovative way": the struggle of good versus evil, "personal responsibility and friendship, the importance of a compassionate life as opposed to a passionate life." Lucas wraps these central age-old themes in a roaring futuristic tale replete with dazzling state-of-the-art high-tech special

14. Ewen, *All Consuming Images*, p. 51.

GM Trying to Bat 1.000

Promoting the planned obsolescence of product styling, Harle Earl of the General Motors Styling Department made this blunt statement in the mid-1950s: "Design these days *means taking a bigger step every year.* Our big job is to hasten obsolescence. In 1934 the average car ownership span was 5 years; now it is 2 years. When it is 1 year, we will have a perfect score."

—Quoted by Stuart Ewen, *All Consuming Images: The Politics of Style in Contemporary Culture* (New York: Basic Books, 1988), p. 245.

---

effects. But the core of the film, and very likely the major part of its appeal, lies in its dramatic content and the likeability and inventiveness of its characters.

What struck the film industry, however, were not only the classic themes but also Lucas's innovations in technique and marketing. In the decade following the release of the first film of the trilogy in 1977, the Hollywood hard-sell brought in more than $1.2 billion from tickets and $1.5 billion from *Star Wars* books, toys, posters, T-shirts, and lunchboxes. Lucas staged, in effect, an artistic and marketing revolution in Hollywood, as Aljean Harmetz explains: "The unprecedented success of a movie set in a galaxy long ago and far away turned Hollywood's attitudes toward science fiction upside down, changed the industry's definition of summer, re-established symphonic music in films, exploded the boundaries of special effects, helped unleash eight years of movies aimed at teen-agers, gave new importance to sound, created a pop mythology, and made merchandising the characters from a movie as important as the movie itself."[15] And all of that because of three films telling one long story. Since 1977 the Lucasfilm company has created and marketed advanced editing equipment, revolutionized special effects, and developed a new sound system for theaters. In the entertainment industry nothing succeeds like success, and success breeds many imitations, all trying to cash in on the rapidly disappearing novelty of the original economic success.

Despite his shrewd business acumen, Lucas differs from most of his film-industry cohorts in his insistence that new production technology serve a higher end than razzle-dazzle style and box-office glitz. Technology, says Lucas, "enhances the tools you have available and

---

15. Harmetz, " 'Star Wars' Is 10, and Lucas Reflects," *New York Times,* 21 May 1987, p. 22.

expands your vocabulary. But they don't make a picture successful. A film is not about technique. It's about ideas."[16] And the success of *Star Wars* argues that no matter how Hollywood pushes marketing flash and newness, audiences still warm to the oldest and deepest of themes. Glitz alone will not carry the day. In the *Star Wars* trilogy the much-ballyhooed innovations take their inspiration from an old-fashioned argument that ideas matter as much as technique, substance matters as much as style. Indeed, it is unlikely that *Star Wars* would have made such an impact at the box office if it had not resonated with a resistance to neomania, even among the young viewers who flocked to see it over and over again. It is equally unlikely, however, that these same viewers would have found the movie gripping if they had not been wowed by its sound and special effects. Thus Lucas's trilogy elicited both resistance and attraction to technical innovation and stylistic flashiness.

The trilogy's repackaging of old myths in new styles and its raising of doubts about innovation in cultural life are two tactics evident in the recent rush to market nostalgia, especially in political strategy. If subsequent trends offer any indication, audiences yearn for what they perceive to be the greater simplicity of the past and feel they have found at least a slice of it in commodities that carry its flavor. It is a real and legitimate longing, especially in times of rootlessness and rapid change. On the production side of popular art, slick marketing of old-fashioned values became a common business strategy during the Reagan era, when nostalgia and pride in traditional images of the United States became public policy. Presently a mélange of innovation and new styling compete with recycled nostalgia as economic strategies of planned obsolescence and perpetual novelty. From a marketing point of view, being old-fashioned might be just one more fad.[17] Movies like *Grease* (1978) and *Dirty Dancing* (1988), the ever-running reruns of TV's *Happy Days,* and "classic" rock music stations vividly demonstrate the marketability of the past.

However, certain facets of the life world of North American culture perhaps impose limits on the success of both nostalgia and new styling. Some ethnic and religious communities believe that values detached from cultural traditions are hardly worth the time and effort. In addition, many people on the margins of society—the homeless, the unemployed, and the working poor—doubt that mere styling will lead them to the promised land. And even those baby boomers who wanted

---

16. Lucas, quoted by Harmetz in " 'Star Wars' Is 10."

17. Randall Rothenberg, "The Past Is Now the Latest Craze," *New York Times,* 29 Nov. 1989, pp. 29, 45.

From Glitz to Glory

Advertisers make the self-fulfilling prophecies of a postmodern age. They foretell shifts in the cultural *Zeitgeist* and help make these happen. In January 1990 *Good Housekeeping* magazine proclaimed the nineties a new "decency decade," a good decade for the earth, the family, corporate ethics, and consumers. The magazine's old-fashioned all-text advertisement in the *New York Times* announced, "The 'health hype' and phony claims will soon be over, as skeptical, caring New Traditionalists ignore the sizzle and demand the steak. They will judge products not only for their quality, but also for the integrity and ethical behavior of their manufacturer. They will look for what is real, what is honest, what is quality, what is valued, and what is important." The magazine's confident prophecy relies on research conducted by Ms. Faith Popcorn, a pop sociologist and a familiar Madison Avenue figure. According to Popcorn, "The 80's was a glitz blitz. That will be an embarrassing place for companies to be in the 90's. We see companies making responsible decisions for society."

—Full-page advertisement, *New York Times*, 2 Jan. 1990, and Randall Rothenberg, "Proclaiming a Decade of Decency," *New York Times*, 2 Jan. 1990, p. 39.

to have it all and have it now find that chasing the grail of novelty provides little lasting satisfaction, even if the latest fad is nostalgia or a recycled value, things that give the feeling of tradition without its substance.[18]

For such groups, the concept of the ever-new seems obsolete. Innovations regularly fail to meet a variety of profound human needs and to show concern for society or nature. Innovative production technology that enhances corporate profit does not necessarily benefit workers or consumers. Nor does stylistic change, no matter how exciting, necessarily benefit anyone or anything but sales. Such considerations are particularly important for North American adolescents. Rapid and superficial changes in the youth culture do not necessarily aid its citizens. Although the youth culture supplies diverse options in adolescents' search for intimacy and identity, the rapidity and abundance of its changes frustrate their most crucial searches. Families and schools must encourage young people to dig beneath the glittering surface of their fast-changing culture to discover what is most important for their lives. However, traditional institutions of nurture cannot easily rival an in-

18. Katy Butler, "The Great Boomer Bust," *Mother Jones*, June 1989, pp. 32-37.

dustrial machine whose prime means of survival is stylistic neomania. The entertainment industry's central role as both a laboratory for testing stylistic change and a stage for dramatizing the effects of innovation places it at the forefront of meeting or avoiding the challenge of nurture.

Integration and Synergy

Attempts to evaluate innovations in production and style must consider the organizational structure of the entertainment industry. One important organizational factor appears in large entertainment companies' desire for systematic control over all elements of production, distribution, and consumption. This top-to-bottom control, called vertical integration, contrasts with horizontal integration, the attempt by each company to expand and coordinate its efforts in different forms of entertainment. Both kinds of integration tend to centralize international economic power within the entertainment industry.

Vertical integration seeks to fuse a given company's production and sales. Prior to the twentieth century, advertising did little more than help manufacturers sell their products at a profit. Indeed, until recently, advertising was but an incidental strategy in distributing goods and services. In consumer capitalism, however, the sales effort "increasingly invades factory and shop, dictating what is to be produced according to criteria laid down by the sales department and its consultants . . . in the advertising industry." Consequently, sales and production efforts have become virtually indistinguishable, and "the distinction between workmanship and salesmanship has been blurred."[19] In the entertainment industry, executives have determined that market should govern product.

In the forefront of this movement has been the rock music industry. The production of rock music usually involves four distinct activities: concert production, recording, radio play, and music publishing. The typical rock-music label sends potentially marketable singers and groups through a "filtering process" that eliminates all but a few would-be stars.[20] Many performers, records, and songs never reach the mass market, having encountered a series of "gatekeepers": agents,

---

19. Baran and Sweezy, *Monopoly Capital,* pp. 133-36.
20. For a relatively early description of the filtering process in rock music, see Paul Hirsch, *The Structure of the Popular Music Industry* (Ann Arbor: University of Michigan Press, 1970).

concert promoters, record producers, and A&R (artist and repertoire) developers at record companies; program directors and disc jockeys at radio stations; and record and music purchasers for store owners and chains. Although the public cannot choose to buy something that never reaches the mass market, the gatekeepers claim to be "giving the public what it wants," and they take this claim seriously. They decide which products to produce and distribute by reading the tea leaves of market research. Given the volatile character of mass taste, it is crucial to try to figure out what the public will want.

This complex process yields a remarkable fusion of "workmanship" and "salesmanship." Like any new entertainer, a garage band playing for high-school dances will try hard to please its local audience. When the band signs a recording contract, however, it must also satisfy the gatekeepers' ideas of what the general buying public wants. Those ideas will thereafter shape everything about the band, from its costumes and interviews to its sound and musical style. That selection process can quickly exclude a band from the rock-music industry, which relies heavily on finding "big hits." Each year American record companies issue thousands of singles and albums, most of them new releases. But less than 10 percent of these releases make it to the radio and the charts, and few of those that do not make it sell at all. In this way the recording industry is like most other industries, for which more than 90 percent of "new products" are "failures." Given such massive overproduction, record companies must "maximize the profits on the records that do sell, minimize the losses on those that don't."[21] The gatekeepers serve to focus time and energy on the potential hit. They preside over the perpetual wedding of production and sales.

Yet gatekeeping alone does not insure increase in profits, which remains the corporate bottom line. The size and complexity of large corporations impede quick and effective responses to unfavorable economic trends. Consequently, they strive to expand marketing reach to a global scale in order to offset with substantial economic power any inflexibility or regional downturns. As a major force in bringing products to consumers and consumers to products, the entertainment industry has helped American corporations expand their global reach. American movies, TV shows, and popular music, like the advertising that accompanies them, dominate entertainment markets around the world. In the last few years, the international concentration of economic power in the entertainment industry has grown rapidly. So great are the stakes and so technologized is the entertainment that the catalyst for global corporate

21. Frith, *Sound Effects*, p. 101.

success, the entertainment industry, has itself become a major player in the world markets for control of economic power.

A prime example of this trend was the 1989 merger of Time Inc. and Warner Communications Inc. One industry analyst suggested that the merger "could prefigure a 21st century in which all of show business is controlled by two or three conglomerates."[22] The stakes are overwhelming. With a $14 billion price tag, the formation of Time Warner Inc. merged two companies whose estimated combined operating profits for 1989 were $1.9 billion. More important than the amount, however, was the source of those profits. Warner brought to the deal a long list of musical talent (including Madonna with Warner Records, U2 with Atlantic Records, and Tracy Chapman and Anita Baker with Elektra Entertainment); the nation's largest record and home-video distributor (WEA Corporation); the world's largest music-publishing company (Warner/Chappell Music); a major Hollywood movie studio (Warner Brothers, which produced the smash hit *Batman*); a television production company (Warner Brothers Television) that had 17 prime-time shows in 1989 including *Dallas, Knot's Landing,* and *Falcon Crest;* the largest producer of home-video cassettes (Warner Home Video); the nation's fifth-largest cable operator (Warner Cable Communications); two-fifths ownership of the operator of seven television stations in major markets (BHC Inc.); and the Licensing Company of America, which leases the right to use names, logos, and the like of clients such as the National Hockey League. Time contributed two cable channels sold to 12,000 cable systems (Home Box Office and Cinemax); a video-cassette distributor (HBO Video); and a four-fifths share of the nation's second-largest owner of cable outlets (American Television and Communications).[23]

As the world's largest media and entertainment conglomerate, Time Warner Inc. now carries formidable clout in nearly every segment of the entertainment industry—the production and distribution of recorded and printed music; movie, television, and video production; cable programming, distribution, and broadcasting; and the production and distribution of books and magazines. The union of Warner and Time

22. Richard Gold, "No Bigness Like Show Bigness," *Variety,* 14-20 June 1989, p. 1.

23. "An Entertainment Engine Takes Shape," *New York Times,* 6 Mar. 1989, p. 37. In addition, the two companies owned publishing enterprises including the many magazines owned wholly or in part by Time (among them *Time, Life, Sports Illustrated, People, Student Life, Fortune, Working Woman,* and *McCall's*), four book companies (Time-Life Books; Little, Brown; Scott, Foresman; and Warner Books), a leading direct-mail seller of books (Book-of-the-Month Club), and a leading distributor of magazines, paperback books, and comics (Warner Publisher Services). Warner also contributed *Mad Magazine* and DC Comics, the nation's oldest publisher of comic books boasting a stable of superheroes that includes Superman, Batman, and Wonder Woman.

Earth Day 1990

Since its formation in 1989, Time Warner has developed many new forms of synergy. For example, it disseminates news, entertainment, and marketing ideas through the whole range of its properties—magazines, movies, cable-TV channels, and home videos. According to Reginald K. Brack, Jr., president of the Time Inc. Magazine Company, Time Warner has been "involved in six or seven sets of negotiations, about putting pieces of this company together for marketers, that are big and multifaceted." A recent example of successful synergy: Time Warner sponsored a network television special on Earth Day 1990 and hyped this event in its magazines. Even news has become advertising—or is it the other way around?

—Randall Rothenberg, "Time Warner Is Marketing Its Synergy," *New York Times,* 15 Feb. 1990, p. C-21.

---

greatly increased the possibilities for synergy—combined operations. According to *New York Times* media analyst Geraldine Fabrikant, "the potential for synergies" was vast. *Variety* commentator Richard Gold agreed, pointing to "new opportunities in global entertainment and communications synergy."[24] For example, the sophisticated marketing at Warner Cable and American Television and Communications, combined with Time's expertise at selling media to people in their own homes, made the merged companies more efficient and persuasive marketers of cable programming to their 5.5 million subscribers. Warner Brothers could easily increase its production of original programming for Home Box Office and also distribute it overseas. In addition, both companies could readily create new cable channels aimed at reaching a world market, while Warner could distribute more records and home videos through Time's mail-order business for books.

Although industry analysts disagreed about the likelihood and profitability of such synergies of diverse corporate expertise, most believed that "the wave of mergers sweeping through the entertainment industry reflects a growing belief among media executives that production and distribution must be under one roof."[25] Entertainment companies wish to exert "maximum domination over their end markets," said

---

24. Fabrikant, "Time-Warner Merger Raises Concerns on Power of a Giant," *New York Times,* 6 Mar. 1989, pp. 1, 37; and Gold, "No Bigness Like Show Bigness," pp. 6-7.
25. Geraldine Fabrikant, "Let's Make a Deal: Entertainment Mergers Show Desire to Run Production and Distribution," *New York Times,* 5 Apr. 1989, p. 29.

David Londoner, an investment advisor at Wertheim, Schroder & Company.[26] This means that film-producing companies like Warner want to own the theaters, TV stations, and pay-TV services that show their movies, and companies like Time that program and distribute televisual entertainment want to own the production studios. Similar business imperatives lay behind other large mergers and acquisitions in 1989, such as the $3.4 billion purchase of Columbia Pictures Entertainment by Sony Corporation of Japan and the $1.45 billion bid for MCA/UA Communications Company by the Qintex Group, an Australian media conglomerate. After acquiring CBS Records for $2 billion in 1987, Sony deliberately set out to acquire Columbia Pictures in order to gain its enormous library of films and TV shows, which provides "software" to serve Sony's hardware, including video-cassette recorders and players, high-definition television, and an 8-millimeter video camera and player.[27] In the words of Richard Gold, "All of show business is now in play."[28]

Producing has become so costly and distribution so competitive that vertical integration has become necessary in order to target markets and maximize profits. Except for the expense of making copies, the cost of producing a film does not go down if fewer people pay to see it. By merging with a distribution company, a production company can insure broad distribution and reduce financial risks. The distributor's interest in a merger differs only slightly. The cost of buying films for distribution varies according to the competition among distributors for the same film. By merging with a production company, a distribution company insures itself a steady supply of films, controls its acquisition costs, and gains better access to the hottest products.[29]

Currently, television does not have the freedom the film industry has to develop vertical control. The U.S. government limits the amount of programming that the broadcast networks may produce. In addition, the networks are not permitted to own cable systems or syn-

---

26. Londoner, quoted by Fabrikant in "Let's Make a Deal," p. 29.

27. Geraldine Fabrikant, "Deal Is Expected for Sony to Buy Columbia Pictures," *New York Times*, 26 Sept. 1989, pp. 1, 40.

28. Gold, "No Bigness Like Show Bigness," p. 6.

29. In "Let's Make a Deal," p. 46, Fabrikant suggests that this is why a company like Viacom, Inc. might wish to merge with a movie studio. Viacom owns TV stations, a television production company, cable systems, and the nation's second-largest pay-TV service (Showtime), but it does not make movies. Until it merges with a movie studio, "Viacom is forced to buy films for Showtime from outsiders, who are well aware that it needs programming. Viacom therefore loses some negotiating leverage." The merging of production and distribution also gives a company additional leverage with entertainers and their agents, who prefer to work for companies "that can promise a certain amount of income from various outlets."

dicate other companies' productions like *The Cosby Show*. Many industry executives expect this to change, however. If that happens, the networks might merge with movie studios, an ideal combination for many entertainment companies. The resulting concentration of economic power would be enormous, involving the broadcasting giants CBS Inc., Capital Cities/ABC, and General Electric, the parent of NBC.

To be sure, merger mania has its detractors in the entertainment industry. Sometimes their comments are no more than smokescreens for backroom maneuvers. Yet there does seem to be genuine concern in the industry that international centralization of economic power could drive out smaller companies and inhibit the "creative freedom" of moviemakers and television producers. This same trend of takeovers and buyouts could create enormous debts that would require an even heavier emphasis on blockbuster products in order to pay off the debts. Nevertheless, the creation of Time Warner Inc. clearly accelerates the drive for other entertainment companies to expand and combine. Mergers and co-ventures will be a matter of survival for independent producers and distributors and for smaller cable operators.

Beyond the immediate fate of the entertainment industry, hard questions arise about the social impact of profit-driven media megalomania. This has become a hot political issue in Western Europe due to an explosion in its number of television stations, a growing demand for American programs, and the need to set uniform broadcasting rules for the European community by 1992.[30] In the United States, more political energy seems to be spent in controversies over the moral content of program offerings than in debates about the structure of the industries that make those products. Few North Americans seem to realize that every concentration of economic power has its winners and losers, and that economic gain for a few often comes at a cultural cost for many.

Although we cannot address all these matters in detail, we want to suggest that the entertainment industry's pursuit of "global cross-marketing synergies," to use Richard Gold's phrase, poses a triple threat to young people. First, huge conglomerates, because they control and shape markets, have sufficient autonomy to ignore the genuine pyschological and social needs and concerns of adolescent consumers. At the same time, such mega-companies have more ways to reach more customers. If such conglomerates do not reach consumers in the movie theater,

30. See Richard W. Stevenson, "TV Boom in Europe Aids U.S. Producers," *New York Times,* 28 Dec. 1987, pp. 21, 23; Steve Lohr, "European TV's Vast Growth: Cultural Effect Stirs Concern," *New York Times,* 16 Mar. 1989, pp. 1, 39; and Steven Greenhouse, "For Europe, U.S. May Spell TV," *New York Times,* 31 July 1989, pp. 19, 26.

It's a Film, It's an Ad, It's Super-Flimflam

Film critic Mark Crispin Miller argues that the goals and methods of advertising have corrupted American cinema. Contemporary Hollywood films are rife with product displays, exaggerated fantasy, and happy endings of the sort promoted by the disposable culture of contemporary advertising. The main purpose of such films, he argues, is to market products whose manufacturers pay to feature them in films. Even worse than this blatant hyper-commercialization, however, is the way many movies, such as Academy Award nominees *Glory, Born on the Fourth of July,* and *Field of Dreams,* strain for empty endings on happy half-notes. In Miller's words, "I worry about a country whose citizens can't tolerate the slightest bit of darkness."

—Randall Rothenberg, "Is It a Film? Is It an Ad? Harder to Tell," *New York Times,* 13 Mar. 1990, p. C-20.

they can always do so through the video store, cable television, or a morning program on network TV. MTV is perhaps an example of things to come: it makes its pitch in cable programming but also promotes itself through numerous spinoffs like MTV-run record clubs and travel tours.

Second, economic centralization impedes or eliminates the cultural diversity that could empower young people and give them a voice in their local communities. If American-based entertainment was eventually controlled by three huge conglomerates, the commercial world would have less space for products that capture and promote racial, ethnic, religious, and underclass concerns and traditions. Although this has been a problem for many years, the high stakes of mass entertainment would demand that companies reach the widest possible audience, thereby reducing the possibility of programming reflective of national cultural pluralism. A variation on this strategy is already in evidence: marketers have targeted narrow slices of the populace with networks or programming, whether it be through MTV or *L.A. Law* or *thirtysomething.* The strategy here is to tailor programming to an economically powerful age group in order to insure the biggest return on production investment. The idea remains the same: less programming and more profit.

Third, increased economic centralization would effectively drive the youth culture even further into the commercial hothouse. Cross-marketing synergy leads to fewer original productions because fewer products are needed to generate sales spinoffs. Furthermore, products are specifically designed—"calculated" might be a better word —to generate as many sales spinoffs as possible. These strategies gather

strength from the commercial nature of radio and television broadcasting, the use of celebrity endorsements and product placement to "pitch"
non-entertainment products, and the recent trend toward promotional
partnerships between media companies and retail companies, such as
that between CBS and K Mart.[31] As we show in a later chapter, MTV has
already taken the youth culture several steps down this road to total
commercialization. It is not hard to imagine a youth culture in which a
few movies and their soundtracks would spawn an entire year of clothing, accessories, slang, parties, and what have you (1989 was already the
year of *Batman*'s Joker)—generating not merely total sound and visual
images but total culture, with hundreds of price tags attached.

This gloomy scenario is not inevitable. Young people are impres-
sionable, but they are not easily duped. If the entertainment industry
treats them as economic pawns, ignoring their needs for identity and
meaning, running roughshod over their passions, and demeaning their
lives, they might simply look elsewhere for fulfillment—chase a different grail than consumerism. All the synergy in the world will not
convince teenagers that they enjoy something that is betraying them. The
building of conglomerates like Time Warner raises the stakes on both
sides of the entertainment industry–youth culture symbiosis. From
either side, we are talking about a risky business.

Consumerism

Indeed, the struggle over the fate of the entertainment-youth symbiosis
may well decide the future of consumerism and traditional institutions
of nurture. The conflict, after all, is over the hearts and minds of each
new generation. We have suggested that the entertainment-youth symbiosis has redefined the role of traditional institutions of nurture. This
symbiosis inducts young people into a life of consumerism that under-
mines attempts by parents, teachers, and community leaders to provide
adolescents with alternative visions of life. Needless to say, the entertainment industry is not unalloyed "evil" pitted against "good" institutions
of nurture. The industry is frequently pilloried for promoting consumerism, yet many popular-art products mount effective challenges to consumerism. And often the industry's consumption-oriented pop-art

---

31. Bill Carter, "K Mart and CBS to Join in Promotion," *New York Times*, 10 May
1989, p. 49; "Fall Promotion Plans Are Outlined by CBS," *New York Times*, 25 July 1989, p. 39;
"K Mart Tie-In Helps CBS in Ratings," *New York Times*, 21 Sept. 1989, p. 39; and Richard W.
Stevenson, "NBC-Sears Promotional Link Is Set," *New York Times*, 24 May 1989, p. 45.

Selling Hollywood via Catalog

In the late 1980s Paramount Pictures launched its own "Special Effects Catalog" of Paramount-related products for image-conscious consumers. Among other things, young people could purchase the following products with the Paramount logo: a water bottle and towel set, backpacks and fannypacks, socks, watches, a director's chair, shorts, shirts, and caps. The company also asked readers to "send us your zaniest snapshots of you or your loved ones wearing or using the products from our catalog."

products merely repeat consumerist patterns that young people have already learned from adults, including parents, teachers, and clergy. Indeed, if the entertainment industry has successfully "pumped" consumerism, it has been able to do so partly because of the failure of traditional institutions to provide compelling visions of life. The struggle lacks clear sides, let alone obvious heroes or villains. Nevertheless, the struggle goes to the very heart of what ordinary people desire for their lives and society.

Consumerism thrives in societies that expect goods and services to fulfill significant drives for meaning, intimacy, and identity. This expectation colors how people pursue their desires, set priorities, view obligations, and make sense of their lives. It is indeed possible for a society to so exalt consumption into a cultural force that it fosters personal obsessions. "Shop till you drop" becomes a credo, and shopaholics a social problem. Scholars suggest that to find the cultural pulse of a society, one need only examine the public spaces around which life is organized. In medieval Europe, the local cathedral provided such a space. In much of late twentieth-century North America, the only community center is the shopping mall. So too, to learn what people find important, one need only look at how they spend their time. For many North Americans, monied consumption has become a preoccupation. According to Laurence Shames, "One of the 1980s characteristic emotional maladies was 'compulsive shopping'—a phrase that moved into widespread clinical use in 1984. . . . There are people out there who literally shopped till they dropped, who spoiled their marriages, wrecked their finances, and occasionally committed felonies because they simply could not stop buying."[32] But compulsive shopping represents only the tip of the consumer-

32. Shames, *The Hunger for More: Searching for Values in an Age of Greed* (New York: Time Books, 1989), p. 148.

ist iceberg. Below the surface lie the realities of deficit spending by governments, the maneuvers and acquisitions of corporate raiders and investment bankers, and health-and-wealth TV preachers. The proverb of the 1980s, the era of the yuppie following upon the "me decade," contended that "It is better to get than to receive."

Social critics of various persuasions agree that consumerism afflicts and even imperils contemporary culture, although they have different reasons for finding this problematic. Judith Williamson argues that consumerism channels our energy toward chasing after superficial objects rather than pursuing what we truly desire. She claims that consumerism allows consumer goods to define rather than to serve our desires: "The need for change, the sense that there must be something else, something different from the way things are, becomes the need for a new purchase, a new hairstyle, a new coat of paint. Consuming products does give a thrill, a sense of both belonging and being different, charging normality with the excitement of the unusual. . . . The power of purchase . . . seems to drink up the desire for something new, the restlessness and unease that must be engendered in a society where so many have so little active power, other than to withdraw the labour which produces its prizes."[33]

Laurence Shames finds consumerism problematic because it encourages consumers to look to products to give meaning and purpose to their lives. Consumerism encourages esteem for "goods not just for pleasure but for meaning. They want their stuff to tell them who they are. They ask that inanimate objects serve as stand-ins for momentous notions."[34] Another critic, Bob Goudzwaard, claims that consumerism leads to the distortion of basic human norms, such as the desire for justice and love. For example, consumerists reduce questions of social justice to questions of financial compensation, as if a society can fulfill its obligations toward the disadvantaged simply by giving them a small slice of the economic pie. Similarly, in a consumerist society, the obligation to love and care for one's neighbor shifts from the individual and the community to professionals and government bureaucracies.[35]

Each of these critics expresses a valid insight. When consumer goods define desire, establish purpose, and distort obligation, consumers

33. Williamson, *Consuming Passions: The Dynamics of Popular Culture* (New York: Marion Boyars, 1986), pp. 12-13.

34. Shames, *The Hunger for More*, p. 146.

35. Goudzwaard, *Idols of Our Time*, trans. Mark Vander Vennen (Downers Grove, Ill.: InterVarsity Press, 1984), pp. 49-59. See also Douglas Frank, "Babes in Babylon: Growing Up Christian in a Society That Consumes Its Young," Calvin College *Dialogue* 20 (March 1988): 10-23.

become slaves of a social system that has failed to deliver what it promises or satisfy the deeper longings of the human heart. But this enslavement does not result from individual weakness or moral turpitude. Rather, it is the consequence of a rampant consumerism which constitutes the dominant ideology of consumer capitalism and a powerful, all-enveloping force in contemporary culture. It sustains economic growth while distracting attention from the inherent problems of a flawed politico-economic system. More serious still, it distorts individual passions and purposes and diverts and subtly reshapes traditional social institutions. More than a set of ideas and attitudes, consumerism offers a dynamic and comprehensive way of life, one that finds confirmation in every act of acquisition. The very power of consumerism, the new consumer capitalist mythos, makes the struggle between economy and culture in the entertainment-youth symbiosis a conflict of potentially dire consequences.

In the 1970s a fashion advertiser invented the slogan "Thou shalt have no other jeans before me." In response, German theologian Dorothee Sölle lamented, "What is blasphemous is not the use of the first commandment for an advertising slogan, but advertisement as such." Every attempt to direct attention to hair spray, cat food, and exotic vacations, she claimed, attacks "the one in whose image I was created."[36] The blasphemy lies in both an irreverence toward what is sacred and an undue reverence toward that which is not. What Sölle says about advertising applies as well to much of the youth-oriented pop art produced by the entertainment industry. Steeped in the charged atmosphere of sales and advertising, popular art inducts adolescents into a way of life where nothing is sacred because everything has its price, including the admonitions of traditional religions.

Appropriately enough, the induction of youth into consumerism has all the marks of an initiation ritual, a rite of passage. Indeed, there is something ceremonial about the way in which American adolescents participate in popular art: carefully prescribed codes govern their conduct; a style of participation counts for more than the substance of any particular product; and the desired outcome can be achieved in no other way. Teenagers do not exaggerate when they say they "just *have* to go" to a video party. Nor do they act out of character when they join the screaming throngs at a Poison concert. In all of this, they simply observe meaningful participatory rituals of American youth culture. They do not

---

36. Sölle, " 'Thou Shalt Have No Other Jeans Before Me,' " in *Observations on "The Spiritual Situation of the Age": Contemporary German Perspectives*, ed. Jürgen Habermas, trans. Andrew Buchwalter (Cambridge, Mass.: MIT Press, 1984), pp. 157-68; the quote is from p. 165.

always realize, however, the means by which participation also inducts them into consumerism.

Ritual Induction

The process of ritual initiation or induction occurs in three ways: through the purchase of popular art, through the consumption of popular art, and through the dominant images in popular art.

The first step toward induction occurs in the purchase of popular art. Even minimal participation in popular art requires countless acts of acquisition. The teenager who goes to a rock concert also has to buy a ticket. But that is far from all. Few self-respecting fans rest content with buying an occasional ticket to an occasional concert. One must buy the group's albums, and one must get the clothes and cosmetics to play one's part as an identifiable fan. Ideally, one would also acquire other complements, including the best sound equipment, the hottest car, and friends to match—everything that money and status can buy. Although many adolescents cannot afford all these things—and, happily, some do not want them—all teenagers in North America live under constant pressure to buy and consume. This pressure comes with the popular-art products themselves. To participate in popular art is to learn the ways of monied consumption and to learn the consequences of not acquiring enough of "the right stuff."

But there are limits to the effectiveness of this induction into consumerism. With each act of acquisition comes the growing awareness that previous acquisitions were not enough or did not satisfy, at least not for very long. Soon many young people become disenchanted with their fervent participation in popular art. Repetitive and compulsive purchases in shopping-mall youth culture never seem to deliver what the products promise. Furthermore, as marketers have lowered the age at which young people are targeted, adolescents have become increasingly sophisticated purchasers: "Studies indicate that most children gain consumer experience at a very early age and have a healthy skepticism about advertising. Today's child watches 30,000 to 40,000 television commercials a year and does a fair amount of shopping alone and with parents. Complaints from children themselves about misleading advertising prompt sponsors to drop four or five commercials every year."[37] The

37. Michael deCourcy Hinds, "Young Consumers: Perils and Power," *New York Times,* 11 Feb. 1989, p. 16.

A Decade of Skepticism

The advertising agency Ammirati & Puris has replaced its glamorous ads for BMW's "Ultimate Driving Machine" with sober ads that explain BMW's technical and design strengths. According to agency executives, a new approach is needed to reach consumers, who are dramatically changing what they expect from products and advertising, producing a "Decade of Skepticism." The agency explains the shift in its strategy by saying that middle-aged baby boomers have become sophisticated consumers, and they are now more interested in the quality of life than the quantity of possessions. Says Martin Puris, the agency's president, "This new adult group of consumers is highly educated. More than 40 percent have attended college. They know hype when they see it."

—Kim Foltz, "As Baby Boomers Turn 40, Ammirati and BMW Adjust," *New York Times*, 26 July 1990, pp. C-1, C-15.

---

same studies show that by the time they are in high school, young people have become deeply skeptical of advertising. Predictably, this skepticism transfers to the hype surrounding popular art. We find, in fact, a variation on the "cry wolf" syndrome. The more often highly touted popular art fails to satisfy, the less likely adolescents are to pin their hopes on it. Although this tendency might not fully deter youth from buying popular art, it does lessen the binding power of popular art.

A second means of induction lies in the actual consumption of popular art. The use of the art piece initiates youth into a consumptive lifestyle. Popular art comes across to teenagers as a rapid-fire array of products designed for easy consumption and quick disposal. Although some teenagers form deep attachments to entertainers, even these attachments are consumptive in style. The teenager who calls a performer "cool," "neat," "awesome," or "rad" ("in" terms change rapidly) thereby announces that popular stars are just as disposable as the latest designer jeans. Breathless Top 40 radio, fast-forward teen films, and high-energy music videos set the accelerated rhythms of a throwaway culture. Popular art products proclaim that they are not here to stay—the consumer must get them while he or she can.

Again, however, there are limits to the effectiveness of this means of induction. By proclaiming their transience, popular-art products explode the hype that exalts their status. Few adolescents rest content with simply consuming the latest fads, although they do offer important vehicles for establishing friendships and personal identity. And rarely do teenagers treat their friends with the same fickleness that the consumptive lifestyle seems to encourage. These facts indicate that youth resort to values from beyond the realm of popular art to determine what meets their needs.

The last path into consumerism lies in the images that dominate youth-oriented popular art. To the extent that the images themselves provide guidance and meaning, much of popular art exposes adolescents to a continual equation: happiness = consumption for the sake of consumption. This equation takes many forms. Negative images of work, school, and family obligations abound; all are pains to be avoided or endured for the sake of unrestricted pleasure. Constant associations of the joy of love with the thrill of sexual possession suggest that what counts in life is personal gratification. In whatever form, the loud and clear message is that in consumption we live and move and have our being. Obviously, this proclamation does not appear only in the youth culture: it pervades the entire cultural fabric of consumer capitalism. The message can be particularly effective in the youth culture, however, because it reaches young, inexperienced people at a time when they are trying to decide what life is all about.

Nevertheless, the relentless equation of happiness with consumption soon runs into the painful realities of adolescent life. Consumption for its own sake leaves an aftertaste of emptiness and lingering desire that few adolescents would equate with happiness. And when friends fight, parents misunderstand, and teachers disappoint, consumption seems like a poor substitute for genuine reconciliation. Indeed, even when popular art promises happiness through consumption, it also sends the message that contentment lies beyond consumerism—in true love, personal integrity, or commitment to social change. Although popular art serves consumerism, it regularly suggests to disillusioned youth that life holds greater rewards than consumerism, thereby undermining the intended induction of adolescents into consumerism.

In the end, none of these ways of induction into consumerism by itself permanently binds. Although their influence can indeed be powerful, neither popular art nor the entertainment industry can dictate how young people conduct themselves. As much as advertisers might like them to be, young people are not passive consumers. They make choices according to values learned from adults and peers, even though they often seem to defy or test those values. Very often, youth turn popular art to non-consumerist ends, and they also see the dark side of a consumptive lifestyle. In this movement toward discernment, they need encouragement and support, not only from the adults in their lives but also from the entertainment industry.

Unbinding the Future

The preceding discussion suggests that popular art within consumer capitalism does not inexorably colonize North American youth culture. The symbiotic interchange between the youth culture and the popular entertainment industry argues that youth exert reciprocal influence on the industry. In the end, colonizers seldom have their way—freedom and independence remain a constant possibility. Moreover, colonizers often undermine their own power through the means they employ. Certainly this is the case with popular art in North American youth culture. On the one hand, popular art effectively inducts adolescents into the economically indispensable ritual of consumption for consumption's sake. On the other hand, young people do with popular art what they want, and they are supported in this behavior by tendencies within popular art itself. Thus there is a fundamental ambiguity in the role popular art plays in the ritual of inducting adolescents into consumerism. The induction seldom occurs without resistance, a significant part of which results from the very means of induction. In this sense, the ritual is no more than a ritual. It is not a divine being with unlimited power. And yet it is a ritual which all of us must understand and evaluate, for it holds secrets to the future of our society. With such awareness, we might learn to share with ease and respect the same subway car.

6. The Heart of Rock and Roll:
The Landscape of a Musical Style

New York, New York is everything they say
And no place that I'd rather be
Where else can you do a half a million things
And all at a quarter to three
When they play their music, ooh that modern music
They like it with a lot of style
But it's still that same old backbeat rhythm
That really, really drives 'em wild . . .

Chorus:
They say the heart of rock & roll is still beating
And from what I've seen I believe 'em
Now the old boy may be barely breathing
But the heart of rock & roll,
The heart of rock & roll is still beating

From "The Heart of Rock & Roll"
by Huey Lewis and the News

No matter what adults say or how they worry, teenagers love their music. They crave it, and they certainly seem to need it. The fifteen-year-old listens to his tape machine after school to find solace from the hurt inflicted by unreasonable teachers, the guys and girls who ignore him, or the parents who pay him too much, or too little, attention. At night, instead of a sitcom, he watches MTV, absorbing the sounds and the images that match the voice and vision of his unspoken dreams, desires, and fears. In the morning, he listens to the radio as he gets up and dresses. At school there is music on portable stereo headsets and in cars on stereos bigger than the engines. Always rock and roll is there, a steady, lively, and varied companion—reassuring, consoling, urging, exulting, defying—constantly defining, reflecting, and changing his moods and ideas.

At the movie theaters, rock and roll has inspired a new and fantastically successful genre of film. For over a decade and a half, movie music has more and more been rock music; increasingly rock soundtracks have become an integral part of films, deftly weaving together and binding reality and fantasy. Rock's first assault on the movies came in B-grade films during the early fifties. Producers sought to make some quick money trading on the star quality of such media idols as Elvis Presley, Frankie Avalon, and buxom ex-Mouseketeer Annette Funicello. In these films, unlike those that were to follow, both the plot and the music were secondary to the celebrity of the stars. That changed somewhat in the mid-sixties with two films that featured the Beatles—*A Hard Day's Night* (1964) and *Help!* (1965). Not until the late seventies, however, did filmmakers fully realize the aesthetic and economic potential of fusing rock and roll with dramas of teen life. Only then did the music itself become a significant "star," enhancing the dramatic appeal and commercial success of a great many movies. This shift made sense: after all, rock music had long since become for teens the prism through which they viewed and understood much of life, the constant backdrop for and interpreter of what they did and felt. The constant presence of music in films simply mirrored an established pattern in their lives. Soundtrack albums often made more money than the films themselves. This was true for numerous youth-oriented movies, including *American Graffiti* (1973), *Saturday Night Fever* (1977), *Grease* (1978), *Apocalypse Now* (1979), *Risky Business* (1983), *Flashdance* (1983), *The Breakfast Club* (1985), *The Big Chill* (1983), *Footloose* (1984), *Ferris Bueller's Day Off* (1986), *Platoon* (1986), *Dirty Dancing* (1986), *Top Gun* (1986), *Good Morning, Vietnam* (1987), and *Batman* (1989). Whether set in a high school or a war zone, movies about teen life would fall flat without rock music to give them authenticity, drive, and feeling. The formula has proven to be a powerful and profitable one.

The power of rock is nowhere more obvious than at a live concert. It is in performance that rock and roll beats the loudest and kicks the hardest, and here much of the heart of rock is laid bare. A concert vividly illustrates the full appeal of rock and roll, for there rock's meanings can be seen as well as heard. Amid a haze of smoke and cascades of multicolored lights thunders rock's hard beat, and in delirious response hordes of enthralled teens scream, sing, and dance. The high-tech rock show aims for a total sensory envelopment that embodies and enhances the absorptive power of the music itself. In a concert, sound, light, image, and performance carry as much power and meaning as any purely musical or lyrical "message." And what that message, the heart of rock and roll, amounts to is best seen in the audience's complete identification with and relish of the "event" happening on the stage and all around them. Especially in their dancing, teens seem to meld with the music, at once expressing themselves, identifying with the music, and enjoying the simple sensory pleasure of sound and movement. Whatever else rock might be—and its inmost meanings are elusive and open to dispute—a concert makes it clear that rock is a dramatic participatory anthem of teen life, freighted with the intense experience of what teens believe, feel, value, and do. Rock is at once a barometer of teen experience *and* the very weather they inhabit, at once the celebration of an ethos *and* the ethos itself.

There is no doubt that rock and roll lives. It has heart and it has soul—an elusive deep-down something that profoundly attracts and affects teenagers. The music pulsates everywhere—on records and the radio, on MTV, in movies, and at dance clubs and concerts all over America. It has an incredibly powerful pull, as even rock's critics admit. Take away the preening antics of "glam" metal bands and the hyped slickness of teenybopper singers, and there is, first and last, the loud, beating heart of rock and roll—strong, driving, and full of sass and sex. While some adults bemoan rock's beat and lyrics and the lifestyle it promotes, the music continues to be a vital presence in the lives of countless listeners, both young and (now) middle-aged. Its influence can hardly be gauged, except to say that rock is far from being an inconsequential musical diversion: for over thirty years it has provided a meaning-laden emotional backdrop for the "coming of age" of young North Americans. It has fostered extremes, from the tumultuous social dissent of the sixties on the one hand to a thriving economic empire on the other. For numerous reasons—among them protest, pleasure, and profit—rock and roll in all its permutations has become a cultural mainstay. The success of "super rockers" in the eighties—Michael Jackson, Bruce Springsteen, U2, Prince, Madonna, and Guns n' Roses—attested to rock's continuing vitality, variety, and freshness; it was bigger, louder, brasher—and wealthier—than ever. In any case, reports of its supposed "death" in the early 1970s now seem, as Mark Twain said upon reading his obituary, greatly exaggerated.

This chapter surveys some of the cultural geography of rock and roll, especially as it both reflects and helps shape the current youth culture. Of foremost concern are the diverse elements of its enormously persistent and deep appeal not only as a kind of music but also as a social movement and a consumer product. All of these identities of rock converge and intertwine; ultimately they are interdependent and inseparable. Nonetheless, for the purposes of analysis, we will attempt to distinguish among them. What we want to do is to try to understand the rock phenomenon in its largest possible context, in its kaleidoscopic fullness. Thus we will look at rock's historical origins and uniqueness, its stylistic variety, its patterns of meaning, its social ethos, and, finally, its cultural functions. By examining different dimensions of this multi-faceted commercial art form, we will try to produce a "gestalt" of the experience and the meaning of rock. These two dimensions are not neatly separable, since it is true of rock—as it is of most art—that its experience contains its meaning. In the end, what attracts adolescents to rock and roll is its emotional immediacy and honesty, its exuberant proclamation of adolescent freedom and autonomy, and its constant dramatization of the human quest, felt with particular urgency during the teen years, for intimacy and identity.

The Music and Where It Came From

Numerous styles and types of popular music have flowered and faded during the past century. Although it had dubious beginnings and a questionable parentage, rock and roll has now become a prominent and seemingly permanent cultural fixture in North American life. While its style and messages have been neither uniform nor simple, from its very infancy rock and roll has consistently spoken directly and deeply to most North American youth.

In many ways rock and roll had no real predecessors. For about twenty years at the turn of the century, ragtime communicated an irrepressibly youthful vigor that other popular music of the time—such as the waltz, the march, and the sentimental ballad of the drawing room—did not. But ragtime, unlike rock and roll, was not an age-segregated music. African-American in origin, this barroom medium was quickly "whitewashed" and marketed to middle- and upper-class white Americans of all ages. It soon became everybody's music.

In the 1920s jazz emerged to become America's first age-specific, generationally differentiated popular music. Its unbridled youthful exuberance (occasionally inspiring excess) and lively danceability gave a name and a spirit to the decade. The sweet dance music of the time, the waltz and the two-step, simply could not match the zest and expressiveness of jazz. But the devotees of the Jazz Age were predominantly white, middle- to upper-class kids beyond high school, often college dropouts or college graduates—a decided minority of America's young people. Jazz appealed to some segments of the American youth population, but it was never significantly marketed toward them, nor did they ever claim it as their own. Even today, jazz fans are typically not young people. And jazz made its primary mark on American life through the rather diluted offerings of the big bands of Benny Goodman and the like. Their work offered a commercially successful fusion of blues, jazz, and dance music, but their audience was a general population of all ages.

And then, in the 1950s, seemingly out of nowhere, came rock and roll. From the beginning, through a special alchemy of sound and feeling, the music captured what youth felt and experienced, although music producers were slow to recognize its attraction. To young people, and almost exclusively to them, the music itself, its steady beat and driving rhythms, expressed and communicated important, peculiarly adolescent feelings, attitudes, and ideas. The sheer sound of rock—apart from its lyrical content—acknowledged, displayed, and even celebrated inchoate and unspoken pubescent fears and desires. Part of that appeal, clearly, was sexual: rock put "it" all out in the open, even though this display was at first deftly sublimated and rarely verbal. The throaty, driving vocal caress and the controversial physical gyrations of an Elvis Presley or a Little Richard spoke volumes, and they did so without ever saying an overt word about the quest for sexual experience, the distinctly hormonal side of the human quest for intimacy. It was but a step from Presley to the Rolling Stones' hard-rock complaint, "I Can't Get No Satisfaction." Amid the tame if not repressed "white bread" culture of the fifties, of Eisenhower and *Ozzie and Harriet*, rock and roll seemed to acknowledge publicly that teens possessed genitals and that it was *all right* to have them. Dancing became a vertical expression of horizontal desire.

Entwined with this earthy strain of rock was the simple, sheer exuberance of being young in North America and enjoying the "good life"—the ritual of cars, dating, "fun," friends, and school. If Elvis Presley brandished the sexual sword of the new music, the Beach Boys represented the more innocent side of rock, although hormonal urgency infused their songs as well. The lighter, less visceral melodies and the simple harmonies of songs like "Be True to Your School," "Surf City," and "Little Deuce Coupe" emphasized a different dimension of the teen experience. If the Beach Boys' music contained a message, both musically and lyrically, it was that it was more than all right to be a teenager— it was great. The Beach Boys enshrined bonding, cruising, and dancing, especially on the beach. Teens seemed to be knocking on the very "gates of Eden," to adapt the title of a recent book on the 1960s. (See Morris Dickstein's *Gates of Eden: American Culture in the Sixties*.) Corporate America would later pick up on this idealization of innocent, hedonistic youth and soak it in an acid bath of commercialism.

Rock seemed to emerge from and play to the experience of growing up, and the music itself—more than lyric, image, or performance—seemed to capture, convey, and promote a specific vision of what was most important to that experience. Musicologists have pondered the enigmas of rock's attraction and have generally gone away mystified, for rock hardly fits into high-culture formalist definitions of musical accomplishment. In the epigraph to this chapter, singer-songwriter Huey Lewis answers as well as anyone the riddle of rock's appeal: "But it's still that same old backbeat rhythm that really, really drives 'em wild." The appeal does not lie in harmony, because most rock-and-roll music consists of no more than four or five very simple chords in a very clearly defined key. Nor does the attraction lie in melody, since the rock-and-roll vocalist does not so much sing as shout and wail. Rock's heralded aural excess does not quite capture its appeal either (150 decibels of ear-splitting roar from the world's largest bank of speakers to the contrary!), because rock can be soft or at least only moderately loud and remain perfectly authentic, as the Grateful Dead, the Eagles, and Bob Dylan have proven. Neither does timbre or tone color, electronically produced and distorted though they may be, account for rock's attraction.

The heart of rock and roll is rhythm and beat—those twin forces which give rock its energy and propel its intentionally simple harmony and melody. Complicated harmony and wild key changes would draw attention away from these elements. Similarly, well-developed tunefulness or operatic vocals would detract from the emotional simplicity of rock's vision of life. Without rhythm and beat, rock would turn to schlock, an accelerated Muzak of mere time-beating, trite chords, and boring tunes. In 1932 a popular song of jazz pioneer Duke Ellington proclaimed, "It don't mean a thing if it ain't got that swing." Much the same is true for rock and roll. In order to be rock, the real stuff, the music must have a strong rhythmic feel, a driving ambience or "groove"; without that, its message is nonexistent or, at best, inconsequential. In some mysterious way, "that old backbeat rhythm" expresses a feel for life that sets teens' pulses racing and their feet moving. The music contains and conveys feelings and moods, a deeply affective sense of life that is best defined as a free, exuberant, and hungry vitality, one that is often but not always hormonal. That feeling is the heart of rock and roll.[1]

No better argument for the creativity, durability, and signifi-

---

1. How rhythm does this is beyond the scope of this discussion. Many social and religious conservatives believe that rhythm is the expression of humankind's baser instincts, its primitive urges, and therefore unworthy of anyone civilized or devoutly religious. It is largely rock's rhythmic foundations that make it the object of harsh criticism.

cance of the feeling of rock exists than its own history. Rock's central apprehension of what life should be has spawned a countless variety of musical substyles. Generally, "rock and roll" refers to the dominant popular music of the 1950s, 1960s, and 1970s—a music that is lively, danceable, often loud and brash, and sometimes sweet and sentimental. Musically, it is distinct from jazz, ragtime, and Broadway tunes. Historically, the meaning of rock and roll is more limited, pointing to a certain kind of music popular at a specific time—the rollicking, (usually) white-performed rhythm and blues and rockabilly coming out of the South in the mid-to-late 1950s. The music that came later, generically labeled "rock," has exhibited much of the spirit, technique, and style of fifties' rock and roll. By and large, however, rock—which has thrived in North America and England from the sixties to the present—has been harder edged and more heavily amplified. As rock has diffused stylistically and geographically over the course of its life, it has grown and diversified, and now bears many adjectival labels, including "country," "folk," "hard," "soft," "punk," "Southern," "psychedelic," "acid," "Motown," and "straight ahead." The music and entertainment industries use all these labels to identify various subgroups within rock and within "the rock audience" or "the rock-and-roll generation"; these labels help segment the buying public into demographic markets. Throughout this chapter, we will refer to both "rock and roll" and "rock" in the structural, musically generic sense, without making fine distinctions between rock styles. The spirit of rock runs through many veins.

What the Music Says

For those teens growing up in the sixties and early seventies, the rock music of the British beat bands (the Beatles, the Rolling Stones, the Who, Led Zeppelin, etc.) and the American bands, whether psychedelic (the Jefferson Airplane, the Grateful Dead) or bluesy (Creedence Clearwater Revival), began to assume the role of a total cultural force. Together these bands and their music flavored, influenced, and shaped just about everything in the youth culture. The music and the performers helped teens decide what to wear, how to act, and who and what to believe—socially, politically, morally, and religiously. During the tumult of the "cultural revolution," rock was both evangel and midwife to a new sensibility, offering a profoundly different apprehension of the central components and goals of life. Its role became all the more crucial if not decisive, because traditional institutions like home, school, and church

Who Likes Rock and Roll?

Rock and roll has been the most significant genre in American popular music over the past thirty-five years, and it continues to appeal to countless teenagers. It must be remembered, however, that rock and roll was and is primarily a music of urban and suburban "white middle class high school students, who really had no native culture of their own, stranded in the Kafka-land of the suburbs, neither country nor city, whose musical tools were the radio, the phonograph, the television set."* In 1951, Cleveland disc jockey Alan Freed introduced his white teenage audience to the music of black rhythm-and-blues artists on his radio show, "Moondog's Rock and Roll Party." The ambitious Freed also arranged live shows featuring black artists for predominantly white audiences. In adopting the vernacular of African-American youth culture, rock and roll brought to the white teenage audience the language, attitudes, and feelings of an oppressed minority. It exposed them to the often tragic and complex side of the American dream.

But what about black American teenagers? Of course, they continued to have their own rhythm and blues and later had soul music, funk, and rap, which were regularly and unashamedly co-opted by the major record companies for sale to their primarily white audiences.** But they couldn't really identify with Buddy Holly, Elvis (black-sounding or not), the Beatles, Bob Dylan, or Fleetwood Mac; nor can they now relate to Madonna or Cyndi Lauper or Tiffany.

Similarly, Hispanic teens can't find an expressive outlet in mainstream Anglo-American rock and roll, unless, perhaps, it is through the culture-straddling music of Linda Ronstadt, Richie Valens, Los Lobos, or Ruben Blades. And how can Native American teens on a North Dakota reservation or in a large Western city identify with this kind of music? It does not speak to or for them, either. Their aspirations, fears, dreams, life stories, and social status are very different from those of mainstream white, middle-class teens.

In general, American teens who belong to minority groups do not find that rock and roll supplies them with maps of reality, functions as a mentor, or aids them in their search for identity and intimacy. Ironically, it was primarily the music of America's largest minority population that gave birth to rock and roll.

---

*William Schafer, *Rock Music: Where It's Been, What It Means, Where It's Going* (Minneapolis: Augsburg, 1972), p. 18.

**One of the rather curious developments in recent years is the rising popularity of black rock and roll. The band called Living Color, for example, plays hard rock—not electric blues or loud and energetic funk or tough rap, the genres stereotypically associated with African-American pop musicians—but just plain hard rock, thought of up until now (although rock was in many ways inspired by black rhythm and blues) as the exclusive domain of white English and American bands.

were beginning to lose their credibility and authority. And through the 1980s and into the 1990s—despite the diffusion of rock styles into punk, metal, glam, thrash, or straight ahead—rock and roll still exerts a major, perhaps unfathomable cultural influence which is no less significant or sizeable for being less overtly rebellious and political than it was in the 1960s and 1970s.

Cumulatively, the many facets of rock, from musical styles to music videos to album covers, tell young people stories about the nature of life, particularly adolescence. The music also offers a variety of prescriptions in response to its depiction of life's challenges and problems. In other words, rock and roll delineates or maps a stage of experience, the territory called adolescence, and then, as a guide or mentor to youth, supplies routes through the new country, guiding its charges through the rocky passages of adolescence toward survival and success in the adult world. At a time when traditional mentors like parents, teachers, and clergy have become irrelevant if not altogether comical to teens, rock and roll gives shape, direction, and meaning to teen experience. One pair of commentators has captured a major facet of rock's influence on teen life: "Produced specifically for youth, much popular music speaks to salient adolescent concerns, from heterosexual relations to rebellion and autonomy. The lyrics, rhythms, and harmonies provide raw materials that youth may draw upon in learning sex roles and composing their sexual identities. Hence music becomes an essential ingredient to the romantic rites of dances, parties, and dating so intrinsic to this transitional period of development."[2]

The point is that most teens are often intensely caught up in a large, interrelated complex of psychological and social struggles over identity and acceptance, love and intimacy, conformity and individuality, and trust and hope. Rock provides some measure of stability and comfort in the midst of family problems, peer pressures, school tensions, and the like. In many ways, for better or for worse, rock and roll helps teens cope with life's struggles as it dramatizes and directs those struggles and connects young people who may feel alone in their problems with peers in similar predicaments. Rock furnishes emotional support and creates an atmosphere of confidence and normalcy. Rock can even supply social status insofar as consumption of its commodities—the style and size of one's wardrobe, or how many tapes and CDs one has—bestows a measure of distinction. For all these reasons, rock and roll was and still is *the* music of the youth culture.

2. Reed Larson and Robert Kubey, "Television and Music," *Youth & Society* 15 (Sept. 1983): 15.

From the beginning, rock strove to create a self-contained adolescent world of values, meanings, and connections. An example comes from the earliest days of rock and roll. Chuck Berry's successful adaptation of rhythm and blues for a white teenage market vividly illustrates how rock began orienting teens to their own culture. In his Chicago-styled rock and roll, Berry used the ordinary realities of the youth culture—cars, music, dating, school, growing up—to paint a picture of contemporary teenage life (in the late fifties and early sixties) and create an atmosphere of carefree living. "Sweet Little Sixteen" (1958) celebrated the phenomenal popularity of rock music by announcing that teenagers were dancing to the same music all across the nation. "School Days" (1957) described the boredom of school, the excitement when the bell rang, and the pleasures of the juke joint. "No Particular Place to Go" (1964) fused popular teen images of freedom and leisure time (nothing in particular to do), music, cars, and romance:

> Ridin' along in my automobile
> My baby beside me at the wheel
> I stole a kiss at the turn of a mile
> My curiosity runnin' wild
> Cruisin' and playin' the radio
> With no particular place to go. . . .[3]

For the guys with "wheels" and girlfriends, only parental mores got in the way of "some enchanted evening." While the lyrics of these songs gave some information to teens trying to figure out what happens when a boy and a girl are out cruising on a date, Berry's inflections—the *sound* of his singing—created a mood that was just as important as any specific lyrical content.

The subsequent history of rock and roll amply details its enormous influence on everything from sex and drugs to politics and peace. One reigning exemplar of the mythic dimensions of rock, Bruce Springsteen, has recounted the influence of rock on his own development:

---

3. These themes have persisted in rock music of the sixties, seventies, and eighties, demonstrating that as a social structure the youth culture has remained essentially the same. The characteristics of the youth culture that Chuck Berry delineated in "Sweet Little Sixteen" were similarly sketched by the Beach Boys in "Surfin' USA" (1963) and by the Who in "My Generation" (1966). The sexual hints that Berry dropped became broader in later songs by other artists. Backseat escapades, usually at the mythological drive-in, were recounted in Freudian fashion by Kenny Loggins and Jim Messina in "Your Mama Don't Dance, and Your Daddy Don't Rock and Roll" (1973) and by Bob Seger in "Night Moves" (1977). And the picture of school as boring and irrelevant compared with the excitement of teen social life can be traced from Berry's "School Days" to Alice Cooper's "School's Out" (1972) to Van Halen's video called "Hot for Teacher" (1984).

"When I was growing up, I got a sense of so many things from rock 'n' roll music. I got a sense of life. I got a sense of *sex*. But most of all, I got a sense of freedom. For me, the best rock 'n' roll always gave me a sense of freedom and expanded awareness."[4] And so it was for countless other adolescents, many of whom were emotionally fragile and searching for identity and meaning. As teen culture became more age-segregated and disengaged from parental control, the culture of rock and roll increasingly gave teens clues to self-identity, intimacy, and self-expression, and offered answers to their pressing questions. Who am I in relation to my parents? What's so important about school? How do I express my own sexuality? Who are my real friends? Rock and roll has always been associated with America's post–World War II youth culture precisely because it was a music that youth could identify with; it was *their* music, performed for kids by kids their own age (or nearly so). The music spoke to them in their terms and on their terms, dealing with inchoate feelings. In the process, the rock phenomenon gave them a distinctive voice and identity apart from the adult world, ultimately giving certain kinds of structure and meaning to their lives.

Nowhere did this become more obvious than in rock's elevation of stars into cultural heroes. The history of rock is peopled with singers and bands that have exerted enormous cultural force because of their musical virtuosity and their potent symbolic alchemy. In retrospect, it is clear that different rock figures from Presley to Springsteen functioned as flash points for the youth culture; they were revered because they embodied the diverse currents of rebellion and longing experienced by the teens of their times. Elvis Presley, for example, seemed like a cultural dissenter from the poor, white, rural subculture of the South. Many saw his hormone-laden popularity as a counterpoint to the venerated social and moral niceties of the Eisenhower era. When in 1958 the Army drafted Presley, consternation and grief beset hordes of teenage fans with whom he had begun to forge seemingly intimate (though electronically isolated) relationships. (See Chapter Three.) Adulation fueled protest. Here was a cultural hero, one who broke the conventional mold of Tin Pan Alley pop star, an outsider, and the system forced him to conform to its demands. Many young people thought Elvis's induction was a thinly disguised attempt by the music industry to squelch this new, irritating music by taking the music's "king" out of circulation for a while.

Teenagers identified with Presley's music because they heard in it expressions of their own nascent longings for intimacy, but they also

---

4. Springsteen, quoted by Mark Fleischmann in "Chimes of Freedom," *Cable Choice*, Dec. 1988, p. 20.

Rock as Idolatry

President Dwight Eisenhower received this letter from three Montana teenagers, which typified the adulation that Presley inspired in his fans.

Dear President Eisenhower,
My girlfriend's [sic] and I are writting [sic] all the way from Montana, We think its [sic] bad enough to send *Elvis Presley* in the Army, but if you cut his side burns off we will just die! You don't no [sic] how we fell [sic] about him, I really don't see why you have to send him in the Army at all, but we beg you please please don't give him a G.I. hair cut, oh please please don't! If you do we will just about die!

Elvis Presley Lovers
Linda _____, Sherry _____, Mickie _____.

—Jean Mueller, "Document of the Month," *Social Education,* May 1985, p. 407.

identified with Presley himself, holding him up as a symbolic older brother. He was both a hero and an anti-hero whose nonconformist lifestyle and unconventional music were considered liabilities by the large record companies to whom "pop music" still meant Tin Pan Alley tunes and published sheet music.[5] By any standard, Presley was an ambiguous cultural figure, at once macho and sentimental. He represented an extreme measure of youthful passion and rebellion that won adult disapproval and teen emulation. More than that, he gave shape to the emerging separate world of adolescence, providing teens with common ground and the promise of intimacy—with their hero and among themselves.

Another later pop figure of untold cultural power was ex-Beatle John Lennon, who had become a cultural and musical hero well before his murder in 1980; indeed, his murder was a direct consequence of his fame. A further measure of his significance was the widespread spontaneous mourning—especially among survivors of 1960s counterculture—following his death. Critic Wayne Hampton explains Lennon's status as a cultural symbol:

> The story of John Lennon is a potent symbol of and for the generation of the 1960's. Because he was a creative giant, former Beatle, rock superstar, and international celebrity, his life story is a source of nostalgia and inspiration for millions of young people in search of personal

5. Daniel Dotter, "Growing Up Is Hard to Do: Rock and Roll Performers as Cultural Heroes," *Sociological Spectrum* 7 (1987): 25-44.

identity. It takes them back to another time and place, to a golden age when flower power, long hair, psychedelics, Oriental mysticism, and mass politics were the rage. It is the hippie version of JFK and Camelot. One stimulates the liberal's imagination, and the other warms the hearts of once young radicals.[6]

In the world of youth, Lennon's life story had all the characteristics of the mythic tale: humble beginnings, passion, individuality, skill, success, romance, and early death. Lennon was the quintessential romantic hero who went his own way, fighting the usual meanings of pop stardom and the easy manipulations of the media and politicians.[7] In the decade since his death, thanks in part to Alfred Goldman's biography and Yoko Ono's honorific film of her husband, the legend of John Lennon has become bigger than the real-life pop singer. Hampton explains this phenomenon by pointing out that the "Lennon legend totalizes a system of values and lifestyle. For like few other popular artists of his era, John Lennon was able to capture, articulate, and embody the fleeting essence of his generation and his era: its madness as well as its brilliance and the inherent contradictions of its dark, nihilistic pessimism and its exuberant, euphoric quest for an impossible utopian ideal."[8] Again, young audiences gravitated to the symbolic ambiguities of a rogue-rebel who flouted conventionality and inspired adoration, solidarity, and intimacy.

In short, rock has provided a new source of youth heroes— larger-than-life figures who embody and shape the ordinary teen's dreams of freedom, autonomy, and intimacy. In any of its numerous forms, rock provides a focal point for individual teenage identity as well as a prime catalyst for defining the youth community.

The extent to which rock captures diffuse adolescent yearnings is evident in two immensely popular teen films. In *Ferris Bueller's Day Off* (1986), the brash and cheeky Ferris and his friends skip school, outwitting the school principal and engaging in some very creative irresponsibility. At the high point of the film, the irrepressible Ferris sings "Twist and Shout" atop a float in the middle of a German-American parade in Chicago's Loop. As crowds and office workers start dancing in enthusiastic response, teen viewers witness an entirely convincing fictional reaffirmation of the power of rock and roll to celebrate life and define community. Similarly, in *Good Morning, Vietnam* (1987), unconventional disc jockey Adrian Cronauer understands the communal

6. Hampton, *Guerrilla Minstrels* (Knoxville: University of Tennessee Press, 1986), p. 10.

7. Simon Frith, *Music for Pleasure* (New York: Routledge, 1988), p. 72.

8. Hampton, *Guerrilla Minstrels*, pp. 10-11.

power and the cheeky, anti-establishment, freedom-loving, sexually provocative nature of rock and roll and its first cousins, soul music and rhythm and blues. While the military brass, the "desk jockeys," want Cronauer to play their music—swing, polkas, and sweet ballads—Cronauer knows that rock is the music of the young fighting man. He knows that these young men, mostly youth still in their teens who are far from home and barely old enough to drink, need their own music in order to affirm their identity and maintain morale. At least this is the movie version of Cronauer's life story. In point of fact, however, the real Adrian Cronauer, on whose experiences the film is loosely based, was not a rock-and-roll disc jockey but only a rather wild and satirical radio announcer. But movie-studio brass knew that injecting rock and roll into the story would give the film a magical appeal that could bring in audiences of teenagers and baby boomers. In these films and in countless others like *Top Gun*, rock and roll is the marching music to which new heroes step and dance. It exerts a strong, enigmatic power that helps define community, shape reality, establish identity, and provide intimacy.

Over time, rock's heroes have become more ambiguous and controversial. Today, the heroic icons that youth emulate are more extreme than anti-heroes like the Rolling Stones, the bad boys of rock in the sixties, who regularly tweaked the nose of the establishment and sneered at its values. Boasting even more overt defiance and contempt are contemporary groups like Guns n' Roses, who on the charts rival the prominence of the Stones in their heyday. According to one critic, the band is "obsessed with the contradictions of adolescence: the unfocused rage and pervasive doubt, the insecurity and cockiness, the horniness and fear. The Gunners' songs don't hide the fact that they're confused and screwed up. 'We know we are,' Axl Rose [the lead singer] says. 'But we're trying not to be.' . . . They are a brutal band for brutal times."[9] Whether their rebellious music and violent persona should be taken seriously or with a grain of salt is almost impossible to assess. Lyrics do not offer a reliable guide to deciphering their public image or the mood of the music itself, which can speak as loudly as any set of words. As mentors and heroes, they hardly warrant emulation, especially considering the extremity of their rebellion; as mirrors of American youth consciousness and values, they are distressingly suggestive of an increasingly deep dissatisfaction among American youth that began quite innocently with Elvis Presley and Bill Haley.

9. Rob Tannenbaum, "The Hard Truth about Guns n' Roses," *Rolling Stone*, 17 Nov. 1988, pp. 60-61.

The Rock Circus

London offers one of the strangest tourist attractions emanating from the world of rock music. Called "Rock Circus," it is a glitzy, glittery museum featuring wax figures of rock stars à la Madame Tussaud. At this circus even the "bad boys" of rock are given the glossy treatment, and the most raucous hits sound like innocent Sunday-school songs. As rock music is institutionalized in the collective memory, particularly at Rock Circus, its revolutionary edge is blunted by commercial success and turned into museum fodder.

Beyond Lyrics: What Rock Does

Road maps come with lines, symbols, and names but not many words. They give directions but through a language of their own. This analogy is perhaps useful for analyzing the effects of rock, especially its lyrics. At best, the words to a song constitute but one expressive element of the multiple effects of rock. The search for verbal meaning within the "gestalt" of the rock product is not easy. The obviousness of most lyrics makes the search look deceptively simple. But often a strict literary analysis of the lyrics is impossible because they are impressionistic, nonrhetorical, or just plain confused. And then a given rock song may carry so much "expressive ambiguity," cryptic symbolism, and buried irony that its meaning cannot be clearly deciphered. Adding to the difficulty is the challenge of simply hearing the lyrics: very often, while the lyrics of some songs may be offensive on paper, they are rendered inaudible by the volume of the accompaniment. As one critic has noted, this blurring of the verbal message seems deliberate: "Heavy amplification and the tricks of the recording studio can add the finishing touches by distorting or drowning the lyrics in the interests of the kind of potential interpretation which can not be checked against a fixed text."[10] And even if lyrics are intelligible, they may convey only one message among several that the "total package" communicates. A performer's live stage show, for example, may "say" something quite different than his lyrics do. Advertising hype may carry yet another message. The problem with trying to pin down lyrical meaning is that rock and roll has always expressed more and meant more than its lyrics alone. The text is but one avenue to the meaning of the song.

10. Bernice Martin, *A Sociology of Contemporary Cultural Change* (New York: St. Martin's Press, 1981), p. 162.

An additional difficulty in assessing the cultural impact of rock music is that so few people seem to actually listen to or understand the verbal content of a song. We interviewed one young woman who, after viewing a video of a song by Prince and reading a copy of the song's lyrics, commented, "I've been singing that song for a while now, and THAT'S what the lyrics mean?" She liked the beat, the sound of the instruments, the yearning voice, but she hadn't contemplated the message of the lyrics because she couldn't quite understand them. In fact, recent research indicates that music fans do not pay all that much attention to lyrics, even when those lyrics, taken literally, often cause major antipathy toward rock music. Further, high-school students generally misinterpret lyrics; at least they give them a meaning different from the literal one. Their interpretations are often based on videos or films using the songs featuring the lyrics. Several older studies have pointed out similar discrepancies between what rock lyrics mean and how listeners comprehend them. One study suggested that the major function of popular music was to provide background noise for teenagers' activities.[11] By and large, young people find it difficult to explain why they like a song or what makes it popular or how it affects them. They simply do not think much about the messages of their music. "Sound" or "beat" rank highest in making a song likeable; lyrics are among the least important factors.[12]

Ironically, attempts by parents' groups to understand the harmful effects of rock have centered mostly on lyrical content. For many critics, lyrics seem to be the only aspect of rock open to rational discussion. The 1988 video "Rising to the Challenge" from the Parents' Music Resource Center (PMRC) bluntly illustrates this point. It explores what the PMRC believes to be the danger that constant exposure to such lyrics poses to formative minds and psyches. But the video doesn't deal substantively with meaning, with function, with what people actually hear or feel. Its argument is *content* specific and not *contextual.* Like most criticism of rock, it reduces meaning to lyrical messages or album-cover art while overlooking the full range of rock's effects. The PMRC is certainly well-intentioned and makes a valid case against some violent and exploitive currents in rock culture and the rock business. Moreover, the efforts that the PMRC has made to educate the public about rock and

11. Walter Gantz and Howard Gartenberg, "Pop Music and Adolescent Socialization: An Information Perspective," paper based on a study conducted in 1977 and presented at the convention of the International Communication Association, Philadelphia, May 1979.

12. Roger Jon Desmond, "Adolescents and Music Lyrics: Implications of a Cognitive Perspective," *Communication Quarterly* 35 (Summer 1987): 278.

to impose certain restraints on the industry have been almost willfully misinterpreted by the media and by rock apologists such as Frank Zappa. Nevertheless, a substantive case against the cultural influence of rock must take into account far more than lyrics or even apparent messages in the music. Rock communicates almost directly to the soul, like so much music over the centuries that has inspired so many social movements. Lyrics are only one of six or seven prominent components in rock production and reception.

Perhaps the biggest limitation on the part of the PMRC and other similar groups is the failure to recognize that the primary mode of meaning and expression in rock music is not "rational discourse." Among the major artistic media for teens, rock in particular is a non-rational mode of communication, dealing with the sensory and the emotional, employing figurative lyrics, musical mood, and symbolic gestures. Since lyrics are often metaphoric, they are not easily accessible to the casual or "outside" listener. In his collection of essays on pop music entitled *Music for Pleasure*, British pop-music critic Simon Frith argues that the primary content of rock music is the communication of moods or generalized states of emotion. "All pop singers, male and female, have to express direct emotion. Their task is to make public performance a private revelation. Singers can do this because the voice is an apparently transparent reflection of feeling: it is the sound of the voice, not the words sung, which suggests what a singer really means."[13]

Perhaps all attempts at determining the specific meaning or the expressive content of particular rock songs will meet with limited success because rock music is the ultimate existential art form. While neat dichotomies are dangerous, it is safe to say that for the most part rock and roll features feeling and experience more than thought and analysis;[14] it cares more about identity and intimacy than knowledge and intellect; it celebrates the here and now, focusing on the experiential rather than the ideological. Rock music doesn't often provide as much specific information as a road map might, although it does do that sometimes; nor does it frequently offer particular guidance as a human mentor might, although on occasion it does this as well. Rather, it appeals and functions primarily on broad emotional and attitudinal levels, as psycho-emotional map and mentor for many. In laying out such a generalized, affective map for great numbers of teens, it establishes for teen culture a supportive atmosphere, an ambience with guidelines for acceptable expression and behavior, at least as far as other teens are

13. Frith, *Music for Pleasure*, p. 154.
14. Martin, *A Sociology of Contemporary Cultural Change*, p. 154.

concerned. By doing so, the music becomes a kind of community, linking and bonding fans of similar tastes, attitudes, and experience. It is a self-contained world in which sensory experience and emotional involvement take precedence over verbal content and rational analysis.

It is clear, then, that part of the great appeal of rock lies in its emotional candor, immediacy, and expressiveness. What a teenager cannot talk about or find words to articulate, he or she can express by dancing to and singing along with rock music, letting the rhythms and words speak and express feelings. Rock frequently communicates feelings of love and camaraderie so that this or that song becomes "our song," giving couples and groups common experience, identity, emotional bonds, and often status. And when things fall apart—the girlfriend leaves or the old man bullies because of grades—and the teenager feels hurt and frustrated but cannot find the words or the behavior to express himself, music can communicate, divert, and provide emotional release. The psychological usefulness of music lies in its almost direct access to the emotional regions of one's being; it penetrates the intellectual and often circumvents the rational. And with the catharsis can come emotional support, for at least someone, some voice—though far away, transmitted by airwaves—understands. Rock and roll performs this dual function for American teens far better than any other kind of music. Especially in the 1950s and 1960s, rock music furnished a new dialect for the tumultuous youth culture. It was a principal means of communication, a *lingua franca* for the postwar generation. Landon Jones described the music as "a language that taught the baby boom about themselves."[15] In a series of videotaped conversations that the authors of this book had with teenagers, the teens indicated the expressive importance of music to them by saying such things as "The music I listen to depends on my mood. I play lively music if I feel happy, slow music if I feel sad." Music is a way for teens to express their personal emotions, to assert their own identity, and to vent inchoate feelings of loneliness, despair, and uncertainty.

Rock as the New Romanticism

To white American young people, rock and roll furnishes a language in and through which they express their feelings and communicate without embarrassment. Rock expresses many contemporary values, mores, and

15. Jones, *Great Expectations: America and the Baby Boom Generation* (New York: Ballantine Books, 1980), p. 72.

worldviews through its use of images, both verbal and visual, and its musical and performance styles and conventions. Since rock and roll is highly "sensation"-al in nature—indeed, is more sensation than it is cognitive expression—perhaps it should not be saddled with the weight of rational content. Furthermore, most rock falls apart under conventional logical analysis; it must be experienced primarily as sensation— driving beats, vocal plaints, loud noises, dazzling lights, and acrid smells—in order to be understood as a cultural force, in order to have meaning. Rock offers a sacrament of sound in which high-decibel noise can function in the same way that reverential silence does in other contexts. At rock concerts and dance clubs, distinctions of melody, harmony, and rhythm are blurred to achieve anarchic, contourless, all-engulfing noise; in plunging into the music, teens largely put aside rational and conventional social limits and distinctions to join a community that celebrates, paradoxically, a number of distinct themes that seem to characterize rock as a whole.[16] All of them, however, reflect a youth-oriented romanticism.

In part because of its contradictions, the best way to understand rock and roll is to see it as a twentieth-century popular expression of Western romanticism. In fact, rock may even be the last gasp of romanticism in this anxious materialistic and scientific age. More than any other contemporary cultural form, rock captures the central elements of the romantic spirit: its individuality, freedom, and rebellion, its search for adventure and originality, its exultation of emotion, physicality, and imagination, and its relish of contradictions, extremes, and paradoxes. It stands in sharp contrast to the classical spirit of integration, order, control, and rationality which makes for a stable and staid society. In just about all ways, rock is a music of extremes that goes for the jugular; it is not usually the sort of music that one goes home to think about or, for that matter, that one hums. It packs into a single song or performance of very simple and traditional musical structures extreme sensations, extreme bodily display, and extreme emotional expression.

This popular romanticism was at its height during the counter-cultural revolution of the 1960s. Rock and roll was its common language in its search for and celebration of utopia, individualism, freedom, imagination, and self-expression.[17] Almost two decades later, American

16. Martin, *A Sociology of Contemporary Cultural Change,* p. 160.
17. According to Bernice Martin, "Romanticism ideologically is the direct opposite of classicism—it is the preference of randomness over plan, for excess over balance, for the subjective over the objective, for emotion over reason, for the ephemeral over the lasting, for the personal or topical over the historically rooted" (*A Sociology of Contemporary Cultural Change,* p. 80).

young people continue to be romantics at heart. As such, they find in rock and roll the perfect visceral dissent from the heavy-handed seriousness and stultifying conformity and consumerism of corporate capitalism. All that they detest is found in the orderly, planned life of suburbs all over the land. The outrageous punk band or the cheeky rap group is not merely "bad" or nihilistic: it is the latest embodiment of the romantic urge to live life free of limits and disentangled from responsibility to society and nature. This urge is sometimes expressed in extreme ways: goat heads, blood, horns, flames, and the like decorate certain album covers, and references to cultic rituals appear in the lyrics of some heavy-metal songs. This is not Satanism, as some of its critics contend; more than likely it is an emphasis that grows out of the romantic desire to view Satan as the one who successfully escaped societal and cultural limitations.[18] Of greater concern is such groups' strong support of violence as pleasure.

Rock as Celebration

While later forms of rock abounded with angry plaints of protest and futility, the early forms of rock captured and expressed one of the purest and most central of romantic impulses. That was, put simply, a kind of innocent and exultant hedonism, a delight in the simple pleasures of the body and of consciousness, of the goodness of being alive. The celebrants of rock did not usually go off to live in the woods or join a commune, which was common in earlier romantic impulses in American life. Instead, they expressed their appreciation within the material progress and established cultural norms of North America. That came first in cars and electric guitars; later it would come in mind-altering drugs and extravagant jet-set lifestyles.

In many ways, the Beach Boys best expressed the "sunny side" of rock music. To them, rock and roll meant unalloyed fun, pure and innocent pleasure. Their music celebrated the vigor of youth and frolicked in the irresponsibility of adolescence. A quick listen to the first few lines of "Catch a Wave," "Surfin' U.S.A.," "Surfer Girl," or "Fun, Fun,

18. Historically there has been among certain groups a fascination with Satan and things satanic, as Roger Lundin explains: "Satan, the arch-negator, was considered a heroic figure by some Romantic poets, because he refused to accept the limits placed upon him by his Creator. In refusing to accept the limits of God and his creation, he turned to the joyful pretense of creating by destroying" ("Grace in the Given," *Reformed Journal*, Jan. 1989, p. 23).

Fun" ("She'll have fun, fun, fun 'til her daddy takes her T-bird away") makes it clear that rock, for all its loud, heavy-handed pretentiousness and macho posturing, can also be just plain fun. The Beach Boys did not advocate social change or espouse nihilistic philosophy; they did not warn, admonish, or rail; theirs was an ideology of fun that emphasized the pleasures of the beach, the sun, girls, and cars. This too was part of the heart of rock. They gave teens playful, danceable music with which to celebrate their youth and their world; their songs were an insistently experiential celebration of the present, a savoring of the eternal now.

That playful, hedonistic side of rock also appears in an earthier form in the earlier rock-and-roll song by Carl Perkins called "Dixie Fried" (1956):

> Well on the outskirts of town there's a little night-spot
> Dan dropped in about five o'clock
> Pulled off his coat, said the night is short
> Reached in his pocket and he flashed a quart
> An' hollered "Rave on children I'm with ya,
> Rave on cats," he cried
> "It's almost dawn and the cops are gone,
> Let's all get dixie fried!"

Here again are the energy and naiveté of rock and roll. The message is as simple as the music: "Have fun while you're young; responsibilities will come soon enough."[19] Indeed, most of the rock-and-roll music from the mid-fifties to the early sixties was light, playful, and easy to dance to, with only mild hints of the anger that was to come later. To many straightlaced elders, it seemed alarmingly frivolous at the same time that it displayed an innocence and exuberance which many of them envied. Early rock suited its audience: a burgeoning white, middle-class teenage market suddenly had increasing amounts of leisure time and disposable income and less and less social responsibility. Robert Snow makes this connection between play, music, and media: "As an arena for leisure, rock also means fun, putting responsibility on hold, enjoying the moment, and being dramatic and outrageous with no apology. It is a world of pure play, where a future payoff is irrelevant and creative experimentation is natural. And this creative experimentation and dramatic play has primarily occurred through electronic media."[20]

Indeed, a large part of the fun and enjoyment of early rock was

---

19. David Hatch and Stephen Millward, *From Blues to Rock: An Analytical History of Pop Music* (Manchester, Eng.: Manchester University Press, 1987), p. 83.

20. Snow, "Youth, Rock 'n' Roll, and Electronic Media," *Youth & Society* 18 (June 1987): 327-28.

made possible by the spectacular rise of North American technology and prosperity. Rock and roll did not spring up magically, nor was the rise of the "youth culture" after World War II entirely surprising. Neither was the phenomenal growth of the music-entertainment-electronics industry mere happenstance. As we explained in Chapter Four, a highly complex symbiotic relationship began to emerge when the industry discovered both the new youth market and the new musical product. The new music meshed perfectly with the new 45-rpm recording format and new radio-programming techniques. When teenagers discovered that they could buy and listen to *their* music on new, inexpensive transistor radios and phonographs, everything took off. It seemed that every teen had a transistor radio; every teen's stack of 45s steadily mounted.

The fact that rock music was a leisure-based, commodity-driven, radio and record-mediated activity for teens did not make it trivial; though in many ways frivolous and superficial, rock profoundly affected all areas of their lives. Rock became electronic fun at home, in the car, at the beach—it was everywhere. This ubiquitousness helped make rock and roll a powerful mode of communication in contemporary culture. As electronics evolved, so did rock music recording.[21] In the late eighties and early nineties, tapes and compact discs have begun replacing vinyl records, and new and improved means of sound reproduction, such as digital audio tape, keep coming. Rock too has continued to change, as has its audience. But these changes have strengthened, not weakened, the symbiotic relationship between the music, the youth market, and the industry. And although the emphases of rock are now more diverse, rock still draws heavily on the philosophy of fun and celebration.

Rock as Protest

Participants in any playful, celebratory activity do not usually ponder the philosophical implications of freedom, youthfulness, and irresponsibility. They just want to have fun. But of course the fun can be all-consuming, the irresponsibility can lead to self-indulgence, and the pleasure can turn into unchecked hedonism. That is precisely what happened to rock after the relative innocence and play of the fifties. It is fair to say that the emphases of rock shifted, moving from a celebration of youth and leisure to rampant self-indulgence and pleasure seeking,

---

21. Martin, *A Sociology of Contemporary Cultural Change*, p. 184.

and from innocent protest to serious rebellion. To some extent, rock has always walked a fine line between fun and excess, between acceptability and subversion. But in the late sixties and the seventies rock lost much of that balance, often becoming excessive in its self-indulgence and outrageous in its anti-authoritarianism. It turned vehemently adversarial, often decidedly macho, and on occasion painfully nihilistic. Since then, those romantic urges gone wild have reverberated through the music and the youth culture.

From its infancy, rock had been cast in the role of rebellious outsider, even in its milder manifestations like that of the Beach Boys. (This mindless music might inspire our kids to skip school and drive too fast!) Early on, the rebellion was often mild protest against conventional adult authority and institutions—a kind of camp critique of social conventions and parental authority. However, over time it took on the role of subversive revolutionary, undermining prevailing customs and traditional morality. On the other hand, commercialization softened its radical qualities. The process by which this all occurred was quite subtle. Musically, rock consisted of very simple, fixed, standard structures and techniques. Chords, blues derivations, drumming, guitar techniques, singing style, lyrical subject matter—all were quite conventional within rock's domain, carrying rhythms, codes, and symbols that wove the fabric and the stories of young people's lives. In its own way, rock held up a mirror to and a map of life in America.

For many, then, rock and roll was one of the major repositories of story and symbol with which to illumine and shape social arrangements.[22] In the youth culture, the car quickly became the "symbol" of freedom; the guitar as "tool" soon represented male sexual potency and prowess. School, another major facet of teen life, suggested repression, and stories of school as confinement or prison have abounded in rock and roll. In the late sixties, drugs became a symbol of openness and a route to increased sensation and sensitivity. All of these and more became conventional symbols within the structure and content of rock and roll, and they have since furnished rebellious rock bands with a ready storehouse of easily understood social and personal meanings.

Rock was able to work its way into North American culture because it deftly mediated social dissent by making it "fun." For all its simple conventions, rock was expressively ambiguous. The contradictory pull of conventional structure and expressive ambiguity made rock and roll the perfect vehicle for anti-establishment, unconventional sentiments. Rock could indict or poke fun and *be* fun at the same time;

22. Ibid., p. 183.

Forms of Protest

Rock music works as a map and a mentor for young people, sending strategic messages, providing individual and communal identity, and supplying a context for emotional intimacy and expression. Even though its precise meanings may be ambiguous and its messages nonintellectual, its gestalt is freighted with ample ideology—if not overtly in lyrical content, then subtly in mode of expression and presentation/performance strategy. Different kinds of rock express distinct feelings, thoughts, moods, and desires, and perform different functions in broader social contexts. What follows is a useful typology that emphasizes function and expressivity as markers of difference (based on the outline of five main types of MTV videos in E. Ann Kaplan's *Rocking around the Clock* [New York: Methuen, 1987]).

Sweet rock is sentimental both stylistically and structurally. The instrumentation is light, the drums are muffled, the star's voice is clear and pleasant, and the lyrics are understandable and often syrupy. The music has a nostalgic, sentimental, yearning quality. The general theme of romance, the ways of love and sex, appears in a narrative pattern of love-loss-reunion that solves all human problems. Authority figures are generally benign, although sometimes mild parent-child conflicts go unresolved.

Adversarial rock runs the stylistic gamut from early rock and roll to soft rock to heavy metal. Rock of this type features mild to heavy criticism of repressive parental/adult authority and often attempts to legitimate a leisure-oriented youth culture. Much of the music of the English bands of the sixties and seventies offered a general criticism of social conditions that affected working-class family life. In the eighties, rockers Bruce Springsteen and John (Cougar) Mellencamp displayed an overt social consciousness in their themes and manner of expression, frequently borrowing the ballad style of folk protest music. Generally dark in tone, adversarial rock sees romantic love as problematic and sex as a struggle for autonomy. Authority figures draw criticism but do not merit destruction.

Nihilist rock is primarily made up of heavy-metal, punk, and (to some extent) new-wave music. Instrumentation is loud and assaultive: drums pound, electric guitars often screech, and the beat is relentless. The singer shouts and screams in an often unmelodious voice, and lyrics are largely undecipherable. In rock of this type, the forms of love and sex referred to are often sadistic, masochistic, androgynous, and homoerotic. Anti-authoritarian themes preach hate, anarchy, destruction, and violence.

Macho rock exalts male virility that exploits female passivity. It is decidedly voyeuristic in its treatment of love and sex. Stylistically it can be country, straight-ahead, or heavy-metal rock. It is basically a hard-driving, no-nonsense rock that celebrates male power and sexuality.

Ambiguous rock is largely new-wave music. Its detached, unemotional tone suits its ambiguous message, which is marked by unclear ideologies, loose narratives, lack of resolution, vagueness of meaning, and a sense of alienation.

it could at once ridicule and amuse; by making protest enjoyable, it could simultaneously rebel and entertain. Protest might well not have been so popular if its musical and social forms—the former setting the tone for the latter—had not been so pleasing. In a way, rock allowed youth to have it both ways: they wished to rebel against a soulless, pleasure-oriented culture, but the means of protest were themselves hedonistic and dependent on the very economic prosperity against which youth were supposedly rebelling. A parallel example appears in the counter-culture's attitude toward individuality, protest, and dress. The jeans and T-shirts ubiquitous in rock culture were meant to be a calculated state-ment against the neat, uniform dress of the big bands, the cute pop stars, and the lockstep business world. Ironically, however, the expressive dress of dissent soon became a dress code in its own right—just as long hair, drug use, and promiscuity became expected "badges" of rock.

What does rock really mean? What are the rockers really singing about? If one knows the symbols, one understands the protest. Whatever the internal ironies of the rock protest, its importance as a defiant *gesture* of the outsider cannot be overstated.[23] Rock stars from Chuck Berry to Mick Jagger to Axl Rose of Guns n' Roses have all assumed the posture of the rebel and have asserted with grand overstatement that rock is not rock unless it is provocative, defiant, and dangerous.[24] As a vehicle for rebellion and protest, however, rock has been far more ambiguous and contradictory than dangerous and violent. More influence has been attributed to it than it has ever been capable of wielding. In retrospect, it can be said that rock fell short of inspiring the sort of political and social change it seemed to be calling for. Instead, rock became a safety valve for the anger, rebellion, and violence that seemed to lurk just beneath the relatively civilized facade of the American youth culture. Rock music may have served, and may still serve, to channel social unrest and latent violence in the direction of political passivity.[25]

One prominent band popularly linked with aggression and social change was the Rolling Stones. Although the band did nothing in

23. Ibid., p. 165.
24. Mick Jagger's actual statement is quoted in the 20th anniversary issue of *Rolling Stone* (5 Nov. 1987, p. 34): "The best rock & roll music encapsulates a certain high energy—an angriness—whether on record or on stage. That is, rock & roll is only rock & roll if it's not safe. You know, one of the things I hate is what rock & roll has become in a lot of people's hands: a safe viable vehicle for pop. Oh, it's inevitable, I suppose, but I don't like that sort of music. It's like, rock & roll—the best kind, that is the real thing—is always brash. That's the reason for punk. I mean, what was punk about? Violence and energy—and *that's* really what rock & roll's all about."
25. John P. Robinson et al., "Protest Rock and Drugs," *Journal of Communication* 26 (Autumn 1976): 125-36.

its radical heyday to discourage that image, by the late 1980s the Stones' celebrated lead singer, Mick Jagger, dissented from the widespread perception of their music and image and commented on the relationship between violence and political change: "I don't think violence is necessary in this society to bring about political change. . . . It's very hard to put your finger on what [the violence of the sixties and seventies] was about. It was a violent period. It didn't seem to have a lot of point to it. There was no great *cause* that was felt. . . . There were a lot of people who wanted violence for its own sake."[26] Jagger's point is well-taken. In fact, a recent study of the British pop and rock-music scene suggests that amid the rise of deviant behavior by youth groups and gangs, rock served as a channel for socially unacceptable behavior. Rock and punk and their derivatives became the arena in which, or the media by which, deviant social behavior, protest, and anti-establishment rhetoric were expressed and vented.[27] The music both encouraged and dissipated youth's frustrations about living in North American society. In other words, adversarial and nihilist rock became an effective opiate, at once providing a safe and ultimately inconsequential outlet for protest and filling the deep pockets of the opportunistic captains of the recording industry.

This failure of rock as protest music distinguishes it from the socialist folk-protest music of the union organizers of the 1930s and that of the fifties' and sixties' anti-war crusaders and freedom riders. Their music was expressively *un*-ambiguous, calling for clear decisions and decisive action. Although the music itself was not defiant, brash, or dangerous, the lyrics did arouse political passions.[28] By contrast, rock protest was often narcissistic, taking the form of anti-social and self-indulgent behavior rather than concern for social and political reform. As one commentator observed, "By helping to translate revolutionary opinions into rhetorical cant, protest rock [of the sixties and seventies] facilitated [merely] token opposition to the status quo."[29]

Regardless of actual social consequence, rock continues to emphasize social themes—sometimes with serious intent. At the present time, for example, the neo folk-rock music of Tracy Chapman, Suzanne Vega, Michelle Shocked, and Lou Reed shows genuine concern for social change. Such singers try to alert their audiences to such issues as economic injustice, political deception, and domestic breakdown. More-

---

26. Jagger, quoted in *Rolling Stone*, 5 Nov. 1987, p. 34.

27. Stanley Cohen, *Folk Devils and Moral Panics: The Creation of the Mods and Rockers* (New York: St. Martin's Press, 1980).

28. See Chapter 5, "Woody Gutherie: The Dust Bowl Balladeer," in Hampton's *Guerrilla Minstrels*.

29. Robinson et al., "Protest Rock and Drugs," p. 135.

over, rock musicians of all stripes often lend their support to charitable endeavors and their influence to social protest groups, whether the cause be the homeless or the rain forests. The "aid" concerts of the 1980s— Band-Aid, Live Aid, and Farm Aid—and the earlier Concert for Bangladesh sought not only to raise money for famine, flood, and farm relief but also to raise awareness of the political and social evils of the twentieth century (and, we might add, to clean up rock's "bad boy" image). Two songs from the early eighties are indicative of the nature of the protest found in rock music: the Rolling Stones' "Under Cover of Night" is a highly critical commentary on American foreign policy, and John Mellencamp's "Crumblin' Down" questions America's consumerist value system and the possibility of breaking free from it. Similarly, the 1988 album by the heavy-metal band Metallica, . . . *And Justice for All,* levels a serious attack against environmental pollution, nuclear war, and the decline of the American legal system.

Despite the media ballyhoo that rock's attention to social problems sometimes draws, and despite how prominently social concern is sometimes used to promote certain pop stars, the actual impact of the music on the attitudes and actions of audiences is difficult to determine. Most indications are that among audiences it is the music more than the message that counts. Crowds flock to protest concerts and benefits not so much because they are politically astute and socially aware but because they want to listen and dance to "that same old backbeat rhythm." During the performance of the rock band the Who at Woodstock in 1969, now deceased Yippie leader Abbie Hoffman climbed the stage to exhort the crowd to political action. After a short time, to the cheers of the approving crowd, Who guitarist Pete Townshend clubbed Hoffman offstage. Even at the height of the countercultural movement, the anthem of which was rock music, fans wanted music, not politics. In hindsight, it seems accurate to say that the Woodstock generation (and all pop-music fans subsequently) believed for the most part in the cult of fun and self-expression; rock was personal and experiential, not social and political.[30] Audiences wanted entertainment, not social change or even a prophetic voice. In sum, the protest of rock was and is more cant and rhetoric than substance.

30. See R. Serge Denisoff and Mark Levine, "Generations and Counterculture: A Study in the Ideology of Music," *Youth & Society* 2 (Sept. 1970): 33-58. See also Robinson et al., "Protest Rock and Drugs," and B. Lee Cooper, "Social Concerns, Political Protest, and Popular Music," *Social Studies* 79 (Mar.-Apr. 1988): 53-60. The "Woodstock generation" has been a ripe group for all sorts of sociological research, and their vehicle of communication, rock and roll, has rightly been perceived as a pretty accurate reflector of sixties' attitudes and values. See Mary Jane Earle Johnson's "Rock Music as a Reflector of Social Attitudes among Youth in America during the 1960's," Ph.D. diss., St. Louis University, 1978.

Usually what rock does is rant about social change without inspiring it. Rock frequently objects to the status quo without changing it.

Nevertheless, a faithful few rock performers remain committed to social change. Belief still runs high, especially among intellectuals, that rock and roll had, at least at one time, the power to actually change society by challenging the authority of the establishment. Belief in the ideological purity and force of rock still abounds. That common notion about the powers of rock is something Gary Trudeau captured in one of his *Doonesbury* comic strips. He spoke through Boopsie, one of his central characters:

> Rock & Roll is all about challenges to authority.
> So instead of B-1's we should be sending them U-2!
> Before using Stingers, we should hit them with Sting!
> Rock & Roll will set you Free!

What authority is Boopsie talking about? Any authority—parental, ecclesiastical, political, legal, military. Authority stands in the way of self-fulfillment and freedom; and if young people can't realize complete freedom from authority to "do their own thing," then at least they can sing about it and wish for it and protest its lack.

Whatever cogency and effectiveness rock and roll might have as an expression of political or social protest, it is certainly a powerful and profound expression of middle-class rebellion against the *cultural* authority of Western bastions of fine art and taste—and all the artifacts and privileges associated with them. Rock attempts more than anything else to break down the walls protecting "elite" culture from the savaging masses. It seeks not to build bridges but to destroy barriers. "Roll over, Beethoven," sang Chuck Berry in his audacious dismissal of the mainstream, elitist culture of adults back in 1956. The implication was that mainstream Western (read: European) music simply did not provide sufficient interest or meaning for teenagers in an industrialized, computerized, consumerist, post-romantic society. Rock music did—it was a fast music for fast times for youth caught in a staid and regimented society, a society to which the classical art establishment gave its blessing in exchange for economic support. Rock and roll gave the youth of America an authoritative and distinctive voice with which to challenge the authority of the gatekeepers of the cultural establishment.[31]

---

31. Classic 1950s rock and roll was viewed as a moral threat by various conservative "concerned" citizens, an economic threat by the established popular-music recording and sheet-music industry, a political threat by right-wing groups, and an aesthetic threat by the cultural elites. (See Hatch and Millward, *From Blues to Rock,* especially Chapter Three.) Even today rock music is perceived as threatening in all of these spheres except the economic: in rock music the industry has found the goose that lays the golden egg.

Rock and roll continues to challenge symphonic music, opera, art museums, Shakespeare and the literary canon, and even the pop music of the twenties, thirties, and forties. Although today's rock music is not so much feared as it is despised by the establishment, it is not loathed because of its occasional violence, its casual references to explicit sex, or its insistent defiance (*that* can be easily co-opted and marketed). Rather, it is despised because it subverts the authoritative hold that the middle and upper social classes supposedly have on mainstream American culture. In that sense, rock is protest that genuinely challenges society.

Rock as Healer

A music full of alienation, angst, and pseudo-rebellion can hardly be expected to be much good for anything—or so many parents and teachers say. On the one hand, rock has been thought to contribute to antisocial behavior and to express nihilistic urges. On the other hand, it contains enormous cathartic power to help youth deal with life's problems and contradictions. For whatever else it might do, rock does at times provide solace and define community—not particularly because it is rock, but because it is music. Today health-care workers and personnel managers have rediscovered what the ancients knew all along and what less sophisticated societies still strongly believe: music is a tool for fostering good physical as well as mental health. Music purifies; music is cathartic. The Greek philosophers taught their students the importance of making music every day in order to cleanse themselves of harmful emotions and attitudes. In Buddhist and Hindu traditions, long, involved chants are employed in healing ministries and in making connections with "universal energy sources." When David the shepherd played his harp to calm the mad King Saul, he simply continued a long, highly respected lineage of singer-poet-philosophers who recognized the relationship between music and human emotions and knew the therapeutic effect that music could have on the human psyche.[32] Music has always shown the power to penetrate directly to the soul, calming or arousing, communicating without words, often purging fear and anger and re-establishing equilibrium.

It is one of the misfortunes of our time that modern academic and fine-art institutions have tended to make music a rationally deter-

32. See 1 Samuel 16:23.

mined and revered fine art, an art which requires education to know and understand, an art which expresses only its own internal structure. A simple emotional music like rock and roll, therefore, has no place in the pantheon of artistic endeavor. Valuing music because of its mystical appeal, the sheer delight of its sounds, or its powerful healing capacity has given way to a rationalistic evaluation of the music itself—its melody, harmony, and structure—a cold, calculating examination severed from music's emotional appeal and cultural function.

Popular music, especially rock and roll, attempts to reassert the position that music once held in the lives of ordinary people. African-Americans, for example, have long sung and listened to the blues precisely because of their healing capacity. To sing the blues is to express emotions for which no mere words are adequate or accurate. Singing the blues is a little like praying—the singer looks for restoration, for redemption of sorts. The blues seem to acknowledge life's hurt and sorrow while purging the soul of bitterness and despair. In doing so, the blues affirm the essential goodness of life. As a descendant of the blues, rock and roll can in whatever form carry that same healing, restorative capacity. Writing about the TV series *Almost Grown*, which was launched during the fall of 1988, reviewer Elvis Mitchell claimed that the show was enjoyable "because it's built around something that TV series have never really acknowledged—the redemptive, life-affirming power of rock & roll. . . . [The show] is about people born at a particular time, who were the first people in America to have music aimed at them and created by them."[33] And in reviewing a new anthology of Chuck Berry's music by Chess/MCA Records, reviewer David Fricke points to "the trademark guitar sting and witty, often barbed lyric narratives with which Berry transformed everyday teenage life, the contemporary black experience, and the healing powers of music into unforgettable pop playlets." According to Fricke, Berry's simple, passionate music has a "continuing influence on everyone and every thing passing in its wake."[34] Indeed, Fricke hits the mark when he goes on to assert that music of all kinds—not just rock and roll—has the capacity to heal. It is the inherent capacity of any well-played, passionately delivered, authentically performed music—from Palestrina to Beethoven to Dylan—to move people who understand and feel its emotional message.

Of course, in order to heal people, music must be accessible, in a language or idiom familiar to its listeners. Rock and roll's claim to heal rests on its accessibility, and it certainly offers that to America's young

33. Mitchell, in *Rolling Stone*, 6 Apr. 1989, p. 31.
34. Fricke, in *Rolling Stone*, 26 Jan. 1989, p. 40.

people. For over thirty years rock and roll has provided a buffer between young people and the cultural establishment; it has channeled youthful expressions of anger and frustration and alienation; it has provided a kind of community ethos; and it has given youth a sense of identity and a pride of ownership in a cultural product created by and for them. In this broad sense, rock and roll brings healing.

But not everything about rock is restorative. Its special preserves of artistic symbols, language, and syntax can create disharmony and foster great suspicion between generations, classes, races, and nationalities. Rock and roll in particular has been associated with deviant social behavior and immorality. Explicit references to sex, drugs, violence, suicide, and Satan by heavy-metal and punk bands may be charged with irony, satire, and humor, but the irony is bitter, the satire vicious, the humor black—and the effects on an unstable psyche may be devastating. Many groups in the more extreme forms of rock seem to defy the very hope that rock might contribute to healing: a metal band struts the stage shouting "F___" and flaunting their sexuality; a punk band spews a nasty mix of fascism and nihilism. Yet these form a part of the baffling paradox of rock and roll: it mirrors the contradictions present in contemporary life more immediately and clearly than any other popular cultural product. It celebrates life and freedom but also wallows in self-indulgence and despair. It heals but it also hurts. Yet in its hurt, it purges; in its outrageousness, it affirms; in its excesses, it pleads for stability; in its romantic contradictions, it tries to make sense out of life's complexities. Great rock and roll—like any great music, really—brings joy, understanding, and healing.

Conclusion

No tidy fences can be put around rock and roll. A heterogeneous and visceral musical expression, its generic name seems strangely apt. Like the music itself, its history in American culture has been varied, vigorous, perpetually surprising, and profound. In rock and roll, subcultural strains in American popular music were intermixed, and this eclectic mélange became *the* mainstream music. Socially, the music has reflected, stimulated, and directed restless currents in American youth culture. On the one hand, it has celebrated the joy of carefree youth, full of sunshine, fast cars, spunk, and hormones. On the other hand, the music has been capable of channeling and perhaps fueling surges of deep social discontent, as it did in the youth rebellion during the Vietnam war era. In addition, this same music has been able to capture and speak to youth's very personal quests for identity, intimacy, and meaning. At times the music has proffered comfort, joy, and hope, even if only in romance, and at other times has seemingly counseled rage and despair at the constrictions of contemporary life. What its moods and lyrics have done, at least in the top songs, is to express and shape the confusions, angst, and dreams of generations of young people trying to figure things out and find their way into adulthood. The prime concerns of this book are the social and economic factors that make rock and roll what it is, and how one determines whether rock music has shed some light for teens as they make their way, sometimes dancing, toward maturity.

7. Rocking to Images:
The Music Television Revolution

The strongest appeal you can make is emotionally. If you can get their emotions going, [make them] forget their logic, you've got 'em.

MTV executive

Now look at them yo-yos—that's the way you do it
You play the guitar on the MTV
That ain't workin'—that's the way you do it
Money for nothin' and chicks for free

Rock group Dire Straits in "Money for Nothing"

When you get down to it, the only thing we have is image.

Tom Freston, 43, President and CEO, MTV Networks

On August 1, 1981, the Warner-Annex Satellite Entertainment Company launched the first full-time rock video network on American television—Music Television or, as it has become known, MTV. Company executives appropriately selected the premiere MTV video from a relatively unknown British rock group called the Buggles. Titled "Video Killed the Radio Star," the video's message and mood were far more important to MTV than was the Buggles' obscurity. After all, this was the channel that would challenge and conquer radio's longtime dominance of the teen audience not only throughout North America but also throughout much of the world. In a montage of exploding TV sets destroying vintage radios, the Buggles sang, "Pictures came and broke your heart . . . video killed the radio star."[1]

Like that first cable-cast music video, MTV's first promotional slogan, carefully selected by company executives, expressed the hopes of a new generation of video-minded business gurus: "You'll never look at music the same way again." As we shall see, the executives' aims were founded on more than dreams and wishes. By MTV's own admission, it was probably the "most researched channel in history." Initially, only 300 cable systems reaching 2.5 million homes carried the network.[2] By 1986, however, it was clear that the market research had paid off, because MTV and its imitators reached 43 percent of all American teenagers every week. In San Jose, California, a harbinger of national youth trends, 80 percent of high school students watched the channel, averaging over two hours daily. Half of the nonviewers offered a simple excuse: they didn't receive the channel in their own homes.[3] For the first few years of music television programming, several hundred local and a few network outlets struggled to repeat MTV's success, but only eight years after its debut, MTV had essentially vanquished all competitors. In less than a decade the channel had stolen teenagers from both radio and conventional network programming. By 1989, 47 million American homes received MTV,[4] and the channel turned some of its energy and capital toward capturing the world youth market.

The rise of MTV was a well-planned business feat. The initial impetus was the recognition that the recording industry was sagging. In the late 1970s, few artists any longer sold recordings with the ease and longevity of Elvis Presley or the Beatles. Record sales peaked in 1977 and 1978, when the soundtracks from *Saturday Night Fever* and *Grease* and Fleetwood Mac's *Rumours* album each sold more than 20 million copies. Overall sales declined from 726.2 million units in 1978 to 575.6 million units in 1982.[5] Young people still listened to the radio, but it seemed to the forlorn industry that music had faded as a potent cultural and economic force in the lives of North American youth. To the recording companies, MTV billed itself as the cure to its economic misfortunes: its

1. R. Serge Denisoff, *Inside MTV* (New Brunswick: Transaction Books, 1988), p. 54.

2. Jay Cocks, "Sing a Song of Seeing," *Time*, 26 Dec. 1983, pp. 63, 56.

3. Se-Wen Sun and James Lull, "The Adolescent Audience for Music Videos and Why They Watch," *Journal of Communication* 36 (Winter 1986): 115, 117, 123.

4. Bob Wisehart, "MTV Is Growing Up and Changing Format as Audience Matures," *Grand Rapids Press*, 23 July 1989, p. H-1.

5. Jon Pareles, "Pop Record Business Shows Signs of Recovery," *New York Times*, 28 Nov. 1983, p. C-13.

promoters boldly claimed that MTV could do for the record companies in the 1980s what radio did for them in the 1950s and 1960s.[6] The new channel seemed to work. "Nothing has rekindled interest in pop music," wrote the *New York Times* in late 1983, "as much as music video—the flashy combination of television commercial and trendy entertainment."[7] By 1983 record companies had become true believers and embraced the idea that their rock bands could get more "exposure per dollar" from videos than they could get by touring.[8]

Another indicator of MTV's well-planned genius was its use of every existing youth-geared form of entertainment. Instead of using film *or* recordings *or* television, it combined all three. MTV rapidly became the most synergistic of all teen media, integrating successful techniques from rock music, popular movies, and live and recorded television programming. MTV was a fast-driven, non-stop drama-music-dance-talk-variety show. In addition, it innovatively combined entertainment and commercials. Thus MTV was not so much a new medium as a synthesis of styles and know-how from many media. And it relied extensively on the same lures of other mass media—sex and violence.

Yet another stroke of genius: what MTV founders took from other media they then took to Madison Avenue. In the early 1980s, few advertisers could effectively reach large numbers of white, middle-class teens. Radio was still alive, but for years it had used local DJs to cultivate only local audiences for local advertisers, from stereo shops to water bed stores and dance clubs. Television had long since usurped radio's status as a medium that won national audiences—but TV audiences were primarily older. Only in the heyday of *American Bandstand,* Dick Clark's immortal Saturday-afternoon dance program, did advertisers have a good shot at a national teenage audience. But MTV changed all that. From the start, it specialized in selling and then delivering the younger teen audience to national advertisers. By 1982, 85 percent of MTV's national audience was between 12 and 34 years of age.[9] Boasted one of the network's creators that year, "At MTV, we don't shoot for the 14-year-olds—we own them."[10]

Before MTV came along, television was "aimed at the broadest possible audience and many adolescents [grew] increasingly distant

6. Denisoff, *Inside MTV,* pp. 1, 31-34.

7. Pareles, "Pop Record Business Shows Signs of Recovery," p. C-13.

8. "Rock Video: Any End in Sight?" *Grand Rapids Press,* 18 June 1983, pp. B-1, B-2.

9. Thomas Doherty, "MTV and the Music Video: Promo and Product," *Southern Speech Communication Journal* 52 (Summer 1987): 353.

10. Quoted by Christian Williams in "MTV Is Rock around the Clock," *Philadelphia Inquirer,* 3 Nov. 1982, pp. D-1, D-4.

from the mainstream focus of this appeal."[11] Listening to the radio, going to the movies, and collecting records —not watching TV—were "most associated with the extent of one's integration into the teen culture." Television put off teenagers largely because it demanded "that the individual be exposed within a family rather than a peer setting."[12] Moreover, youth-oriented TV was merely a hodgepodge of programs. As a result, youth watched little television during early and mid-adolescence.[13] By contrast, MTV offered teenagers a channel designed just for them, and it was always there. As one MTV executive put it, "[The] key to MTV is that you can watch for a while, walk away, go down to the store, come back, and you haven't missed anything."[14] MTV joined music, radio, and television in establishing national target markets, doing so in a way that would insure the likelihood of "generational disjunctions."[15] It soon proved a siren to the high-stakes media planners perched on Madison Avenue hot seats. Sociologist R. Serge Denisoff explains why: "By innovative conceptualizing, timing, and luck, MTV . . . tapped into the youth culture written off by the television industry."[16] Success was quick and clear: the network's ad revenues rose from $7 million in 1982 to $150 million in 1984.[17]

MTV's youthful executives, who grew up watching TV, shrewdly anticipated the expanding role of popular entertainment in North America's youth culture. Teenagers had long enjoyed rock music and had ritualistically flocked to movie theaters and drive-ins. Entertainment invaded nearly all areas of youth life—home, school, church, work, and free time—and increasingly shaped and reflected it. "Music tends to be a predictor of behavior and social values," explained an MTV executive. "You tell me the music people like and I'll tell you their views on abortion, whether we should increase our military arms, [and] what their sense of humor is like."[18] In other words, young people lived in the

11. Reed Larson and Robert Kubey, "Television and Music: Contrasting Media in Adolescent Life," *Youth & Society* 15 (Sept. 1983): 15.

12. John W. Johnstone, "Social Integration and Mass Media Use among Adolescents: A Case Study," in *The Uses of Mass Communications: Current Perspectives on Gratification Research,* vol. 3 of Sage Annual Reviews of Communication Research, ed. Jay G. Blumler and Elihu Katz (Beverly Hills: Sage Publications, 1974), pp. 41, 46.

13. Jack McLeod and Jane Delano Brown, "The Family Environment and Adolescent Television Use," in *Children and Television,* ed. Ray Brown (Beverly Hills: Sage Publications, 1976), p. 207.

14. Bill Barol, "The Sight of Music," *Newsweek on Campus,* special issue, Nov. 1982, p. 13.

15. Larson and Kubey, "Television and Music," p. 28.

16. Denisoff, *Inside MTV,* p. 193.

17. Bernie Ward, "Music Video Grows Up," *Sky,* Apr. 1985, p. 80.

18. Quoted by Williams in "MTV Is Rock around the Clock," p. D-1.

cultural trenches dug partly by the entertainment industry, and the founders of MTV knew that those trenches would only deepen and expand. Sociologist Robert Snow catches the dynamic interplay and interdependence of the entertainment media and the youth culture:

> The inescapable conclusion about the role of radio and television in youth culture and rock music is that they are inexorably bound together in a harmonious triad. Members of youth culture and rock music require and depend on these electronic media to foster and maintain the character of their music and life style. As such, media are seen as serving and symbolizing a sense of identity and community among like-minded people. The net effect is that it is difficult to imagine what would happen to youth culture or electronic media if either were to disappear.[19]

As we shall show, MTV eagerly and profitably inserted itself into the contest between generations. In its planners' self-interested vision, the marketable "good life" depicted in its great program variety offered consumerist identity, fabricated intimacy, and generational discontinuity.

As the nineties begin, MTV and its spin-off businesses, all part of Viacom, Inc., the successful entertainment empire, have become mentors for an expanding youth culture in North America and, increasingly, for youth cultures in the rest of the world. Potential MTV viewers are nurtured by the company's kid-oriented Nickelodeon channel, a hodgepodge of old network sitcoms, adventure and game shows, older and newer cartoons, and numerous other specials. Most of the daytime programming is directed at very young viewers; later every evening, Nickelodeon transforms its program schedule into a package of shows called Nick at Nite, which captures the older kids looking for a "halfway house" on their way to MTV. Like MTV, Nickelodeon has not put much emphasis on high night-by-night ratings or weekly audience stability. Its goal has been to initiate long-term viewer commitment to a channel designed "just for them."

Nickelodeon and Nick at Nite share MTV's values and sensibility. Early on they became parts of a unified world of youth-oriented television. That world includes a cynicism about the "adult" culture and greatly esteems consumption-based novelty and change. All three channels affirm a visual universe where seeing is believing and where mood and image are more important than narrative and dialogue (a point we will return to later). Moreover, these channels provide their viewers with a hollow intimacy and a shallow identity, both grounded in viewing the

---

19. Snow, "Youth, Rock 'n' Roll, and Electronic Media," *Youth & Society* 18 (June 1987): 332.

programs and purchasing products. These emphases are in keeping with Viacom's goals: to attract young audiences, keep them, and sell them to advertisers. In May of 1989 Viacom announced the launching of yet another new channel—the "HA" TV Comedy Network.[20] Presumably it, too, would serve advertisers.

Viacom's latest channel venture, Video Hits-1 (VH-1), has carried on, albeit rather haltingly, the rock-video "tradition" for the post-MTV audience. VH-1 is MTV warmed over for older "kids" in the 25-49 age group. Unlike MTV, which emphasizes irreverence, zaniness, and instability, VH-1 is meant to communicate comfort, stability, and friendliness.[21] Started in 1985 and frequently overhauled by a succession of new management teams, VH-1 soon became known as a "dumping ground for videos not hip enough for MTV."[22] In the late 1980s viewership declined, but Viacom continued tinkering with the format in hopes of finding a way of capturing older viewers who no longer watched MTV. In 1987 the channel was revamped specifically for the baby-boom generation, a move which held out some promise, given that group's insatiable appetite for music, movies, and shopping. The channel is visually more sedate than MTV and oriented more toward pop music than rock music. "If VH-1 succeeds," wrote one industry observer in 1989, "it will be because it can convey the rock 'n roll attitude matured for graying rockers."[23] In 1990 VH-1 was still trying to figure out how to make that happen.

This chapter examines the keys to MTV's success in North American youth culture. Along the way it draws heavily on the themes developed in previous chapters. Specifically, we will examine MTV's central commercial impetus, its consumerist ethos, its marketing of "video" intimacy and community, and lastly, the cultural consequences of its controversial "style." (One cultural consequence of MTV, of course, is generational discontinuity, something very upsetting to parents. Ironically, parents paid MTV's early bills. The channel was heavily capitalized by American Express, which plowed credit-card profits into the cable system.)[24] We believe that MTV's success will long echo through the

20. Bill Carter, "An MTV Comedy Channel," *New York Times,* 19 May 1989, p. C-14, and "HBO and MTV Begin a Serious Battle over Comedy," *New York Times,* 22 May 1989, p. C-6.

21. Erik Hedegaard, "MTV's VH-1: Music Video for the Housewives," *Rolling Stone,* 17 Jan. 1985, p. 38.

22. Jeremy Gerard, "An MTV for Grown-Ups Is Seeking Its Audience," *New York Times,* 7 Aug. 1989, p. Y-13.

23. J. Max Robins, "Into the Groove," *Channels,* May 1989, p. 29.

24. Denisoff, *Inside MTV,* p. 1.

One Hour of MTV

Morning of February 15, 1990

9:00:00   video: The Fine Young Cannibals sing and dance to the tune "I'm Not Satisfied" from their album *The Raw and the Cooked*. Key lyrics: "There must be more to life."

9:03:40   video: Legendary rock guitarist Eric Clapton plays and sings "Bad Love" while popular singer/songwriter Phil Collins plays the drums in this black-and-white performance video. Key lyrics: "I've had enough bad love/I need something I can be proud of."

9:08:10   promo: The channel plugs its own Sunday-night video program, "Unplug," which features acoustic performances.

9:08:40   promo: MTV serves up its own "Awake on the Wild Side" promo complete with sunrise images of African animals in the wild.

9:08:50   veejays: Morning veejays Jonathon and Lisa plug a new movie and play with a small ceramic dog. When Jonathon touches the dog's mouth to Lisa's, she complains, "You got dog on my lipstick."

9:11:35   video: Jane Child sings "Don't Want to Fall in Love" while sitting, standing, and dancing in a variety of locations. The camera returns repeatedly to her face, and the viewer sees the three delicate chains that extend from a ring in her nose to her ear. Key lyrics: "Love is just like a knife/You made the knife feel good/I'll fight you till the end/You have started sinking in."

9:15:38   promo: Rock star Neneh Cherry plugs MTV.

9:15:48   video: Young MC performs the rap video "Bust a Move," which shows one close-up after another of female dancers' undulating hips and bouncing breasts. The lyrics say that guys should "bust a move" on girls.

9:20:07   promo: The channel promos its own "Ben Stiller Show."

9:20:27   promo: MTV promos the upcoming "HA Comedy Network," which is owned by MTV Networks.

9:20:54   ad: A local advertisement comes on, hyping an upcoming professional wrestling pay-per-view program.

9:21:34   promo: The channel runs a promo for reruns of "Murder, She Wrote" on USA Network.

9:22:00   promo: The channel promos the upcoming Janet Jackson world tour, listing dates and places.

9:22:28   veejays: Jonathon and Lisa offer a childish imitation of Janet Jackson dance moves.

9:23:22   video: Janet Jackson, Michael Jackson's sister, sings and dances to "Pleasure Principle," imitating many of the dance steps popularized by her brother.

9:28:29   promo: The channel runs another safari-like promo for its "Awake on the Wild Side" morning program.

9:28:42   video: Billy Joel, singer/songwriter/pianist, sings and plays "I Go to Extremes" in a performance video. Key lyrics: "Darling, I don't know why I go to extremes."

9:32:43   video: The group Junkyard sings "Simple Man" while standing in front of an old Western ranch house in the middle of nowhere. Women magically appear on the ranch during the video. Key lyrics: "Lord, I'm a simple man/Ain't too much I need/Ain't asking for all of your love/ Gimme whatcha can and set me free."

9:37:07   promo: The channel runs yet another "Awake on the Wild Side" promo.

9:37:18   veejays: Jonathon and Lisa answer a letter from a viewer in California who wants to know such things as where MTV's main office is, where MTV veejay Julie Brown gets her clothes, and if viewers get free tickets for concerts.

9:39:15   video: The group UB40 performs "Here I Am." Key lyrics: "Here I am, baby/Come and take me by the hand/Ooooh show me."

9:42:28   video: Rock star Peter Gabriel sings "Big Time" while his face is transposed from one scene to another in a "claymation" video. Among other things, monsters' faces grow out of simulated earth and moss.

9:46:56   promo: Rock star Richard Marx plugs the channel.

9:50:59   veejay: Lisa sits alone at a desk, telling viewers about a newspaper article on aphrodesiacs. In the article one person suggests that sex requires only two warm bodies and a cold bottle of champagne. Lisa complains that that might promote drinking. After a hand from off-camera offers Lisa some bananas, she says, "Maybe there's other things you could do with the champagne bottle."

9:52:38   promo: Once again, the morning show promotes its "Wild Side."

9:52:43   ad: A local ad for auto shows at malls comes on.

9:53:13   ad: A local ad for a vocational school is featured.

9:53:45   news: MTV's hourly news show runs a few clips from films nominated for Academy Awards. That's the news.

9:57:00   promo: The channel plugs itself (so to speak).

9:57:08   video: The group Whitesnake performs "The Deeper the Love" on stage with an elaborate light show; interspersed with footage of their performance are scenes of a woman taking a bath. Key lyrics: "The deeper the love, the stronger the emotion/And the stronger the love, the deeper the devotion."

corridors of Hollywood, New York, Nashville, and wherever else the entertainment industry sets up shop. Films, TV shows, musical recordings, and every other entertainment vehicle will be shaped by the lessons MTV has taught to growing numbers of young media moguls in the expanding world of cable television.

MTV as Commercial Entertainment

MTV is often described as a television version of a rock radio station. This is partly accurate. MTV uses "veejays," the video counterpart of deejays; it plays the audio tracks of rock music recordings, most of which are played on the radio; it includes many short commercials, the economic lifeblood of rock radio stations; and it offers short news programs generally focusing on the rock music scene, just as rock radio's own news has been focused increasingly on the interests of young people. Like rock radio, MTV uses extensive on-air promotions to attract and retain audiences, and it alters its programming during 24-hour cycles to match the changing activities and moods of youth during the day. Both rock stations and MTV are principally in the business of playing "free" recordings that will attract teenagers for advertisers and help generate consumer demand for audio recordings. And finally, just as teens tune in rock stations primarily for the music, they watch MTV at least partly because of its musical component.[25]

Like radio stations, MTV has big sales at the heart of its commercial being: it unquestionably helps recording companies sell cassettes, discs, and records. Not since *American Bandstand* in the 1950s has a regular TV program had such an impact on recording sales.[26] By 1983, MTV was even able to sell a particular song or album in markets where it had gotten no radio airplay. Groups such as Duran Duran, Flock of Seagulls, and Stray Cats found commercial success in the United States not through radio airplay but through MTV videos.[27] Some successful artists, especially Michael Jackson, benefitted enormously from video exposure. The play of Jackson's "Thriller" video on MTV boosted weekly album sales from 200,000 to 600,000. Moreover, in the mid and late 1980s MTV's power to generate record sales spilled over into film. As one film

25. Sun and Lull, "The Adolescent Audience for Music Videos and Why They Watch," p. 120.

26. Denisoff, *Inside MTV*, p. 33.

27. Ibid., p. 117.

producer put it, "If you have a really hot soundtrack and you can get MTV playing it all day long, you're in business."[28] The success of the video-styled movie *Flashdance,* which was inspired by MTV, "brought all of the studios into the music video field," where they have since exerted a major presence with such movies as *Top Gun* and *Dirty Dancing.*[29]

However, MTV is even more commercially driven than are rock radio stations. MTV was born out of the belief that recording companies would create promotional videos specifically for the new medium, which the network could then use at no cost to successfully "pitch" recordings. Already in 1983 a Nielsen survey found that 63 percent of MTV's audience bought an artist's album after watching an MTV video featuring a cut from that album.[30] From the beginning, videos were intended to be the means to greater recording sales. The music video was not, from the perspective of MTV, a worthwhile production in and of itself. As one writer for *Billboard* put it, "Unlike all other forms, video music clips exist to sell a product. Regardless of their look, regardless of whether or not the artist makes an appearance, virtually all are advertising for albums and artists." Their sole reason for being was not art, self-expression, or entertainment but sales.[31] Indeed, rock videos started in Europe, where "conservative, government-controlled radio stations forced pop-music groups to seek exposure on television. Acts looking for spots on national TV shows . . . created and submitted videotapes of their performances."[32]

A major hurdle for MTV was to convince recording companies to spend from $30,000 to $60,000 to produce a polished video. The channel did so by eventually persuading the companies that video airtime was as valuable as sponsored commercial time. In other words, MTV persuaded recording executives that video time was equivalent to commercial time, that videos were, in fact, "free" commercials. As a result, promotional budgets skyrocketed for rock groups deemed by record companies to be visually attractive fodder for the video channel. Appropriately enough, most American rock videos were produced and directed by successful advertising personnel, not by recording artists, marketing specialists from record companies, or even people from the film business. Video directors were powerful shapers of video style and content, but they remained relatively obscure, like the directors of TV commercials. One critic argues that the commercial genealogy of rock

28. Quoted by Denisoff in ibid., p. 246.
29. Ibid., p. 247.
30. Doherty, "MTV and the Music Video," p. 354.
31. Laura Foti, quoted by Doherty in ibid., p. 357.
32. Barol, "The Sight of Music," p. 12.

videos dictates that they be called "rock promos" because they are designed to sell recordings and because they use many of the "avant garde" techniques of many broadcast advertisements.[33] So commercially oriented are they that MTV did not require recording companies to produce videos that necessarily had anything in common with the original audio track. Image and effect guided production philosophy. Like regular product commercials, rock videos are yet another device with which to sell to the public. "We refer to most TV as 'commercial' television," writes Richard Gehr. "Actually only MTV can lay claim to that title because that is precisely what it is: ersatz commercials punctuated by 'real' ones."[34]

Still, however commercial in intent and design, rock videos entertain viewers. The videos themselves attract an audience by satisfying some of the human urges displayed in different leisure activities, from attending films to listening to the radio to reading novels. Adolescents generally turn to television for entertainment, relaxation, and relief from loneliness.[35] In the wake of MTV, North American youth now listen to audio recordings as a means of rekindling the experience of watching rock videos. Listening to recorded music transports youth to a realm of moods and emotions communicated not by the music alone, as was once the case, but by its video on MTV. To put it differently, the musical recording and its promotional video fuse in the minds and hearts of teenage viewers. Like participating in a rock concert that frames a musical experience, watching MTV powerfully fuses recorded sounds to specific visual stimuli. The promotion and the product meld within the same entertainment experience. The video promo not only promotes the musical product but also shapes the purchase, use, and appreciation of that product.

Needless to say, since the advent of MTV, the rock recording industry has scrambled to take full advantage of MTV, because videos can play a decisive role in making, distributing, and selling their products. New rock groups receive contracts partly on the basis of how "videogenic" they are, while established artists, sometimes leery of the video concept, face making themselves available for videos over which

33. E. Ann Kaplan, *Rocking around the Clock: Music Television, Postmodernism, and Consumer Culture* (New York: Methuen, 1987), p. 13.

34. Gehr, "The MTV Aesthetic," *Film Comment* 19 (July/Aug. 1983): 40.

35. Jack Lyle and Heidi R. Hoffman, "Children's Use of Television and Other Media," in *Television and Social Behavior*, ed. Susan Lloyd-Jones et al., vol. 4 of *Television in Day-to-Day Life: Patterns of Use: A Technical Report to the Surgeon General's Scientific Advisory Committee on Television and Social Behavior* (Rockville, Md.: National Institute of Mental Health, 1972), pp. 181-82.

they have little or no control. As mentioned earlier, videos can sometimes sell audio recordings that might not get radio airplay or might not do well on the radio. This combination of promo and product, video and music has led many rock music critics and some artists to complain about the impact of MTV on the artistic integrity of the music. Wrote Jon Pareles in the *New York Times*, "[Rock video] shifts the role of the musician from creator to actor, and a video clip often costs more to produce than the song it is based on."[36] Furthermore, claimed scholar Lawrence Grossberg, by placing rock and roll still further into "the hands of commercial corporations [music television] increases the distance between the fan and the musician, and decreases the ability of both to control the production of the music."[37] "After watching hours and days of MTV," lamented one writer in *Rolling Stone*, "it's tough to avoid the conclusion that rock & roll has been replaced by commercials."[38]

The age of rock videos unites artists, media, and recording companies in a self-interested bond of youth-oriented commercial entertainment. "More than other programs," says E. Ann Kaplan, "MTV positions the spectator in the mode of constantly hoping that the next ad-segment . . . will satisfy the desire for plentitude. . . . MTV is more obviously than other programs one nearly continuous advertisement, the flow being merely broken down into different *kinds* of ads."[39]

MTV and Consumer Identities

MTV's success also resulted from the channel's careful cultivation of consumption-based teen lifestyles. Rock videos were, after all, only part of MTV's commercial entertainment strategy, which was to promote the purchase and display of consumer products. The aim of the channel's founders was to encourage youth to join a particular subculture that openly challenged traditional sources of authority and invited youth to join their "own" world of fun and games. MTV's carefully researched marketing concept sought to provide youth with a lifestyle, not just entertainment. Rock music was the entrée to the broader teen culture. Said Bob Pittman, one of MTV's creators, "I'm concerned not only with

36. Pareles, "Pop Record Business Shows Signs of Recovery," p. C-13.
37. Grossberg, "MTV: Swinging on the (Postmodern) Star," in *Cultural Politics in Contemporary America*, ed. Ian Angus and Sut Jhally (New York: Routledge, 1989), p. 257.
38. Steven Levy, "AD Nauseam: How MTV Sells Out Rock & Roll," *Rolling Stone*, 8 Dec. 1982, p. 33.
39. Kaplan, *Rocking around the Clock*, p. 143.

how people use a product, but what is going on in their lives. . . . When you're dealing with a music culture—say people aged twelve to thirty—music is something beyond entertainment. It's really a peg they use to identify themselves. It's representative of their values and their culture. You're dealing with a culture of TV babies. They can watch, do their homework, and listen to music at the same time."[40]

From its beginning—by design, not accident—MTV was a vehicle intended to bring youth beyond music to the heart and soul of consumerism. As Jay Cocks of *Time* magazine put it, MTV used music "as a marching band for materialism."[41] Added Lawrence Grossberg, "Rock videos are not only self promotion but advertisements for consumption itself. . . . [MTV] sells not only advertisers' products but lifestyles and a commitment to consumption."[42] Everything on the channel, from the videos to the game shows, from the ads to the veejays, was deliberately linked to MTV's own version of youth-oriented consumerism. Viewers were encouraged not only to watch videos, purchase recordings, and attend rock concerts, but also to participate in the culture depicted on the channel. American youth were offered a seemingly exciting and meaningful alternative to their restrictive and parochial styles of life—to stake their identities, who they were, on the acquisition of products, whether music, clothes, beer, or cologne. Material goods promised entrée into a magic kingdom of excitement, status, and well-being.

The particular success of MTV lay in the fact that it was geared to youth—those consumers most susceptible to peer pressure and suggestions about how to spend their time and money. In North America, teen life occurs to a large extent in the entertainment arena, where youth gather with their friends and try out various identities through fashion, language, manners, and other ritualized behaviors. American youth "consume" entertainment partly as a way of establishing who they are in relation to their friends. MTV harvested this pliable audience for advertisers, recognizing that a 24-hour video channel could shape youth identities more powerfully than old-fashioned rock radio. MTV told youth that *they* could decide who they were and what life was all about, and that the easiest way to do that was through consumption. It was a mentor unlike the others vying to influence youth. The video channel was dynamic, fun, and unpredictable. It established no moral obligations, required no educational accomplishments, and issued no parental

40. Quoted by Denisoff in *Inside MTV,* p. 45.
41. Cocks, "Sing a Song of Seeing," p. 63.
42. Grossberg, "MTV," pp. 259-60.

rules and regulations. MTV accepted all who had the time and money to buy into the lifestyles portrayed on the channel.

The founders of MTV clearly intended to exploit the ease and "indiscretion with which [youth] part with their discretionary income."[43] Youth are fickle but hungry consumers who follow carefully the latest fads and fashions. More than adults and younger children, youth want to follow current cultural trends because they provide maps to an ever-changing teen world. MTV's task was to create an attractive consumerist channel that appeared to be free of corporate control and parental authority—a station for teenagers featuring individuals their own age (or a little older) who could be trusted to tell it straight. The challenge within this was to cloak the hard sell, to make the pitch subtly. As one MTV executive put it, "You have to be careful that you stay this side of the line of being perceived by the consumer as a sell out."[44]

In order to shape consumerist identity, the programming format of MTV, from the videos to the commercials, blurred the lines between advertisement, entertainment, consumption, and leisure. "Music videos give the product a new location on the consumers' landscape," wrote Pat Aufderheide, "not as messages of a potential purchase or experience but as an experience in themselves, a part of living."[45] Thus MTV forged a stronger but less overt link between salesmanship, marketing, and promotion on the one hand, and entertainment and leisure on the other. The point was to make the commercial indistinguishable from the programming. "Once commercial reality becomes primary in daily life," explained Aufderheide, "the direct appeal to buy can be submerged."[46] To many teenagers, MTV appeared to be created for *them* rather than for the advertisers and the record companies. MTV even started its own record club, which satirized traditional record clubs. The message was clear—consume MTV's way.

The trick MTV used to achieve its goal of almost total commercialization was to make all telecast elements look alike. In short, MTV began to make its commercials look like rock videos. It peddled the usual products—soft drinks, gym shoes, chewing gum, jeans, and the other paraphernalia of youth—through "spots" that were a hybrid of typical network advertisements and rock videos. The ads used the impressionistic images of rock videos, which communicate feelings and moods more than rational or discursive messages. The images were

43. Doherty, "MTV and the Music Video," p. 352.

44. Robins, "Into the Groove," p. 25.

45. Aufderheide, "Music Videos: The Look of the Sound," *Journal of Communication* 36 (Winter 1986): 63.

46. Ibid., p. 63.

The Sayings of Chairman Bob

Probably no one put more creative energy into the development of the MTV network than Bob Pittman. His quotes speak for themselves. (Citations for the quotes are included in the text of this chapter.)

"[We're] dealing with a culture of TV babies. They can watch, do their homework, and listen to music at the same time."

"People in Podunk, Iowa, think [MTV's] more theirs than it is mine. It's a cult."

"Our core audience is the television babies who grew up on TV and rock & roll. . . . The strongest appeal you can make . . . is emotionally. If you can get their emotions going, [make them] forget their logic, you've got 'em."

"[MTV's mood] is greater than the sum of its parts."

"What we've introduced with MTV is a nonnarrative form. . . . We rely on *mood* and *emotion.* We make you feel a certain way as opposed to you walking away with any particular knowledge."

"It's the style, not the substance."

"At MTV, we don't shoot for the 14-year-olds, we own them."

"The only people who can understand the new way to use that television set are the people who grew up with it. . . . They . . . will accept almost anything over that screen."

"I think all the fashions and styles that are being introduced by MTV are just that—fashions and styles."

brief and rapid fire, often carefully synchronized with music. Even more than most TV network commercials, MTV's ads were often difficult to distinguish from the "programs"—the rock videos—themselves. Commercials were meant to be entertaining and fun, not dull or preachy. The sales pitch became part of the flow of entertainment on the channel.

Predictably, over the years MTV's on-air promotions have worked to reinforce the channel's consumerism. According to Howard Polskin, "Promotions on MTV enhance the network's identity, sell albums for rock stars, create a strong bond between the artist and the audience and promote good will among advertisers, many of whom vie fiercely to sponsor the promotions."[47] Many promotions have involved wild fantasies that have integrated rock music, the ostentatious life of rock stars, and personal consumption. One such promotion featured a "hedonism" weekend with rock celebrity Jon Bon Jovi in the tropics; another promotion offered a winner the one-day property rights to an entire town.[48] In one way or another, MTV's promotions have captured youth-oriented versions of the American dream of personal fame and fortune. On VH-1, the MTV for baby boomers, one promotion promised the winner a collector's edition of each of the 36 models of Corvettes produced annually by Chevrolet since 1953.[49] The Beach Boys wrote a song specifically for the sweepstakes' commercials. In return, VH-1 promoted the group's summer tour in 1989. The price of such promotion is high: the Corvette promotion alone cost MTV an estimated $5 million.[50]

For some young people, MTV became an attractive consumerist island amid the stormy and gloomy world of their everyday lives. Not surprisingly, youth who were unhappy at school were more likely to be avid MTV viewers during the week.[51] Everything on the channel was at once fun *and* commercial, and the way to the fun was through buying the product. Craig Reiss, news editor for *Advertising Age,* correctly predicted in 1985 that advertisers would "learn the same lesson that came with MTV—that in a music/video oriented show they are better off cutting a special commercial that fits in with the flow of the video imagery rather than cut that flow to go to a straight sell."[52] Pat Aufderheide confirmed Reiss's prediction. "Advertisers have been quick to take a cue from music video's appeal, just as the videos have built on a stylistic base created by commercials," she noted. Both equate "the product with an experience to be shared, part of a wondrous leisure world."[53] Few young people could afford to buy all of the trappings of the identity depicted on the channel, but the dreams and fantasies persisted—and still do. As the fashion director of one department-store chain admitted, "Kids see what the stars are wearing tonight, and they want to wear it tomorrow." Added the children's fashion advisor for J. C.

47. Howard Polskin, "You Can Win a Pink House—Or a Camel Ride in Egypt with Tom Petty," *TV Guide,* 5 Dec. 1987, p. 12.

48. Barry Walters, "Like It or Not MTV Lives!" *Village Voice,* 2 June 1987, p. 39.

49. Gerard, "An MTV for Grown-Ups Is Seeking Its Audience," p. Y-13.

50. Janet Stilson, "Latest VH-1 Promotion Puts Pedal to the Metal," *Electronic Media,* 5 June 1989, p. 29.

51. Sun and Lull, "The Adolescent Audience for Music Videos and Why They Watch," p. 118.

52. Quoted by Ward in "Music Video Grows Up," p. 84.

53. Aufderheide, "Music Videos," p. 62.

Penney, "Rock video is really driving the children's market. . . . Whatever the rock stars are wearing, kids are trying to emulate."[54]

MTV and Fabricated Intimacy

Television's success as an American popular medium results partly from the ways it has blended into the lives of viewers. Watched in the privacy of the home, and communicating most effectively the human face and its "personal" expressions, television has always been a rather "intimate" medium that creates for the viewer a sense of relationship with on-air personalities. This manufactured "intimacy" encourages viewers to like and trust its stars, from news reporters and anchors to talk-show hosts and soap-opera characters. Indeed, television more than other media fosters one-way "relationships" in which viewers have intense feelings about stars, often believing that the stars care about them personally. Sometimes this leads to neurotic jealousies and bizarre fantasies, many of them sexual, but more commonly TV's capacity for artificial intimacy—what we might call delusions of closeness—simply builds viewer loyalty to particular personalities, programs, and commercial sponsors.

Building on television's ability to suggest closeness, MTV helps entertainers to establish appealing public personas in order to encourage commercial allegiances. The channel breeds rock stars, especially veejays, whom viewers like and trust. Every day, around the clock, the channel makes "real" stars out of obscure people, stars who become commercial objects. As one scholar suggests, with MTV "the music business is increasingly incorporated into multinational corporations with diverse, trans-media interests in entertainment. The production of a hit song is less important than the production of the star as a marketable commodity."[55] From its earliest stages, MTV carefully planned to exploit TV's capacity for intimacy in order to make viewers feel like they were privileged friends or, more likely, voyeurs of these stars. "Tuning in is like dropping a quarter into a peep show," said one critic. "It doesn't matter when you watch because it's always the same and the only variation comes in who's doing what in which position."[56] In fact, the network's explicit sexuality more than anything else attracted youthful

54. Quoted by Denisoff in *Inside MTV,* p. 258.
55. Grossberg, "MTV," p. 261.
56. Walters, "Like It or Not MTV Lives!" p. 39.

viewers, providing a quick erotic blitz whenever they wanted it. As one study of the channel concluded, "Music video sexual content may have a decidedly adolescent orientation, suited to its audience; fantasy exceeds experience and sexual expression centers primarily on attracting the opposite sex."[57] The sexual emphasis is pervasive: a study done several years ago indicated that over three-quarters of rock videos depicted sexual intimacy, and over half of all women in videos were dressed provocatively.[58]

Whether or not the connection was sexual, viewers felt "involved" in MTV programming. This had been part of MTV's plan: the MTV executives knew that this sort of viewer "involvement" would mean greater audience loyalty, which would benefit recording companies and advertisers as well as the channel itself. In fact, within a year of its debut, MTV was receiving nearly 100,000 letters every month, many of them written personally to veejays.[59] Consistent intimacy was methodically crafted out of the channel's rather unique combination of "revealing" videos, homey sets, informal veejays, fantasy promotions, and local MTV tours.

Sets in particular helped create "a meticulously designed fantasy. The idea was to create a gestalt of comfy limbo, the basement or rec room of a family that cared enough to adopt you as one of their own."[60] The set's visual appeal, from dark lighting to rec-room furniture, established an informal, conversational atmosphere. Since the set looked as if it could be another room in the viewer's own house, the viewer had little difficulty feeling relaxed and open—and thus was vulnerable—while watching MTV. Once the TV was turned on, MTV credibly meshed with the ambiance of the typical middle-class or upper-middle-class household.

Within this homey setting, veejays were ready to relate personally with each viewer as if they were members of the same family. Veejays themselves were carefully developed "products." They needed "human faces that [viewers] could relate to," said one channel executive.[61] Also, it was important that they dress fashionably but casually, conveying a sense of informality while at the same time selling the

57. Richard Baxter et al., "A Content Analysis of Music Videos," *Journal of Broadcasting & Electronic Media* 29 (Summer 1985): 336.

58. Barry L. Sherman and Joseph R. Dominick, "Guns, Sex, and Rock and Roll: A Content Analysis of Music Television," paper presented at the annual meeting of the Speech Communication Association, Chicago, Nov. 1984, pp. 13-16.

59. Levy, "AD Nauseam," p. 34.

60. Ibid., p. 33.

61. Quoted by Denisoff in *Inside MTV,* p. 47.

consumption-oriented lifestyle of the channel. One MTV executive noted that early research explored "the way the channel should feel, the image, the style, what the Veejays should wear—should they wear suits, or punk clothes?"[62] MTV's overall goal, rare at the time, was to create the impression that the programming was a "live" experience being shared by the individual viewer and the individual veejay, both of whom were watching the videos together in the privacy of their own places. In fact, however, "the only live presence as the videos are being aired is the technical director at 'the uplink facility' . . . who sits at a console beside a Rolodex that lists the opening and closing shots of every videoclip and promo in the library. The technical director consults a playlist and provides a proper visual segue from clip to clip."[63]

Predictably, network promotions sought to enhance this sense of involvement by involving individual viewers in programming and with personalities. Eighty percent of the network's contests involved "putting winners together with rock stars for several days at a time."[64] As one MTV executive put it, "MTV was almost larger than life when we started, so we had to have grand fantasy promotions. . . . [They] mean our viewers are involved in MTV." Another added that promotions would "help build an emotional bond through the fantasies they develop."[65]

MTV's first major promotion was the "One Night Stand," which awarded the winning viewer a limo ride to the airport, a flight to a major city, another limo ride to a gourmet restaurant, and a limo ride to a local rock concert. After the performance the winner went backstage to meet the rock group. Then it was back to the airport via limo for the return trip home—and all this in one day. Another successful promotion featured a "House Party" contest, which offered winners a free party for 200 people in their own home. MTV supplied videos, veejays, food, drinks, and other "necessities" for a party designed to impress peers and strike fear in the hearts of most parents.[66] In yet another contest, the winner got to work for a week as a "roadie" on a Bruce Springsteen tour.[67] It was almost as if the obscure MTV viewer would suddenly actually *live* the kind of life depicted in teen films. These types of promotions generated mail bags filled with entries, but they were just the beginning.

62. Levy, "AD Nauseam," p. 33.
63. Ibid., p. 34.
64. Polskin, "You Can Win a Pink House, " p. 13.
65. Quoted by Levy in "AD Nauseam," p. 34.
66. Denisoff, *Inside MTV,* pp. 65, 87.
67. Polskin, "You Can Win a Pink House," p. 12.

In 1989 MTV actually gave away the boyhood home of rock superstar Jon Bon Jovi. The network bought the New Jersey house from the star's mother, who still lived in it, for an estimated $300,000. In the first two minutes of the contest alone, over 192,000 calls were made to the contest number by viewers attempting to enter. By the end of one evening, some 800,000 calls had been made to the contest number by viewers attempting to be one of the few callers who would get through the jammed lines.[68] All told, viewers made some 3.5 million calls in hopes of claiming the singer's house as their own.[69] In promotional spots for the contest on MTV, Bon Jovi told excited viewers, "This isn't just a house, man, it's the place where I grew up! It's my boyhood home, man. This is the place where I learned about the finer things in life. Like rock 'n roll. And women."[70] Bon Jovi's comments characterized MTV's goal of fostering quasi-intimate fantasies to capture the imaginations of young viewers. In one way or another, MTV promotions steered youth toward the people and products peddled on the channel. Intimacy enhanced the cult of rock celebrity and served consumption.

MTV also encouraged fabricated intimacy between viewers and the channel through "personal" appearances in cities across the country. During spring break, MTV broadcast from student-filled beaches in Florida; in this instance, the channel inserted itself into one of the major "fun" rituals of college-age teens in North America. Students who were unable to go to Florida could experience the beach parties through their "friends" at MTV. In 1989 MTV launched a forty-city concert tour called "Club MTV Live . . . The Tour." The stage and set for the live performances were designed to resemble the show's home set at the Palladium in New York.[71] Hosted by an MTV personality, each local performance played on the image and notoriety of MTV instead of the names of the performing artists, few of whom had any music on the national charts.[72] MTV's college tour, the "Museum of Unnatural History," combined new products and MTV in a shopping mall museum.[73] Other tours included the "MTV Headbangers Ball," which featured several heavy-metal bands performing in thirty cities, and a live version of MTV's "Remote

68. "Fan Wins Singer's House," *New York Times*, 31 Mar. 1989, p. B-3.

69. Jim Pettigrew, "MTV Network Strives to Broaden Video Base," *Electronic Media*, 22 May 1989 (Special Report), p. 12.

70. Quoted by Wayne King in "Fan Will Win Bon Jovi's Jersey Roots," *New York Times*, 28 Mar. 1989, p. B-2.

71. "MTV Dance Show Going on Road," *Variety*, 14-20 June 1989, p. 71.

72. William R. Macklin, "MTV Revue Misses Key Elements," *Grand Rapids Press*, 31 July 1989, p. D-8.

73. "MTV Dance Show Going on Road," p. 71.

Control" game show which toured college campuses in the fall of 1989.[74] These kinds of "outreach marketing" were usually combined with on-site sales of MTV-related merchandise, which were designed to further solidify the personal commitments of viewers to the celebrities and lifestyles associated with the channel.

In 1989 the MTV networks, which included MTV, VH-1, and Nickelodeon/Nick at Nite, signed an agreement with a company that manufactured "mass-audience interactive telephone technology."[75] "We're going into interactive in a huge way," said MTV's general manager.[76] The telephone was already an important part of the MTV networks' promotional strategy. On VH-1, a segment called "Album Covers" was designed to "flash the cover" of a particular album and open up the phone lines for viewers to "tell us what was going on in their lives when that album came out."[77] Although it was not altogether clear how the MTV networks would use the high-tech equipment beyond tabulating contest calls or viewer responses to particular videos, clearly the channels were far ahead of others in fostering audience response and involvement. One report suggested that MTV was planning a live show where viewers would use their telephones to determine the outcome of particular segments.[78] In any case, MTV had already mastered some of the most successful techniques for fabricating intimacy.

MTV and Generational Community

In commenting on the impact of MTV on the viewers' personal lives, one channel executive remarked, "People in Podunk, Iowa, think it's more theirs than it is mine. It's a cult."[79] Just a few years after its debut in 1981, MTV became an important part of the national youth culture. As one critic lamented, MTV is "a permanent, evolving part of the teen machine."[80] MTV executives geared the channel for youth, especially the lucrative twelve- to twenty-four-year-olds, whose tastes and values were at once reflected in and shaped by the programming. For youth, MTV

74. Pettigrew, "MTV Network Strives to Broaden Video Base," p. 12.
75. "Briefs," *New York Times,* 30 Mar. 1989, p. D-5.
76. Robins, "Into the Groove," p. 29.
77. Gerard, "An MTV for Grown-Ups Is Seeking Its Audience," p. Y-13.
78. Pettigrew, "MTV Network Strives to Broaden Video Base," p. 12.
79. Levy, "AD Nauseam," p. 33.
80. Walters, "Like It or Not MTV Lives!" p. 39.

publicly represents and embodies their communal experiences, moods, longings, and feelings. Pat Aufderheide believes that MTV has provided a kind of social glue for North American youth: "Music videos have animated and set to music a tension basic to American youth culture: that feeling of instability which fuels the search to buy and belong. . . . For young people struggling to find a place in communities dotted with shopping malls but with few community centers, in an economy whose major product is information, music videos play to the search for identity and an improvised community."[81]

Clearly, MTV has become an important force in an expanding national teen culture. By offering, nationwide, new identities and intimacies, however contrived, the channel largely transcends ethnic, religious, and geographical distinctions among American youth. Like college dormitories, MTV has little respect for the distinctive backgrounds of its inhabitants. In the world of MTV all youth are equal parts—consuming ones—of the same musically separate and visually distinct cultural landscape. Pat Aufderheide has suggested that music videos work to "abolish history (along with other real-world constraints), offering in its place a set of aids to nostalgia."[82] By nostalgia Aufderheide means that teens come to "experience" the past merely as a set of personal memories elicited by recognizable music and images; the past loses its force as a substantive determinant of the present or one's identity or fate within it. Without history, free from the shackles of tradition and the realities of the past, MTV has constructed "an atmosphere that causes an artificial sense of community."[83] From its privileged position in the lives of youth, MTV seeks nothing less than to shape the future of youth by replacing history with its own version of the world. By "encouraging recording artists to expand their creativity both visually and conceptually," one executive asserted, "the music industry can become the predominant art form through which the new generation seeks to express itself. We—music video—can monopolize the imagination of a new generation."[84]

The generation that MTV seeks to influence is the perpetual national youth culture. While not a community in any geographical or organizational sense, the world of teenagers resembles a community in terms of age, lifestyle, and prevailing ethos. MTV is the cheerleader for this new "community" of young consumers who dance to the same

81. Aufderheide, "Music Videos," p. 63.
82. Aufderheide, "Music Videos," p. 71.
83. Levy, "AD Nauseam," p. 33.
84. Quoted by Denisoff in *Inside MTV*, p. 117.

music, wear similar clothes, and chant common shibboleths about life. A senior vice-president and creative director of MTV predicted that "MTV will continue to feed off culture and to feed into it."[85] MTV is not merely in the entertainment business. The channel is part and parcel of the culture industry, paying close attention to the fears, dreams, and longings of teen lives in order to discern common threads of meaning and significance. Said a president of MTV Networks, "If its market position is to be a kind of window on the present of the music world, and the youth culture. . . . The biggest challenge is to really try and remain as close as we can on a commercial basis to what's going on in the music scene and youth culture scene that's new."[86] MTV's antennas in the teen world, the market researchers, constantly look for signals and tremors to use as bases for programs to win back "lost" viewers. As a catalytic cultural agent for a new, generationally distinct "community" of youth, MTV leads the way for its other channels that seek to do the same for children and baby boomers.

In the daily rituals of North American youth, MTV has assumed a prominent and competitive place amid film, radio, and music. Before the introduction of MTV—and its partner, the VCR—television viewing was a relatively unimportant activity for most teens. TV was associated with family life, and teens were much more attracted by other, more youth-oriented media than by the comparatively dull ritual of sitting in front of the TV set with parents and siblings. But MTV changed all that, and now it has joined radio, music, and film as an exciting and compelling focus of youth leisure and entertainment. Thus MTV exerts enormous power in its ability to dictate the youth agenda—what youth talk about, what they do, and what they deem relevant and significant in life.

To make sure it misses no one, MTV offers an entertainment smorgasbord: it supplies youth with a great variety of specialized programming. By 1989, in addition to the rock videos, MTV had created its own game shows, comedy program, and daily rap-music show. It was also planning a soap opera, a variety show, and a "lightning-paced" international pop-culture program called "Buzz."[87] Along with MTV's traditional rock videos, rock news, interviews, music specials, video countdowns, syndicated comedy, and other shows, the channel's diverse, innovative programming made it very lively and unusual. While most cable-TV networks were identifiable by the particular kind of

85. Quoted by Michael Freitag in "Judy McGrath: Television Executive," *New York Times,* 9 Apr. 1989, p. 38.

86. Quoted by Wayne Robins in "Video Woes: A Midlife Crisis for Music Television?" *Grand Rapids Press,* 23 Feb. 1987, p. C-14.

87. Freitag, "Judy McGrath: Television Executive," p. 38.

Watching More and Knowing Less

A 1990 study found that youth consume a lot of media but tune out the news. The under-thirty generation "knows less, cares less and reads newspapers less" than any generation in the past fifty years. They even watch less TV news than youth in the past, despite the success of cable TV's all-news channels. Also, youth today are far less interested in major news stories than were youth in the 1950s and 1960s. The study, titled *The Age of Indifference*, warned that young people are an "easy target of opportunity for those seeking to manipulate public opinion."

—*Time*, 9 July 1990, p. 64.

---

programming they offered—e.g., sports, news, or films—MTV was notable for its breadth of programming. Like a college campus, where nearly all of the public activities address specific student-interest groups, MTV's smorgasbord pitched itself relentlessly and directly to youth, and in the process endowed them with a common identity. And a large part of MTV's common ground—like that of the youth culture itself—was consumerist. MTV's offerings typified the consumption-oriented pleasures and preoccupations of the expanding youth culture, and thus the channel rapidly became the culture's own generationally restricted community center. If nothing else, MTV provided nonstop relief from the boredom of life. Commented a delighted teenager when his rural Virginia town received MTV on the local cable system: "MTV is new. There are not that many new things that come to Emporia."[88] MTV brought New York to Emporia. Almost overnight, teenagers across the country transcended localism by linking themselves with the distant but seemingly personal and sophisticated world of MTV.

While MTV's programming diversified and its own national community solidified, the channel reached for a global audience. By 1989 MTV was available in 24 countries.[89] MTV Europe, started in 1987, gathered 13 countries and 7 million viewers into MTV's increasingly broad community. Forty percent of the homes in West Germany were wired to MTV, and 33,000 viewers in Budapest, Hungary, joined the roster.[90] Meanwhile, the interactive telephone system promised to pro-

---

88. Quoted by Denisoff in *Inside MTV*, p. 291.
89. Robins, "Into the Groove," p. 22.
90. Sean Kelly, "Parting the Iron Curtain: MTV Europe in Talks with East German TV," *Electronic Media*, 15 May 1989, p. 16.

vide MTV's growing international audience with its own hot line to the channel's capital in New York. Global democratization, U.S.-Soviet détente, and the outbreak of democracy in Eastern Europe appeared to guarantee that the telephone lines would be used by young people in most technologically developed countries.

At the same time, however, it was not nearly so clear that the new world community, what Marshall McLuhan optimistically called the "global village," would genuinely advance the causes of peace and harmony. Thanks to MTV, youth in Emporia, Iowa, might indeed have more in common with those in Gedansk, Poland, but such a superficial internationalization could hide a growing separation between generations and a dangerous memory loss in the media-rich West. By and large, the real economic and political problems of the world received no attention from MTV. Even the gaps between rich and poor groups and between nations were largely invisible. What sort of political future might emerge at the hands of those weaned in the electronic community known as MTV? What sort of democracy and what visions of a just society could be fashioned out of the world of MTV? Given the channel's consumerist youth ideology, it is very possible that MTV might exacerbate rather than alleviate worldwide tensions.

Mood and Image over Statement and Reason

If MTV captures the interest and reflects and shapes the sensibilities of youth, as we believe it does, the channel merits serious adult concern. Behind all of the legitimate public expressions of dismay and outrage over MTV's incessant sex and violence lies a much deeper issue: what kind of adults and citizens will MTV produce? Can a world of beguiling, fabricated intimacy and consumerist identity ever break free of its own self-imposed generational limitations? Can MTV kids mature to assume their responsibilities in a democratic society? Is MTV merely a teenage fad or a harbinger of a new kind of mass-mediated society?

Many scholars and critics believe that the success of MTV foreshadows deep and wide-ranging changes in the broader culture. One of the few optimists about MTV, Sue Lorch, argues that "rock video is . . . the herald of a new age of human understanding, the signal of a new Weltanschauung." In her judgment, MTV "marks the large scale knowledge, the awareness in the collective consciousness, of truths heretofore known only to the academy and to a relatively small artistic community."[91] Michael Shore similarly concludes that MTV represents the rise of a new artistic impulse and aesthetic sensibility, but he is far more ambivalent about its repercussions:

> Modern art and culture have been about remaking, circumventing—or destroying—established traditions and conventions of narrative logic and pictorial representation. In a sense, rock video—with its emphasis on image and montage over genuine emotion—just may represent the ultimate triumph (or debasement, depending on your perspective) of this modern artistic impulse, or at least the assimilation of that impulse. Rock video is a popular medium, not an esoteric one. It has brought avant-garde attitudes and techniques into the mainstream.[92]

E. Ann Kaplan, most critical of all, worries about the fate of the audience's sense of history. "MTV blurs previous distinctions between past, present, and future," she claims. In her estimate, MTV "refuses to take up a secure critical position from which to speak." The channel lacks a "historical frame" and provides "pastiche" rather than real "parody."[93] Lawrence Grossberg concurs, focusing on MTV's propensity to manipulate mood and emotion at the expense of intellectual and moral substance: "The uniqueness of music television's communication is defined by the fact that the construction and dissemination of moods is increasingly separated from the communication of particular meanings or values."[94]

Kaplan and Grossberg offer convincing and telling critiques of MTV's own self-imposed limitations. MTV may indeed feature a popular avant-garde aesthetic, but the channel fails to provide any reflection on the personal or social effects of that aesthetic. As one MTV executive put it, "We told our production staff to throw out the rules. We want to develop our own spirit and personality so we will relate to our target . . . group."[95] Another one of MTV's founders stated that MTV was designed to create a mood which "is greater than the sum of its parts."[96] Appeal has been emphasized over substance. Admits an MTV executive, "What we've introduced with MTV is a nonnarrative form. As opposed to conventional television, where you rely on plot and continuity, we rely on *mood* and *emotion*. We make you feel a certain way as opposed to you

91. Lorch, "Metaphor, Metaphysics, and MTV," *Journal of Popular Culture* 22 (Winter 1988): 143.

92. Shore, *The Rolling Stone Book of Rock Video* (New York: Rolling Stone Press, 1984), p. 36.

93. Kaplan, *Rocking around the Clock*, pp. 144-45.

94. Grossberg, "MTV," p. 262.

95. Quoted by Denisoff in *Inside MTV*, p. 54.

96. Quoted by Levy in "AD Nauseam," p. 33.

walking away with any particular knowledge."[97] The result is what Grossberg calls MTV's "authentic inauthenticity," which "refuses to locate identity and difference outside the fact of temporary affective commitments." What makes MTV so powerful, he concludes, "is not the particular videos but its hip attitude, its refusal to take anything—itself, its fans, and the world—seriously, even as it appears to do just that."[98]

It is our conclusion that MTV is one of the most powerful forms of contemporary propaganda. By directly manipulating human emotion while hiding the strings, by creating an appealing, impressionistic mood that devalues logical analysis and rational critique, MTV gives young viewers what they want without clarifying what it is they get. MTV is proof of Jacques Ellul's argument that the most effective forms of modern propaganda are created to satisfy the desires and wants of individuals in mass society.[99] Such propaganda does not so much impose its "truths" upon people as it reaffirms existing attitudes, values, and beliefs. MTV's elaborate market research established the channel's own cycle of propagandistic communication; MTV and the youth culture are locked in an enormous feedback loop in which MTV responds quickly to the latest fads and fashions, trying to stay on top of what teens want while never questioning the value or propriety of those wants. MTV's goal as a propaganda machine is not open control of the *beliefs* of youth but the guidance of youth's emotional needs and psychic energy in directions that benefit the channel. Like a moral eunuch, MTV cares little about its emotional and moral impact on the teen culture and the wider society. It has always accepted teens where they already were—in the middle of a media world—and made them even more that way. According to E. Ann Kaplan, MTV has helped transform rock music's ideology of youthful freedom and dissent "into the new era of the 'look,' 'style,' [and] 'self-as-commodity.' "[100] The consequences are troubling.

One of the network's creators rightly described MTV as a "mood, not a show." He and other co-creators wanted MTV to be "irreverent," so they "messed up the set a bit," dimmed the lights, and accepted sloppy verbal delivery by the veejays. "We had to give [MTV] a rough edge," he continued, "because that's what rock and roll music is. . . . It's loud, distorted, irreverent music."[101] While this irreverent attitude has freed MTV from the programming formulas of traditional television and made the network the epitome of a popular avant-garde

97. Quoted by Denisoff in *Inside MTV,* p. 241.
98. Grossberg, "MTV," p. 265.
99. Ellul, *Propaganda* (New York: Alfred A. Knopf, 1971).
100. Kaplan, *Rocking around the Clock,* p. 54.
101. Quoted by Denisoff in *Inside MTV,* p. 59.

aesthetic, it has simultaneously locked viewers into an anti-critical, pre-intellectual, juvenile response to culture and society. MTV treats viewers like spoiled babies who "grew up on TV and rock 'n roll," admitted an MTV co-founder.[102] An MTV executive boldly proclaimed that the channel is "not linear, like normal television; we're not dealing with plot and continuity, we're dealing with emotion, which is an entirely new way to use that television set. The only people who can understand the new way to use that television set are the people who grew up with it. . . . They . . . will accept almost everything over that screen."

The MTV "community" is a remarkably shallow culture based far more on fabricated, mass-mediated emotions and experiences than on tradition, logic, and reason. "In MTV," said one of the channel's co-founders, "we're talking about dealing a mood to you. It's the style, not the substance."[103] Although some songs and artists attempt to make statements about life, politics, and the environment, the channel's carefully crafted ambiance isolates those statements from any kind of meaningful community discussion or debate. They have the same status as the glut of ads, promos, and videos, meriting no more attention or concern. MTV "evokes an intense euphoria, a kind of 'high' that partakes in an experience rather than responding to an artist's statement."[104] At the same time, the network thoroughly ignores traditional community life grounded in ethnicity, religion, race, or locality. Youth participate in the MTV community only indirectly through the marvels of media technologies, not directly as influential citizens. In this way MTV reflects the broader trend in North American politics toward propaganda and emotional appeal. Like the wider society, MTV trades community discourse and analysis for monologic mass communication, swaps discussion for passive experience, and bypasses reason for emotion. It encourages rapid, perpetual consumption, not reflection. As Richard Corliss puts it, "Each MTV video says: I got three, four minutes, and in that time my sights and sounds are gonna blitz your brain. The next video says the same thing, and the next and the next. MTV doesn't exhale, doesn't allow for relaxation. It's like a 24-hour dance marathon where no one's allowed to drop out."[105] In fact, MTV videos are carefully crafted for non-thinking consumption. Russell Mulcahy, one of the top rock-video producers, says that for a video to succeed on MTV, "the most important thing is

102. Quoted by Levy in "AD Nauseam," p. 33.
103. Quoted by Williams in "MTV Is Rock around the Clock," p. D-4.
104. Aufderheide, "Music Videos," p. 58.
105. Corliss, "The Medium Is the Message," *Film Comment* 19 (July-Aug. 1983): 34.

repeatability, and a piece gets boring if it becomes too literal."[106] One study found that music videos are "punctuated by rapid shot changes, averaging 19.94 shots per minute."[107] MTV combines "high-tech" electronics and "high-concept" visuals that flaunt montage cutting of music sequences, swish pans and flashy camera movements, dissolves between zoom shots, and rack focusing.[108] In short, it keeps the images changing rapidly and unpredictably.

Of course, it would be unfair to hold MTV responsible for the propagandistic plight of modern democracies, where the image-makers increasingly rule the political roosts and where mass-mediated public debates are increasingly vacuous. Our point is far less obvious and much more troubling: MTV is setting the trend for public communication and establishing a new metaphor for social life. Throughout the United States and increasingly around the world, MTV is transforming people's conception of and tastes in public communication and shaping their lives. "The effect of rock videos is insidious," sighs one researcher. "It doesn't require that the viewer be consciously aware, yet the videos influence real-life judgment regarding appropriate behavior."[109] Like the political image-makers, the MTV directors are nearly invisible. It is time to focus the public spotlight on the new image merchants to the youth culture.

MTV's most obvious impact has been on segments of the entertainment industry and the news media, many of which have adopted MTV's style, mood, and look. One of the most successful TV programs of the 1980s, *Miami Vice,* was originally conceived of by an NBC executive as "MTV Cops."[110] A director of *Vice* confessed that the show was written "for an MTV audience, which is more interested in images, emotions, and energy than in plot and characters and words."[111] Thanks partly to MTV, Americans are fed more and more kinds of entertainment that emphasize "disjunctures of time and space, odd interrelationships, connections without apparent channel . . . , synesthetic interplay, [and] a blurring of distinction between subject and object."[112] "High concept" films such as *Flashdance* (1983) and *9 1/2 Weeks* (1986), for example, used

106. Quoted by Barol in "The Sight of Music," p. 16.

107. Donald L. Fry and Virginia H. Fry, "Some Structural Characteristics of Music Television Video," paper presented at the annual meeting of the Speech Communication Association, Chicago, Nov. 1984.

108. Justin Wyatt and R. L. Rutsky, "High Concept: Abstracting the Postmodern," *Wide Angle* 10 (Fall 1988): 46.

109. Ned Miller, "Sex Roles in Stereo," *Health,* June 1988, p. 24.

110. Denisoff, *Inside MTV,* p. 242.

111. Quoted by Denisoff in ibid., p. 253.

112. Lorch, "Metaphor, Metaphysics, and MTV," p. 152.

increasingly rapid movement and emphasized fashion and style over message and narrative.[113] Similarly, we see more and more highly stylized, visually rapid commercials that tie products to particular moods, images, and feelings rather than to specific sales messages or rational product appeals. As Justin Wyatt and R. L. Rutsky have pointed out, "MTV, with its emphasis on startling, provocative and disjunctive images, has been a major catalyst for this convergence of advertising, film and video."[114] R. Serge Denisoff correctly concludes that the channel's success has "transformed many segments of the entertainment and news print media with its style, *film noir* mood and abbreviated span of attention."[115]

It might be, as Sue Lorch suggests, that the new video aesthetic can convey truths that are "inexpressible discursively."[116] Our goal in this chapter is not to attack visual forms of expression and to venerate the written word as the only possible conveyer of truth. Nevertheless, we seriously question how worthwhile the new commercial-entertainment aesthetic really is without a genuine community of self-critical discourse. The art world has long had its critics. So have the academy, the religious and theological communities, and even the general public. MTV and the youth "community" it fosters have little patience with critics and little room for them. As a result, the expanding world of MTV is evaluated only by those who have no voice within the community that consumes its products. MTV will permit the public to experience its moods and to see and hear its style but not to address the MTV "community" in any meaningful way about those moods and styles. MTV "is all about the death of context," says Richard Corliss. "It is the shotgun annulment of character from narrative, the anaesthetizing of violence through chic, the erasing of the past and the triumph of the new."[117] The new community has not only challenged the authority of others, but also, more profoundly, has rendered irrelevant the concerns and even the questions of communities that existed for decades before the use of music television. "If any one trope sums up the rhetoric of rock video," argues Richard Gehr, "it's that of discontinuity and disjunction. Gestures, actions, and intentions are nearly always divorced from a systematic context. . . . MTV is a context that seems to abolish context, removing the freedom of the record listener to edit his or her experience."[118] As Sue

113. Wyatt and Rutsky, "High Concept."
114. Wyatt and Rutsky, "High Concept," p. 45.
115. Denisoff, *Inside MTV,* p. 241.
116. Lorch, "Metaphor, Metaphysics, and MTV," p. 143.
117. Corliss, "The Medium Is the Message," p. 34.
118. Gehr, "The MTV Aesthetic," p. 39.

Lorch argues, MTV says to all of us that we are little more than "the art which we ourselves have made."[119]

Conclusion

MTV's first promotional slogan declared the response it hoped to elicit— "I want my MTV"—and North American youth heard the message. Decades earlier, a television advertiser had tried a similar slogan for hot breakfast cereal: "I want my Maypo." MTV's version of the slogan appropriately assigned the channel's teenage viewers the whine of children at the breakfast table. The "babies," however, were mostly between twelve and twenty-four years old and their "food" was hardly so nourishing. MTV is the tube's latest cultural gruel for teens of all backgrounds and beliefs. "Come unto me, all who are bored, insecure, and lonely," says the new video prophet, "and I will give you identity, intimacy, and fun. My images are attractive, and my sounds are catchy."

By its very nature, MTV can only temporarily soothe the souls of youth. Like much popular art, the channel has no anchor in a real community and little or no historical permanence. Not even gender is fixed: "male and female are fractured into a kaleidoscope of images."[120] Nor do the proffered identity and intimacy provide cultural depth and emotional stability. In turning youth into ever greater consumers, the network further erodes the social institutions that have formed the personal and collective anchors for so many teenagers for centuries. As an agent of socialization, MTV cares about little beyond the immediate needs of advertisers, the goals of the rock music industry, and especially its own financial condition.

In short, MTV has no cultural home. It struggles to establish its own traditions, but the marketplace is too fickle and the teen world too dynamic. Compared with earlier youth-oriented media, even the music and radio industries, MTV is caught in the wild flux of its own creation. Built on research and "high concept," the network is forever locked into the need for additional research, prognostication, and reassessment. It places youth on a whirligig of change that spins ever faster as the conditioned consumers scream for more speed and more "stuff." As the ratings swing up and down, as fads and fashions shift, as youth continue searching for themselves amid the rubble of modern society, MTV will

---

119. Lorch, "Metaphor, Metaphysics, and MTV," p. 154.
120. Aufderheide, "Music Videos," p. 70.

Consumer Reports Rates MTV

In 1987 the magazine *Consumer Reports* asked its readers to rate the "overall quality" of basic cable-TV channels. MTV came in dead last, even behind such unknowns as the Financial News Network and the Weather Channel. Not surprisingly, MTV was rated slightly higher by younger viewers. Oddly enough, however, MTV was one of the few channels rated higher by women than men.

—*Consumer Reports*, Sept. 1987, p. 551.

---

have to keep slaving for its success. If MTV actually met the deepest personal and social needs of youth, there would be little need for constant innovation or, for that matter, competing social institutions like the family and the church. MTV could raise the "television babies" on its own. Nothing would please the channel more, but nothing is less likely. MTV will be plagued by the same social instability and cultural flux that it has found so profitable to exploit and promote.

On MTV the individual has little worth except as a viewer and a consumer. One study concluded that nearly half of all "concept" (i.e., nonperformance) videos depict nihilistic images such as sacrifices, murders, self-destruction, brutality, theft, drug use, and skin punctures.[121] Youth hope for more, but all they get is a chance to tune in and to buy. Meanwhile, the products and styles change so fast that even the energetic, savvy, and wealthy cannot keep up with them. If consumption leads to nihilism anyway, what good is it? The despair evident on rock videos appears to be the fruit of the consumption portrayed on the commercials.

MTV is the most thoroughly commercial—and artificial—attempt yet to create an entire subculture founded on personal consumption. No one knows for sure what will happen to that subculture in the decades ahead, but there is little reason to assume that MTV will completely replace its competitors in the business of raising young adults. There will be more symbiosis and more synergy, more media and more ways to reach youth with the message of despair. Like its predecessors in Hollywood and Nashville, MTV must read the tea leaves of cultural change in a society where change is endemic. If it fails to do so, it may be dethroned, but it will not be crushed. MTV, like rock and roll, is here to stay.

---

121. Donald M. Davis, "Nihilism in Music Television," paper presented to the Mass Communication Division of the Speech Communication Association at its annual meeting, Chicago, Nov. 1984.

The problem with MTV is not that it mixes music and images or even that it must make a profit. MTV's plague is the same as that of the youth subculture generally—no sense of home. The network refuses to commit itself to anything other than consumption and cultural change, and these are hardly adequate bases for true community, meaningful identities, strong intimacies, and high moral purpose. Without a change of heart that brings institutional transformation, MTV will never enrich the youth culture as much as it will corrupt it. Its empty consumerism breeds nihilism, a bleak viewpoint perhaps reflected in its bizarre images of death and destruction. If youth need their MTV, they need still more a new kind of video network that truly celebrates life and gives hope. Such life and hope come with authentic community and true faith, not with a frantic consumerism, no matter how hard it rocks.

8. Looking at Teen Films: History, Market, and Meaning

While TV networks, radio programs, the music world, magazines and the world video all cater to the young, the strongest attempt to win the minds and souls of young people probably occurs in the film industry.

Dora Albert in <u>Variety</u>, 16 Jan. 1985

Teenagers love movies. For years now, roughly from the mid-seventies, ever-mounting box-office receipts for Hollywood's flow of products have shown exactly how much adolescents like movies. Not since early filmdom's nickelodeon and then the forties' and fifties' matinee fare have teens been so devoted to the cinema. In fact, the adolescent audience has been so eager and receptive that the last fifteen years have seen the emergence of a whole new genre, or a revamped set of old genres, specifically oriented toward adolescents. Indeed, the "teen pic" or "kidpix," as they have been called, have swept Hollywood and now, with no significant challenge in sight, continue to dominate the film industry.

Not only have teen pictures sustained movie theaters across the continent, but they have invaded and in many instances conquered the home. The VCR, a low-cost technological wonder, turns just about everyone's family room into an "entertainment center," a slightly smaller version of the shoe-box multiplex theaters that occupy shopping malls. An intensely market-sensitive industry, Hollywood has been quick to plunge into the home video market, and the results have been staggering. As much as the public still imagines the theater to be the prime showplace for movies, in 1987 income from video rental and sales was nearly twice the income from theatrical release (7.2 billion dollars

211

total, with 4.4 billion of that coming in rentals).[1] Those with leisure time but little money (the price of a ticket in a city theater is now about six dollars) can now bring home virtually any Hollywood offering for 99 cents (or twice that for a new release). In addition, for those who choose not to go so far as the local video store, cable movie channels such as Home Box Office and Showtime provide a virtually endless supply of old and new movies, many of which fall in the teen film category. The new Pay-Per-View channel pipes films directly into individual households for a mere couple of dollars (films that viewers can tape on their VCRs).

Given the huge adolescent appetite for films, it is no wonder that Hollywood is more than appreciative and eager to satisfy the teen market, although the major studios recognized its potential rather belatedly. In the mid-seventies the movie industry seemed to stumble across, accidentally or at least reluctantly, the enormous profit potential of the emerging teen audience. Astonishing profit margins convinced a conservative industry of the gold that lies in the adolescent audience. George Lucas's *Star Wars*, released in 1977, cost $10 million to make and quickly returned ten times that amount; some analysts suggest that its profitability over time is essentially unmeasurable. (Twentieth Century-Fox estimated that in the three years following the film's release, *Star Wars* toys alone brought in half a billion dollars.)[2] The well-known *Porky's* (1982), a high-jinks sex and vengeance romp, cost $5 million to make and has returned over $180 million. The first three releases in New Line Cinema's low-budget gore-and-horror series called *Nightmare on Elm Street* (1984), featuring Freddy Krueger, together brought in more than $100 million. In the summer of 1988, the fourth episode fetched over twice its production cost in its first weekend in the theaters. The profitability of the teen market is indicated by the additional fact that over half a million video cassettes of the *Nightmare* series have been sold—and that at roughly 60 dollars apiece.[3] New Line Cinema has also taken in close to $4 million in licensing fees for Freddy Krueger paraphernalia that ranges from masks to board games to bubble gum.[4] So large and potent is the teen market that 40 percent of Hollywood's annual profit

1. David A. Cook, *A History of Narrative Film,* 2nd ed. (New York: W. W. Norton, 1990), p. 898.

2. Ibid., p. 888.

3. Richard Corliss, "Did You Ever See a Dream Stalking?" *Time,* 5 Sept. 1988, pp. 66-67.

4. Aljean Harmetz, "Another 'Nightmare': A Studio's Sweet Dream," *New York Times,* 13 July 1989, p. 11.

comes from roughly two months of summer releases, all of which are overwhelmingly oriented to the youth market.[5] For example, the summer of 1989 saw the big-budget *Batman*, which cost $30 million to produce, take in $250 million, including $60 million for actor Jack Nicholson. Eventually the gross is expected to exceed $1 billion.[6]

The love affair between the American film industry and the American adolescent was not always this strong and constant. In the past, it was at best a sporadic dalliance. In the early days of the silent film, when the medium was new and fascinated everyone, adolescents provided a large chunk of the audience, but they were not catered to in any particular fashion. After the advent of sound and through the Studio Era, the "B movies"—which included formulaic Westerns, war films, and comedies—drew large audiences, including teens, but they were not being targeted. Even the kinds of films that appealed especially to adolescents were aimed at the whole family, and if adolescents seemed to like them more than others, that fact was incidental rather than primary in the minds of moviemakers.

This chapter will survey the emergence of the contemporary teen film as a popular art form within cinema, a development that roughly parallels the rise of rock and roll within music. The social and demographic conditions that gave rise to the music also provided the backdrop for the flourishing of the teen film. While the lineage and development of the teen film is relatively easy to trace, the great variety, appeal, and worth of these films present difficult interpretive and evaluative problems; those will be the focus of the last portion of the chapter. There we will briefly survey the prevalent teen-film genres and explore in greater depth the role and worth of two of those, the teen-experience film and the horror picture. This interpretive undertaking will readily demonstrate the complex interactions of the art-audience-business symbiosis that pervades and shapes the world of adolescent culture.

The wide spectrum of teen pictures, ranging from the therapeutic dramas of teen life to the diabolical tales of monsters and mutilation, gives cause for both hope and alarm. What is certain is the tremendous influence that film exerts in the lives of teenagers. Partly deriving from its great aesthetic clout—mixing as it does narrative, visual image, and music—its gargantuan influence upon the young cannot be ignored.

5. John Greenwald, "Shooting the Works," *Time*, 21 May 1990, pp. 64-66.

6. Jack Egan, "Hollywood's Numbers Game," *U.S. News and World Report*, 2 Apr. 1990, p. 40.

Puberty Comes to the Movies: The Rise of the Teen Film

During Hollywood's golden heyday from 1930 to 1945—what is commonly called the Studio Era or the Classic Period—the movie audience doubled in size, increasing from 31 percent of potential moviegoers to 73.6 percent. At the peak of this period, roughly 95 million Americans went to the movies each week. As Hollywood would soon learn, the composition of the typical movie audience had slowly shifted from urban working-class people to include the educated young suburbanites of the middle and upper-middle classes.[7] By the 1940s Hollywood had begun studying itself and discovered a departure from past patterns: those with higher income and more education went to the movies most often, and among that group young people predominated. Needless to say, that was great news for the movie industry. And the future looked very bright. After all, postwar prognostications indicated that in the years to come education would increase, income would grow, and the population would boom.

While all these happy predictions did indeed come true, unexpected problems appeared that derailed the movie industry's hopes. The decade following World War II was not profitable or promising for Hollywood; it suffered marked audience decline and comparative bad times. As the Cold War settled into a deep freeze and America looked for homegrown communists, the Un-American Activities Committee of the House of Representatives (HUAC) investigated both the State Department and Hollywood. The effect was at the very least a great quantity of smoke (historians still debate how much "red heat" there actually was in the film industry). In any case, public enthusiasm for film cooled. Worse still, anti-trust judgments by the Justice Department forced the major film companies to divest holdings of exhibition monopolies. Major theaters in large cities, ideal for premieres and publicity, were by law sold off. That in turn spurred a bidding war among theaters for exhibition rights. This new competition forced up ticket prices, effectively excluding the lower-income groups that had been the most reliable consumers of Hollywood's product. From 1946 to 1956, over four thousand big-city theaters closed, essentially abandoning the urban audience. In addition, the postwar baby boom dramatically curtailed leisure expenditures among the young marrieds who would otherwise go out to the movies. Staying home was simply more convenient and

7. See Robert Sklar, *Movie-Made America: A Social History of American Movies* (New York: Random House, 1975), p. 271; and Susan Mary Donahue, *American Film Distribution: The Changing Marketplace* (Ann Arbor: UMI Research Press, 1985), p. 29.

less expensive. And then there was television, an innovation whose impact on leisure habits and expectations is virtually unmeasurable. It came on the scene when the average North American might have had suspicions about Hollywood, and, coming as it did right into the home, it seemed to offer safer, nonsubversive entertainment. Virtually overnight, then, mainstream Hollywood found itself severed from its traditional audience and reluctant if not unable to tap the potential of the new youth market that the surveys had foretold.

Faced with an ebbing audience, Hollywood gambled with a number of different strategies to again fill the theaters. First came the musicals, most notably *Singin' in the Rain* (1952) and *The Bandwagon* (1953). The Western found fresh life with *High Noon* (1952) and *Shane* (1954), the former a disguised satire of the HUAC investigations. Acting on the assumption that audiences craved novelty and spectacle, studios improvised the cumbersome 3-D gimmick. Of the technical innovations from this period, wide-angle projection—CinemaScope or Panavision—proved the most successful, accentuating the difference between movie theaters and the small, black-and-white TV screen. Again in the effort to offer potential audiences what they could not find on television, the film industry began to loosen the bonds of self-censorship. Violent gangster films and *film noir*—a somber cinematic style that featured grim urban settings and themes of disillusionment and despair—became staples of the theater. Despite all these stratagems, movie attendance continued to dwindle. It would take some time and the emergence of a new clientele for Hollywood to realize where its treasure lay.

"Youth films" were not new to the Hollywood repertoire, but prior to the fifties, these films were always tutorials on how youth might fit into the adult culture. For example, films like *What Price Innocence?* and *Enlighten Thy Daughter*, released in the 1930s, were highly formulaic morality plays. As the titles suggest, they warned young women to flee from fornication and encouraged parents to provide their corruptible offspring with adequate sexual instruction. Between 1937 and 1947, MGM produced a popular series of Andy Hardy films that starred Mickey Rooney. While Andy invariably fell into confusions and predicaments, each film ended happily and, in case the audience did not catch the story's moral, with a lecture from Andy's all-knowing but sympathetic father, Judge Rooney (God was never so nice). In this series, as with the more gritty *Our Gang* series, teenagers were portrayed as lighthearted, innocent, and always respectful of adult authority. Although it was appealing and safe, the Andy Hardy series began to fade in the early fifties; an attempt at reviving it late in the decade flopped. Instead, other kinds of films were becoming popular. As a noted market researcher of the time put it, "It's all James Dean and werewolf stuff."[8]

Sensing something different afoot, major Hollywood studios devised some films that targeted a distinct youth market as opposed to the family. Before long, "restless youth" became a cinematic cliché: they were personified by Marlon Brando as a motorcycle gang leader in *The Wild One* (1954), angry and violent teenagers in *Blackboard Jungle* (1965), and James Dean as an alienated teenager in *Rebel without a Cause* (1955). Trying to exploit a developing trend, Twentieth Century-Fox cast heart-throb singer Elvis Presley in a slew of predictable movies, beginning with *Love Me Tender* (1956). These fell relatively flat, not only because Presley could not act but also because these movies simply recycled old plot formulas and stuck Presley in the prominent role. Westerns and Civil War movies, even with Presley starring, had little appeal for adolescents. Thus, in the fifties, Hollywood had mixed success with teens; for the most part, the road into the youth market proved elusive. Always looking for certainty at the box office, mainstream Hollywood preferred business as usual, employing its time-worn formulas to court the tastes of the family.

Nonetheless, a study done in 1958 by the Motion Picture Association of America showed that the percentage of people in theater audiences was inversely proportionate to age. Sixty-eight percent of box-office receipts came from those under twenty-five, while 19 percent came from those over forty-five.[9] Translated into economic terms, those figures meant that 80 percent of the industry's annual billion-dollar box-office take resulted from purchases by those between the ages of twelve and twenty-four. With still more baby boomers on the way, Hollywood again had cause for optimism. On top of that, this new audience was, thanks to television, far more visually oriented than earlier generations. It was also better educated and possessed more discretionary spending power. Despite audience research, however, it would take some time for mainstream Hollywood to tailor productions for the emerging youth market.

Part of the movie industry urged moviemakers to take a different tack. In its battle with television, Hollywood invested much of its money and creativity in the production of mega-dollar spectacles like *Ben Hur* (1959) and *The Ten Commandments* (1956). Exhibitors, on the other hand, sent moviemakers another message. Theater managers rec-

8. Quoted by Dwight MacDonald in "Profiles: A Caste, a Culture, a Market-1," *New Yorker,* 22 Nov. 1958, p. 60.

9. See "Film 'Future': GI Baby Boom," *Variety,* 5 Mar. 1958, p. 1.

ognized that teenagers were their best customers and began calling for more short films with specific teen appeal. Admittedly, those few teen-oriented pictures in the market did not draw the ideal tame audience that theater owners hoped for; reports included claims of "riotous conduct, police protection, slashed seats, and general damage to theaters." But more important was the fact that these movies filled the theaters and brought in dollars at the box office.[10] Nonetheless, the big studios continued to ignore the youth market, preferring to pursue their traditional audience by recycling old genres.

Into this gap between teen audience desire and Hollywood offerings leaped a number of small, independent film companies, and to those independents the first outright teen films were a major boon. Film producer Alan Katzman and disc jockey Alan Freed both capitalized on the rock-and-roll explosion by producing low-budget films that featured rock singers. Katzman's *Rock around the Clock*, released in 1956, is especially noteworthy. "By showing that teenagers alone could sustain a box office hit, *Rock around the Clock* pushed motion picture production strategy toward the teenpic," observed one industry analyst. "Its own history and promotional campaign provided a model fit to be imitated."[11] Katzman made each of his many films for under half a million dollars, and reportedly never lost money on a picture. By 1958, in a fundamental reversal of the traditional marketing pattern, 65 percent of Hollywood releases came from independents, although they were to be distributed by the majors, a trend that would continue to grow.[12]

Among the independents, American International Pictures proved the most successful and influential in exploiting the new teen market. Samuel Arkoff and Jack Nicholson formed AIP in 1952 and built the company around theater owners' need for short double-bill features for the drive-in circuit, which itself was a popular new format on exhibition avenue. An AIP sales director explained the company's motives and rationale: "We'd like to make nice family pictures, but we're in this for the money. If the kids think it's a good picture and the adults don't, that's all right. Seventy-five per cent of the drive-in audiences are under twenty-five, and seventy per cent of our gross comes from drive-in theaters. God bless the whole 5000 of them."[13] The beauty of teen films was that they could be quickly and cheaply produced: an AIP picture

10. "Teenage Biz vs. Repair Bills," *Variety*, 19 Dec. 1956, p. 20.

11. Thomas Doherty, *Teenagers and Teenpics: The Juvenilization of American Movies in the 1950s*, no. 3 in the Media and Popular Culture series (Boston: Unwin Hyman, 1988), p. 74.

12. Donahue, *American Film Distribution*, pp. 28-31.

13. Quoted in "Z as in Zzz, or Zowie," *Newsweek*, 5 May 1967, p. 61.

could usually be completed during a two-week shooting schedule with a budget ranging from $100,000 to $200,000. The picture usually reached the theater three months after production was complete. In a little over a decade, AIP made over 130 low-budget features for the youth market; from this venture, the company reportedly grossed about $250 million, with about 75 percent of that figure ending up as profit.

As this hefty rate of profit suggests, the executives for AIP were not stupid; they realized that, by standard Hollywood accounting formulas, their profit tripled the size of the production investment. And these men were not only economically shrewd; they also knew what kinds of strategies and stories to use to hook teenagers. AIP pictures were the result of extensive investigation into American youth. Executives received reports on teen culture from twenty-eight offices across the country. From this research, Arkoff and Nicholson developed a shrewd marketing strategy for teen audiences which they called the "Peter Pan Syndrome." The strategy was based on these assertions:

1. A younger child will watch anything that an older one will watch.
2. An older child will not watch anything a younger child will watch.
3. A girl will watch anything a boy will watch.
4. A boy will not watch anything a girl will watch.
5. In order to catch the biggest audience, the film must focus on the 19-year-old male.[14]

In film plots, AIP exploited the curiosities, sometimes morbid, and the fantasies, usually sexual, of the drive-in theater crowd. "As for tastes they rate action first followed by horror stuff, then rock 'n roll," Nicholson explained. "They like stories about people of their own ages . . . which automatically generates a need for new faces. James Dean arose from this requirement. While not a teenager, his appeal was to that age bracket."[15] In short, AIP pioneered the notion of the youth-oriented film.

In many ways, AIP remains the direct ancestor of many of today's teen genres. The company produced a host of movies focusing

14. Quoted by Alan Levy in "Peekaboo Sex, or How to Fill a Drive-in," *Life*, 16 July 1965, p. 82. Until recently the rule of thumb in Hollywood was that a movie had to attract the young male audience in order to be a blockbuster hit. In the late 1980s, however, several films scored big at the box office by drawing a higher percentage of females than males in their initial theatrical run: *Dirty Dancing, Rain Man, Three Men and a Baby, Cocktail, Working Girl,* and *Big.*

15. Nicholson, quoted in "Birth of an Action-Pic Nation," *Variety*, 17 Oct. 1956, p. 1.

on favorite teen topics, horror films, and an Edgar Allan Poe series. In the early 1960s, AIP launched a series of beach-party films that *Newsweek* described as "one long round of beach bunnies undulating to rock 'n' roll."[16] Most of the beach party films, such as *Beach Party* (1963) and *Bikini Beach* (1964), cost less than $200,000 to make, and several grossed over $2 million. As the times changed, Arkoff and Nicholson developed tales of social turmoil and student unrest. Films like *The Wild Angels* (1966) and *The Trip* (1967) sought to reflect "exciting social changes, crises, rationalizations and adjustments of society" in their depiction of student revolution, the counterculture, and drug experimentation.[17]

Despite the success of independents like AIP, the major studios continued to ignore the youth audience throughout the sixties. Avant-garde director Richard Lester and the Beatles, the decade's hottest rock group, brought a measure of respectability to youth-oriented films with *A Hard Day's Night* (1964) and *Help!* (1965), both produced by United Artists. Respected *Village Voice* film critic Andrew Sarris called the British group's first offering "the *Citizen Kane* of juke box musicals."[18] But United Artists was far more interested in the soundtrack rights to Beatle songs than in the Fab Four's potential on the movie screen. And instead of taking a cue from the success of those two films, the major studios continued to spend enormous sums of money on spectaculars that might prove to be smash hits, as *The Sound of Music* had been in 1965.

When the major studios did finally discover the youth market, its existence came as a big surprise. *Bonnie and Clyde* (1967), *The Graduate* (1967), *2001: A Space Odyssey* (1968), and *Easy Rider* (1969) were responsible for the first turnabout in box-office figures since World War II. These and other films like them clearly reflected the social concerns, values, and aspirations of the postwar generation in the last half of the sixties, and this group flocked to the theaters again and again. Suddenly the content and themes formerly relegated to the exploitation film became standard fare in mainstream movies. *Bonnie and Clyde* romanticized youthful Depression-era bank robbers into simple Robin Hood rebels; *The Graduate* depicted the toll that the spiritual and moral vacuity of affluent America took on an alienated student; the sci-fi *2001* wrestled with themes of humankind's origins and destiny in images that youth could understand; and *Easy Rider* exalted counterculture rebels while indicting the country's widespread social bigotry. However ennobling or serious these themes might be, for Hollywood nothing talked like

16. "Z as in Zzz, or Zowie," p. 61.
17. Ibid., pp. 61-62.
18. Sarris, "Bravo Beatles!" *Village Voice,* 27 Aug. 1964, p. 13.

profit. *The Graduate* was made for only $3 million and grossed more than $35 million after six months in the theaters. *Easy Rider* cost a mere half million to produce and worldwide grossed over $60 million. Mainstream Hollywood had finally gotten the message: low-risk, low-budget youth movies could reap fantastic profits.

Nevertheless, big-budget pictures could still make a lot of money, as did *Airport* in 1970. In fact, production budgets continued to rise throughout the seventies, culminating finally in the *Heaven's Gate* debacle that bankrupted United Artists in 1980. Michael Cimino's film cost in excess of $40 million, was yanked after initial release for recutting, and in second release closed out of the theaters after one week. Grosses amounted to no more than 10 percent of the studio's investment.

Throughout the seventies, a number of films made by young baby-boomers drew large audiences of baby boomers: Francis Ford Coppola's *The Godfather* (1972), George Lucas's *American Graffiti* (1973), Steven Spielberg's *Jaws* (1975), Sylvester Stallone's *Rocky* (1976), Michael Cimino's *The Deer Hunter* (1978), and Coppola's *Apocalypse Now* (1979). As discussed in Chapter Four, the entertainment industry's courtship of the baby boomers culminated in 1977-78 with *Saturday Night Fever* (1977) and *Grease* (1978), both of which starred heartthrob John Travolta. Next audiences turned to George Lucas's *Star Wars* saga and Steven Spielberg's enormously successful string of films, *Close Encounters of the Third Kind* (1977), *Raiders of the Lost Ark* (1981), and *E.T.: The Extra-Terrestrial* (1982). With the fable-like *Star Wars*, teenagers initiated a pattern of repetitive viewing, seeing a particular film two or more times. As a result, George Lucas's space western became the third top-grossing film of all time. "The older generation was mystified," noted Landon Jones. "Why see a movie three times if you get the message the first time? But that was precisely the McLuhanesque point: for this generation, the medium *was* the message."[19] The communal experience at the theater—visiting galaxies far, far away via extraordinary special effects or sitting ringside cheering for Rocky and the triumph of the American dream—was the message. For many teens, repeat viewings became a way of hanging on to a unique visual experience, and those numerous viewings became, in some circles, a status symbol to be reckoned with.

In 1984, another study by the Motion Picture Production Association showed that 54 percent of the movie-going public were between the ages of twelve and twenty-four. Moreover, 51 percent of those from twelve to seventeen went to a theater at least once a month, compared

19. Jones, *Great Expectations: America and the Baby Boom Generation* (New York: Ballantine Books, 1980), p. 139.

with only 21 percent of those over eighteen. Strikingly, the 24 percent of the public who were frequent movie-goers accounted for 84 percent of paid admissions. Thus, as a Los Angeles marketing executive commented in 1985, a producer wishing to make some money stood an excellent chance of doing so if he made a "film for people from the ages of 10 to 30." Market analyses indicated that these people were "not only the largest segment of those who go to the movies, but they're the repeaters who often go to the same movies two to ten times."[20] And repeaters became an important market ingredient, since they made up for the eroding attendance of the aging baby-boom population.

In general, the term "teen pics" refers to a broad collection of diverse and usually intertwined film genres that are designed to appeal to and capture that large body of customers called "youth," an audience that spans the twelve to twenty-five age spread. Teen-oriented films span the traditional movie genres. However, it is fair to say that some of the most popular teen films use elements of as many different genres as possible in order to "maximize" their audience appeal. Thus, a part of the appeal of a movie like *Star Wars* is that it includes elements of a wide range of genres, including adventure, war, western, initiation, romance, sci-fi, fantasy, comedy, techno-thriller, and horror. Nevertheless, few teen films are so expansive in scope, nor do such diverse genres often blend as well as they do in *Star Wars*. Few filmmakers have the creative capacity of George Lucas. By and large, teen films tend to ride one track or, at the most, two or three from start to finish. For instance, the film *Predator* (1987), starring muscle man Arnold Schwarzenegger, consists of combat and adventure with big doses of fantasy, high-tech thrills, and horror. That formula first worked for Schwarzenegger in the futuristic *Running Man* (1987) and was repeated in 1990's $50 million Schwarzenegger vehicle, *Total Recall*. A robotic version of the Schwarzenegger hero appears in the urban crime setting of the hit *Robocop* (1987) and *Robocop II* (1990). Sylvester Stallone is a well-muscled "war version" of the same hero in *Rambo: First Blood II* (1985).

In marked contrast, John Hughes's *Some Kind of Wonderful* (1987) employs romance, initiation, and comedy. A predecessor, *Saturday Night Fever* (1977), did much the same, easing up on the comedy but incorporating still another powerful track—the soundtrack, in this case the disco beat of the mid-seventies. In doing so, it paved the way for a host of other profitable serio-comic initiation tales of music-laden romance: the Broadway musical adaptation *Grease* (1978), *Flashdance* (1983), *Foot-*

20. Quoted by Dora Albert in "Youth May Be Wasted on Young But Its Appeal Is Showbiz Asset If You Understand What It Is," *Variety*, 16 Jan. 1985, p. 7.

Youth and the R-Rated Film

Every year Hollywood produces more R-rated movies than any other type. In 1989, for instance, 67 percent of movies rated by the Motion Picture Association of America were given an R rating. These films, which supposedly restrict youth from attending, actually attract teenagers. To the MPAA, "R" signifies a fair amount of explicit sex, violence, and/or profanity. To teenagers, who flock to these movies in droves, it means attractive adult entertainment. It appears that the movie rating system, designed by moralistic film critics to protect youth from questionable fare, actually attracts some young people to it.

—*Variety*, 29 Nov. 1989, p. 7

---

loose (1984), and *Dirty Dancing* (1987). The adventure tale was combined with initiation and comedy in sex farces like *Porky's* (1982) and *The Revenge of the Nerds* (1984). The redoubtable horror genre, the stuff of R-rated series like *Halloween* (1978) and *Nightmare on Elm Street* (1984), mixes terror, gore, sex, and initiation. That genre is played on with somewhat campy cynicism in "PG-13" horror films like *Gremlins* (1984) and *Gremlins II* (1990). And on and on go the seemingly endless combinations and mutations of genre, endlessly derivative and inventive, in eager search of the happy alchemy that will translate film stock into pure gold.

Life in the Teen Ghetto: Formula Sitcoms with Acne

A major genre within teen movies, sometimes called *the* teen pic, is the film about teenagers growing up. These films play directly to the primary adolescent quests for identity and intimacy, which are very often inseparable. While traces of such yearnings probably run through all teen films, this variety of teen film plays out its themes in the youth culture itself, utilizing it for setting, characterization, and plot. For the most part, as AIP discovered, these pictures do not require a great screenplay, great acting, or great direction. Consequently, they cost relatively little to produce. One screenwriter, perhaps somewhat jaded, described how tempting a genre like this can be: "It's easier because you don't need Redford. You need a bunch of kids, girls in tight jeans with ample breast works and some sort of thin thread of a story. . . . If you can design . . . a teenage film where they're watching somebody through a peephole . . . and there are enough car chases and enough Perils of Pauline and there's enough titillation for teenage libidos, you'll get [a studio to make it]."[21]

In any case, the Hollywood perspective is clear: adolescents have the time and the money that often deliver spectacular returns on minimal investment in low-budget features. The miniscule capital required for production and the "repeater" crowds for these growing-up films make them very lucrative for Hollywood studios. For example, *National Lampoon's Animal House* (1978) cost a mere $2.9 million to make and grossed over $150 million. Perhaps the classic in the genre, if such a term befits the product, was *Porky's* (1982), which cost $4.8 million and brought in $180 million; it became the all-time top-grossing Canadian-financed feature film. Another film of teenage rebellion, John Hughes's *Ferris Bueller's Day Off* (1986), earned Paramount almost $27 million.

Through adventure, comedy (sometimes farcical), and romance, these films of growing up dramatize the tensions of the adolescent world, focusing on the unchanging preoccupations of youth—popularity, identity, and the desire for intimacy, especially sexual intimacy. The greatest appeal of these films perhaps lies in the fact that they directly address and emphatically affirm adolescent experience. As rock and roll often endorses teenage experience by singing about it, these films endorse teenage experience by dramatizing it. They strive to tell the teen story using a set of criteria that teens affirm. In short, they validate the "felt ambiguity" of life as a teenager, those curious struggles that result from dwelling in a pyscho-emotional land between childhood and adulthood. The preoccupations of that adolescent world are not only publicly presented and acknowledged but also enjoyed and even flaunted, often in gleeful defiance of adult perspectives on such things as taste, language, morality, mores, intelligence, and maturity. Thus films like *Porky's, Animal House,* and countless others detail a long stream of "gross" jokes and gags about sexual appetite and assorted bodily functions. In these "stories," and in those focusing on wars of status and mating, struggles often indistinguishable from one another, many forbidden attitudes and behaviors are displayed, dramatized, and approved. The segregated teen ghetto is described and sanctioned—a public document is about them and for them. Often, that alone is enough to attract teenagers' attention and appreciation. As one historian of the teen film has observed, teenagers will "go to most any film about teen-agers."[22]

---

21. Quoted by Mark Litwak in *Reel Power: The Struggle for Influence and Success in the New Hollywood* (New York: New American Library–Plume, 1987), p. 114.
22. Doherty, *Teenagers and Teenpics*, p. 186.

Teen films generally use close depiction and drama, however predictable at times, to show what it is like to be a contemporary teenager, giving countless cues and clues on exactly how to be a teenager. In short, teen films offer a greatly varied smorgasbord of old and new ideas and values for self-definition and strategies for living. One critic suggested that for "teens in search of tips on language, behavior and all the right moves," John Hughes's *Sixteen Candles* functioned as "a therapeutic documentary, a sort of survival kit of '80s cool."[23] Put in simpler terms, teens learn what is cool and what is not, what is nerdy and what is not. Many of the films serve as a kind of primer or *ad hoc* etiquette guide on teenhood. Many adult critics have lamented the disappearance of "role models" for teenagers; what they really mourn is the disappearance of adult-sanctioned role models. There are few resplendent heroes in the mold of John Wayne or Jimmy Stewart. Teen films are still, and by their nature probably always will be, replete with characters for teens to emulate, but more often than not those heroes accentuate the unique value of the teen world in opposition to an adult world that is portrayed as more than dubious.

Troubled Lives and Troubling Films

Parents often protest the raucous vulgarity, sexual titillation, gory morbidity, and general superficiality of the adolescent world portrayed in teen films, and those are indeed legitimate concerns about real moral and aesthetic problems. The adult hubbub is aggravated by the screen personas and private lives of many a teen-film actor, whether Rob Lowe or singer-actress Madonna. As salacious or decadent as some screen roles might be, those are often surpassed by the unsavory notoriety of stars' alleged real-life roles; gossip magazines regularly "tell all" about stars' drug habits or sexual exploits. Of course, Hollywood has always had this decadent underbelly, which is reflected in all of filmdom, not just the teen film. Nevertheless, parents have cause to be more anxious than ever, given the rise in sexual diseases, some of which are fatal, and given the increase in and availability of drugs and alcohol, which can be addictive and sometimes lethal. Hardly any adolescent is likely to go astray because of a single film or even a host of pictures about the teen world, but teen films support broader social change that greatly—and legitimately—concerns adults.

23. Richard Corliss, "Well, Hello Molly!" *Time*, 26 May 1986, p. 69.

Troubled youth usually have larger problems than going to the movies. In fact, to a surprising extent, many films about teens, even those depicting drug use and promiscuity, are conservative in nature, ultimately advocating traditional sorts of values. Some very popular teen films have been cautionary tales about the pitfalls of life in the teen ghetto. *Less than Zero* (1987) offered a grim portrait of drug addiction amid the privileged youth of Los Angeles; and *Clean and Sober* (1988), starring Michael Keaton, depicted the denials and evasions of drug dependency in a harsh light. It should also be remembered that a teen audience frequently finds something very different in a film than do parents and critics. In one of the more infamous teen pics, *Porky's,* liquor, promiscuity, rebellion, and bad language abound and, indeed, are extremely repugnant. However, along with these elements, alarming as they might be, comes a strong tale about peer acceptance and community and a fight against bigotry and parental tyranny. While the film exploits and exalts dubious teen mores and values, it at the same time asserts another set of positive values, ones that to many teens seem more pertinent than explicit sex and bad language.

What critics and parents often fail to realize, then, is that teenagers usually see something different from what adults see in teen films. The films of life in teendom help give meaning, worth, and emotional context to experience in the youth culture, often transforming the mundane and drab routines of life into an exciting adventure. For many teenagers, watching movies about contemporary teen life in a suburban mall theater is like looking into a cinematic mirror. In these pictures the struggles of young people occur in the age-segregated world of high school and various teen hangouts. School serves a much more important role as a hub for extracurricular activity than as an institution for learning. Home is portrayed as a source of tension in the life of a teenager. Characters are drawn from the variety of social subgroups that form around particular interests and skills—athletic, academic, social, artistic, and so on. On the screen appear—in shorthand, stereotypical fashion— nerds and geeks, dumb jocks, "brainiacs," beauty queens, horny dorks, lonely maidens, and handsome studs, to name a few. The innocent, the shrewd, the strong, and the vulnerable fumble their way to self-esteem, relational success, and personal meaning, at least on occasion. When adults do intrude into this cinematic kingdom of youth, they usually prove to be hypocritical, idiotic, sweet but terribly out of touch, uncaring, or tyrannical. More often than not, plots revolve around a young person's search for identity and the desire for intimacy, social acceptance, romance, and sexual experience, which are exactly those issues that psychologists pinpoint as especially significant during the teenage years.

Sex and Capitalism in the Teen Film

A popular teen film starring Tom Cruise, *Risky Business* (1983), combines initiation, prostitution, and the marvels of free enterprise. Joel Goodsen (Cruise) is a high-school senior living in a wealthy suburb of Chicago. Because his parents have expectations of him that exceed his abilities, Joel feels inadequate and fears failure. He is haunted by sexual nightmares tied to his academic performance; admission to Princeton, the school of his parents' dreams, is highly unlikely.

While his parents are away on vacation, Joel decides to break loose. He begins by helping himself to the scotch in his parents' liquor cabinet, and works his way up to calling a prostitute named Lana whose sexual powers are equal to his daydreams. He is temporarily the envy of his friends.

But Joel quickly becomes embroiled in a series of unfortunate but comical events. The key event occurs when he takes Lana out for ice cream and ends up putting his father's precious sports car at the bottom of a lake. Suddenly he needs several thousand dollars to repair it.

Feeling desperate, Joel yields to Lana's imaginative suggestion that they turn his parents' house into a brothel for one night in order to get the money he needs. He invites Lana and her co-workers over and then invites his male friends, who have plenty of cash to spend. On the night that this free-enterprise scheme is in operation, a Princeton representative comes to the house for a personal interview with Joel. Joel's GPA isn't good enough for the Ivy League, the counselor tells Joel. But on his way out, the counselor can't resist the temptation of Lana's friends, and he subsequently revises his opinions of Joel. Shortly after his parents' return home, Joel receives a letter of acceptance from Princeton.

Although this film is in many ways a clever spoof, its tongue-in-cheek message is clear: He who is wise in sex and free enterprise will be successful in life. *Risky Business* both affirms the culture of adolescence and applauds the values and cunning of a successful capitalist enterprise.

A wide variety of films inhabit this category, ranging from more serious explorations of adolescent life to mindless exploitations of teen-age fantasies. Unfortunately, for every film that genuinely examines the challenges of adolescence, there are a dozen exploitation films that blatantly sensationalize their subject matter—"formula sitcoms with acne," one critic called them.[24] Capitalizing on pubescent daydreams and familial conflicts, these pictures all rely on the same ingredients: dirty jokes, crude gags, and especially the teenage equivalent of a home

24. Armond White, "Kidpix," *Film Comment* 21 (July-Aug. 1985): 11.

run, the sexual triumph. "They're basically about guys trying to get laid," explained Jeff Kanew, director of *The Revenge of the Nerds* (1984):

> When I became involved with *Nerds*, the script already had a party scene, a peekaboo scene, a panty raid, a food fight, a beer-guzzling contest. The studio's instruction to me was "Give us *Animal House*." I gave it to them but tried to layer it with some humanity and real characters. I didn't think anything was tasteless as long as it was funny.[25]

A veritable host of movies supplied, and resupplied, simple cheap thrills for box-office lure: *Porky's* (1982), *Porky's II: The Next Day* (1983), *Porky's Revenge* (1985), *Private Lessons* (1981), *Private School* (1983), *Zapped!* (1982), *My Tutor* (1983), *Spring Break* (1983), *Mischief* (1985)—the list goes on *ad infinitum*. Most of these films were resolutely vulgar and, at that, mediocre, either derivative (at best) or baldly repetitious (witness the two sequels to *Porky's*).

The Better of the Teen Films

Still, a few films in these fanciful chronicles of teen life transcended the hackneyed limits of genre in treating high-school culture and adolescent experience. The first notable exception, a landmark film about high school and contemporary adolescence, was United Artists' *Fast Times at Ridgemont High* (1983). Writer Cameron Crowe spent a year undercover posing as a senior student in a southern California high school before writing a book and then the screenplay for the movie. Many of Crowe's characters were actually composites of several people he befriended at Clairemont High School in San Diego in 1979. Some members of the graduating class of that year were upset by stereotypical treatments, others were angered at close facsimiles, and still others considered the story and characters on the mark. As the ten-year reunion for the class approached, one former student commented, "Cameron did portray me accurately in the film, though it sort of stereotyped cheerleaders—and everyone else. But I liked the movie a lot overall; . . . he did a good job showing what high school life is really like."[26] One of the things that Crowe observed and translated effectively to the screen was the fact that, despite the affluence of the students' families, the students still main-

---

25. Kanew, quoted by Gerald Clarke in "And *Animal House* Begat . . . ," *Time*, 15 Apr. 1985, p. 103.

26. Quoted by Jamie Reno in "Ridgemont Redux," *Premiere*, 25 Sept. 1989, p. 24.

tained part-time jobs to pay for their consumerist lifestyles. As one might expect, this altered socio-economic reality changed teen hangouts. Instead of the malt shop or the drive-in burger stand of the fifties, the shopping mall was now the new center of extracurricular life, a teen home-away-from-home utopia with an abundant source of part-time jobs, amusements, multi-screen theaters, restaurants, and retail stores. The film's documentary-like style and realistic teen setting and social portrait soon made *Fast Times* the benchmark in the teen-film genre. United Artists earned almost $16 million in domestic rentals against production costs of about $9 million.

The plot follows a teenage girl's quest for intimacy in an age-segregated world of peer advice, useless classes, and part-time jobs, reflecting real adolescent life and issues. A rock soundtrack provides continuous background music. Subplots involve a series of sexual misadventures that expose the adult-like facades that effectively cover the tender emotions and uncertainties of teens as they struggle for identity and peer acceptance. As one reviewer notes, "What makes it appealing (yet may upset some parents) is that the kids rely on one another," pretty much excluding traditional authority and counsel:

> They've gained independence from the adults at home. The kids are there to catch each other after the falls, and to console each other—they function as parents for each other.
>
> It's not surprising that the movie is a success: for the kids in the audience, the feeling of being in an autonomous world of high-school kids must be wonderful. . . . The world of this film is a kids' network, where their choices, whether surfing or studying or just getting stoned, aren't judged.[27]

While *Fast Times*, directed by Amy Heckerling, shows the awkwardness and pitfalls of teenage sex, it nonetheless ignores some of the larger difficult realities of teen life. When one character becomes pregnant, she rather simply procures an abortion. The decision is devoid of religious, ethical, and medical considerations—those larger issues that lie beyond the usual scope of adolescent investigation. The film presents abortion as a convenient means of overcoming an unexpected and unfortunate happenstance in the sexual pilgrimage. Nevertheless, there is a suggestion of right and wrong: the father of the unborn child is ridiculed for reneging on his promise to pay half of the fee charged by the abortion clinic.

Cameron Crowe's teen classic was followed by a series of mov-

---

27. Pauline Kael, "The Current Cinema: Rice Krispies," *New Yorker*, 1 Nov. 1982, p. 146.

ies by writer-director-producer John Hughes, whose work has combined social realism with psychological insight. Hughes's productions have regularly starred various members of the "brat pack," a group of young actors and actresses cast repeatedly in Hollywood's outpouring of teen films in the 1980s. In the mold of *Fast Times*, Hughes's pictures have focused on the emotional and social struggles of the middle-class suburban teenagers who went to see the pictures, often several times. The films have assumed a kind of classic status and remain popular at teenage "video parties."

Sixteen Candles (1984) is a lighthearted comedy about a teenage girl who struggles with family, high-school social life, and her own appearance and emotions. In *The Breakfast Club* (1985), teens from diverse social strata spend a Saturday at school in detention and share common struggles over strained relationships with absentee or overbearing parents. The characters are clearly stereotypes, but they are convincing and strike lively chords of wonder and reflection in young audiences. In an interview, one recent high-school graduate commented that she liked to analyze things in movies like this: "How would I be in that situation? I always do that. How am I different from that person? Who do I know that would play that role? Or you want to be like someone. Like in *Breakfast Club*." Hughes's *Pretty in Pink* (1986) also invites reflection by focusing on social and emotional tensions and the adolescent cruelty that results from young people coming to terms with their different socioeconomic backgrounds in the same social setting.

Hughes's success has to do with both the stars he chooses and the world he creates. All three of these Hughes films starred teen princess Molly Ringwald. For Hughes and for countless others, the young actress somehow typified average middle-class suburban teens. Ringwald, said one reviewer, "mines the emotional convulsions that make every teenager feel he or she is the first lonely explorer on the dark side of the moon." About Hughes, *Time* film critic Richard Corliss wrote that at thirty-six,

> he provides no adult's-eye view of teen problems. Instead, he gets spookily in sync with the swooning narcissism of adolescence: that teachers are torturers, that parents are sweet but don't quite understand, that friends and lovers are two distinct species, one domestic, one alien, that I feel all these things I can never express, that there must be someone out there who will love me to pieces. Hughes gives teens what they want in life and movies: romance, passion, pleasure, commitment—and a little sex. His pictures are like teen psycho-therapy with guaranteed happy endings.[28]

28. Corliss, "Well, Hello Molly!" p. 67.

Movie Identification Quiz #1

DESCRIPTION: The bosomy blonde begs and screams. The hero watches, smiling, relishing. Clamped flat in an iron sling, spread-eagled, the blonde is lowered, slowly, horrified, over a cauldron of boiling lava. Repeatedly the camera cuts between the hero's leer and the lady's terror. And this scene is an encore.

Earlier, with like relish, drawing out their torture even more than that of the blonde, the villains lowered a boy in the sling—while the audience watched his excised, fearstruck heart beat ever more furiously as he sank toward the lava. The sling returned empty. These scenes, like the movie as a whole, come amply stocked with implements of torture: whips, chains, knives, spiders, potions. Body parts and blood abound.

Sex and violence, violence and sex—they are brewed up together with a titillating mix of voodoo dolls, magic rocks, and blood drinking. Nice stuff. This does not emerge from the commercial sewers of kiddie or hardcore porn. A PG film, it is, according to the rating code, acceptable for kids about eight and older.

IDENTIFICATION: Steven Spielberg's *Indiana Jones and the Temple of Doom* (1984) ranks eighth in all-time box-office receipts, right behind *Raiders of the Lost Ark* (1981), the first in Spielberg's trilogy of tales of fear, pain, horror, and black magic. Full of snakes, knives, burnings, and Nazis, the plot of *Raiders* features the rather implausible notion that Hitler wanted to find the lost Jewish Ark of the Covenant so he could use its supposed occult powers to further his anti-Jewish cause. The third offering in this series, *Indiana Jones and the Last Crusade* (1989), follows Jones and his father in their quest to locate the Holy Grail, the cup from which Christ drank at the Last Supper. Again, the morality informing Christianity, the truth of which is indicated by the quest itself, is not honored by either Spielberg or his main characters.

Although perhaps somewhat harsh in his judgment, Corliss nonetheless catches some of the flavor of Hughes's world and how and why it appeals to its teen audiences. Hughes's art seems to work because he so adeptly packs so much into his simple but searching serio-comic tales of the psycho-social landscape of contemporary adolescence.

Probably the freshest of Hughes's films, and the quintessential film about teendom, is *Ferris Bueller's Day Off* (1986). In this movie Hughes works within the conventions of the teen-film formula, summarizing its central themes, but changes its angle of vision so that *Ferris Bueller* avoids the witless repetition and clichés common to the genre. As the title suggests, the key to it all is the character of Ferris Bueller, an upper-middle-class high-school senior living in a posh Chicago suburb.

Ferris is a happy and zestful rebel who, in his clever antics, mixes teen bravado with a winsome affection for adolescence and his peers. Hughes turns the film into a frolic, full of whimsy and fun, making it an elaborate and at times surreal improvisation of what life might be and should be like. On the day the movie documents, Ferris decides to play hooky. Ferris, after all, feels trapped, bound mind and foot by the silly banality and coercion of the American high school, which is deftly satirized in the film. Ferris readily sees through the false deference, necessity, and baloney that characterize the relations between authority, learning, and studenthood. His insight accounts for both his plight and his appeal. Seventeen going on seventy, Ferris knows what the adult world is like, and he knows too that he is on the verge of passing irretrievably into that realm where everyone thinks pure hokum is the good, normal, serious stuff of living. So Bueller will have one more day off before giving himself over to the homogenizers.

To begin the lark, Ferris fools his parents with extravagantly feigned illness, goading his sister to distraction; coaxes his long-suffering hypochondriacal buddy, Cameron, into borrowing his father's museum-piece Ferrari; and elaborately springs his girlfriend from school. With the stage set for fun, he lights out for the city, a pal on each arm. And so it goes, with Ferris pulling all the ruses and pranks that teens yearn to play on their pompous and gullible elders. While there are some close calls along the way, especially with the nerdy principal who is Ferris's nemesis, Ferris's day is a happy and successful homage to teenhood. By its end, Ferris's effervescence and joie de vivre quite literally start the whole city dancing and singing. With his mastery, Ferris triumphs over obnoxious people and negative circumstance. "Everything works for him," says his woeful buddy Cameron. In *Ferris Bueller*, the teenage desires for freedom, control, identity, intimacy, and meaning are fulfilled, however momentarily, and relished. Here the dream, so often thwarted by an obtuse if not malignant adult world, is realized. Given the chance, Ferris controls his world, thus playing out a common fantasy, especially of teenagers. His rebellion is not an angry revolt but a gleeful romp, a frolic. Nor is Ferris mean or macho like Stallone, Schwarzenegger, or Eastwood. Ferris seems to recognize that people—even high school principals—are not so much vicious as they are vain, foolish, and simply out to have a good time.

For many years, before he moved on to adult comedy, Hughes's teen films were all the rage. This is not surprising. Especially when compared with most other teen films, his movies are vivid, telling, and fresh, and full of both comedy and poignance. As a whole his work seems to distill and clarify the angst and calamity of youth's woe-ridden journey toward what we call maturity. He recognizes that initiation is a tough business. Always his films feature trenchant and often touching depictions of teen survival amid contemporary America's wild mix of identity, caste, and sex, each a potentially lethal pitfall.

What, finally, do Hughes's movies and most other teen films provide that is of value to teens? This is a very difficult question, and asking it highlights the elusive role of teen films in adolescent culture. Examining Hughes's films shows that even the best of the genre are uneven. It is easy enough to see and praise the comic realism of Hughes's portraits of kids absorbed in teen crazes and adolescent anxiety. The major thematic preoccupations of *Sixteen Candles* seem to be self-acceptance, intimacy, and social success, although these are all caught up in the rush to lose one's virginity. And who dares do what with and for whom—again, questions of intimacy and acceptance—seems to be at the center of *The Breakfast Club*. Often, however—and this is true of most teen films—whatever good things the movies may be saying about friendship and self-affirmation seem to be lost in the superficial events of plot and sensation. Here again, business imperatives, especially mining a proven formula for box-office gold, have enormous impact on the content of teen-oriented films. Hughes, for example, seems to approve of the often facile strategies that his teens embrace to fulfill their individual quests. And he endorses their desperation when perhaps he should be trying to defuse it. Not having a date, after all, is not terminal or even of ultimate significance, and its bad effects usually subside or are outgrown. And even nerds have friends, even if they are only other nerds. In his films Hughes plays out the struggles and conflicts of youth; whether any light shines, any problems are solved, or any reconciliations are reached, perhaps only teens and time can tell.

The Ghoul in the Closet: Understanding Horror Pictures

It is not always difficult for teens, parents, and critics to understand the fundamental appeal and role of movies about adolescent life. Their themes and values are often relatively transparent. Nor is it difficult to see the offensiveness of some of the films. Their vulgarity, bawdiness, and "sexploitation" can be hard to take, no matter how redeeming their plots. Among the really perplexing teen-oriented films, however, is the genre known as the horror movie. To most adults of moderate temperament and taste, the genre seems at its core sociopathic, expressing a prurient interest and delight in carnage in general and sexual mutilation in particular. The horror movie appears, even to cinematically untrained adults, to be an entirely different beast than the more playful comedy-romance genre.

Commonly called "slasher" or "slice-and-dice" films, the genre has proven to be enormously successful in the last decade and a half. Among the steady and ample flow of horror films since the early 1970s, three major series—*Halloween, Friday the 13th,* and *Nightmare on Elm Street*—have dominated the market and generated sequels, tirelessly retreading old plots with new special effects and varieties of assault and gore. Despite the genre's apparent crass commercial exploitation and its myopic and repetitive content, it cannot be written off as socially unimportant; indeed, numerous critics from both church and academy contend that the horror film is a terribly important barometer and index of North America's cultural mood. The opening sentence in a recent book on the horror film proclaims, "[The] modern horror film is an extraordinarily diverse group of texts that epitomize the tangled workings of American popular culture, which is at once business, art, and purveyor of entertainment and ideology."[29] However, exactly what horror films mean and what constitutes their appeal and cultural role and effect are matters very much open to question.

Surely the most puzzling dimension of horror films, and a major facet of their appeal, lies in their content. Most of the discussion about horror films has focused on their graphically violent content and the effect it has on audiences. Just about everyone is extremely upset about it—except teens. Individuals and organizations from the full range of the political and social spectrum have decried the genre, although according to somewhat varying criteria. Some have seemed primarily concerned with the genre's explicit sexual content, some with its violence, some with its violence against women, and some with the political agendas allegedly "buried" in the films. Predictably, perhaps, conservative religious groups and alliances have probably raised the most fuss, usually objecting to the prominent sexual content of the genre. Donald Wildmon's National Family Association has monitored values throughout the media and has won national attention through its promotion of boycotts of sponsors of problematic network television programming. The National Council of Churches, which consists primarily of mainline Protestant denominations, has funded a study and report entitled "Violence and Sexual Violence in Film, Television, Cable and Home Video."

29. *American Horrors: Essays on the Modern American Horror Film,* ed. Gregory A. Waller (Urbana: University of Illinois Press, 1988), p. 1.

But the objections come from more than the religious quarter. As part of a widespread protest against the victimization of women in pornography in general, many feminist groups have complained loudly about the slasher films, citing their constant and brutal victimization of women. (A lot of males die too, but their deaths involve much less visual anticipation, detail, and relish than the deaths of females do.) In addition, groups of health professionals such as the National Coalition on Television Violence collect and publish information on violence throughout the media in an effort to point out its deleterious effects on children in particular. Film critics have joined the hue and cry as well. Prominent film scholar Morris Dickstein has called the R-rated horror film "hardcore pornography of violence made possible by the virtual elimination of censorship," a view which is shared by well-known Chicago film critics Gene Siskel and Roger Ebert.[30] Even conservative syndicated columnist George Will has pondered the phenomenon, wondering if the national "fixation" on "savagery" does not signal "a desensitization of the mass audience."[31]

The popularity of horror films is indeed startling. One measure of their popularity is the sheer number of them now available. In 1947, horror films were but .004 percent of the world's annual release; by 1967 the number had grown to 7.6 percent; and by 1987 one out of every six films made in America could be classified as a horror film. According to *Variety*, revenue from theatrical rentals of horror films increased from $6 million in 1979 to $230 million in 1987. But these figures give only a partial indication of audience, since many horror films bypass the theatrical-release route and go straight to video stores. As one watchdog newsletter reported, "While theater viewership of uncut and graphic horror has increased approximately 15-fold since 1979, *total viewership of horror, including home viewership, has increased roughly 300-fold.*" Critics fear that the volatility of the subject matter is greatly increased by the slack enforcement of rating codes in theaters and the virtual absence of enforcement of the age restrictions that are supposed to guide rentals in video stores.[32]

So what is the fuss about? The typical plot of a horror movie runs something like this. A deranged and hideous man prowls in the night, hunting down victims, usually teens, whom he then proceeds to mutilate and kill one by one. Always the camera's eye is the attacker's

---

30. Dickstein, quoted by Waller in the introduction to *American Horrors*, p. 7.

31. Will, "Scary to Consider Horror Fixation," *Grand Rapids Press*, 12 Dec. 1989, p. A-17.

32. *National Coalition on Television Violence News* 9 (June-Oct. 1988): 3.

Movie Identification Quiz #2

DESCRIPTION: In another PG film, a strange, winsome creature (an early Christmas present) that looks like a teddy bear come to life goes to live with an ideal teen in an idyllic American village. When wet, the pet spawns clones that soon mutate into snarling pests, half human and half reptile. The cackling brood savors killing as much as playing their endless practical jokes, usually mixing the two. The picture's last half features the inventive, graphic ways in which the humans and creatures stalk and kill each other using blenders, chain saws, microwaves, catapults, crossbows, decapitation, and incineration. And all of this action takes place on Christmas Eve. (The violence quotient of these Yuletide misfits makes Ebenezer Scrooge look like St. Francis.) With its combination of gore and cute, cuddly creatures and sentiment, the movie is pitched straight to the young teen market.

IDENTIFICATION: *Gremlins,* another Spielberg production of 1984, ranks twentieth in all-time box-office receipts. Admittedly, saying bad things about Spielberg, the sweet fellow who brought us lovable E.T., is like impugning Mom and apple pie. It also qualifies the critic for a free test for hysterical paranoia. As much as the characters he has given us, like E.T. and Indiana Jones, Spielberg himself is a contemporary cultural icon, a kindly and trusted guru, for parents as much as for kids. After all, "kid" films directed or produced by Spielberg account for five of history's top ten money-makers (and seven of the top twenty) and have hauled in well over a billion dollars. While it clearly took awhile for Hollywood to see the gold in *Gremlins,* a sequel hit the screens in the summer of 1990 and proved to be one of the most financially successful films of the season. Where are you, Mr. Rogers?

---

as he spies and closes in on the first unsuspecting and then terrified woman. (The attacker's male victims do not merit this close cinematic attention.) The audience repeatedly participates in his pursuit, slowly approaching couples or girls caught in vulnerable activities such as bathing, dressing, or making love. Blades of all sorts—knives, axes, and chain saws—slash, gouge, and dismember. The camera then pauses to appreciate the carnage pinned to walls or littered all over. The monster turns away only when butchery finally sates his appetite for pain and murder. And there is no ending this phantasm from hell. Although the beast is "killed" at the end of the movie, there are ample suggestions that it will resurrect itself for ever-gorier escapades of carnage in who-knows-how-many sequels.

By summer 1990, *Nightmare on Elm Street* had reached number five in its series and *Friday the 13th* had spawned its eighth horror. The malevolent superhuman and indestructible monsters—Jason, Freddy Krueger, and Michael Meyer—return over and over again, no matter what the suggested finality or gruesome mode of their previous departure (and one can hardly imagine more painful and permanent destructions). Until they are permanently dispatched, they will inflict a vast, abominable amount of pain and violence on teens, mostly girls. With unfathomable malice and relish which the audience participates in vicariously, the stalker terrorizes, tortures, and kills. His strength and his weapons flash, threaten, coerce, subdue, and invade. Always the violence done to women clearly represents phallic assault, an obscene predatory distortion of any semblance of normal male sexuality. Women are the inviting game, and the audience becomes involved in the hunt. As the violence in slasher films is portrayed more and more positively and provoked with less and less motivation, it is ever more graphically depicted, both visually and verbally. These films exhibit every conceivable sort of mutilation, most of it done to women. The fate of victims and victimizer forms the chief narrative interest: who will get killed next and how, and how will the "monster" finally be defeated? The body count for one of these films ranges from four to twenty. The level of brutality astounds at times but is generally made to seem fun. Since the monsters are always male, sexual arousal mixes with the "pleasure" of assault.

Not surprisingly, most of the critical comment on these films deals with the extent and nature of their violence. The experimental research of numerous social scientists, most notably Edward Donnerstein, has shown with some certainty that aggressive violent sexuality like that depicted in the slasher films has measurable short-term consequences on male attitudes about violence toward women. Those who have researched the effects of watching violent pornography, a category into which the slasher films fall, agree that the material negatively affects college-age males: it reduces their sympathy for rape victims, increases their willingness to coerce women sexually, increases their levels of anger, and "disinhibits" them from expressing that anger toward women generally. Since these films all feature a crazed male aggressor and a "plot" that's a mix of sex and violence, they effectively model and advocate aggressive male sexuality. Psychiatrist Thomas Radecki, director of the National Coalition on Television Violence, argues that regular doses of even small amounts of violence produce harmful behavioral effects. He cites one research study from UCLA which indicates that middle-class husbands "noted a 25 percent decrease in angry feelings and lost their tempers 35 percent less often after just one week of limiting their television viewing to non-violent programs."[33]

The apparent ease with which media violence influences attitudes and behavior, even for "normal" adult men, suggests that there is ample social justification for concern about the moral and political ramifications of depictions of sexual violence. The more radical critics of media violence such as Radecki argue that sufficient statistical evidence exists to link 25 to 50 percent of contemporary social violence to violent entertainment.[34] While it involves only speculation, critics can but wonder, for example, about how pubescent boys will be affected by long-term exposure to violent pornography. The message is more than clear: it's all right, even fun to hurt women to get what every male desires and deserves. If viewed repeatedly, as much of this material is, by those whose notion of sexual relations is just forming, it may prove to be a particularly volatile conditioning apparatus. Psychically and socially corrosive attitudes and practices may become deeply entrenched. To be sure, not many boys will grow up to be crazed rapists and murderers, but the spread of violent films will certainly spread hurt and suffering and increase the fraying of any social fabric, whether of family, town, or nation.

The extremity of the slasher film, both its nature and its apparent effects, represents something new in the mainstream of Western culture, at least in the modern world. Spectacle barbarism, if that is what we can call staged brutality, was featured in the coliseums of ancient Rome. And from the Middle Ages up through the present progressive industrial ages, dark folk tales of forbidding, supernatural forests full of ogres, goblins, and witches have exerted a strong presence on the fringes of Western cultures. But the eruption of bloody, atavistic impulses at this stage of modern life perplexes many, secularists and religionists alike. The least that can be said about the production and the popularity of the blood feasts of the horror film is that they run counter to central Western cultural notions of the origins and purposes of human life. One prominent Western moral and social ideal has its roots in the biblical creation narrative. That account sets forth a grand vision of intimacy and harmony conceived by God, in whose heart lies a deep aversion toward, and a fundamental ban on, violence and violation. In Eden, before it was lost, the very texture of being was infused by mutuality and care—reverence toward, delight in, and adoration of every living creature. Neither violence, predation, pain, nor death had any place. In short, love reigned.

33. Radecki, "America: Culture of Violence," *Action,* Nov.-Dec. 1987, p. 7.
34. Ibid., p. 8.

Such an ideal, needless to say, stands some distance from the ethos of the contemporary horror film.

The stark contrast between this notable social and cultural ideal and the content and effect of the horror film gives ample reason for caution if not outright alarm in response to this genre, especially as it affects the nurture of adolescents. On this score, the findings of modern social science on the effects of mixing violence and sex only reinforce what the moral and spiritual traditions of Judaism and Christianity have argued from their start. Images and stories do shape mind, mood, and imagination, and influence thought and behavior. The current wave of horror movies makes obscene violence seem feasible, interesting, and passionate; it promotes erotica with a punch and a slash, and its point is the pleasure of watching and inflicting pain. Nor is the mood or approach in these films different, except in degree, from those of countless other films in supposedly "milder" genres, particularly war and adventure films like *Rambo* and *Indiana Jones and the Temple of Doom*. The aggressive taste for violence and gore has increasingly set the tone for "mainline" entertainment, forcing it to incorporate lurid elements in order to appear adult or grown-up to young audiences. One film scholar has observed that by "continually pressing the boundaries of both PG- and R-ratings, the modern horror film has violated taboos with a monsterlike ferocity unprecedented in the contemporary American cinema, and in the process horror has increased freedom of expression and affected the codes of commercial television as well as [of] the motion picture industry."[35]

While the nature of the action in horror films is clear, and social scientists are gaining a clearer grasp of its effects, the fundamental appeal and meaning of horror films continue to perplex most adults and critics. Just about every facet of modern learning and theory, from psychological to political, has been evoked as an interpretive filter to explain both the appeal and the meaning of these films. Academic inquiries sometimes seem insightful but at other times seem only slightly less ludicrous than the films themselves. Often academic soothsayers overlook simple and obvious explanations in order to cite horror films as the latest proof of this or that social or psychological theory. Certainly modern progressive theorists are not well disposed temperamentally to consider the darker possibilities of making sense of the horror "fixation," as George Will calls it. In any case, it often seems that no sooner does an academic show insight into a facet of the appeal or cultural function of a film genre than that insight is exalted into a monolithic perspective. Academics tend to

---

35. Waller, introduction to *American Horrors*, p. 6.

be quite confident of their ability to know the function and meaning of films for audiences: one remarks that "while we may not be able to locate what exactly it is within the horror myth that attracts different audiences, we do know what it is within this specific audience that keeps it interested."[36] Rather than proclaim such certainty, it is perhaps more useful, on this and other matters, to forge a composite view that allows for a complex series of observations and insights that collectively might suggest the full mystery of the way in which art products, good and bad alike, affect and shape the ideas, attitudes, and actions of their users. What follows, then, is an effort to survey some major interpretive approaches to the phenomenon of horror films.

The first we might call the minimalist or naturalist point of view, and a number of different reasons for the appeal of horror films might be subsumed under this label. "Minimalist" seems to offer as good a label as any for this approach, because its perspective does not rely on intricate social data or theories; rather, it is emphatically commonsensical. Or it might be called "naturalistic" because it fastens on the seemingly natural features of youthful development, particularly those that are more than obvious to observers of teenagers. First, most teens want to feel and look grown-up. Tired of kidhood, they sooner or later reach for whatever will make them feel "old" or look "mature" in the eyes of their peers. Like part-time jobs and cars, horror films are among those things that teens were once too young for, and thus, having once been proscribed, are very popular among teens seeking badges of their coming of age. So going to horror films can help teens feel like they belong, like they are participating in a cultural ritual that "everyone does." The needs for identity and social acceptance can hardly be underestimated, and these two needs usually go hand in hand. There is, too, natural pubescent curiosity about two facets of adult life, namely, sex and death, from which teens were earlier protected. In this way too, horror movies serve a distinct function: like initiation films, horror films contain ample quantities of anatomy and sex but also throw in large doses of morbidity. This voyeurism of violence, the sense of being allowed into forbidden territory, the realm of assault and murder, is as important as sexual voyeurism. Lastly, for many teenagers, horror films make good dates. A boy likes a girl clinging to his arm in fear, and a girl likes an arm to cling to, especially the arm of a "manly" boy who does not blink at the bloody spectacle on the screen.

Beyond this important commonsensical analysis lies a thick

36. James B. Twitchell, *Dreadful Pleasures: An Anatomy of Modern Horror* (New York: Oxford University Press, 1985), p. 68.

Movie Identification Quiz #3

DESCRIPTION: Authorities give a life-term rock-pile prisoner freedom so that he can go on a secret mission. During that mission he single-handedly kills about a hundred enemies, a gruesome body count of buffoons and demons. The success of the mission is hardly the point, nor is plausibility. What stands out is assault—varied, graphic, and continual: it includes burning, carving, impaling, gutting, garroting, bludgeoning, exploding, hanging, and plummeting *ad nauseam*. Even though the only woman in the movie is killed, the bulging and bloodied hero shows clearly enough what all the muscle and gore is really about: sex and power.

   This film, R-rated (children under seventeen not admitted without parent or guardian), was in large part responsible for making its star the favorite actor of teens in 1985. This phenomenon poses an interesting conundrum: the star made it to the top of the teens' list primarily because of a movie that many teens were not, according to the rating code, supposed to see. A couple of summer afternoons in a movie theater showed well enough that this blood-drenched pageant of ritualistic machismo found its most fervent devotees amid pubescent boys.

IDENTIFICATION: Sylvester Stallone's *Rambo: First Blood II* ranks number twenty-two in all-time box-office receipts and is one of a successful series of seven Stallone films (four *Rocky*'s and three *First Blood*'s, earning more than half a billion dollars). These movies, most of them with scripts written by Stallone, exalt the capacity to endure and inflict pain as the sole means of establishing manhood. The motive for both taking and giving hurt lies not in the desire for justice, what the old western hero perhaps sought, but in the desire for retribution, what we might call the "make-my-day" syndrome also popularized by Clint Eastwood, Charles Bronson, and Eddie Murphy. And a glorified route it is, full of muscle, sweat, blood, defiance, and exalted brutality.

tangle of interpretive perspectives that trace patterns of individual symbols or networks of symbols. In all these different approaches, the suggestion is that horror films, despite their seeming simplicity of plot and meaning, carry enormous cultural freight as they play out for audiences important cultural, social, political, and psychological conflicts, issues about which audiences care deeply but oftentimes cannot address consciously or straightforwardly because of the issues' very weightiness, depth, and centrality. For example, a common view of science fiction and horror films is that their appeal lies in the dramatization of ordinary "repressed fears and desires"; specifically, according to film scholar Patrick Lucanio, the horror film "relies on the presentation within an irrational milieu of symbols that easily bear a Freudian interpretation and thus delineate the psychological workings of repressed fears."[37] Lucanio describes the horror film as a self-contained entity:

> One must view and interpret the meaning and value of the horror film on *its* terms; we will discover its true meaning and value only by fathoming its charged symbolism. We must learn to speak its language. The genre thus unites its . . . presentational qualities to form a singleness of effect: horror. By presenting this effect in terms of an alternate reality—a self-contained world with an inner logic—the entire tale, as evidenced by images, becomes symbolic and therefore asks us at the outset to discover its meaning.[38]

In other words, while horror films are what they seem, they are also more than what they seem, and it is that "more" which accounts for their deep appeal, whether that be social, political, or psychological. Different films and subgenres in science fiction and horror, often overlapping, seem to exhibit particular kinds of appeal and meaning, very often depending on who is doing the interpreting.

The most common and most lasting interpretation of the symbology of horror films is psychological. According to this interpretive perspective, horror films display and express normal, deep-seated human fears, usually ones that are too unwieldy or scary to bring to the surface because they are "too painful for us to deal with consciously and directly."[39] Those can be fear of threats, fear of fear itself, fear of mutilation, fear of unbridled sexual desire, and fear of death, which are comparatively new subjects and matters of curiosity for adolescents. Usually psychological discussions of horror films plunge headlong into the theoretical constructs of Freud and modern psychoanalysis. Critics of this school usually see horror films as expressing fears of unrepressed sexuality, the inability of the id to control the dark hungers of the libido. Critic Margaret Tarratt argues that "the horror film is most often the dramatization of the individual's anxiety about his own repressed sexual desires, which are incompatible with the morals of the civilized life."[40] Along this line, critic James Twitchell claims that the horror film has "little to do with fright; it has more to do with laying down the rules of

37. Lucanio, *Them or Us: Archetypal Interpretations of Fifties Alien Invasion Films* (Bloomington: Indiana University Press, 1987), pp. 5-6.

38. Ibid., p. 11.

39. Charles Derry, "More Dark Dreams: Some Notes on the Recent Horror Film," in *American Horrors*, p. 163.

40. Tarratt, quoted by Lucanio in *Them or Us*, p. 5.

socialization and extrapolating a hidden code of sexual behavior. Once we learn these rules, as we do in adolescence, horror dissipates."[41] This viewpoint explains common reactions to the typical horror-film plot. For example, the fear of the typical horror-film monster, usually rapacious and bloodthirsty, becomes fear of a well-repressed, unrecognized part of the self that the psyche senses but cannot acknowledge or tame. Whether the recent crop of "slasher" horror films works in peculiar ways to defuse and resolve inward apprehension or, as some social-scientific research now suggests, foments or aggravates antisocial behavior has not yet drawn much comment from academic scholars and theorists of cinema.

Just as the symbology of the horror film taps into and explores the unacknowledged and repressed interior fears and conflicts of its audience, so also the genre moves outward to chronicle more public and socially shared tensions and fears. Just as the horror film can speak to private inward anxiety, so also it can speak "to shared fears, to a culture's anxieties."[42] Given this expansive frame of interpretation, just about every facet and level of sociocultural function can serve as an interpretive reference point for horror films. For some scholars, even the most seemingly banal horror films, from *The Texas Chainsaw Massacre* to *Friday the 13th,* offer a "thoroughgoing critique of American institutions and values." This has been said of *The Night of the Living Dead,* for instance, which according to one analyst criticizes "the nuclear family, the private home, the teenage couple, and resourceful individual hero . . . media, local and federal government agencies, and the entire mechanism of civil defense."[43] Even the stalker films pick up on the "inefficacy of old ideas"—specifically, those having to do with the status of women in society and the status of America in the world—to forge a new "modern-day myth . . . that imparts to the members of its society an explanation for the ongoing conflicts within it."[44] For example, many critics see the extreme violence against women in slasher films as a cinematic depiction of and response to the major social dislocations and anger resulting from the rise of feminism. Similarly, in the past, critics attributed horror films with a kind of political meaning. During the early Cold War, amid the "red scare" in America, many critics saw the alien invasion film as a metaphor for subversion either from without or from within, generally catching the mood of siege and the paranoia about a looming, unseen enemy. Likewise, the recent slasher movies featuring apocalyptic

41. Twitchell, *Dreadful Pleasures,* p. 66.
42. Derry, "More Dark Dreams," p. 163.
43. Waller, introduction to *American Horrors,* p. 4.
44. Vera Dika, "The Stalker Film, 1978-81," in *American Horrors,* p. 99.

carnage supposedly reflect adolescent apprehension about nuclear weapons and international conflict.

One of the most persuasive if overlooked perspectives on horror films and horrific art in general is that the "gothic" elements of horror supply viewers with a sense of the numinous in an age that temperamentally disdains religious experience. For example, one literary critic, S. L. Varnado, suggests that the gothic tale has lasting appeal because it exists on a different "ontological plane" than other kinds of fantasy tales. He argues that ghost stories and the like impart, like few other forms of art, "the *feeling* of the supernatural." Their aesthetic verisimilitude provides immediate felt experience of something quite beyond the ordinary or natural in experience—"the grounds of which cannot be made conceptual" and lie outside the confines of the rational and scientifically understandable.[45]

Varnado invokes German religious philosopher Rudolf Otto's analysis of religious or numinous experience, what Otto calls the *"mysterium tremendum et fascinans."* For Otto, the Latin phrase suggests—for that is the most language can do—the nature and contours of an encounter with the supernatural or extrahuman: some suddenly tangible mystery occasions profound awe to the point of fear and trembling but also compels attention or fascination. The phrase "rapt wonderment" describes the human response and thus defines the character of the event, and where horror tales are concerned describes the response prompted by the encounter with the creature, be it a zombie, an alien, Frankenstein, Dracula, or Freddy Krueger. The numinous encounter has at its core a paradoxical element insofar as it contains elements of both dread and fascination and insofar as its object can be either benign or hostile. Otto's phrase defines the ontological and metaphysical status of the encounter, not its moral character. Thus the event or creature might be friendly or malignant, as the difference between the sociable alien E.T. and the horrific monster in *Alien* well illustrates, but both trigger essentially the same initial response: surprise, amazement, fear, and curiosity.

What perplexes so many parents and cultural critics is the persistence of youthful fascination with superhuman monsters and creatures. After all, the reasoning goes, we live in an educated, scientifically sophisticated age—why the appeal of such comparatively "primitive" beings? One explanation offered is that horror films might be a last gasp of childhood fancy, the love-hate relationship with the "thing in the closet" or "things that go bump in the night." There is no doubt some

45. Varnado, *Haunted Presence: The Numinous in Gothic Fiction* (Tuscaloosa: University of Alabama Press, 1987), pp. 6, 9.

truth in this view. On the other hand, the sum of this and all other critical perspectives, whether feminist or Marxist, do not account for the adolescent fascination with horror. Rather, the reason for youth's current interest is that modern culture lives in a spiritually denuded world, one shorn of all signs of the supernatural or transcendent. Theologians argue and anthropologists such as Clifford Geertz confirm that resolute modernist secularism has produced a deep human appetite—comparable to the instinctual needs for sleep, food, and sex—for a sense of a supernatural or an ultimacy of some sort beyond the self and society. The more a culture denies, suppresses, or tames the yearning for a real live here-and-now divinity, the more its members, especially its young, will seek to satisfy that yearning. With their insistent assertion of an irrepressible and lasting supernatural "something" beyond the human, horror films satisfy, however temporarily, the nonrational desire and quest to encounter and affirm the reality of a transcendent other. That "other," as suggested, can be benign, as it is in *E.T., Cocoon, Close Encounters of the Third Kind, Superman,* and *The Abyss.* Or it can be horrific, as it is in *Rosemary's Baby, The Exorcist* (a series), *The Omen* (a series), *Alien* and its sequel, *Aliens,* and the numerous slasher-ghoul series. All these films posit the reality of an ultimacy beyond the ordinary; in the case of the horror films, it is most often radical evil that seeks to devour everything in its path.

Similarly, horror films seem to offer an oblique route via which youth can acknowledge that the world is indeed a dark and chaotic place and that evil is indeed real, which is a message that goes strongly against the resolute optimism of consumerist North America. Contemporary novelist John Updike has acknowledged such in his comment that modern culture only grudgingly admits the reality of evil in that it pictures "a minimal supernatural, clean, monotonous, hygienic, featureless."[46] Young people correctly suspect that not all is well behind the cheerful facades of innumerable TV commercials and the happy endings of countless sitcoms. As ghost stories and nighttime fears argue, the world is perhaps a tragic place where devouring forces loom and burst forth when least expected. Thus the horror film is an oblique acknowledgment—a hieroglyph, perhaps—of the dread that, if not prompted specifically by monsters, is elicited by a world not less threatening and hostile to human happiness. Film scholars generally concur that a chief feature of the contemporary horror film is its insistence on the danger of the ordinary. As R. H. W. Dillard puts it, modern horror tales typically depict a "group of people [who] are besieged by an apparently harmless

---

46. Updike, "Introduction to *Soundings in Satanism,*" in *Picked-Up Pieces* (New York: Alfred A. Knopf, 1976), p. 87.

and ordinary world gone berserk."[47] Horror can summarize a kind of pop nihilism—stylistically almost punk at times—that results from a recognition of the fundamental aloneness and terror of life.

Key to this perspective is the awareness that each person has within an unfathomable capacity if not thirst for doing evil in very direct, intentional ways. Updike wonders if there are "not tendencies in our private psychologies" that work "within as a positive lust, an active hatred."[48] Such tendencies are only worsened by the remarkable prosperity of North America: Updike speculates that "the more fortunate our condition, the stronger the lure of negation, of perversity, of refusal."[49] In a peculiar way, horror films offer to adolescents still another mirror, a fun-house mirror *in extremis* in which they observe and explore a dramatic corollary to their own dark suspicions about their own worst selves. The horror stories become parables of predation that capture unconscious fears about individual potential for destruction. However, if recent social-scientific research is accepted, then the films are not only parables of dark inner exploration but also visions of violence that foment fear and hostility.

Oh Be Careful, Little Eyes

The exact appeal, meaning, and influence of teen films remain uncertain. Movies are not easy cultural products to assess, either for their artistic merit or for their social influence. For adults, at least, a more enigmatic and exasperating form of entertainment would be hard to imagine. That adult frustration has probably always been piqued by various youth activities, for youth perennially seek their own identity, and often choose their own varieties of entertainment so as to create a sense of distance between them and their parents. On the other hand, it is probably true that no previous culture saw such an enormous and potent youth culture as North America now witnesses. Movies feed the distinctiveness of this culture: no small part of the appeal and power of youth-oriented films derives from the exclusive angle of their approach. Ever mindful of the financial bottom-line, moviemakers use the social and economic structure of the youth culture both as a guide for shaping their products and

47. Dillard, "Night of the Living Dead: It's Not Like Just a Wind That's Passing Through," in *American Horrors*, p. 26.
48. Updike, "Introduction to *Soundings in Satanism*," p. 89.
49. Ibid., p. 90.

Movie Identification Quiz #4

DESCRIPTION: In one of the most profitable teen films ever made, rated R, a group of fifties' teenage boys pillage both the high school and a local roadhouse, not to mention the local female population. These boys, depicted as healthy and fun-loving, spy on the girls' shower room, befuddle the police, enrage the porcine bigots, booze continuously, and "score" as often as they want to (even the wimpiest one is a stud). In addition to these violent visual and attitudinal assaults, the language throughout is relentlessly abusive of people, God, and sex, of the whole of the loveliness of creation. This is male teen heaven, and their girls love it too.

IDENTIFICATION: *Porky's,* released in 1982, cost less than $5 million to make and earned roughly $180 million. While clearly the most successful, it is only one of a spate of teenage sex films that border on soft-core pornography. A kind of middle-class high-school *Animal House* (which cost $3 million to make and made $150 million), *Porky's* abounds in raunchy groin humor that rationalizes, normalizes, and then sentimentalizes adolescent randiness and promiscuity. Any means of dealing with a hormonal drive other than immediate and frequent copulation is abundantly ridiculed. No one in this fantasy world ever experiences bad sex, let alone any unhappy consequence thereof, such as guilt, disease, or pregnancy.

Besides constantly and raucously pursuing sex, the teens in *Porky's* booze continually and ridicule everyone who would stymie their heedless carnal revel. When verbal put-down fails as a response, felonious violence is an acceptable alternative. If another offend thee, smite him or her, by word or blow. And here the offensive are defined as either "old" (meaning "adult") or nerdy, which are usually one and the same—they are all hypocrites and buffoons.

Porky's is simply the best known of a horde of money-making "teen pics" whose shape and focus resulted from studio research into adolescent male sexual fantasies. Two of the more famous, *Private Lessons* and *Risky Business,* which gave Tom Cruise his start, put such fantasies at their center. Such films pack the shelves of video stores and fill the early morning hours of cable stations.

as a marketplace in which to pitch them. To an extraordinary degree, the subject matter and narrative strategies go right for the "ragged edges" of the adolescent psyche, those problematic areas like sex, status, and "cool." In other words, teen films are primarily designed for box-office appeal; emotional and social impact are secondary considerations at best. By now, Hollywood has essentially mastered the "formula" for the teen film. Its main premise, first hit upon by American International Pictures, is that teens will go to see just about anything about teens.

Indeed, a large part of the clout of teen films comes from the very familiar youth-culture or teen-ghetto setting, which gives the pictures a veneer of realism, no matter how preposterous the story. That holds true for a spectrum of pictures, from *Star Wars* to John Hughes's movies to slasher films. Like rock and roll and MTV, these films are "just for them," and there is no higher compliment or better way to win youth's attention.

In taking this approach, most youth-oriented films exploit their audiences by emphasizing particular subjects for the purpose of box-office appeal, and therein lie some of their more troublesome messages. Sex is almost always a principal subject, represented as a teenage obsession and, more often than not, the primary source of teenage identity. With few exceptions, teen films gratuitously exalt sex, picturing it as the chief goal and pinnacle of human experience. According to these films, sex is the best toy in the playpen of adolescence. The only genuine tragedy is chastity or, worse than that, virginity. The sexual act itself is romanticized, imbued with salvific qualities that can supposedly transform a young person's life. This storybook portrayal prevails despite the fact that initial sexual experiences are almost always awkward, embarrassing, and emotionally (if not physically) unfulfilling. Within the world of teen film, then, sex becomes a panacea, but it is one that ignores the larger issues of unwanted pregnancy, sexual disease, and social and emotional tragedy.

Similarly troublesome is the treatment of rebellion in teen films. In almost every case, rebellion is inspired not by social idealism but by personal resentment or the quest for self-fulfillment. For example, a dark cynicism motivates John Rambo in the *First Blood* series, and the pleasure of revenge dominates the shreds of idealism that haunt his character. In many of these films the heroes and heroines do not rebel against the establishment; on the contrary, they are often upholders of the status quo celebrating a teenage consumer party. In *Risky Business,* Tom Cruise's character rebels against his wealthy, upper-class parents, but his purpose is to outdo them in thrill-seeking and consumerism—and he wins big by spending a night as a pimp. The *Porky's* series features an autonomous group of teens whose values differ little from those of the indulgent hypocrites against whom they rebel—and they rebel not to right any wrongs but to gain power and control. By and large, Hollywood producers have attracted the teen audience with films that reflect the surface-oriented "fun and beach party" values that have been gaining popularity ever since the 1960s, culminating perhaps in the glib hedonism of the yuppies of the 1980s. No doubt this resulted in large part from the dramatic shift in American culture and its subsequent impact on youth. The postwar baby-boom generation reached adulthood dur-

ing a period of unprecedented prosperity that financed the liberal progress of the Great Society. While economic recessions in the late 1970s and
early 1980s cast a brief shadow, the sense of ever-increasing economic
benefit and leisure has not suffered any chastening. For rebellious youth,
the goal now seems to be outdoing adults in gaining—preferably with
minimal or no effort—the comforts of the North American consumerist
lifestyle. Teen films tell youth to get it and enjoy it now because there is
no life after college—only work, marriage, routine, more work, and
senility.

Nor do most teen films seek to correct or push beyond gender
stereotypes of male dominance and female submission. Even in the
adventure pictures that have little or no romance or sex, characterization
emphasizes traditional images of maleness. Rocky, Rambo, and other
macho heroes like Tom Cruise's Maverick in *Top Gun* are men, generally
young, whose attractiveness and mastery of their particular skill is
without parallel. If there is a prominent and successful woman in the
picture, such as the female engineer in *Top Gun,* she eventually succumbs
to the boyish machismo of the hero. Only John Hughes's films and some
of the horror pictures present somewhat independent women or women
who control the action of the film.

In addition, North American teendom appears to be the exclusive domain of white adolescents. Perhaps as a consequence, in many
films directed to this audience, racial and ethnic minority groups are
unfairly represented and unrealistically portrayed. From teen films audiences would never learn that America has had an unsavory history of
slavery, segregation, and discrimination. Nor would they learn of the
extraordinarily high rates of unemployment in inner-city America. Although this seems to be changing with the modest success of writer-
director Spike Lee, most filmmakers are less concerned with minorities
because the dollars lie elsewhere; white, suburban, twelve- to twenty-
five-year-old males compose the major share of the audience for teen
pictures.

Adolescent horror pictures are bad, if not puzzling and repugnant, but as this concluding discussion suggests, they are not the only
cause for alarm. Given the pervasiveness and availability of the adolescent film—in theaters, through video rentals, on cable channels—many
adults want to shout from the rooftops the lines from the old children's
cautionary hymn "Oh Be Careful, Little Eyes, What You See." The fact
is that teenagers will see movies—probably many movies—and very
few of those will depict faithfully what it is like to live in an adolescent
skin; others will make living in that skin more difficult, both for the
adolescent and for others. Parental prohibition generally can go only so

far; thorough-going prohibition is not physically possible or psycho-logically sensible. Moderation and cautious adult engagement in the selection and viewing process do hold out some hope. Simply put, adults must make the effort to engage themselves with the world of youth; they must care enough to enter youth's enclave, breathe the same air, learn the language, and exchange reports on what the world, life, and the movies are like.

9. Chasing the Grail: Youth in a Culture of Leisure

The end of labor is to gain leisure.

Aristotle

A perpetual holiday is a good working definition of hell.

George Bernard Shaw

Liberty is being free from the things we don't like in order to be slaves of the things we do like.

Ernest Benn

To be able to fill leisure intelligently is the last product of civilization.

Bertrand Russell

On the one hand, parents sometimes complain that teenagers have never had it so good. In parents' eyes, the world of middle-class kids looks a lot like an old-fashioned carnival or amusement park: an endless midway of "fun," games, goodies, rides, and sideshows. Or, better yet, for teenagers today life is more like a circus with numerous wild rings. Not only have amusements multiplied—they have become flashier than ever. What strikes most everyone about the youth culture, beyond its sheer quantity and variety, is its texture of glitter, high excitement, and perpetual diversion. Occasionally school and work intrude, but not for long or very seriously. As usual, teens "hang out"—a lot. That is something they have always done and always will do. Now, however, they seem to devote more of that "hang-out" time to electronic entertainment, regardless of form or setting. Indeed, some critics argue that the hallmark of teen culture, no matter what brand of it, is an addictive devotion to the electronic media. Teens swim in an electronic sea, mesmerized by the ever-changing spectacle of strange and colorful shapes and sounds. Enrapt, they readily forget about the dangers of drowning. Their delight might prove to be their destruction.

It is an easy case to make. Statistics on media use, both viewing and listening, indicate its pervasive allure. Teenagers watch less broadcast television than younger kids, but the time they used to spend watching network shows they now spend watching cable programming, especially MTV and the movie channels. Tens of millions of teens watch MTV for over an hour every day. The average teen watches about two movies a week, and those usually at home via cable or rental cassettes.[1] In effect, the family rec room can become, at the flick of a thumb, a diverse dramatic world of heroes and hookers, singers and monsters. At home and away, car radios, boom boxes, and disc players make rock and roll a ubiquitous anthem to every facet of ordinary life—an emotional backdrop for the unwieldy process of growing up. Besides listening to the radio, teens purchase hundreds of millions of dollars of recorded music every year. And they "buy" live performances too: in cities small and large, the largest communal gatherings are expensive, hi-tech rock concerts that mimic the gods' own thunder and lightning. If anything, there seems to be a surfeit of amusement, more than anyone can take in—circus overload, we might call it—and it never ends (unlike those annual itinerant carnivals or seasonal parks that move on or close down). Images and sounds, all telling some sort of story, are constant and pervasive. Rock radio and rock-band tours, dance clubs, MTV, cable movies, and movie emporiums (now housing as many as twenty theaters) form the flashy bedrock of youth's cultural landscape. Kids never had so much so good.

As parents know, however, this is not the whole picture. Behind the electronic circus are the hourly data of America's social wreckage. For all their leisure and unprecedented amusements, North American youth suffer a host of plagues: boredom, fatigue, addiction, narcissism, anomie, abuse, and suicide. What to older people sometimes looks like heaven feels, for them, more like hell. For many youth (and adults as well)—including not only the poor and disenfranchised but the well-to-

---

1. Se-Wen Sun and James Lull, "The Adolescent Audience for Music Videos and Why They Watch," *Journal of Communication* 36 (Winter 1986): 117.

do and powerful—the electronic utopia has turned dystopian. Both reactionaries and revolutionaries have pointed out that the more time, wealth, and amusement teens have, the worse off they seem to get: their lives are marred by alcohol, drugs, violence, gangs, divorce, greed, ostentation, classism, pornography, disease, and suicide. The hard truth of this lamentable predicament, contradictory and puzzling as it seems, slowly seeps into public awareness. Stranger yet, in today's media-dependent world, public knowledge of these sad tidings comes mostly by the very means that abetted their rise. TV and film often glamorously dramatize social problems, selling their sensational stories like hawkers at a circus sideshow. The broadcast media eagerly, even proudly bring news of the mischief and tragedy.

The media may indeed bear some responsibility for fostering various social calamities, whether abortion, abuse, or teen suicide. However, a more fundamental cultural ailment underlies North American teen dis-ease: a surfeit of leisure. More and more teenagers seem to have more and more time for leisure and enjoyment. They have an abundance of leisure time scarcely imaginable in the past. If they work, it is usually only to procure the economic means to purchase those goods that enhance free time—cars, clothes, stereos, junk food—supposedly to make the good times even better. Even impoverished youth frequently acquire all the accoutrements of media culture, sometimes at the expense of meeting basic physical needs. Such a predicament foments the perennial worries of "old fogies" who fear that, as the old adage puts it, "idle hands are the devil's playground." "Spare time" and boredom breed trouble, or so the media tell us, nurturing what has become a major myth about youth. From *West Side Story* to *Grease,* from *The Wild One* to *Animal House* and *Risky Business,* whether in the ghetto or the suburbs, bored teens invariably create havoc. As shown in Chapter Two, hormones and "spare" time don't mix, except for the profit of the entertainment industry.

While that view has great appeal and some historical cogency, it greatly oversimplifies a condition that afflicts not just youth but the whole of American culture. The challenge of leisure, of so much for so many, is comparatively new and looms very large. What plagues youth also hounds adults, and it is part and parcel of a broad cultural upheaval whose outcome we still await. The media-oriented lifestyle of youth is in fact only the most conspicuous outcropping of a deep transgenerational confusion about the uses and purposes of time, whether in work or in play. Never have so many partaken of so much, either temporally or materially. What to do with this new "extra," this new cultural bounty, confounds almost everyone; social data of abuse and excess suggest one

---

A Foxy Network Attracts Youth

Fox, the so-called fourth commercial TV network, has learned how to court young viewers—with heavy doses of sex and violence. While the big three networks (ABC, NBC, and CBS) have significantly larger audiences, Fox generally has a higher percentage of younger viewers. Called "brash, young pirates" by the *Wall Street Journal*, Fox's programmers openly admit that "blood and sex" attract the most viewers, especially young ones. Programs such as *21 Jump Street*, *Married . . . with Children*, and *America's Most Wanted* gave Fox the highest percentage of young viewers of all networks on Sunday night.

—Dennis Kneale, "Can Fox Cool Down and Stay Hot?" *Wall Street Journal,* 25 May 1989, p. B-1.

---

index to a broad cultural perplexity. The problem of leisure forms a major element of modern cultural confusion: what to do with ourselves when we have the time. And consigned as youth are to a special, protracted limbo between infancy and maturity, they suffer acutely the human quests for identity, intimacy, and meaning. Very often parents caught in the economic scramble choose to divert their adolescent offspring with the very thing they themselves are after—more leisure toys, whether cars, stereos, movies, clothes, recordings, or whatever. Neglect instead of nurture only worsens the aimlessness of youth lost in the elusive glitter of the electronic carnival.

As a whole, Western culture has not fared well amid this new historical dispensation. Rather than broad social contentment—a fair of delight and mutuality—cultural paradoxes haunt virtually every social group and institution. Appetite, variety, and pleasure abound while satisfaction lags far behind. The great leisure circus, enticing and abundant, promises more pleasure but delivers less delight and contentment to its dazed clientele. The electronic carnival has never been so enormous and well-hyped, but it delivers less, and in the wake of disappointment it fuels still more desperate searches. Thoreau's charge a century ago that industrial affluence bred lives of "quiet desperation" seems painfully apt.

This chapter explores the background of modern leisure and how its pursuit and its promises, amid disorienting cultural flux, have become salvific for legions of devotees. The public en masse, and especially its children, now turn to electronic entertainment, perhaps the chief promulgator of the "good life," for more and more purposes and satisfactions, many of which were once served by other myths, customs, and institutions of Western culture. This recourse appeals particularly to youth because they especially feel the lack of a cohesive tradition in a mobile and pluralistic world. To be sure, humankind has always sought leisure, enjoyment, and entertainment. In the present predicament, however, numerous socio-economic and cultural circumstances have whetted the appetite for the ultimately chimerical ideal of intense sensate life, an ideal shaped, promoted, and mined by the entertainment industry. The entertainment industry, especially in the case of MTV and the movies, now flaunts its extraordinary hold upon the expectations of audiences. Finally, the chapter surveys the bewildering landscape of the roles of popular art, concluding with a benchmark for evaluating popular art's capacity for cultural nurture. We argue not against leisure and media but for wise and fruitful use of them.

The Newness of Leisure

Leisure is not the creation of modernity, but never has it been enjoyed by so many. There is, however, more to leisure than the length of the workday or workweek or the amount of "self time." Equally important is the certainty, regularity, and security of our leisure. Here the difference between modernity and the past is clear and telling. Most employed Americans can confidently anticipate and plan the use of nonwork time. Moreover, they expect to enjoy it for years, during a long life of basic comfort and health. This expectation in itself constitutes a major historical change. For everyone from teenagers to "golden oldies," expectations about what life might yield and what it is for have dramatically shifted. That is evident in the variety, elaborateness, and expense of the leisure revolution, which encompasses an ever-increasing number of things— entertainment, travel, collecting, sports, fitness, fashion. The habits and mind-set of today's consumers of leisure diverge starkly from history's norm, of which they know little.

A notable consequence of pervasive leisure is that most moderns, teens especially, consider it normative and ordinary, something commonplace—a "right," in fact—and cannot imagine an era when the conditions of daily life were even slightly worse. Yet the scale of modern leisure surpasses even the wildest fantasies of the commoners of the past, whose lives have received little historical attention. Needless to say, the desire and struggle for ease—the dream of leisure—has always been a central cultural preoccupation. Even the beginnings of Western culture, as documented in Greek drama and biblical narratives, attest to a peren-

Leisure Then and Now

Only a hundred years ago in the United States, working and living conditions and health problems were, by today's standards, horrendous; the life of the average person was marked by long work hours, grinding labor, overcrowding, stench, filth, malnutrition, disease, poverty, and caprice. In 1793, a yellow fever epidemic killed 10 percent of the population of Philadelphia, and smallpox and other contagions regularly ravaged American cities.* So constant were hardship and disease that during the American Civil War twice as many soldiers died from disease and starvation as from battlefield injuries.**

The demands of ordinary life and making one's way were severe. In seventeenth-century America, most unprivileged adolescents were either apprenticed or indentured to other families. At the height of the American Industrial Revolution in the late nineteenth century, and early in the twentieth century in England, the average workweek for working-class urban children, who often began working at age nine or ten, was well over sixty hours. Working conditions were both unhealthy and dangerous. Life on the farms proved little better, with intense seasonal labor and year-round morning and evening chores. Child labor laws gradually eased the labor burden for urban youth, as unionization and improved technology later did for adults. Before the Industrial Revolution provided more leisure, it first extracted vast quantities of time and health from the working class. Only as recently as 1930 did the workweek finally shrink to the current forty hours. By and large, the conditions of survival were far more arduous and capricious, and lives were far shorter: as late as 1900, the average life span was only 47 years.

*Jack Larkin, *The Reshaping of Everyday Life, 1790-1840* (New York: Harper & Row, 1988), pp. 78-81.
**Daniel E. Sutherland, *The Expansion of Everyday Life, 1860-1876* (New York: Harper & Row, 1989), p. 19.

nial struggle between toil and rest, suffering and enjoyment. On such crucial matters have rested for countless epochs the central contours of daily life. But never before was leisure the pervasive and ungoverned territory it is today. In seventeenth-century England, for example, the role, content, and control of leisure activity provoked deep political, religious, and social turmoil. Traditional societies enjoyed leisure, to be sure, during seasonal and religious festivals, but these interludes were intermittent and short-lived. The circuses of the past largely set up shop, opened their gates for a short time, and then moved on. With few exceptions, history's countless faceless generations have lived lives that have fit the Hobbesian description of "nasty, brutish, and short."

It is difficult to overstate this point, for its neglect in contemporary culture aggravates the culture's confusion about leisure. Modernity's historical amnesia largely overlooks even the most elementary facts of history—that, for example, the forty-hour workweek is but a few decades old. The progress toward leisure is new and, comparatively speaking, very dramatic.

The dramatic changes in conditions of work and leisure reflect the historical oddity of modern life. On many fronts, modern science, technology, and industry have seemingly reversed the effects of the biblical Fall: hardscrabble toil for food, pain in childbirth, and the sway of early death. If these burdens—"curses" is not too strong a word—have historically described the general tragic harshness and brevity of life, then indeed the fortunate Western world has managed to surpass some of the limits that have bound civilization from its beginnings. Lives marked by physical health, longevity, ease, and abundance have replaced short, bleak lives of drudgery, pain, and poverty.

Indeed, the lifestyle of the average Westerner exceeds the luxurious lifestyles of bygone economic elites who largely escaped most of the hard daily struggle for survival—the aristocracies of Jerusalem, Athens, Paris, Boston, and the like to whom historians have given most of their attention. In hindsight, however, it looks as if those small, privileged groups suffered some of the same puzzling cultural maladies we now face. Modern culture, too, is rife with historical peculiarities, both opportunities and calamities, that only increase in number and strangeness, for never in history have so many for so long enjoyed such steady and abundant leisure. It is clear that contemporary youth have more leisure, and greater affluence with which to enjoy it, than the vast majority of adults only a hundred years ago ever dreamed possible, at least in this life.

The Paradox of Leisure, or
The Hard Work of Finding Fun

Actually, the development of Western leisure has not been nearly so benign or idyllic as it sounds. The rise of mass leisure and the availability of ever increasing electronic options have been decidedly mixed blessings. Technologically based leisure has exacted its price; it has bestowed but a patina of real human freedom, and that at a high cost. Instead of being freed by the scope and scale of leisure, young and old alike have become slaves of the electronic carnival. As inmates of adolescence, youth are confined to their own special prison—to a realm of leisure, pleasure, dreams, and peers. With the rise of easily consumed, widely available leisure "products" have come the shackles of modern youth culture.

In the four decades since the end of World War II, North America's corporate-industrial economy has flourished, producing both leisure and affluence. At the same time, however, numerous popular books and films have persistently pointed to the costly psychological and ethical toll of pursuing the grail of leisure. Again and again, people have questioned what the very quest for glorious leisure does to the minds and souls of humankind. From Sloan Wilson's *The Man in the Gray Flannel Suit* (1955), a best-selling novel about success in corporate America, to the prolonged current of dissent in such films as *The Graduate* (1967), *Network* (1976), *Broadcast News* (1988), and *Wall Street* (1988), one piece of popular art after another has pondered the personal cost of obtaining leisure and material reward.

The ironies are obvious. On the one hand, scads of best-selling self-help books—from Robert Ringer's *Looking Out for Number One* and *Winning through Intimidation* to Norman Vincent Peale's countless positive-thinking inspirationals—have explained how to climb the ladder of success. On the other hand, innumerable self-help best-sellers—ranging from sex manuals to psychologist Leo Buscaglia's guides to feeling and loving—suggest how to repair the infinite variety of frozen and blighted selves of countless adults and children damaged by success. *The Hurried Child*, the best-selling book by child psychologist David Elkind, indicted the common middle-class practice of imposing adult standards of competition and performance on young children, who then grow up to be fretful adults. Elkind's impressionistic hunches in the 1970s were empirically confirmed by social research. While most Westerners enthusiastically endorse capitalism's remarkable benefits, a strong subcurrent wonders about the value and old-fashioned moral correctness of work whose reward is contemporary leisure. The villain seems to be a byproduct of capitalism—namely, affluence.

In spite of the growing suspicion of the real fruits of consumption-oriented leisure, a significant cultural shift does not seem to be in the offing. Unparalleled leisure and affluence seem only to fire the appetite for more. One carnival leads to another, grander display of electronic leisure. The 1980s seemed the era of greed and "me," the time of yuppies, enormous stock scandals, and widespread governmental deceit and corruption. Even the Rolling Stones, the bohemian countercultural heroes of the 1970s youth revolution, fully "capitalized" their 1989 North American tour with the generous sponsorship of a brewery. Statistics further corroborate the mood. American adults seem willing to sacrifice more and more for "goods" and leisure—ironically, even time itself, a sacrifice which cuts into leisure. Today many work so hard and long to acquire the conditions and accessories of "genuine" leisure—second homes, power boats, snowmobiles, and electronic gadgetry—that they have little time to actually enjoy the rewards of their labor. At best the things of leisure have become taxing symbols of a dream rather than a means of realizing that dream. With such labors, who has time for play? Where is the land of leisure?

This points to a central paradoxical irony of our time: more and greater technology does not notably increase free time. Quite to the contrary, numerous studies have shown that the more technologized a culture becomes, the less leisure its workers enjoy.[2] Both the acquisition and maintenance of costly, exotic electronic gadgets and symbols demand ever greater amounts of time and resources, just those commodities that we wish to expand and enhance. As one observer has succinctly put it, "The time commitment our consumption requires snatches away the very leisure we thought we were gaining."[3] The constancy and rigor of our pursuit of leisure threatens to overwhelm us, and on this front youth have learned well from the models of their parents. It is a dubious legacy at best. Relegated to a world of leisure and affluence, the fun palace of adolescence—what F. Scott Fitzgerald calls "purposeless splendor"—youth consume and drift.

To be sure, our techno-industrial economy serves its workers, but those same workers increasingly serve the incessant demands of the economy's planned obsolescence of up-scale consumerism. The labor force works ever harder and longer to obtain those items that will save time, provide leisure, and help everyone enjoy everything more efficiently and intensely—that is, when time allows. The predicament, then, seems to be that we work longer and harder to achieve the well-off life of ease and idleness, which only recedes as we chase it. The circularity of the predicament recalls Fitzgerald's sad benediction in the last sentence of *The Great Gatsby* (1925): Ahead lies an "orgiastic future that year by year recedes before us. It eluded us then, but that's no matter—tomorrow we will run faster, stretch out our arms further. . . . So we beat on, boats against the current, borne back ceaselessly into the past." If we could but step out of the flood tide of pursuit, we might find the time to breathe and enjoy it all. With the techno-economic means of the electronic Eden, a whole culture lives in mutual, reciprocal submission.

2. Leland Ryken, *Work and Leisure in Christian Perspective* (Portland, Ore.: Multnomah Press, 1987), p. 51.

3. Ryken, *Work and Leisure in Christian Perspective*, p. 51.

In Pursuit of the Good Life?

In the fifteen years between 1973 and 1988, the average workweek has expanded from 41 hours to 47, with many professions, like law and medicine, demanding an 80-hour week. The optimistic forecasts of the 1960s that in twenty years the workweek would dwindle to 22 hours and the work year to 27 weeks now seem fantastic. With increased work commitments, the average American's actual leisure time has shrunk by 37 percent. In over half of American marriages, both spouses work, and that burden of family care doubles for the sizeable number of single parents.

—Nancy Gibbs, "How America Has Run Out of Time," *Time*, 24 Apr. 1989, p. 58.

It is safe to say, then, that affluent leisure has become a commercial and popular icon by which modern Western culture now steers its way. The appetite for leisure often embraces irrationality as hordes chase the newest fad—whether it be tanning parlors, winter trips, snowmobiles, or CD players—to enhance and intensify the experience of leisure. Youth exhibit the same appetite in their headlong rush to buy the latest album, see the hottest movie, wear the trendiest styles, or sample the coolest beer. Western culture has indeed received a marvel-filled gift, alluring, intoxicating, and new in the long history of the race. Oddly, as social data clearly indicate, youth have inherited and adopted a mind-set that offers, at best, mixed satisfactions. Still, for youth as for adults, the shiny commercial promise of new and greater delight continues, and the search for satisfaction finds ever-new impetus. If teens learn anything from their parents these days, it is that leisure is a holy grail to be relentlessly pursued.

The Exaltation of Modern Leisure

The peculiar paradox of modern leisure—at once involving greater labor, pursuit, and dissatisfaction, a condition particularly evident among youth—results in part from the unthinking ahistoricism of contemporary culture: the failure to recognize the uniqueness of the modern moment. The habitual parental song of "You never had it so good" or "When I was a kid in the fifties . . ." may be true, but it does not do much to raise anyone's historical awareness. In any case, this mood partakes of strong antimodern intellectual currents, liberal and conservative alike, that have often romanticized the past in order to demystify mass culture and modern techno-industrial accomplishment. As one historian of leisure has commented, work has always been work, and people have always perceived it as such. There never was some bygone ideal era when work was so infused with meaning and joy that it was other than work. Always there has been a dividing line between work and leisure, except perhaps in animistic societies. That does not mean, however, that the conditions of labor in relation to leisure, community, and self have always been the same. Rather, it is important to see any given setting of work and leisure within a spectrum or continuum of mixtures of content and discontent.

In contemporary North America, the bifurcation between work and leisure has grown sharper. From early industrialism in the eighteenth century to the present, the demands of "work time" or "punching the clock" have routinized work. The relative discretionary freedom of the pre-industrial worker to work or play on a given day no longer exists; exercising such freedom today involves considerable economic sacrifice and risk. Obligation and routine, the much-lamented workplace "rut," dominate. The standardization of work tasks, specialized and repetitive—whether in a law firm, on an assembly line, or at MacDonald's—has made work less meaningful, with high numbers of American workers feeling unchallenged and unfulfilled. The social atmosphere of the workplace, driven by profit and flavored with quotas and competition, makes many contemporary work settings drab, impersonal, and forbidding. Finally, for most of modern culture, going to work entails increased travel time, distance, cost, and, very often, stress, thus removing work even farther, geographically and psychically, from one's non-work world. The combination of these factors—regularity, standardization, impersonality, competition, transport, and stress—have demeaned and separated work from locality, community, freedom, and self-worth. Work has become "labor" and "wages," simply putting in one's "time." Moreover, standards of affluence—food, clothing, housing, sanitation, transportation, and entertainment—have become so high for many middle-class youth and their families that they often must work long and hard to obtain those standards.

By and large, given the structure of modern corporate work, employees simply cannot take a brief leave of absence or an extended holiday. The employee who does so loses the job, the house, the cars, and the money for the kids' educations. Those brief annual respites, vacations, have become frenetic, requiring that huge amounts of energy and money be expended on recreational "getaway" vehicles or stays at exotic retreats or other "purchasable" intense experiences. Opting out of the economic climb, either by choice or by social standing, insures a life within the social welfare "safety net" of poverty, crime, and boredom. Only a few manage an alternative lifestyle. The consequences of the few available choices are not inviting.

The effect of this regimented, corporate-industrial "workstyle" has been to exalt the value and significance of leisure. Leisure activity—whether watching TV, eating out, fishing, or going to art galleries—has increasingly supplied compensations for the deficiencies of work. As work has become constrictive and regimented, less a domain of choice, pleasure, and significance, adults and youth alike have searched ever harder for "good times," as a beer commercial put it, which promise clear and densely "packed" enjoyment and significance, whether physical, social, or aesthetic. It is this appetite and the quest to satisfy it that the commercial entertainment media, especially advertising, continually fuel and exploit.

The conditions of modern labor, then, have notably increased the economic cost of leisure and exalted its significance, since leisure is made to compensate for the contemporary deficiences of work. A century and a half of industrial advancement have greatly increased the resources for leisure but have not necessarily increased the level of human freedom, contentment, or ease. Contrary to long-standing expectations, leisure has apparently become less relaxing and restorative because the modern work world has made the increase and "use" of leisure more necessary and more desperate. We have much pleasure but little satisfaction or content. The commercial media, including entertainment, have prospered by marketing to this dis-ease, accentuating its reality and promising multiple consumerist solutions. And of course, since youth are beset by the natural developmental problems of identity and intimacy and have ample amounts of disposable income, they have proven to be an especially fertile market for entrepreneurs capitalizing on discontent.

This tenuous relationship between work, leisure, entertainment, and consumption takes place within a larger, century-old cultural disorientation (some would say crisis)—the loss of an intellectually and symbolically cogent and cohesive cultural vision. In the place of the univocal cultural force of the Judeo-Christian tradition, whatever its deficits and lapses, has emerged a smorgasbord, a broad pluralism of competitive, salvific "isms": scientism, secularism, hedonism, consumerism, Jungianism, New Ageism, aestheticism, capitalism, Marxism, *ad infinitum*. There is an "ism" for every taste, class, age, and educational background. In this philosophical supermarket, in which many of the choices are proffered by the media, people generally look for an "ism" by which to understand and steer their lives, although this search is only rarely undertaken as a programmatic philosophical venture. Victorian poet Matthew Arnold aptly expressed this cultural fix when he described himself as "Wandering between two worlds, one dead,/The other powerless to be born." Arnold mourned the loss of a Christian vision of the world, one he could no longer accept, but he sensed the profound and lasting cultural confusion that would follow its demise. With the old Christian world gone, rendered no longer credible by Darwin, Western culture possessed nothing of commensurate intellectual or imaginative stature or "force," to use Henry Adams's term, to take its place. For better or worse, the cultural glue of the West had lost its hold, throwing the culture's members into disarray and confusion.

Many cultural critics suggest that Arnold's depiction describes a lasting condition of confusion and aimlessness. That legacy afflicts youth in particular, suspended as they are between an eroding cultural coherence and today's bewildering, hydra-headed pluralism. Arnold's hope for a new compelling vision that would yield a new coherence has not been realized, nor does there seem to be much prospect for such. Instead, in North America in particular, adults and youth cast about in that multi-ringed circus with which we began this chapter—diverted and entertained but unsatisfied and searching. Novelist-philosopher Walker Percy has explained the modern consuming self in the darkest of terms, as a creature without center or aim. Because of the loss of a transcendent focus and meaningful cultural cohesion, the everyday "self sees its only recourse as an endless round of work, diversion, and consumption of goods and services."[4] The only common ground seems to be a vision of the "good life," a consumerist sensate ideal allowed by our leisure and affluence and fostered by Madison Avenue, a myth in which children are thoroughly immersed by endless commercials. Percy believes that we live during a stage of civilization in which the self is wholly defined by the empirical realities of the objects, experiences, and entertainments it acquires. As Percy himself has suggested in such novels as *The Moviegoer*, at least part of what has filled the vacuum of meaning, bondedness, and delight has been electronic entertainment, and youth in particular have turned to the media for light and warmth.

4. Percy, *Lost in the Cosmos: The Last Self-Help Book* (New York: Farrar, Straus & Giroux, 1983), p. 122.

What to Do with Leisure, or
Six Uses of Entertainment, Historic and Contemporary

Entertainment has given contemporary youth a way to spend their time and their money. The modern leisure smorgasbord offers TV, music, movies, and even interactive video games. Academic researchers, journalists of TV and print, and anxious parents have endlessly argued whether these fillers of time be friend or foe. The points of contention touch everything from the nature of the medium and the morality of program content to appropriate amounts of use. The more theoretical debates about the content, nature, significance, and influence of popular entertainment, especially that designed for teens, do not seem likely to abate any time soon. Most people agree that the electronic carnival contains too much violence and sex, but there is virtually no consensus on who should say what is too much or how to go about combatting the bad. However, the question of what should supplant these staples is rarely asked. In spite of the volumes of words lavished on this subject, there is little clear understanding, let alone consensus, on exactly what entertainment is or what it should accomplish. Consequently, it is perhaps useful to review both historic and current understandings of the uses of entertainment.

Although we can only hypothesize about certain developments in the distant human past, it seems safe to conclude that with the emergence of stable society came entertainment. In other words, entertainment has always been at least a part of other activities. The history of human cultures suggests that the desire to be entertained constitutes a basic appetite and activity, as central and vital as the need for sleep and food. As soon as humans had some free time, they no doubt tried to amuse or enjoy themselves, and that was entertainment. And amid their work of survival and child-rearing, they no doubt discovered activities they enjoyed, and that was entertainment, or at least partly so. Similarly, they took pleasure and satisfaction in their worship, their feast days, and their devotional art. In legends and sagas, sacred and otherwise, that were told, sung, and drawn, ancient peoples learned their own histories that depicted their place in the world, in the process enjoying the tale's substance or the skill or artfulness of the narrator. In laying out fields or adorning pots, tents, or clothes, these peoples took pleasure and satisfaction in design, representation, and color. That, too, was entertainment. In short, they not only devised entertainment but also *were entertained* by many of the common activities of their lives. Anthropology and ethnography abound with accounts of the multiple purposes and almost infinite variety of entertainment, from cockfights to opera-going, in both ancient and modern cultures.

In other words, this hunger for entertainment has long existed, even before there was a word for leisure. Humankind's desire for enjoyable physical settings and meaningful psychological settings, two profoundly intertwined needs, is not a unique feature of modern life. It is more than likely that the convergence of contemporary leisure and the chaos of meaning in modern society has simply whetted the human hunger for meaning and enjoyment. A chief feature of the biblical Eden, the central myth of Western culture, one that forecasts a principal historical preoccupation, was the sensuous plenty and delight of the garden: trees were good to look at, their fruit was good to eat, and the sun and the moon took their galactic places in order to mark festivals in which the great gift of the created world, life itself and its immense fecundity, might be regularly celebrated. Thus the biblical account's mythic calling to know and delight in the earth and all its creatures betokens and summarizes a realm of meaning and experience after which humankind has ever since been striving. In the delight of the senses and social mutuality lies meaning, and in the meaning lies mutuality and delight.

The long and toilsome journey after the tragic fall from paradisal felicity has only accentuated the human quest for meaning and delight. And in our current cultural fix, the varied conditions of the modern world—philosophic, social, economic, and technological—have very likely, at least for many adolescents, only worsened the ageless, restless quest for understanding, identity, intimacy, and delight. We have vast resources for leisure and amusement but lack a personal or collective vision to undergird them. As Western culture has become more technologically advanced, socially fragmented, and ideologically disoriented, the quest for what entertainment has historically provided—maps of meaning, delight, and diversion—has only intensified. Correspondingly, entertainment makers have been more than eager to meet the demand with whatever will sell, however tawdry. In this we find a symbiotic interdependence between audience and industry, consumer and producer.

Entertainment still flourishes, performing its old functions. In our modern cultural plight, however, we have asked the realm of art to assume new authoritative functions that were previously performed by religion or kinship. Some of the new major forms of entertainment such as violent pornography suggest a grave imaginative distortion if not a reversal of the biblical paradigm of delight and intimacy. Recognizing this, it is useful to reflect on the different functions of art and entertainment—how and why we fill our leisure time.

The Mythic Function

One understanding of art looks at popular entertainment as supplying consumers with an imaginative realm or refraction of life that contains clues, signs, and routes for interpreting the tangled welter of experience that life presents. Mythic narratives—whether they be of Odysseus, Abraham Lincoln, or Rambo—tell us much about what the world might be like and how we should behave in it. Adolescents, too, seek this vital information about life. Cultural analysts repeatedly point to these mythic constructions, for they potentially chart the way for a variety of human pursuits. Full of terror and ecstasy, guile and innocence, horror and beauty, iniquity and virtue, life itself challenges us all to survive and prosper. We are, after all, as novelist/playwright Thornton Wilder has suggested, "thrown into existence, like dice from a box," and we spend much of our time thereafter trying to understand life's obstacles and solve its riddles. Much of art, then, works to describe the nature of the world and one's place within it, and from these dramatic depictions, in story and image, we learn.

This function of popular art is now heightened insofar as Westerners for the most part live without traditional religious certainties and communities, and in such a setting most people confront questions, usually starting in adolescence, to which there is now a plethora of answers. North American culture now churns forth a multiplicity of attractive solutions and claims, ranging from Christian fundamentalism to New Ageism to rank hedonism. Young people may not start quite from scratch, but the inquiry assumes much more urgency and confusion when we live in a philosophical supermarket where appeal depends on packaging and much shelf space is devoted to snack food.

In an electronic world, a single, binding myth no longer can shape and beckon pluralistic societies. The instinctive human appetite to imbibe images and stories that impart some measure of clarity, delight, and hope has, amid our sea of uncertainty, turned voracious; we scramble and hunt ever harder for satisfaction. For many people, especially those with the leisure and affluence that allows for the quest, our popular entertainments have become, unconsciously exalted though they may be, forceful practical laboratories for cataloging and testing life's options.

The Aesthetic Function

The question of what in popular entertainment an audience enjoys is a harder one to answer. A partial rejoinder from the highbrow bastions of

Art and the Church

There is neither a simple nor a clear way to gauge the impact of art. Most often audiences sense or feel its mysterious alchemy transform their perception of the world and themselves. Beauty and ugliness, the glory of creation and the horror of fallenness, hope and despair depicted—these affect everyone every day, in countless small or large ways.

We are continually immersed in art through the forms and textures of all the things we have created—cars, homes, clothing, entertainment, and so on. More than that, our relationship with art is not casual; we make it and absorb it with fascination and delight. Indeed, the pervasiveness of art and our fascination with it reveal a central and insatiable human appetite for imagining, enjoying, and understanding life. And art is a prime means to that end.

This recognition is nothing particularly new for the historic church, which has long known the power of artistic forms. For millennia Christians have fought over the inclusion and meaning of the details in the narrative of God's action in the world, particularly the details about the character and role of Jesus Christ—what and how he said or did this or that to one group or another. Those centuries-old arguments have not only been a matter of getting the "facts" straight, as indispensable as those are. Many of the enduring creedal disputes have gotten their fire from the profound recognition that assertions about and images of Christ are matters of enormous import for faith and devotion. What is in the story—the question of canon—and how one tells it—the substance of creeds—have been of pivotal importance in determining the life of the believer, the church, and the culture. Through the work of the Spirit, the holy story, its incidents and images, shaped the life of faith—how the faithful understood, believed, felt about, and lived those stories.

Like its struggles with canon and creed, the church's historic ambivalence toward visual images, dating to ancient Israel, reflects a profound apprehension of and anxiety about the power of art. Foes and advocates alike have recognized the shaping and even transfixing power of visual representation—an allure and force that the discipline of aesthetics still labors to fathom. Ardent Calvinists have destroyed cathedrals and churches, thus dramatically exhibiting their suspicion of the visual arts specifically and of imaginative creation in general. On the other hand, one of the major traditions of Christian faith, Eastern Orthodoxy, has emphasized the devotional use of icons, and it has flourished and endured, even amid the oppression of the Soviet Union. The enormous power of story, image, and imagination was amply illustrated recently in the firestorm over *The Last Temptation of Christ*, a film made by two seemingly earnest Christian artists. The same power and influence of visual appeal can be seen in the marketing strategies and controversial scandals of televangelism.

educational and moral privilege suggests that at least part of the appeal of popular art lies in its constant replay of mythic elements, in countless melodramatic ways, and that this repetition accounts for some audience satisfaction. The implication of this answer is that popular art is but a pale shadow of high art. Television, pop music, and movies will very likely never be as cerebral and serious—whatever that means—or as "complex" and nuanced as high art, but that recognition says very little about the success, worth, or influence of an imaginative venture. Unfortunately, the canons of criticism have in effect dictated that the only significant or true art—whether musical, visual, or dramatic—is that which is susceptible to extensive and complex verbal analysis of form and content, a set of criteria that invests professional specialists with cultural authority and exalts their knowledge.

Such a bias toward distillable meaning (or, in the case of modernism, anti-meaning) or verbal amplitude—what some would call logocentric interpretation and evaluation—has prompted great masses of people to regard their taste, intelligence, leisure activities, and even mores as necessarily inferior simply because they have not won approval from a long-entrenched, self-inflating, and self-protective critical establishment. Furthermore, the high critical stance has virtually forgotten that a prime intention or effect of all art, at least that which is good enough to be called entertainment, is pleasure or enjoyment. Despite what elite critics might say, popular audiences should remember that it is appropriate to like the simple and unsophisticated tales, legends, fables, myths, parables, melodramas, and fantasies. Moreover, both elite critics and popular audiences should recall that some of the works that now make up the classical galaxy either were once very popular or borrowed some of their most renowned material from popular forms. In music this applies to Bach, Beethoven, and Copland; in literature, to Franklin, Melville, Dickens, and Fitzgerald; in film, to Griffith, Eisenstein, and Hitchcock.

With this in mind, it is perhaps safe to venture that a chief function of art, in its clarifying and intensifying of the perception of the "stuff" of life, is simply to heighten one's awareness of and pleasure in being alive, and that can be accomplished equally well by simple or complex forms, by tragedy or comedy, by realism or fantasy. At perhaps its most minimal level, in the vitality and virtuosity of performance, popular entertainment prompts a simple relishing of the sensuous goodness of life—of the marvelous timber of voice and expression, of the close mimicry of life in acting, of the facsimile and surprise of visual composition. The gift of feeling good about being alive is no small present—nor is its acceptance a trifling thing.

Lost notions of the Christian tradition illustrate the gist of this line of thought. Calvinism and some sacramentalist strains of Roman Catholicism have always emphasized the notion of general or common grace, a texture of love and beauty infused into the very fabric of creation and the patterns and rhythms of ordinary daily life. To a great extent, traditional philosophical humanism has simply secularized this age-old Christian strain. In any of these perspectives, all humankind has the capacity to enjoy and revel in the ordinary beauty and glory of life and nature. The glory persists, and even amid tawdry distortions of primordial beauty, vestiges of splendor remain. In an early novel by John Updike, the protagonist's minister-father, upon hearing drunken laughter coming from a bar, comments, "All joy belongs to the Lord." The modern experience of alienation and horror has rightly sobered our joy in being alive, but the numerous terrors of our century remain horrific violations precisely because they do so diminish how fine life can be.

There is, after all—though the pessimism of modernism would deny it, at least in print—the plain fun of expressing and viewing and hearing the revel of being alive. In our most unthinking enjoyment there can be a kind of aesthetic enraptment, whether that is prompted by a rock beat, a dance move, a camera sweep, or an inane joke. There is also the plain delight we can take in seeing life rendered fully, freshly, vigorously, humorously, or triumphantly, even if that is only in a rerun or a retelling of old stories in new ways. In unfathomable and untraceable ways, ways that are largely unchartable routes to destinations in the human psyche, seeing and hearing intensify awareness, wonder, and relish—or, when appropriate, horror. Life becomes more dear.

The Excursionary Function

Insofar as art enwraps its audience in aesthetic enjoyment and participation, it offers two more very important and probably necessary aids to the human circumstance. First, there is the very real necessity to get away, to leave the immediate concerns, obligations, and worries of daily survival in order to enter, at least for a short while, another mode of thought and experience. The human psychological mechanism must simply "shut down" at times, do something else, to allow time and rest for reflection and healing. The simple act of attending a concert or a movie, of focusing one's attention on another sort of expression, allows the spirit to recoup and renew itself for the practical toils of everyday life. That benefit is very likely gotten regardless of the artistic medium, although the entertainment has to be of sufficient quality to capture and sustain attention. These aesthetic vacations refresh and enliven the spirit and nurture the resiliency and creativity important to the ordinary tasks of life. Modern poet T. S. Eliot suggested that "human kind cannot bear very much reality." There are those who, using Eliot as a starting point, would contend that the human spirit seeks simple escape and renewal in popular entertainment. To some extent, the harried nature of modern life creates a pervasive kind of stress that makes our psyches demand that we spend some nights being "couch potatoes."

A more subtle explanation of the crucial cognitive and emotional necessity of "getting away" through popular entertainment comes from anthropologist Clifford Geertz. In a famous essay on the Balinese cockfight, Geertz argues that seemingly incidental entertainments are in fact—through images, stories, and songs—metaphorical distillations, relevant but not frighteningly rendered, of the crucial experiences and issues of life. These inviting metaphors catch up important themes of "death, masculinity, rage, pride, loss, beneficence, chance." Regardless of medium, says Geertz, the purpose is simply to "display," not to dilute or agitate, an emotionally charged portion of experience. Put simply, such excursions constitute stories that people "tell themselves about themselves."[5] They enter another world, an imaginative and fictive one, in order to understand this one. In getting away, audiences see and feel played out before them the essential dramas and questions of life, and such "display" clarifies and resonates with the world in which they find themselves.

As an elaboration of what Geertz suggests, and an echo too of the mythic function previously discussed, it is worth looking at what many popular entertainments provide. In the simpler forms of narrative—usually called fables, romances, or melodramas—good seemingly always triumphs. With hopeful climaxes, the tales suggest that all things will end well. This optimistic cast in popular art has endured relentless criticism by the elite critics, who believe that such entertainment is naive, fanciful, and stultifying. Those of a political bent contend not only that the happy endings of popular art are insufficiently realistic, but also that the facile hopefulness of good-always-winning-out-in-the-end dulls, diverts, or saps audience reaction to evil. Such art, it is claimed, is delusory and propagandistic, serving as the pie-in-the-sky opiate that religion once was before it supposedly died away.

It can be argued, however, that these excursions into hope and triumph might ultimately renew resolution and prompt action. Not all incentives toward good come from desperation; much is fueled by the

5. Geertz, *The Interpretation of Cultures* (New York: Basic Books, 1973), pp. 443-48.

hope that good and kindness might in the end win out, if only steeled by idealism and determination, which is the usual content of the popular dramas of movies and TV. Criticism of this optimism says much about the naiveté of "high culture" in estimating the naiveté and intelligence of those who are heartened by such tales. Average people today are tired and harassed, yes, but most are not simpletons or fools. Most audiences, both adult and teen, can readily enough tell the difference between what is and what we wish. We know full well that happy endings are not all that frequent, that life is full of tragedy, but still we watch, because melodrama and happy endings give us hope that maybe things will somehow turn out all right in the end. Popular entertainment may amount to escape, but it is escape with a purpose, whether refreshment, new perspective, or hope.

The Function of Cohesion

While the old Christian glue has loosened in Western culture, popular art still does provide various shared—by virtue of their popularity—images and tales that allow for social connectedness and larger cultural cohesion. Perhaps the most widely shared religious experience in recent decades came via the immense popularity of, first, the continuing *Star Wars* saga, begun in 1977, and then, in 1982, the story of *E.T.: The Extra-Terrestrial*. It seemed that everyone responded to the spiritual appeal of "the force" in *Star Wars* and something about the lostness in E.T.'s plaintive appeal to "phone home." These are perhaps fragmentary and transient linkages, but they do supply referents, much like sports, politics, and soap operas do, that together constitute a core or pool of common experience whose meanings are clear, articulable, and forceful.

This dimension of popular art appeals particularly to teens who are, comparatively speaking, new to the world and eagerly, sometimes desperately trying to figure out the riddles of identity and intimacy. They absorb images, lyrics, musical beats, jokes, and stories like sponges and then weave those data into the fabric of their own dreams and relationships. Tastes in music, for example, can form the basis for "something to talk about" or orientations or criteria for social grouping. The stuff of popular culture has become increasingly important as almost every cultural setting has become ethnically and religiously diverse and marked by transition rather than permanence. The average American family moves every four years, making geographical, social, and cultural ties hard to establish and sustain. Tradition exerts relatively little hold on youth. It is little wonder, then, that a national electronic culture has increasingly displaced older means of cultural transmission and allegiance. For better or worse, entertainment itself now supplies the historical continuity and sociocultural glue necessary to perpetuate a society. It supercedes tradition, ethnicity, religion, and locality to make itself the stuff of historical and national cohesion.

The Function of Distraction

We live in an unusual culture that simultaneously generates enormous quantities of stress and boredom. The demands and excesses of a highly technological consumerist culture, as described earlier, take a hard toll on its workers. Assembly-line work full of repetition, monotony, and blandness wearies and deflates the spirit. Huge numbers of underpaid, unemployed, and untrained people, usually young, lifelong members of the new underclass, live desperate, futureless lives marred by boredom, crime, and drugs. Meanwhile, in a vastly different economic caste, the executives and middle managers, likely candidates for the leisure class, flag and falter, expending enormous amounts of time and energy in the race for success and status. And so it goes. The cultural direction of America, like that of many of her economic allies, both western and eastern, seems now to have a sort of relentless and irreversible momentum. Leisure, wealth, and the abandon of youth—what looks like the permanent exaltation of the yuppie—increasingly summarize American cultural aspirations.

This grim cultural forecast features the bleak blending of both fatigue and temporary satedness that leads only to greater dissatisfaction. The world of work exhausts, both physically and psychically, whether it involves manual, skilled, or managerial labor. And the prizes in the great consumeristic free-for-all on which we increasingly gorge offer only momentary satisfaction, and at a very dear cost. The effort of acquiring the ever-mounting glut of material blandishments profoundly disorients the central and deeper psychological and spiritual needs of the self: relatedness, calm, reflection, and meaning. In this context, we increasingly use popular entertainment to fill the void, dull the ache, or mask the confusion—however one wishes to describe treating (or mistreating) the malady. Popular art forms now function less for diversion and more for mindless distraction, another addictive route that keeps the self from contemplating its own confusion and emptiness. The arts become, finally, hypnotic, a perpetual whirl and chant to induce a trance that serves simply to take the mind off things it should be considering.

The New Video Leisure

The rise of the VCR in North America has changed leisure habits across the land. The impact of the new technology will be seen especially among the new generation of youth raised with the VCR. So far some of the effects are already clear. Between 1984 and 1987 alone, the following changes in leisure habits took place among adults in the United States:

VCR ownership:	+234%
museum attendance:	+24%
movie attendance:	+9%
dance attendance:	-14%
theater attendance:	-25%
attendance of classical and pop concerts:	-26%
attendance of opera and musical theater:	-38%

—*Newsweek*, 28 Mar. 1988, p. 69.

Increasingly, electronic pop art supplies the bright images and loud sounds we crave to stupefy awareness.

The Function of Compaction

So enamored are we of the consumerist ideal of an abundant Eden that we consciously set out to glut ourselves on the enticing pleasures of goods and entertainment that the commercial world promises us. The gods of work and economic success loom large, breeding frenzied efforts to absorb as much entertainment as possible, as much of the good life as we can, in order to confirm the essential rightness of the consumerist ethos. In another way, one that probably has more to do with the heart, our enjoyment mania offers compensation for the drudgery or stress of the work that provides the affluence that allows the compensation. Ironically, in either case, the frenzy of the economic scramble spills over into leisure and dominates it. Consequently, hordes of people in all social classes grasp for more and splashier leisure and leisure products despite shrinking quantities of free time and resources: big-screen, high-definition TVs; surround sound quadraphonic digital Dolbyized high-definition interactive multi-screened VCRs; laser digital audio and video players; wall-sized sound machines (speakers) and entertainment centers; cars with more speaker power than horsepower; and a plethora of other technological wonders: cordless, go-anywhere speakers, headphone radio-cassette players, compact audio players, and wrist-watch TVs. In the worst extremes, what is heard or seen becomes irrelevant. Style and effect count for more than content or form—and this may be truer of the devotee of opera than of the lover of boom-box rock. For larger and larger audiences, it is the fullness of the reproductive capacity and the force of the illusion that dominate. The techno-personal quest for the chimera of multiple perfect sounds and perfect pictures for perfect moments seduces, drives, and becomes an end in itself.

In such a culture, satedness is impossible. One can gain satisfaction only by taking more and more in. The premises of a consumer culture—based on fashion, status, and obsolescence—undercut the very prospect of gaining any sort of lasting satisfaction. As the goods and activities we pursue became increasingly less satisfying, their elaborate bells and whistles multiply. The latest, hottest fads seem to combine two or more entertainments or distractions at once, especially as time, affluence, and gadgetry allow, to stave off boredom, futility, and fear. We do not now simply sail or fly, we parasail. We do not merely fish, wily and patient; we plumb the deeps with sonar to find the prey. Sports stadiums now have domes, air conditioning, and big-screen instant replay. Movie complexes house twenty screens, thousands of seats, and huge sound systems such as the THX system designed and licensed by George Lucas. The all-purpose, hyper-sensory anything jolts us into being: I vibrate; therefore I am.

Cultural Criticism, Popular Entertainment, and the Quest for Leisure

Anthropology and sociology have done much to delineate the multiple cultural roles of art. It is now relatively easy to delineate with some precision the different functions of art and entertainment in different cultures. Questions of value—the relative emotional health or rightness of those cultures, or of the arts that inform, shape, reflect, and sustain them—generally do not concern social scientists. By and large, they restrict their analysis to questions of how cultures function. At the same time, aesthetic or art criticism has become rarefied, preoccupied as it is with theory; it long ago relegated questions of value to psychology and politics. In any case, traditional art criticism does not prove helpful in the assessment, whether aesthetic or moral, of popular art, especially when it focuses on an established canon of elite masterpieces. Calls for the examination of popular art usually elicit references to its general unworthiness; specifically targeted are its alleged lack of seriousness or depth, complexity, and innovation. Critics with marked ideological perspectives, whether conservative, Marxist, or feminist, often see popular art as the new electronic opiate that binds the masses to dullness and passivity.

So deeply entrenched is this elitist bias that the evaluation of popular art is not likely to muster much attention for some time to come. The reasons for this are complex, and space does not allow us to examine them here. In any case, the larger challenge is to formulate some sensible criteria for the aesthetic, intellectual, and moral evaluation of popular art, a topic to which we devote our concluding chapter. Any critical filter must sensibly take into account the rich fullness of human culture—especially appetites for myth, art, and play—provided by contemporary anthropologists of the stature of Clifford Geertz and Robert Darnton. To do otherwise is to ignore on behalf of ideology what modernity itself has taught. Not only must an informed view take into account the functional multiplicity of popular art, but it must also appreciate the significance of aesthetic simplicity, the depth of metaphor, the resonance of allusion, and iconic intensity. Most of all, amid the nightmarish political and psychic landscape of the twentieth century, any view must assert an inclusive prescriptive norm that promises to distinguish cultural health from cultural decay. By some means or another, Western culture must begin to ponder the significance and impact of the kinds of stories we tell ourselves. At the same time, we must avoid the narrow moral and political guidelines that would give rise to a new constrictive legalism.

Numerous traditions can be mined for fresh perspectives for this task. One of the most lively perspectives available in the West stems from the Jewish-Christian notion of creation. It gives us a simple retrospective ideal that successfully resolves a variety of questions about the shape, texture, and purposes of human culture—what the world at its best might and should be.

The Genesis account of creation clarifies divine intentions for human life—specifically, what God wanted not *from* but *for* humanity. Hardly any other piece of Western story-telling, religious or secular, has been so subject to misinterpretation and misemphasis. Popular lore and religious nurture based on the creation story seldom venture beyond prattle about birds, fishes, and fig leaves. Usually the world is deemed "good," as God declared it, only because God said so, and that pretty much settles the matter. Readers most often cannot explain why it is good for humankind, let alone why it is good for God—why God bothers and what God likes about the world. Within the Christian tradition, there has been much theo-biblical talk of order, hierarchy, dominion, and sometimes harmony, but not of what God intended for human life.

Close attention to the creation account allows for a clear fix on divine intentions for life in Eden. And what we find there says more about God than about humanity per se. The Holy One fends off void and chaos to establish and consecrate for humanity a history and a teeming place in which to live it. The divine intention for humankind is already evident on the fourth day, about halfway to the point at which God actually created a human. God lets his ultimate desire be known by placing lights in the sky to mark seasons *and* festivals, the latter being a grateful revel in which only humans partake (Gen. 1:14, REB). As he is shaping the world, God knows where it is all headed. Already, so early in the account, God has in mind the good pleasure of humanity for which he brings into being that whole plenteous world. Food drops from trees, and flesh does not devour flesh. And there is too the demand that all creatures procreate and thrive.

The second chapter of Genesis fleshes out this scheme still farther. There we find the heralded details of God forming man from the dust of the earth. More importantly, numerous details reveal the emphasis that God places on a fitting habitation for humankind. This is ground for meeting and delight, a place that Creator and creatures might together enjoy and relish. We are told that Eden is full of fruitful, beautiful trees and that there is a river to water the garden (2:8-10). Adam and Eve, helpmates together, care for the garden and increase its fruitfulness and glory. In return, the garden provides physical nurture and sensuous delight for the eye and the palate. As Adam and Eve live in harmony with animal and plant life, so also they abide in ease, a quiet intimacy of trust and gratitude, with the Creator, Who walks the garden in the cool of the evening. Seen so, Eden becomes a habitation of delight, harmony, and mutuality, the hallmarks of creation. Its uniqueness is emphasized by the stark contrast with what soon follows after the Fall: the pointless, jealous slaying of Cain and the predatory violence that occasions the Flood, acts that God plainly abominates. In Eden there was no violence or contention. Rather, there was only celebration of and delight in the glory, mutuality, and harmony of a world that moved in glad, gracious concert with all things—plant, animal, human, and divine.

The point here is that a primary intention of the creation was to provide an arena of unceasing delight, a spectacular show at once aesthetic, moral, psychological, social, and political. Although it is important to note that one Old Testament scholar has suggested that the repeated "good" of the first chapter connotes aesthetic more than moral judgment, one suspects the two meanings are here conflated and indivisible.[6] In any case, what God likes and provides for humankind says much about God and about the texture God intended for human life—its daily "stuff" should occasion constant relish, gladness, and gratitude. It is this sensibility that provides the backdrop for the psalmist and the prophets, who compare God's greater glory to the self-evident splendor and majesty of the natural world. The continual invocation of glory and beauty assumes that the world is resplendent with the creative fire and fineness of divine love and that, accordingly, beauty and aesthetic delight do and should inform our sense of what surrounds and animates life—namely, God; at the very least we should recognize that it is the hand of God that shapes the beauty that exalts all things, including people.

The delight is clearly aesthetic, a psychological response to color, form, texture, and rhythm. It is far more than that, however. Aesthetic pleasure is not "pure" and does not transpire apart from a "packed" human setting, a circumstance freighted with social, intellectual, and moral pressure, as the Fall amply demonstrates. Rather, delight is experienced within, partakes of, and even depends upon conditions of harmony and intimacy, which are moral and relational categories, each informing the other. Aesthetic pleasure, then, flows from and hinges upon, is interdependent and co-extensive with moral and relational qualities. Biblical scholar Walter Brueggemann labels this a "theology of blessing" wherein the whole creation manifests the "friendly disposition" of God.[7] Reciprocal, interwoven, co-extensive—beauty has at its inmost core a texture of welcome and assent, of intimacy and trust.

This perspective not only sheds light on the complex interplay of elements that make successful art but also restores to art and aesthetics a central role for moral reflection and affirmation. Questions of formal value cannot be separated from questions of moral and social value. The Genesis creation account provides, then, a practical benchmark for approaching and reflecting on the nature, enjoyment, and purposes of art. There is no delight without intimacy and trust, and no trust without intimacy and delight, and no intimacy without delight and trust. A fully developed art cares desperately for these interwoven categories, and, if effective, illumines, inspires, and shores up awe, delight, welcome, and assent. This perspective can be but suggestively outlined here. But even

6. Bernhard W. Anderson, "Mythopoeic and Theological Dimensions of Biblical Creation Faith," in *Creation in the Old Testament*, ed. Bernhard W. Anderson (Philadelphia: Fortress Press, 1984), p. 15.

7. Brueggemann, *Genesis: A Bible Commentary for Teaching and Preaching* (Atlanta: John Knox Press, 1982), p. 37.

this outline reveals its value: it posits a full domain for art that draws critical attention away from the prevailing silliness of elite and popular antagonisms, which is a first step in opening long-closed windows of perception in the understanding and criticism of art.

We will not do away with art, whether it is that of consumer-driven Hollywood, bedtime stories, or Puccini. Teens in particular, unhampered and with ample leisure time, draw it in like air. Their predicament is not unlike that of their parents but is more acute, given their inexperience, immaturity, leisure time, and relative isolation from the adult culture. Driven by their own longings for intimacy, identity, and delight, cast into that circus of enjoyment, artistic and otherwise, beset by a voracious and wily entertainment industry, and lost in a welter of competing ideologies, youth flounder, and it is no wonder. Their human callings to delight, intimacy, and love at once beckon and baffle. They wonder and they wander, latching on to the nearest icon or soporific that promises some surcease, no matter how brief, from confusion, boredom, and pain. And the magic grail of leisure ever recedes, no matter how they chase it. They "beat on, boats against the current"; they press on, dancing in the dark.

10. Zappa Meets Gore: Evaluating Popular Art

Hey, Mr. Tambourine Man, play a song for me. . . .
In the jingle, jangle morning, I'll come followin' you.

Take me for a trip upon your magic swirling ship
All my senses have been stripped
And my hands can't feel the grip
And my tongue's too numb to sip. . . .

I'm ready to go anywhere, I'm ready for to fade
Into my own parade
Cast your dancing spell my way
I promise to go under it. . . .

From "Mr. Tambourine Man"
as sung by the Byrds

In September 1985, at a U.S. Senate Committee hearing on record labeling, rock musician Frank Zappa squared off against Tipper Gore, the president of the Parents' Music Resource Center, and the classic American conflict between artistic freedom and community standards entered the age of image politics. The hearing before the U.S. Senate Committee on Commerce, Science, and Transportation was not intended to produce federal regulation or legislation, but few participants seemed to mind.[1]

---

1. This was true with the exception of Senator J. James Exon of Nebraska, who complained that members of Congress "indulge in too many publicity events that are far beyond the scope of regulation and legislation, which I think is our primary purpose" (quoted in "Record Labeling," Hearing before the Committee on Commerce, Science, and

Both Zappa and Gore understood that projecting an image of conflict was more important than resolving any real dispute, and that public opinion frequently sides with the most likable and evocative image. Prominent celebrities had to appear concerned about the impact of heavy-metal music. Further, the antagonists had to engage in public dispute over freedom of expression and the maintaining of public morality. The congressional hearings were a media event, a symbolic court in which the public became judge and jury while the media presented the cases.

Despite all of the symbolic posturing, the transcript of the first session shows that genuine issues were at stake. The committee heard testimony from a variety of interest groups, both parental associations, which sought to shore up public morality, and representatives of the music industry, which hoped to ensure its freedom to market its products. Strikingly absent were those who listen most to rock and to heavy-metal music in particular. According to representatives of the Parents' Music Resource Center (PMRC) and the National PTA, someone had to do something about the lyrics of some heavy-metal rock songs. In the words of Susan Baker, parents were justly "concerned by the growing trend in music toward lyrics that are sexually explicit, excessively violent, or glorify the use of drugs and alcohol."[2] Tipper Gore recommended that the record companies label their own products, using a uniform set of ratings similar to the movie industry's rating system (X, R, PG-13, PG, G). She also asked that the lyrics of labeled music products be available for perusal before purchase. These recommendations gained support from a music professor and a youth psychiatrist who emphasized the adverse effect of heavy-metal music on teenagers' attitudes.

Not surprisingly, representatives of the music industry had little sympathy for the PMRC's recommendations. Three musicians spoke out against them and in favor of artistic freedom. In Zappa's words, "The complete list of PMRC demands reads like an instruction manual for some sinister kind of toilet training program to house-break all composers and performers because of the lyrics of a few."[3] Stanley Gortikov, president of the Recording Industry Association of America, suggested that record companies use the warning "Parental Guidance—Explicit Lyrics" to label future releases which warranted adult supervision, but he opposed any further measures. Representatives of the radio broadcast

---

Transportation, U.S. Senate, 99th Congress, First Session on Contents of Music and the Lyrics of Records, 19 Sept. 1985, p. 50).

2. Baker, quoted in ibid., p. 11.
3. Zappa, quoted in ibid., p. 53.

Banned in the U.S.A.

In March 1990, facing the prospect of increased regulation by at least nineteen states, the Recording Industry Association of America agreed to place the black-and-white warning label "Parental Advisory—Explicit Lyrics" on the lower right corner of records, cassettes, and compact discs with questionable lyrics. This agreement does not extend to small, independent companies that are not members but that release many of the recordings deemed objectionable.

In June 1990, Skyywalker Records, one of the most successful small independent record companies in the United States, made headlines when *As Nasty As They Wanna Be*, the controversial album by the Miami-based rap group 2 Live Crew, was ruled obscene by a federal judge in Florida. Soon afterward a record-store owner in Fort Lauderdale was arrested for selling the album, and three band members were arrested for performing a song from the album. Luther Campbell, owner of Skyywalker Records and lead singer of 2 Live Crew, replied by releasing a single set to the music of a Bruce Springsteen hit. The single is titled "Banned in the U.S.A."

industry gave conflicting testimony. One urged all segments of the music industry to form a "National Music Review Council . . . to achieve self-regulation on the issue of offensive or pornographic lyrics."[4] Another encouraged individual broadcasters to make their own decisions about how to respond to local concerns about "porn rock."[5]

Despite obvious disagreements about specific solutions, most witnesses agreed that children and young teenagers should not be exposed to certain lyrics. For whatever reason, some rock lyricists focus on violent, profane, vulgar, obscene, and even sadistic images—a fact that apparently disturbed many witnesses. For example, none of the witnesses at this hearing wanted their own children to listen to the words from Judas Priest's "Eat Me Alive."[6] Among other things, that song depicts the sexually stimulated male as a panting animal whose "gut wrenching frenzy" conquers the female. The female is forced "at gun point" to "eat" the male as his "rod steel injects"; while the male "groan[s] in the pleasure zone," the female is sodomized. These lyrics clearly seem to turn sex into rape. But the various participants disagreed about how common, how offensive, and how significant such lyrics are.

4. William J. Steding, executive vice president of the Central Broadcast Division of the Bonneville International Corporation, quoted in ibid., p. 137.

5. Edward O. Fritts, president of the National Association of Broadcasters, quoted in ibid., p. 133.

6. "Eat Me Alive," from the album *Defenders of the Faith*, quoted in ibid., p. 37.

The congressional hearing on record labeling illustrates well the problems of evaluating youth-oriented popular art. Often it seems that each individual has his or her own preferences, and that we share no common standards for our various preferences. At the same time, most people agree that popular art sometimes violates community prohibitions against such things as pornography and blatant racism. Yet few concur about sensible responses toward or public policies on controversial art.

Such debates raise three questions about popular art and youth in North America. First, who judges aesthetic or moral value? Who should assess the worth of popular music, movies, and rock videos? Second, what is being decided? What do we mean when we say certain products are or are not desirable? Third, by what means do we decide? By what standards should we evaluate popular art? This chapter discusses each of these topics in turn, using rock music as a touchstone for its reflections.

Perspectives in Conflict

In the early seventies, Herbert Gans argued that the United States is divided into five "taste cultures," each with its own films, music, literature, visual art, and so forth, which express different aesthetic standards.[7] Relying on the socio-economic factors of income, occupation, and (especially) education, Gans distinguished high culture, upper-middle culture, lower-middle culture, low culture, and quasi-folk low culture. Instead of pitting these taste cultures against each other, Gans recognized the legitimacy of each. He argued that every taste culture is socially desirable provided that it meets the demands of its users, rewards its creators, and does not hurt its users, creators, or society. By refusing to participate in the perennial war over taste, Gans set forth an important case for cultural pluralism and corrected the worst mistakes in elitist critiques of mass culture.

Interestingly, Gans suggested that ethnic, racial, and youth subcultures "may only be temporary offshoots" of the dominant taste cultures.[8] In recent years, however, two developments have dramatically changed Gans's portrait. First, the youth culture has come to dominate

7. Gans, *Popular Culture and High Culture: An Analysis and Evaluation of Taste* (New York: Basic Books, 1974).
8. Gans, *Popular Culture and High Culture*, p. 94.

much of the cultural landscape, and second, boundaries between taste cultures have eroded, partly under the pervasive impact of a youth-oriented entertainment industry. Thus, in considering the value and role of popular art, one cannot ignore the presence and perspective of North American youth. At the same time, one must note the tensions between this perspective on the one hand and the perspectives of adult entertainers and guardians on the other. As the hearing on record labeling illustrates, significant conflicts over popular art occur between three different groups: the entertainment industry, the youth culture, and the adult "guardians" of education and tradition, including parents, teachers, and ethnic, racial, and religious leaders. (The difficulties of evaluation demand that we distinguish between three groups rather than the two contained in the notion of symbiosis.) We shall briefly summarize the perspective of each group and then suggest how to broaden each perspective in order to move toward consensus about controversial popular art such as heavy-metal music. Public accord demands that each group not only understand the perspectives of other groups but also broaden its own perspective.

Entertainment industries are first and foremost business enterprises. These businesses produce and distribute art, information, and entertainment in order to make a profit. Their overriding consideration is the rate of return on their investment. As a result, the industry wants popular art that is well-made and easy to market. In a normal business year, a major studio produces and markets a wide range of films, some cheaply made but having broad appeal (which describes many teen films), others expensive to make and having little appeal (except to many critics). A major music company functions much the same way. In the record-labeling controversy, one fact too seldom noted is heavy metal's high rate of return on investment. Its importance is as much economic as artistic.

Because of its complexity, the entertainment industry embraces endless compromises between competing forces—the artists, the agents, the production companies, and the distributors, not to mention the public. Although power shifts from one group to another (agents have gained more clout in recent years), the basic interests of each group remain fairly constant. Generally, the most dramatic conflicts of interest erupt between artists and production companies. Very often artists wish to express their own vision of life, and they tend to see movies or records as means to this end. The production companies, in contrast, look for products that fit or expand their market, even if that means refusing or revising the artists' work. What is good for the artist might not be good for the company, and what the company wants might not mesh with the artist's wishes. Compromises emerge from the shared need to promote the artist's work and reputation in a way that captures a big enough market to sustain both artist and company. Just as it is important for many artists to become stars, so it is important for most companies to work with artists who will do what is necessary to become stars.

In sum, then, the entertainment industry has an enormous stake in popular art, and its perspective clearly cannot be ignored. Business imperatives and an environment of cutthroat competition often constrict that perspective. Consequently, the industry needs constant reminders that talent, marketability, and profitability do not guarantee desirable products. A product may have all these qualities but still be racist or prurient in intent and effect.

When we consider North American youth, we note that their perspective on popular art differs from that of the entertainment industry in two significant respects. First, adolescents prefer popular art that fits their experience. Market prognosticators in the entertainment industry can come up with astute guesses, but these can never substitute for the adolescent's own evaluation about this fit. Often the industry misreads adolescent experience. Second, youth use popular art as eyes and ears in their passage into an adult world. They constantly check to see whether the world of popular art mirrors the adult world they know. Sometimes popular art seems more honest and real; sometimes parents, teachers, and community leaders seem more trustworthy and wise; sometimes there is no conflict between the two worlds; and sometimes neither world seems worthwhile.

Consider the way rock music can reflect and illumine virtually every facet of human experience, as filtered through the highly emotional experience of teenagers. Lyrics run the gamut of themes, while the music itself ranges from smooth to raucous, from gentle to angry. Rock expresses sorrow and pain as well as joy and pleasure, and every emotion and attitude in between. It is sensitive as well as mean-spirited; mystical and spiritual as well as dirty and terribly earthy. Rock music fastens on contradictions and conflicts in life that don't yield to easy resolution. Adolescents hear their own hurts and disappointments as well as joys and excitement expressed in the rhythms of rock and roll; the music serves to affirm their experiences and validate their feelings. In its function as "eyes and ears," however, rock often becomes a vehicle for misunderstanding between generations, races, religious groups, and economic classes, for rock music echoes and reinforces polarities in contemporary culture.

Parents, teachers, and community leaders frequently worry about the effects of popular art on the character and behavior of youth.

Many also think that more substantial things merit youth's time and attention, such as education, jobs, and needy people. Understandably, adults feel puzzled or put off by youth-oriented popular art, even though they themselves grew up in a youth culture. For one thing, such art fits a stage of life the adults have left behind, if only a few years before. Just as teenagers would feel silly playing with tricycles, so adults feel out of place amid the latest youth-oriented popular art. In addition, adolescents use popular art to test the lives and values of their elders. Adults find being role models tough enough without suffering negative comparisons to pop stars like Madonna and Tom Cruise.

Inevitably, conflicts arise between such distinct attitudes toward popular art. A "great" movie by entertainment industry standards might strike teenagers as heavy and stupid. An "awesome" rock concert will seem lewd and much too loud to parents and teachers. A "good" video by parents' or teachers' standards will flop for the industry and bore teenagers. Such differences in taste create clashes when adults and youth must live together. Indeed, these clashes occur on a small scale in every home, school, and ethnic, racial, and religious community. They take on larger proportions when disputes arise over public policy about such things as heavy-metal lyrics. Although we do not have specific advice for resolving such disputes, a few observations may clarify the issues.

1. The entertainment industry often relinquishes its responsibility in two respects. First, in its drive to exploit the youth market, the industry all too frequently ignores the values of those who provide young people with their primary nurture. Adolescents are not merely randy consumers with lots of cash. They too are people—the children of parents, the students of teachers, and members of ethnic, racial, and religious communities. Their adult guardians have legitimate worries about how popular art affects North American youth. Given the great pedagogical power of popular art, entertainment companies have an obligation to pay attention to these worries, just as corporate America has an obligation to prevent plant closings and environmental damage.[9]

Second, the structure of the entertainment industry allows young people very little direct influence on what popular art gets produced. While they can "vote" with their time, interest, and dollars, the industry has not encouraged adolescents to undertake actual production. In this respect, the industry is not much different from many schools, where teenagers have little say about what and how they should

9. This is the issue raised by *Roger and Me* and all too frequently ignored in debates about its merits as a documentary film.

learn. One of North America's most creative industries could use a little more imagination in this regard.

2. North American youth are distressingly naive about popular art. First, they have little understanding of how the entertainment industry and the arts work. One reason for this lies in the fact that the industry puts a high gloss on everything it does, making it tricky to decipher fact from fiction. Furthermore, parents, teachers, and community leaders do too little to explain the entertainment industry and its roles in North American society.

Second, teenagers show little awareness of the larger contexts of popular art. Again, neither the industry nor other institutions of nurture have provided much help. As a result, young people remain entranced by the immediacy of each new experience and have little grasp of the history or social significance of various types of popular art. They also lack exposure to other types of art, whether folk art and high art within Western culture or such traditions in other parts of the world. All too often their evaluations of popular art remain shallow and parochial.

3. Usually adults simply ignore youth-oriented popular art and accept only their own views as legitimate. By ignoring youth art, however, adults ignore the children in their care. It would be better for adults to acknowledge their ignorance or discomfort and let young people help them understand why they enjoy certain movies and music. Unfortunately, even this approach can backfire: some adults may use this kind of exchange as a forum in which to insist that their perspective is the only legitimate one after all. This happens easily, for adults regularly tell children how to think and what to do, and are unaccustomed to treating children with mutual respect. During adolescence, young people undergo the often painful process of deciding for themselves what they should think and how they should behave. They need all the encouragement they can get, especially in evaluating popular art.

Content, Form, and Function

Clearly, different people have different reasons for calling the same song "good." Some will cite an important issue or theme. Others appreciate its rhythm and performance. Still others refer to the role it plays in their experience, perhaps stirring a sorrowful memory or giving them a tune to dance to. The first group approves the song's content or meaning; the second group focuses on the song's form or structure; and the third group latches onto the song's context or function.

The teenage panel on TV's long-running *Dick Clark's American Bandstand* graded each new song they heard according to two standards: "It's got a good beat and you can dance to it." This may sound like a silly cliché, but it deals precisely with the two large issues of artistic form ("It's got a good beat") and function ("You can dance to it"). Of course, there's much more to a song's form than its rhythm, and dancing is not the only activity for which pop music is suited.

Young people interviewed by the authors revealed that they too had thought about why a particular song was good. Invariably they used formal and functional standards. Comments such as "I like the sound of the voice," "The bass lays down a nice beat," or "I thought their light show was fantastic" are in effect formal evaluations. Comments such as "I listen to this because it relaxes me" or "It makes me feel good" assess a song's functions. These responses present no astutely articulated criteria, yet they deal with rock music's form—its structure, techniques, and conventions—and the music's function—how it fits into young people's lives. While the content or meaning of music is often elusive, the interviewees did venture opinions about the themes and issues of movies and videos.

Little did they realize that their responses reflected the three main ways in which philosophers in Western culture have evaluated art. In the ancient and medieval worlds, when state-sponsored religions dominated, art was evaluated primarily by its content. The early philosopher Plato thought that good art must tell the truth about reality. Since very little art did this, Plato held a rather dim view of art, an attitude that has influenced much of Western Christianity. During the rise of industrial capitalism and democratic nation-states, philosophers began to emphasize form more than content in art. Clive Bell, for example, asserted that good art must display "significant form" and stir up an "aesthetic emotion."[10] In this approach, the moral stance or political effect of a work of art became irrelevant for deciding its goodness.

In recent years philosophers have begun to stress the importance of context and function. How art is produced and how it functions in life and society are crucial for deciding its goodness. This approach, sometimes called contextualism, stands apart from the formalism of Clive Bell.[11] It has played a strong role in our discussion of youth-oriented popular art. We do not argue that function is the only important factor or even the most important factor in evaluation, but that function

---

10. Bell, *Art* (London: Chatto & Windus, 1914).

11. See Marcia Muelder Eaton, *Basic Issues in Aesthetics* (Belmont, Calif.: Wadsworth, 1988), pp. 76-103.

is just as important as content and form. Each factor furnishes a legitimate basis for evaluating popular art, and recognizing this helps one see the strengths and weaknesses of perspectives that emphasize one factor over others. A brief discussion of each of these three factors may prove helpful.

Content. It is notoriously difficult to say what many popular art products are about. Most movies, songs, and rock videos do not make straightforward statements. They explore and suggest, often in non-verbal ways, more like body language than like newspaper articles. As Calvin Seerveld puts it, art tends to have "a parable character, a metaphoric intensity, an elusive play in its . . . presentation of meanings. . . . Art calls to our attention in capital, cursive letters, as it were, what usually flits by in reality as fine print. There is a type of exploratory, uncovering, at-the-frontier element prevalent in art."[12] Consequently, different people can see or hear different content in a single piece of popular art. In the hearings on record labeling, for example, Tipper Gore had cited "Under the Blade" by the group Twisted Sister as an example of a song whose lyrics promoted sadomasochism, bondage, and rape. But according to Dee Snider, the song's writer and a member of the band, "The lyrics she quoted have absolutely nothing to do with these topics. On the contrary, the words in question are about surgery and the fear that it instills in people."[13]

This example suggests another complication in interpreting popular art: the meaning of a song or movie derives in part from the context in which it is experienced. Because of their different expectations, Gore and Snider interpreted the same set of lyrics differently. One can only wonder what the typical teenage fan thought "Under the Blade" meant. Social changes can also affect the meaning of popular art. A song that once expressed anger over the Vietnam war might later prompt a vague nostalgia that an advertising agency wants to translate into baby-boomer purchases of its client's product.

While music by itself presents numerous ambiguities, a given popular art form can complicate interpretation by employing many different media at once in varying ways, thus allowing different "messages" to be conveyed. In the case of the Christian rock band Stryper, for example, three different meanings stand out. On stage the band strikes a pose of male power and domination; the lyrics and music of their albums preach Christian commitment and personal salvation; their "In

12. Seerveld, *Rainbows for the Fallen World: Aesthetic Life and Artistic Task* (Toronto: Tuppence Press, 1980), p. 27.
13. Snider, quoted in "Record Labeling," p. 73.

What Do You Hear?

What are the lyrics to Twisted Sister's "Under the Blade" about? Tipper Gore says they promote rape. Dee Snider says they express the horror of surgery. Who's right? Here are the lyrics, as presented on p. 84 of the transcript of the congressional hearing on record labeling:

> A glint of steel
> A flash of light
> You know you're not going home tonight
> Be it jack or smith
> Doctor's or mind
> Nowhere to run, everywhere you'll find
> You can't escape
> From the bed you've made
> When your time has come
> You'll accept the blade!
>
> You're cornered in the alley way
> You know you're all alone
> You know it's gonna end this way
> The chill goes to the bone
> Now here it comes that glistening light
> It goes into your side
> The blackness comes
> Tonight's the night
> The blade is gonna ride
>
> CHORUS:
>
> > Cause you're under the blade
> > Oh, you're under the blade
>
> It's not another party head
> This time you cannot rise
> Your hands are tied
> Your legs are strapped
> A light shines in your eyes
> You faintly see a razor's edge
> You open your mouth to cry
> You know you can't
> It's over now
> The blade is gonna ride
>
> CHORUS

You've tried to make it to the front
You're pinned against the side
A monster stands before you now
Its mouth is open wide
The lights go on, the night explodes
It tears into your mind
When the night does end
You'll come again
The blade is gonna ride

CHORUS

God We Trust" poster suggests veiled androgynous sexuality and an unholy alliance of male power, sex, and religion. Is the band saying "It's all right to flaunt it as long as you don't do it"? This would not exactly be a helpful message for young people trapped amid confusing mores, beset by shaky sexual identity, and unsure of their own religious commitment. Given the fact that Stryper's message seems to vary from medium to medium, it is hard to discern precisely what the band is trying to say.

However, the difficulties of interpreting popular art do not suggest that we should not try to assess its content. Rather, the difficulties serve as a reminder that popular art calls for interpretation, and that evaluation of content always involves interpretation. Among the three groups discussed earlier (the entertainment industry, teenagers, and adult guardians), it is the parents, teachers, and community leaders who worry most about the content of youth art. They know that destructive views can encourage destructive attitudes and actions, and that the absence of constructive views can undermine life-affirming values and commitments. But if adults truly care about questions of content, then they must learn to look and listen with sympathy and discrimination. They must better understand the subtleties of artistic form, and they must learn about cultural contexts. The former will make them better able to address the entertainment industry, and the latter will help them understand the youth culture. In order to achieve some measure of wisdom about artistic content, adults must undertake both tasks.

Form. Those who study music, literature, or visual art tend to pay more attention to questions of form than the average listener, reader, or viewer. Yet it is not always clear what they mean by "form," nor is it immediately obvious that traditional approaches to artistic form help reveal which products best nurture North American adolescents.

When applied to popular art, "form" refers to one of four things: how various subjects or themes are presented (presentation); how various materials are used to make this product or event (construction); how the elements of a product or event are organized (organization); and how the product or event characteristically looks or sounds (surface qualities). A student of *Batman,* for example, can look at the way the film treats the theme of good versus evil (presentation). He or she can examine how the film crew employed set design, lighting, sound, camera angles, and editing to make this movie (construction). He or she can figure out how elements like plot, character, setting, and dialogue coordinate to create unity (organization). And he or she can discuss how this film appears to the viewer—its tension of technical polish and chaotic pace, for example, or its juxtaposition of impending catastrophe and slapstick humor (surface qualities). These studies need not conflict with one another; indeed, they are frequently done in concert. A thorough study of form determines whether presentation, construction, organization, and surface qualities all gel.

Many traditional approaches to artistic form focus only on the organization and the surface qualities of an art product at the expense of how it is produced and how it fits into a larger event. Traditional musicology provides finely tuned descriptions of the harmonic, melodic, and rhythmic structures of individual compositions, and it develops sophisticated classifications of musical genres such as the symphony or art song. Unfortunately, it tells us little about the process of composition or a piece's role within a concert or recital. These considerations become even more important within rock music because studio production and live concerts play a major, sometimes decisive role in the form and success of rock music.

Of course, organization and surface qualities do tell a good deal about rock music. For one, they help us distinguish rock from other popular musical genres. Rock consists of very simple elements and very basic techniques and conventions—distinct from those of, say, jazz or ragtime or Broadway songs—such as harmonies made up almost entirely of three-note chords, melodies with narrow range, duple meter and heavy backbeat rhythms, a blues-guitar strumming technique, a rough, almost shouting singing style, oft-repeated words and phrases, and the predominance of electronic instruments and equipment. So much of rock is sheer sound, even noise, which often overwhelms the ears. It is primarily a vocal music in which lyrics are not as important as the sound of the voice, the power of the amplification, and the energy of the entire experience.

While such purely musical characteristics of rock emerge plainly in recordings, the form of the rock phenomenon has as much to do with nonmusical as with musical elements, as much to do with the visual and the dramatic as with the aural. In short, rock must be seen as well as heard, performed as well as played in recorded form. Part of rock is theater—wild costumes, choreography, lights, smoke. Another part is rhetoric—strident claims designed for their shock value. Very often a rock concert looks and feels like a religious event—rock stars are idolized, their music the rousing hymnody of a new type of revival meeting. The live event often takes on a political tone and character—it involves the promotion of confrontation and anarchy, anti-establishment slogans, and calls for social change.

And all the while, rock remains a commodity, a product manufactured, marketed, and sold as a piece of cultural goods by the entertainment industry. Like T-shirts and lunch meat, it is produced and packaged to sell and make money, and it is played and promoted everywhere—on radio, on TV, at concerts.

The phenomenon of rock is most clearly displayed at the live rock concert, especially a concert held in an arena. Everything is there—the ear-shattering music, the shouted lyrics, the frequent four-letter words; the swaggering, leaping, hair-tossing performers; the jumping, swaying, reveling crowd of young people; scantily dressed girls and rag-clad boys; leather, lace, and tank tops; fist-clenching, finger-pointing, hand-waving; posing, posturing, parading on arena floor and on stage; posters, recordings, T-shirts, photo albums, biographies, fan-club memberships—all for sale at premium prices along with mountains of popcorn and candy and gallons of pop or beer, depending on the venue and the audience's age. A rock concert is part baseball game, part revival meeting, part county fair—to name just a few of its components—where excitement abounds, spirits are high, and everyone goes home a winner.

While traditional studies of form have not paid much attention to production and performance, the entertainment industry clearly has, and it has done so far more than young consumers and their elders have. Without a doubt, the entertainment industry recognizes that quality and innovation in form, in all its dimensions, are keys to marketable products and commercial success. Because this is the case, representatives of the industry quickly become uneasy when faced with any proposals that smack of censorship. Although it is understandably leery of certain kinds of regulation, the industry needs to recognize and respect the fact that the power of artistic form, especially in the kingdom of rock and roll, places tremendous responsibilities in its hands.

Needless to say, rock recordings that are imaginatively produced can make a lasting impression on millions of listeners. The continued popularity of the Beatles' music is due in no small part to the formal excellence of their recordings. The Beatles employed familiar musical materials but did not trivialize them. One need only recall such imaginative instrumental touches as the use of the string quartet in "Yesterday," the bass harmonica and soprano recorder in "The Fool on the Hill," the trumpet trio in "Strawberry Fields," the unhackneyed harmonies in "Eleanor Rigby" and "Michelle," or the many simple and plaintive tunes that fill their repertoire. Consistent high-quality production greatly enhanced the fresh style and treatment.

So too, rock concerts—although lacking the permanence of recordings—can have an overwhelming effect through choreography, lighting, costumes, and staging. When their overall effect is considered, rock concerts are clearly more than haphazard mélanges of razzle-dazzle. Through careful planning and at great expense, the Michael Jackson tours of the 1980s emphasized *the show*. Essential to these extravaganzas was Jackson's superb dancing, integrated into the music, lighting, and larger concert structure. Creatively conceived and staged, the shows became theatrical events. Jackson and his producers exploited the inherent theatrical potential of rock music.

With such power come countless opportunities to manipulate the audience for commercial or other ends. Although in extreme cases a government might intervene to balance the interests of producers and consumers, it is preferable that the entertainment industry acknowledge its own responsibilities and act accordingly. Moreover, adolescents should learn to evaluate the formal qualities of rock, movies, and MTV in order to become more aware of how these media work their beguiling magic. Parents, schools, and community organizations can raise awareness by discussing popular art with teenagers, by developing courses or units on popular art in the school curriculum, and by having youth leaders pay more attention to the formal aspects of youth-oriented popular art. An educated consumer is better able to separate exploitation from entertainment.

Function. Throughout this book we have stressed the point that popular art performs many legitimate functions in the lives of North American adolescents. We have emphasized that some of its most important functions for youth have to do with the formation of identity, intimacy, and purpose. Like families, schools, and community organizations, popular art helps young people discover who they are, develop peer groups and friendships, and explore the purpose of their lives. In each of these functions, popular art enjoys certain advantages over other institutions of nurture. It does not usually impose the obligations and assert the authority that young people so often resist from their elders. Instead,

Canned Heat

State legislators in New York and New Jersey have proposed laws regulating the use of recorded music at live concerts. It has become increasingly common for leading performers such as Milli Vanilli, Janet Jackson, and Paula Abdul to move their lips or fingers while machines do the actual singing and playing. The proposed legislation would require advertisers and ticket agents to tell consumers that the performance is not completely live. According to Jon Pareles, music critic for the *New York Times,* the trend toward canned music reflects the desire for superhuman perfection among performers who gained their reputations through video clips built around studio recordings. It will be very tricky to develop appropriate legislation for all the different uses of canned music in live concerts, and perhaps unnecessary as well—if audiences aren't getting what they want, the performers will soon find out and change their routines.

—Jon Pareles, "Canned Music at Live Shows: Should Audiences Be Warned?" *New York Times,* 10 July 1990, pp. B-1, B-12.

popular art supports rather than supervises interactions among youth. It also gives them more exposure to current questions of purpose than many parents and teachers can provide, and does so in a more provocative way. Rarely can an adult match the fun and relevance of popular art as it guides youth in the search for identity, intimacy, and purpose.

One unfortunate aspect of all this, however, is that popular art cannot deal with young people as individuals. Nor can it address the specific texture of their lives. Rather, it generally leaves the mistaken impression that all adolescents are basically the same, and that the local institutions and influences in their lives, such as families and racial and religious traditions, do not matter very much. The mass-produced and mass-distributed nature of popular art makes these limitations inevitable.

Beyond the immediate context of youth culture, popular art can fulfill other important functions. It can serve, for example, as an agent of sociocultural memory, as a means whereby the record of the struggles and triumphs of past generations can be kept alive by a new generation. Although not targeted to a teenage audience, films like *Glory* and *Driving Miss Daisy* have just such an effect. Without films like these, the struggle to achieve civil rights could easily be forgotten. In much the same fashion, popular art can perform political functions. It is clear from the history of rock and roll that, when combined with other social forces, popular music can promote both engagement and apathy. Many rock songs deal with flying away or dropping out. This theme of escape, which abounds in all of American popular music, reflects a particularly American attitude toward freedom and individualism. This emphasis can work two ways: "escapist" songs can encourage people to dream of a better world and take up a political pursuit of that dream, or they can foster just the opposite—a resignation that inclines people to leave everything the way it is. Much depends on a song's mood and social context.

Consider "Mr. Tambourine Man," the lyrics of which appear at the beginning of this chapter. With its appealing call to escape a constricting reality and enjoy a heightened awareness through the magic of imagination, the song can have more than one political function. The trip, perhaps drug-induced, can inspire either action or evasion. In its original version, Bob Dylan's song promotes political activism. In its remake by the Byrds, "Mr. Tambourine Man" promotes political apathy, for the challenge of the trip is minimized by the sunniness of the Byrds' delivery and the lighthearted, down-home character of the musical accompaniment.

Or take one of the most popular songs by the Eagles, "Hotel California," which flirts with cultural criticism but actually tends to celebrate an appealing type of escapism. While it is difficult to know for sure how youth interpret the song's lyrics or experience its musical expression, "Hotel California" appears to condone cultural resignation—what the song refers to as "checking out." On one level the song is a description of the moneyed, decadent California lifestyle, with its iced champagne and mirrored ceilings. More broadly, however, "Hotel California" may be a commentary on American culture as reflected in the leisure and consumption-oriented lifestyle of California, perhaps the contemporary locus of the American dream. In the song, the "Hotel California" is a "lovely face" that attracts people all year long. Inhabitants become "prisoners" of their "own device," lured by the place's facade and eventually trapped by its addictive and dark-sided glamour. All that the inhabitants can do is "relax" and "receive" what comes their way, as the hotel's night man indicates. They have become victims trapped by their own misdirected desires; they can "check out" of the life that leads them, but they "can never leave." Expressing this kind of cultural fatalism may have been an attempt to critique the American dream, but it seems instead to encourage and prolong the very condition that it condemns. Despite the impressive guitar work that concludes the song, both musically and lyrically "Hotel California" offers little more than resignation and acceptance.

The list of popular art's functions could go on. It is clear from

Chapter Five that popular art has important economic functions, both as the product of a powerful entertainment industry and as a purveyor of consumerism. Popular art also plays a part in people's morality and religion, as we suggest throughout this book.

The many different functions of popular art occur within specific contexts that help determine these functions and provide a basis for evaluating them. People find some movies, records, and music videos more worthwhile than others partly because of their hopes and fears about various social contexts. Since there are many different contexts and many different attitudes toward each context, evaluations based on context tend to be messy and controversial. Nonetheless, they form a vital part of the assessment process. Function and context should have as much weight as content and form in evaluations of popular art.

Context is particularly important to adolescents. For them, the ability of popular art to work on a social-psychological level counts most. Music must have more than a good beat—can you dance to it? A movie should do more than address some burning social problem—would it be good to see on a date? Parents and teachers will better understand teenage preferences in popular art if they keep in mind the weight of social-psychological factors in adolescent evaluations. The entertainment industry, by contrast, must keep in mind that other contexts equal or surpass the importance of the social-psychological, even though teenagers themselves do not usually give other contexts as much weight. In other words, the industry's decisions about production and marketing should consider more than the immediate social-psychological desires of teenage consumers. Social problems, politics, morality, and religion— to name some of the more prominent features of contexts in which teenagers live and by which their adult lives will be marked—are of equal or greater importance. The most effective pedagogy, for adults and for the entertainment industry, helps teenagers connect their immediate concerns and environment with the issues that face all of us in the full context of our lives.

Avoiding the pitfalls of moralism and formalism. Approaches to evaluation that emphasize only content or form do not aid the complex decisions all of us must make about the desirability of various types of popular art. An overemphasis on content—especially common among parents, teachers, and community leaders—easily degenerates into moralism. Moralism regularly fails to appreciate the wonderful fun and inventiveness of much popular art. It also regularly praises shoddy products whose only redeeming value is a supposedly wholesome

Say Anything

Writer and director Cameron Crowe, who made *Fast Times at Ridgemont High* in 1983, brought the adolescent world to the screen again in 1989 in *Say Anything*. Instead of simply recycling the teen-film formula, this unlikely love story focuses on the tensions and limitations of the teenage world constructed by North American society. *Say Anything* is a movie about two teenagers who demonstrate their maturity, although society does not recognize them as ready for adulthood.

The movie begins at that mythical threshold of the adult world—high-school graduation. The valedictory address is delivered by Diane Cort, a brilliant and beautiful young woman whose promising future is filled with endless opportunities. Her father's single-minded plans for and rigid guidance of her life, however, make Diane into an academic overachiever. She forfeits a normal and healthy social life and emotional self-awareness for her scholastic success.

Lloyd Dobler is the exact opposite. He is not among the academic elite and has no plans beyond graduation, but he is emotionally sensitive and extremely popular among his peers. Predictably, Diane and Lloyd fall in love, but their romance is not simply a matter of opposite personalities being attracted to one another. Different as they are in certain ways, Diane and Lloyd both demonstrate that they genuinely care about other people. Both have the values and the determination to transcend the limitations of their youthful existence. Although the portrayal of them is exaggerated, the adult world and its values pale in comparison to the honesty and truthfulness these two young people struggle to maintain amid familial and societal conflicts that result from their love for each other. They in their trustworthiness provide a sharp contrast to the main adult character, Diane's father, who, though adamantly opposed to their relationship for ostensibly "good" reasons, is dishonest and corrupt. Ultimately Diane and Lloyd discover that they can "say anything," or be completely vulnerable, only to each other. This is symbolized in their sexual encounter; although it occurs outside the bonds of marriage, it does occur within the bonds of a strong emotional relationship.

The story ends with Diane leaving to pursue her academic career; Lloyd goes with her in a supportive role. The gender-role reversal is not out of context within the film, but it is unique among teen films, most of which are geared to nineteen-year-old males. Perhaps that is one reason why *Say Anything* was only a mild box-office success during the spring/summer of 1989. Probably a more significant factor was competition: the film no doubt drowned in the flood of record-breaking releases that year, including *Indiana Jones and the Last Crusade*, *Ghostbusters II*, and *Batman*. Whatever the reason for its limited appeal, *Say Anything* shows the trials of maturing adolescents with integrity (though the characters may be exaggerated) instead of merely exploiting the genre with a formulaic story about fleeting sexual conquest.

message, however poorly communicated. Most damaging, perhaps, is the moralists' tendency to impose their standards on everyone else, including teenagers and the entertainment industry. Such imposition not only overlooks the democratic framework of a pluralistic society but also proves an ineffective way to promote ethical standards.

Often those who see the dangers of moralism will counter by overemphasizing artistic form. Such a position, especially common in the entertainment industry, easily turns into an empty formalism. Under attack from some parents and educators, artists and industry executives occasionally cloak themselves in the mantle of formal purity, which is comparable to the claim of total impartiality by the news media or the assertion of complete objectivity by scientific researchers. While it is true that artists and producers have a responsibility to make the best popular art possible, it is not true that formal factors are the only acceptable basis for deciding which art is best. And while the entertainment industry must have the freedom to make its own decisions about production and marketing, it must admit that these decisions are not merely artistic. Because the industry is a powerful educational, economic, political, and moral force in North America, it has public responsibilities that go far beyond mere entertainment and commerce. At the very least, as a fountain to which young people flock for nurture, it has educational obligations.

A contextual view of evaluation provides a necessary antidote to both moralism and formalism. In fact, the authors of this book believe that neither adult guardians nor the entertainment industry will properly discharge their responsibilities toward youth unless they respect the contextual basis for adolescent preferences in popular art. Nor will young people develop mature responses to popular art and their elders unless they learn to place their own youth culture in the larger contexts and demands of contemporary society. Although this can be painful, draining some of the simplicity and spontaneity from the enjoyment of popular art, such recognitions are part of the price of becoming an adult. A broader understanding of popular art and its functions will follow, as well as a deeper appreciation of the best that the entertainment industry has to offer.

Standards of Evaluation

Thus far we have discussed the different views and attitudes of the entertainment industry, the youth culture, and adult guardians, and we have considered the role of content, form, and function in evaluations of popular art. We have seen that no single group has a monopoly on evaluating the worth of popular music, movies, and rock videos. Instead, each group has a legitimate interest and point of view, and must learn to cooperate with the other groups. So too, neither content nor form nor function has proven more important for evaluating popular art; each has equal weight, and each must be informed by the others. We are left with one big question. How do we decide whether certain products are desirable? In other words, what should be our standards?

Before attempting to answer this question, we wish to make two comments. First, in a democratic and pluralistic society, no individual or group has either the right or the duty to dictate standards, although everyone is entitled to suggest or advocate various standards. To remain vital, however, a democratic society must address the question of shared standards. Educators and scholars have an important task in this re-gard—namely, to help determine which standards are generally accepted. Second, practice does not always follow belief; nor do deeply held beliefs always result in consistent behavior. Educators and scholars should look hard for such discrepancies, and they should call them to everyone's attention. This is a valuable way to find out whether the standards people espouse are also the ones they ought to follow.

"Standards" refer to a group's expectations of actions and effects within a social sphere or institution. For example, the comment "That was a bad movie; the acting was lousy" appeals to a standard of good acting. It is hard to define good acting, but most everyone can recognize bad acting and believes that paid actors should do their job well. As this example suggests, most standards are implicit in our talk about art. They become explicit in the work of art critics, educators, and scholars, who try to point out exactly why and how certain art products succeed or fail. Please note, however, that standards of evaluation do not simply float down from the ivory tower to popular art. They operate as well in ordinary conversations. The discussion that follows considers technical, aesthetic, social, economic, political, moral, and religious standards or expectations. Although it has been aided by the work of art critics and the like, it tries to start with the standards which ordinary people actually follow and to which they actually appeal when they make and enjoy popular art. But it also suggests ways in which these standards need to be broadened or deepened.[14]

14. These standards are formulated in such a way that each one could be used to evaluate not only the *form* but also the *content* and *function* of popular art. To demonstrate this in detail would require a longer and more technical chapter. A further complication is

Technical excellence. In North America one of the most widely shared beliefs about popular art holds that it should be competently made or performed and presented. Indeed, sometimes this expectation reflects a cultural obsession with proficiency. Movie actors and directors compete for Academy Awards, teenagers argue about the best rock group, and adults try to outdo each other with the best home-entertainment units. Often, "the best" refers primarily to such factors as skill, professionalism, and equipment quality. North Americans have little patience with shoddiness in popular art, although we seem more tolerant of it in other areas of craft and manufacture.

However, technical excellence has other dimensions besides proficiency, ones which are harder to identify and about which there is less agreement. For lack of better terms, let's call them "freshness" and "fit." Freshness has to do with the extent to which a tradition or genre or medium has been explored, reworked, and revitalized. "Fit" refers to the extent to which the production or performance of a piece of art matches the uses and users for which it is intended.[15] Some critics hold that too many popular art products and performances, while proficient, lack freshness or fit: they do not turn up anything new, or they engage in overkill, sometimes almost literally. As a result, audiences find such products boring or forced—just ask teenagers who have seen the third installment of *Rambo, The Karate Kid,* or *Back to the Future.*

Aesthetic expressiveness. Although philosophers disagree about what gives one art product more aesthetic value than another, nearly everyone involved with popular art expects it to express something and voices disappointment when it fails. Almost everyone wants art to capture something about the world and to present it in an effective way. The best art in this regard engages and sometimes deeply moves. All of us have gone to gripping movies that haunt us for days afterward. Every one of us can mention popular songs that bring pure joy to hear or sing and that seem just right for a particular mood or occasion. Usually we cannot explain why these art products have such importance, but we nevertheless prefer them.

Expressiveness seems to be a hallmark of all great artists and entertainers. It is a matter of timing, of finding exactly the right mix, of looking and listening in unexpected ways and then making these seem

---

that each standard has different implications for different art forms and media (e.g., recorded rock music, network television programs, Hollywood movies).

15. Nicholas Wolterstorff's *Art in Action: Toward a Christian Aesthetic* (Grand Rapids: Eerdmans, 1980), pp. 91-121, has some useful things to say on these topics, although most of his examples come from high art.

exactly right. But there is more. To make expressive art, the performer must also sense deeply the joys and sorrows of human life and offer a compelling vision of life's purposes and dreams. To enjoy such art, audiences must have a similar acuteness and vision. Without such artists and audiences, popular art becomes a dull affair. All the high-tech equipment and clever marketing gimmicks in the world cannot make up for a lack of keen sensibility. When mainstream popular art has become dull, it has looked to minority subcultures—which seem to retain their richness and freshness—to renew its vitality.

Social scope. It goes without saying that everyone involved in popular art expects it to be popular. Still, it is not at all obvious exactly what "popularity" means, and there are at least three different ways to think about its meaning. The entertainment industry usually regards popularity as a quantitative measure of distribution and sales as indicated by trade charts, sales figures, and box-office receipts. A second measure of popularity gauges consumption as distinct from distribution and sales. For example, one might call the Beatles' album *Sgt. Pepper's Lonely Hearts Club Band* very popular not because of the number of copies initially sold or because of profits made but because of how many people have enjoyed the album through the years. A third definition of "popularity" refers to a more qualitative standard of production as distinct from distribution and consumption. For example, the movie *Full Metal Jacket* could be called popular not because of box-office receipts and not because of how many people have enjoyed it, but because of how well the filmmakers have captured the experience of many Vietnam veterans. In such instances, the degree of popularity depends on the extent to which a particular group or subculture recognizes and supports the vision presented.

As a matter of fact, however, the first meaning has gradually come to dominate talk about popular art. All of us, producers and consumers alike, now tend to equate the "popularity" of a popular-art product with its cash value for the entertainment industry. Ironically, this may mean that our emphasis on popularity has elitist implications. By praising a product for a popularity equated with the number of albums or tickets sold, one says in effect that whatever rings up the most private profit for the relatively few industry owners is also the art that best represents what the people *(populus)* want and need.

By contrast, it may be useful to think of popularity as "social scope." The social scope of an art product is its reach in the society or audience for which it is intended. Social scope has two dimensions— breadth and depth. An art product whose reach is broad will speak to and for many segments of the intended audience; a product with depth will burrow beneath the surface of their lives. Often these two dimensions are in tension. Thus a work of art may be popular in that it reaches many people in a relatively superficial manner, but unpopular insofar as it does not embrace or interpret their experience in any substantive way. Alternatively, a movie or song may have depth but lack accessibility. The most popular products are neither superficial nor inaccessible. Although there may be some connection between popularity in this sense and the number of tickets or albums sold, sales figures are not always the best indicator of social scope. Poor sales figures might simply indicate inadequate marketing strategies and say little about the quality of the product itself.

Economic worth. Although social scope is not equivalent to commercial success, this does not mean that popular art should not do well in the marketplace. If commercial products fail commercially, then all their technical, aesthetic, and social merits become irrelevant, because they will not reach their intended audience.

Let's say a rock album hits the airwaves and the record stores— the latest effort of a big-name rock star known for her imaginative guitar licks, daring harmonic excursions, and high-tech production. The album begins to sell well and receives wider and wider air play. The video of the album's title song offers a dazzling display of the video-maker's art, and the national tour that the rock star launches to promote the album is an absolutely stunning theatrical tour-de-force. People everywhere go wild over the music—singing along with it in their cars, dancing to it at the concerts—and it racks up a tidy profit for the makers and sellers.

How does one evaluate the music's worth? The album is a carefully crafted, well-integrated collection of songs that are thematically unified and technically brilliant. This is good. The traveling show is also well-conceived, innovative, exciting, and smoothly executed. The music energizes countless ordinary consumers, making them sing and dance and feel good. The performers on tour interact with their audience to create a spine-tingling atmosphere where the message of hope sounds loud and clear and where "community" and "commitment" take on new meaning. And this is good. The album, the video, and the tour pay off handsomely for thousands of employees at all levels and help fill the coffers of the production company, allowing them to underwrite some struggling new groups and take some artistic and financial risks. And this, too, is good.

But let's imagine another scenario—that the album doesn't sell, and the heroic efforts to craft a good recording, make an excellent video, and create an exciting tour do not attract the expected audiences. The music may be a good product in many respects, but the entire project fails, perhaps because it doesn't touch the public with any urgency, perhaps because the musicians, record company, and concert promoters misunderstood what the public wanted. The album is a commercial bust, and in that respect it is a bad product.

Two temptations appear in this sort of economic evaluation of popular art. One temptation is to make commercial success the primary or sole criterion for the *general* worth of a product or an event. Although this temptation afflicts industry executives more strongly than artists and their audiences, the system of consumer capitalism pressures everyone to reduce questions of overall value to measures of commercial success. This pressure exerts particular force in popular art, which is so strongly market-*driven*. It is important to remember, however, that commercial success does not make a popular-art product good in all respects, nor does commercial failure make it generally worthless. A commercial flop can be technically, aesthetically, and/or socially worthwhile, and a commercial hit can be technically, aesthetically, and/or socially worthless.

A second temptation is to equate *economic* worth with mere commercial success. According to Bob Goudzwaard, an economist and social critic, people who pursue financial profit regardless of who or what may be damaged in the process readily turn production and consumption into meaningless activities. He argues that businesses should be evaluated as public stewards rather than as mere profit-makers. In other words, society should expect businesses to preserve and enhance the many different resources with which human beings have been entrusted. A company that turns a huge financial profit but pollutes the environment, wastes energy, damages employees' health, and creates local economic havoc is an economic fiasco.[16] Similarly, the economic worth of popular art involves more than commercial success. Movies, rock concerts, and music videos that squander artistic talent and whose consumption damages the audience's lives and community become economic disasters, no matter how much money they bring in. Debates over pornography, racism, and sexism in popular art would be more fruitful if critics utilized broad standards of economic stewardship rather than narrow measurements of commercial success. Perhaps this suggests an important dimension overlooked in the exchange between Frank Zappa and Tipper Gore.

Political significance. Earlier we claimed that popular art performs political functions. This may strike some readers as odd, since

---

16. Bob Goudzwaard, *Capitalism and Progress: A Diagnosis of Western Society,* ns. and ed. by Josina Van Nuis Zylstra (Grand Rapids: Eerdmans, 1979), pp. 211-12.

popular art in North America typically does not address specific government policies or promote the platforms of particular political parties. Yet popular art does perform functions that are "political" in an extended sense of the term: it serves to encourage or discourage motivations, attitudes, and behaviors that might liberate disadvantaged groups and work toward justice for everyone. The political functions of popular art depend on the context of its origin, construction, and use. Music that has had few obvious effects on political motivations in North America has proved explosive in South Africa or Eastern Europe.

The history of rock and roll well illustrates the political functions of popular art and their dependence on context. During the civil rights movement and the Vietnam war, rock quickly became an anti-establishment music. Indeed, political protest now seems built into the medium, a musical mood and style that mocks conventional attitudes, values, and lifestyles. Says Mick Jagger of the Rolling Stones, "Rock & roll is only rock & roll if it's not safe. . . . The real thing is always brash. Violence and energy—that's really what rock & roll's all about."[17] In other words, real rock threatens the status quo. But rock protest can function in various ways, depending on its audience and the setting in which it is performed. According to Canadian rock musician Bruce Cockburn, much protest rock simply serves as a means of middle-class rebellion and poses little threat to the North American status quo:

> Because rock music has the ear of so many people it can be an effective medium for getting information out, or for swinging people's feelings, at least temporarily. It's also the "opiate of the masses" in a way that the church has never been successful in being. . . . You can have a rock band—like Run DMC—that is extremely revolutionary in their attitude but has a sort of dual function of rabble rousers on the one hand and social drug on the other.[18]

While Cockburn tries to provide in his music a progressive voice on political issues, he recognizes that the political functions of rock and of other forms of popular art depend to a large extent on the context in which they are made and used.

In addition to performing obviously political functions such as expressing and channeling protest, popular art helps weave more subtle threads into the political fabric of North American society. For one, it serves to reinforce or challenge accepted gender roles, and it has undeni-

17. Jagger, quoted in the twentieth anniversary issue of *Rolling Stone*, 5 Nov. 1987, p. 34.

18. Cockburn, quoted in "Talking with Prometheus," Calvin College *Dialogue* 20 (Dec. 1987): 11-12.

Waiting for a Miracle

Bruce Cockburn (pronounced "Coh-burn") is Canada's premier songwriter-guitarist. By recording with True North, an independent label, he has been able to follow his own path in the world of popular music. This path has taken him from country-folk recitals in Toronto coffeehouses to rousing rock concerts in Tokyo, Italy, Germany, and major cities across North America, and from early themes of escape and personal authenticity to later themes of social protest and solidarity with the oppressed. All along the way Cockburn has given his listeners exquisite guitar work and provocative lyrics rich in imagery and meaning.

Waiting for a Miracle (1987) gives a retrospective of Cockburn's twenty-year career. This album shows his consistent pursuit of depth and integrity. Although such qualities limit his mass appeal (few of his songs make the Top 40), they create a loyal following among those who find him singing for them of hope amid brokenness and political commitment amid complacent consumerism. And, by incorporating elements from the music of the people he sings about, he gives a moving expression of solidarity with the oppressed. Cockburn is a Christian, but his music does not preach. It echoes an honest struggle with life's questions, both personal and social. This is clear in the lyrics of the title track of *Waiting for a Miracle:*

> Look at them working in the hot sun
> the pilloried saints and the fallen ones
> working and waiting for the night to come
> and waiting for a miracle
>
> Somewhere out there is a place that's cool
> where peace and balance are the rule
> working toward a future like some kind of mystic jewel
> and waiting for a miracle
>
> You rub your palm
> on the grimy pane
> in the hope that you can see
> You stand up proud
> you pretend you're strong
> in the hope that you can be
> like the ones who've cried
> like the ones who've died
> trying to set the angel in us free
> while they're waiting for a miracle.
>
> Struggle for a dollar, scuffle for a dime
> step out from the past and try to hold the line

so how come history takes such a long, long time
when you're waiting for a miracle?

You rub your palm
on the grimy pane
in the hope that you can see
You stand up proud
you pretend you're strong
in the hope that you can be
like the ones who've cried
like the ones who've died
trying to set the angel in us free
while they're waiting for a miracle.

—Words and music by Bruce Cockburn

ably shaped attitudes toward different ethnic and racial minorities. Popular art has also influenced expectations of various professions and occupations as well as of social institutions, governments, and nations. In fact, some correlation might exist between popular art's depiction of poverty, homelessness, unemployment, and discrimination and audience willingness to tackle such problems.

Because popular art performs numerous political functions, audiences should strive to assess the political significance of various popular-art products. After all, various movies, rock albums, and music videos seem either to promote or to downplay various political changes. Obviously, how one judges these products reflects one's convictions about who needs to be liberated and how to accomplish justice. In that sense, the political is personal, just as the personal is political, as feminists have rightly insisted. Consumers with certain political convictions will find one movie or one album more suitable than another for promoting political awareness and change. Those critics who claim that popular art has an apolitical character naively see it as just another commercial product or source of personal enjoyment. Indeed, consumerism often blinds North Americans to the political dimensions of popular art, thereby making evaluations of political significance seem either arbitrary or overstated. As a matter of fact, however, audiences make such evaluations in the act of deciding what popular art to consume.[19]

19. Although this chapter distinguishes between political and moral evaluations,

Moral and religious integrity. Pluralistic societies contain a variety of sometimes competing moralities and religions. Such heterogeneity makes public discourse about moral and religious matters endlessly complex. The difficulty is only increased by the powerful individualism that shapes North American society, which treats moral and religious concerns as wholly private matters. At the same time, one cannot help but observe that the seemingly private issues of morality and religion are influenced by national and international forces of technology, economy, and polity. In the end, the private character of morals and religion is more illusory than real. Just how widely we share certain moral expectations and religious convictions becomes clear when a leader in medicine, business, or government flagrantly violates codes of professional ethics.

Given this rather schizoid state of affairs, North Americans fumble about in a quandary about moral and religious evaluations of popular art. Some say that such evaluations are inappropriate, especially when the evaluators wish to turn their own moral and religious beliefs into public policy. If the moral and religious fanatics get their way, can book burnings, witch-hunts, and pogroms be very far behind? Others insist that moral and religious evaluations are crucially important, especially when an entertainment company or advertiser shows a callous disregard for all that some people revere. If amorality and irreligion win the day, can sexual perversion, satanism, and anarchy be very far behind? Although no witness at the congressional hearings on record labeling went to either of these extremes, the tension between these two camps made itself felt throughout the proceedings, and it has subsequently become stronger in public discourse about popular art. In this supercharged atmosphere, it becomes difficult to say much of anything meaningful on the topic with any hope of being heard. "A plague on both your houses," although to the point, would not be very helpful. Perhaps the following three observations will be of some value.[20]

First, moral and religious evaluations are no less appropriate than technical, aesthetic, social, economic, and political judgments, even

---

we are not suggesting that the political is amoral or that morality is nonpolitical. For example, the political struggles to achieve civil rights for women and ethnic minorities are motivated in part by a moral conviction that injustice is wrong. So too, recurring debates about the effect of popular art on public and personal morality are motivated in part by struggles for political power. We have tried to use the terms "political" and "moral" in roughly the same sense in which they are used in contemporary public discourse, without thereby endorsing any usage that separates the political from the moral or vice versa.

20. Similar observations are made by Wolterstorff in *Art in Action*, pp. 172-74, although we disagree with his approach to cases of conflict between aesthetic merit and moral corruption.

though moral and religious evaluations might stir up more controversy or might not readily translate into appropriate public policies. To be sure, it is hard to imagine anyone completely refusing to make such evaluations. Even the strictly amoral or irreligious person finds certain products of popular art commendable or reprehensible on moral or quasi-religious grounds. Perhaps such people prefer art that celebrates the goodness of humanity over art which suggests that everyone is selfish, mean-spirited, and ignorant. Or they might find pornographic "snuff" movies repugnant, not only because these lack technical and aesthetic merit but also because they radically violate the dignity of individual human beings.

Second, while popular art demands moral and religious evaluations, they are neither the only evaluations needed nor always the most important evaluations. As products that have technical, aesthetic, social, economic, and political dimensions and that function in various contexts, rock albums, movies, music videos, and the like elicit many different kinds of evaluations. In general, no single kind of evaluation is always more important than any other kind, since the appropriateness of an evaluation depends on the context and the angle from which one evaluates. Indeed, if a popular artist thinks that political ideas always form the most important motives and ends for making art, that artist's songs or films will soon degenerate into ineffective propaganda—ineffective insofar as they lack the excellence, expressiveness, and scope needed for popular art to function well in a political context. Or if a teacher thinks that moral concerns always outweigh other factors in selecting popular art for enjoyment and study, she or he will end up shielding students from much challenging popular art and thereby constrict the sensitivity and maturity of the students' moral discernment.

Third, the debate between, say, libertarians and fundamentalists cannot become a genuine discourse until all recognize that we bring some shared expectations to our debates. Pluralism makes vigorous debate possible but at the same time makes difficult the task of discovering the hopes and fears that bind us together. Still, deep in the ethical and religious fiber of North American society lies a desire for mutual respect and personal integrity. All take offense when an individual or a group refuses others the respect that this individual or group wants. And every community wants its members to live with integrity, even though everyone fails from time to time to act with integrity.

Accordingly, given this moral-religious vision, audiences generally expect integrity in popular art in North American society. In this context, "integrity" means that artists and producers will not try to ply audiences with products that ignore distinctions between right and wrong. Further, adults hope that producers will not deliberately inundate youth with material wildly inappropriate for their stage of moral development. At the same time, adults expect that adolescents will not shirk the burden of deciding what is morally and religiously appropriate. Lastly, we expect adult guardians not to be popular-art hypocrites, preaching one view to the young while practicing something quite different. The common thread uniting all sides argues that the products should be sincere in intent, trustworthy in use, and capable of sustaining a sense of goodwill and human dignity. Although these expectations are often disappointed and for many are inadequate, they suggest a crucial orientation for evaluating youth-oriented popular art.

Pluralism and Pedagogy

Despite its circus-like atmosphere, the congressional hearing on record labeling put many problems of evaluation on center stage in the North American public square. At the forefront stood the conflicting interests of the entertainment industry, adult guardians, and youthful consumers. Just offstage, fussing about in the wings, were the supporting cast of form, content, and function, sometimes donning the costumes of formalism, moralism, and contextualism. From backstage, invisible and barely audible, came the promptings—as if from a coded script—of different kinds of evaluation and the standards on which these rely. But as one looks back, it seems as if the drama has just begun and the main act is still to follow. And this is indeed the case, for the main act involves all of us in our daily interactions with popular art. Before the curtain closes on our prologue, however, consider two final stage directions.

The first concerns the notion of pluralism. Up to now the discussion has referred to the pluralism of diverse groups in North American society. But there is another kind of pluralism, equally important but less obvious to the casual observer. This pluralism involves various kinds of evaluations and the standards on which they are based. Against elite aesthetics, one does well to acknowledge that all popular-art products function in multiple ways, and that no product is merely or primarily an aesthetic object. Against crude populism, one must note that few products of popular art will rank high according to all six standards discussed here. Those few that do are the ones that nearly everyone judges to be outstanding. One challenge for all, from maker to consumer, is to learn to discern the various ways in which a popular-art product is better or worse than we expect it to be.

This observation leads to the second point, which has to do with pedagogy. There are many strategies for encouraging young people to evaluate popular art and to articulate their rationale for evaluation. One strategy, promising but too little tried, involves young people in the production of their own popular art. As cooks and carpenters have known for centuries, there is no surer way to learn what makes for good cooking or good cabinet-making than to try it oneself. The same would seem to apply to popular art. In addition, creating and performing a rock song or scripting, shooting, and editing a short video takes adolescents out of their consumerist passivity and unleashes their energy and imagination. If combined with research, discussion, writing, and other traditional modes of instruction, producing popular art could refine and advance adolescents' evaluative abilities. This route would also open up a whole new terrain for adolescents to explore with their peers and with their parents, teachers, and other leaders. And as they explore this new ground, young people will find their own voices in their own local settings.

Not long ago a teenager drowned in the icy waters of a lake in Ontario. His untimely death shocked his community and devastated his parents and peers. All of Mark's friends from school, including his hockey teammates, came to his funeral. Some students with their own rock band provided the music. Amid the wail of the guitars and the smashing of the drums arose the anger and grief of death, the pain and mystery of life. Although this nontraditional mode of expression startled some of Mark's relatives and their friends, this group of mourners together found a voice, were united in sorrow through the power of popular music. And in an unexpected way, the electronic sounds became the heartfelt celebration of Psalm 150.

Nothing we say or do can diminish the tragedy of a young person's death. But all of us need ways to speak and act in response to our suffering as well as our blessings. It is in situations like this, when teenagers and adults are truly open to themselves and to one another, that popular art acquires its deepest significance.

Selected Bibliography

Adair, Gilbert. *Vietnam on Film: From the Green Berets to Apocalypse Now*. New York: Proteus, 1981.

Adorno, Theodor W. *Aesthetic Theory*. Trans. C. Lenhardt. London: Routledge & Kegan Paul, 1984.

_____. "Culture Industry Reconsidered." *New German Critique* 6 (Fall 1975): 12-19.

_____. "How to Look at Television." *Quarterly of Film, Radio and Television* 8 (Spring 1954): 213-35. (Reprinted as "Television and the Patterns of Mass Culture." In *Mass Culture*, ed. Bernard Rosenberg and David White, 474-87. Glencoe, Ill.: Free Press, 1957.)

_____. *Introduction to the Sociology of Music*. Trans. E. B. Ashton. New York: Seabury Press, 1976.

_____. "On the Fetish-Character in Music and the Regression of Listening." In *The Essential Frankfurt School Reader*, ed. Andrew Arato and Eike Gebhardt, 270-99. New York: Continuum, 1982.

_____. *Prisms*. Trans. Samuel and Shierry Weber. Cambridge, Mass.: MIT Press, 1981.

_____. "A Social Critique of Radio Music." *Kenyon Review* 7 (Spring 1945): 208-17.

_____. "Transparencies on Film." *New German Critique* 26 (Spring-Summer 1982): 199-205.

Adorno, Theodor W., with George Simpson. "On Popular Music." *Studies in Philosophy and Social Science* 9 (1941): 17-48.

Albert, Dora. "Youth May Be Wasted on Young But Its Appeal Is Showbiz Asset If You Understand What It Is." *Variety*, 16 Jan. 1985, pp. 7, 92.

Alloway, Lawrence. *Violent America: The Movies, 1946-1964*. New York: Museum of Modern Art, 1971.

Altheide, David L. "The Mass Media and Youth Culture." *Urban Education* 14 (July 1979): 236-53.

Alther, Lisa. *Kinflicks*. New York: Alfred A. Knopf, 1976.

American Teens Speak: Sex, Myths, TV, and Birth Control—The Planned Parenthood Poll. New York: Louis Harris and Associates, Inc., 1986.

Anderson, Bernhard, ed. *Creation in the Old Testament*. Vol. 6 in Issues in Religion and Theology series. Philadelphia: Fortress Press, 1984.

_____. "Mythopoeic and Theological Dimensions of Biblical Creation Faith." In

Creation in the Old Testament, ed. Bernhard W. Anderson. Philadelphia: Fortress Press, 1984.

Andrew, Dudley. *Concepts in Film Theory.* New York: Oxford University Press, 1984.

_____. *The Major Film Theories: An Introduction.* New York: Oxford University Press, 1976.

Appleton, Clyde. "Black and White in the Music of American Youth." *New York Education Quarterly* 4 (Winter 1979): 24-29.

Aries, Philippe. *Centuries of Childhood: A Social History of Family Life.* New York: Vintage Books, 1965.

Armour, Richard A. *Film: A Reference Guide.* Westport, Conn.: Greenwood Press, 1980.

Ashby, LeRoy. *Saving the Waifs: Reformers and Dependent Children, 1890-1917.* Philadelphia: Temple University Press, 1984.

Atkins, Thomas R., ed. *Graphic Violence on the Screen.* New York: Simon & Schuster, 1976.

_____. *Sexuality in the Movies.* Bloomington: Indiana University Press, 1975.

Aufderheide, Pat. "Music Videos: The Look of the Sound." *Journal of Communication* 36 (Winter 1986): 57-78.

Ausband, Stephen C. *Myth and Meaning, Myth and Order.* Macon, Ga.: Mercer University Press, 1983.

Bach, Steven. *Final Cut: Dreams and Disaster in the Making of Heaven's Gate.* New York: William Morrow, 1985.

Bailey, Beth L. *From Front Porch to Back Seat: Courtship in 20th-Century America.* Baltimore: Johns Hopkins University Press, 1988.

Baker, M. Joyce. *Images of Women in Film: The War Years, 1941-1945.* Ann Arbor: UMI Research Press, 1980.

Balio, Tino, ed. *The American Film Industry.* Madison: University of Wisconsin Press, 1976.

Balswick, Jack, and Bron Ingoldsby. "Heroes and Heroines among American Adolescents." *Sex Roles* 8 (1982): 243-49.

Banner, Lois W. "Religion and Reform in the Early Republic: The Role of Youth." *American Quarterly* 23 (1971): 677-95.

Baran, Paul A., and Paul M. Sweezy. *Monopoly Capital: An Essay on the American Economic and Social Order.* Harmondsworth, Middlesex: Penguin Books, 1966.

Baranowski, Marc D. "Television and the Adolescent." *Adolescence* 6 (Fall 1971): 369-96.

Barol, Bill. "The Sight of Music." *Newsweek on Campus*, special issue, Nov. 1982, pp. 12-16.

Bart, Peter. "Hollywood Finds Gold on Beaches." *New York Times*, 22 June 1965, p. 25.

Barthes, Roland. *Mythologies.* Trans. Annette Lavers. New York: Hill & Wang, 1957.

Basinger, J. "America's Love Affair with Frank Capra." *American Film* 7 (Mar. 1982): 46-51, 81.

_____. "Meet Frank Capra." *American Film* 13 (Dec. 1987): 59-62.

Bataile, Gretchen M., and Charles L. P. Silets, eds. *The Pretend Indians: Images of Native Americans in the Movies.* Ames: Iowa State University Press, 1980.

Baxter, John. *The Cinema of John Ford.* New York: Barnes, 1971.

Baxter, Richard, et al. "A Content Analysis of Music Videos." *Journal of Broadcasting & Electronic Media* 29 (Summer 1985): 333-40.

Baym, Nina. *Novels, Readers, and Reviewers: Responses to Fiction in Antebellum America.* Ithaca, N.Y.: Cornell University Press, 1984.

_____. *Women's Fiction: A Guide to Novels by and about Women in America, 1820-1870.* Ithaca, N.Y.: Cornell University Press, 1978.

Beales, Ross. "In Search of the Historical Child: Miniature Adulthood and Youth in Colonial New England." *American Quarterly* 27 (1975): 379-98.

Bearison, David J., Jean M. Bain, and Richard Daniele. "Developmental Changes in How Children Understand Television." *Social Behavior and Personality* 10 (1982): 133-44.

Becker, Howard S. *Art Worlds.* Berkeley: University of California Press, 1982.

Beja, Morris. *Film and Literature.* New York: Longman, 1979.

Bell, Clive. *Art.* London: Chatto & Windus, 1914.

Bell, Daniel. *The Cultural Contradictions of Capitalism.* New York: Basic Books, 1976.

_____. "Sensibility in the 60's." In *Youth: Divergent Perspectives,* ed. Peter K. Manning, 27-44. New York: John Wiley & Sons, 1973.

Bellah, Robert N., et al. *Habits of the Heart: Individualism and Commitment in American Life.* Berkeley: University of California Press, 1985.

Belz, Carl. *The Story of Rock.* 2nd ed. New York: Harper & Row–Colophon Books, 1969.

Benjamin, Walter. "The Work of Art in the Age of Mechanical Reproduction." In *Illuminations,* ed. Hannah Arendt, trans. Harry Zohn, 217-51. New York: Schocken Books, 1969.

Bennett, Tony, and Janet Woollacott. *Bond and Beyond: The Political Career of a Popular Hero.* New York: Methuen, 1987.

Berger, Bennett M. "The New Stage of American Man—Almost Endless Adolescence." In *The Contemporary American Family,* ed. William J. Goode, 202-20. Chicago: Quadrangle Books, 1971.

Bernstein, Richard, "John Irving: 19th-Century Novelist for These Times," *New York Times,* 25 Apr. 1989, p. C-13.

Betterton, Rosemary. *Looking On: Images of Femininity in the Visual Arts and Media.* London: Pandora Press, 1987.

Bezilla, Robert, ed. *America's Youth: 1977-1988.* Princeton, N.J.: Gallup Organization, 1988.

Bigsby, C. W. E., ed. *Approaches to Popular Culture.* Bowling Green: Bowling Green University Popular Press, 1976.

"Birth of an Action-Pic Nation," *Variety,* 17 Oct. 1956, p. 1.

Blake, Richard A. "Catholics and the Media Sleeze Factor." *America,* 1 Aug. 1981, pp. 15-18.

Bogle, Donald. *Toms, Coons, Mulattoes, Mammies, and Bucks: An Interpretive History of Blacks in American Films.* New York: Viking Press, 1973.

Bohn, Thomas W., and Richard L. Stromgren. *Light and Shadows: A History of Motion Pictures*. Port Washington, N.Y.: Alfred, 1975.

Bonomi, Patricia U. *Under the Cope of Heaven: Religion, Society and Politics in Colonial America*. New York: Oxford University Press, 1986.

Boorstin, Daniel J. *The Americans: The Democratic Experience*. New York: Random House, 1973.

_____. *The Republic of Technology: Reflections on Our Future Community*. New York: Harper & Row, 1978.

Bottigheimer, Ruth B., ed. *Fairy Tale and Society: Illusion, Allusion, and Paradigm*. Philadelphia: University of Pennsylvania Press, 1986.

Bowers, Wendy. "Violent Pornography." *Humanist* 48 (Jan.-Feb. 1988): 22-25.

Boyum, Joy Gould. *Double Exposure: Fiction into Film*. New York: St. Martin's Press, 1985.

Brady, John. *The Craft of the Screenwriter: Interviews with Six Celebrated Screenwriters*. New York: Simon & Schuster, 1981.

Brannigan, Augustine, Dolf Zillmann, and Jennings Bryant. "Pornography and Behavior: Alternative Explanations." *Journal of Communication* 37 (Summer 1987): 185-93.

Brantlinger, Patrick. *Bread and Circuses: Theories of Mass Culture as Social Democracy*. Ithaca, N.Y.: Cornell University Press, 1983.

Braudy, Leo, and Morris Dickstein, eds. *Great Film Directors: A Critical Anthology*. New York: Oxford University Press, 1978.

Bremner, Robert H. "Other People's Children." *Journal of Social History* 16 (1983): 83-103.

Brody, Stephen. *Screen Violence and Film Censorship*. London: Her Majesty's Stationery Office, 1977.

Brooks, Tilford. *America's Black Musical Heritage*. Englewood Cliffs, N.J.: Prentice-Hall, 1984.

Brown, Charles T. *The Art of Rock and Roll*. 2nd ed. Englewood Cliffs, N.J.: Prentice-Hall, 1987.

Brown, Elizabeth, and William Hendee. "Adolescents and Their Music." *Journal of the American Medical Association* 262 (22-29 Sept. 1989): 1659-63.

Brown, Jane D., Kenneth Campbell, and Lynn Fisher. "American Adolescents and Musical Videos: Why Do They Watch?" *International Journal for Mass Communication* 37 (1986): 19-32.

Brown, Peter, and Steven Gaines. *The Love You Make: An Insider's Story of the Beatles*. New York: McGraw-Hill, 1983.

Browne, Ray B., ed. *Popular Culture and the Expanding Consciousness*. New York: John Wiley & Sons, 1973.

Brueggemann, Walter. *Genesis: A Bible Commentary for Teaching and Preaching*. Atlanta: John Knox Press, 1982.

Buckley, William F., Jr., et al. "Freedom to Read: 5 Authors' Letters to Attorney General's Commission on Pornography." *Society* 23 (Sept.-Oct. 1986): 72.

Buechner, Katherine A. *Whistling in the Dark: An ABC Theologized*. San Francisco: Harper & Row, 1988.

Buhel, Paul, ed. *Popular Culture in America*. Minneapolis: University of Minnesota Press, 1987.

Bumsted, J. M., and John E. Van de Wetering. *What Must I Do to Be Saved? The Great Awakening in Colonial America*. Hinsdale, Ill.: Dryden, 1976.

Bürger, Peter. *Theory of the Avant Garde*. Trans. Michael Shaw. Minneapolis: University of Minnesota Press, 1984.

Burgin, Victor, James Donald, and Cora Kaplan, eds. *Formations of Fantasy*. New York: Methuen, 1987.

Burke, Kenneth. "Literature as Equipment for Living." In *The Philosophy of Literary Form: Studies in Symbolic Form*, 3rd ed., 293-304. Berkeley: University of California Press, 1973.

Bushman, Richard L. *From Puritan to Yankee: Character and the Social Order in Connecticut, 1690-1765*. Cambridge, Mass.: Harvard University Press, 1967.

Butler, Ivan. *The Cinema of Roman Polanski*. New York: Barnes, 1970.

_____. *Religion in the Cinema*. New York: Barnes, 1969.

Butler, Jerry. *Raw Talent: The Adult Film Industry as Seen by Its Most Popular Male Star*. Buffalo, N.Y.: Prometheus Books, 1989.

Butler, Katy. "The Great Boomer Bust." *Mother Jones*, June 1989, pp. 32-37.

"Cable Porn." *America*, 13 June 1981, p. 175.

Calder, Jenni. *There Must Be a Lone Ranger: The American West in Film and in Reality*. London: Hamilton, 1974.

Calkins, Ernest Elmo. "Beauty: The New Business Tool." *Atlantic Monthly* 140 (Aug. 1927): 145-56.

Callahan, Jean. "WB's Cornyn Tells Tribunal of Cost Fears." *Billboard*, 12 July 1980, p. 4.

_____. "Women and Pornography: Combat in the Video Zone." *American Film* 7 (Mar. 1982): 62-64.

Cameron, Ian. *Adventure in the Movies*. New York: Crescent, 1973.

Campbell, Lloyd P., and Betty Roether. "Suggested Guidelines for Television Viewing for Children and Adolescents." *Contemporary Education* 55 (Summer 1984): 220-21.

"Can Any Good Thing Come Out of Hollywood?: An Interview with Producer Ken Wales." *Christianity Today*, 21 Sept. 1984, pp. 19-25.

Cantor, Joanne, and Sandra Reilly. "Adolescent's Fright Reactions to Television and Films." *Journal of Communication* 32 (Winter 1982): 87-99.

Capra, Frank. *The Name Above the Title: An Autobiography*. New York: Macmillan, 1971.

Carey, James W. *Communication as Culture: Essays on Media and Society*. Boston: Unwin Hyman, 1989.

Carney, Raymond. *American Vision: The Films of Frank Capra*. Cambridge, Mass.: Cambridge University Press, 1986.

Carter, Bill. "HBO and MTV Begin a Serious Battle over Comedy." *New York Times*, 22 May 1989, p. C-6.

_____. "K Mart and CBS to Join in Promotion." *New York Times*, 10 May 1989, p. 49.

"The Case Against Porn." Editorial. *America*, 15 Mar. 1986, p. 198.

Cavallo, Dominick. "Social Reform and the Movement to Organize Children's Play during the Progressive Era." *History of Childhood Quarterly* 3 (1976): 509-22.

Cavell, Stanley. *Pursuits of Happiness: The Hollywood Comedy of Remarriage.* Cambridge, Mass.: Harvard University Press, 1981.

Cawelti, John G. "Notes toward an Aesthetic of Popular Culture." *Journal of Popular Culture* 5 (1971): 255-68.

Chaffee, Steven H., and Albert R. Tims. "Interpersonal Factors in Adolescent Television Use." *Journal of Social Issues* 32 (Fall 1976): 98-115.

Chaffee, Steven H., Jack M. McLeod, and Charles K. Atkin. "Parental Influences on Adolescent Media Use." *American Behavioral Scientist* 14 (Jan.-Feb. 1971): 323-40.

Chiarelott, Leigh. "Cognition and the Media-ted Curriculum: Effects of Growing Up in an Electronic Environment." *Educational Technology* 24 (May 1984): 19-22.

Christensen, Ferrel, Dolf Zillman, and Jennings Bryant. "Effects of Pornography: The Debate Continues." *Journal of Communication* 37 (Winter 1987): 186-89.

Christenson, Reo. "It's Time to Excise the Pornographic Cancer: The Notion That Pornography Is a Victimless Crime Has Allowed It and Its Peddlers Leniency under the Law." *Christianity Today,* 2 Jan. 1981, pp. 20-23.

Clarens, Carlos. *Crime Movies: From Griffith to the Godfather and Beyond.* New York: W. W. Norton, 1980.

Clarke, Gerald. "And *Animal House* Begat . . . ," *Time,* 15 Apr. 1985, p. 103.

———. " 'I've Got to Get My Life Back Again.' " *Time,* 23 May 1983, p. 66.

Clarke, Peter. "Introduction: Some Proposals for Continuing Research on Youth and the Mass Media." *American Behavioral Scientist* 14 (Jan.-Feb. 1971): 313-22.

Cocks, Jay. "Sing a Song of Seeing." *Time,* 26 Dec. 1983, pp. 52-64.

Cohen, Stanley. "Contexts and Background: Youth in the Sixties." In *Folk Devils and Moral Panics: The Creation of the Mods and Rockers,* 177-204. New York: St. Martin's Press, 1980.

Coleman, James S., with John W. C. Johnstone and Kurt Johnassohn. *Society: The Social Life of the Teenager and Its Impact on Education.* New York: Free Press of Glencoe, 1962.

Collins, Douglas. "Ritual Sacrifice and the Political Economy of Music." *Perspectives of New Music* 24 (Fall-Winter 1985): 14-23.

Collins, Jim. *Uncommon Cultures: Popular Culture and Post-Modernism.* New York: Routledge, Chapman & Hall, 1989.

Comer, James P. "Television, Sex, & Violence: 11 through 13 Years of Age." *Parents Magazine,* July 1986, p. 160.

Compton, Mary F. "Television Viewing Habits of Early Adolescents." *Clearing House* 57 (Oct. 1983): 60-62.

Congressional Reference Division. *Rock Music Lyrics IP0342R.* Washington: Congressional Research Service, Library of Congress, Feb. 1986.

Conroy, Stephen S. "Popular Technology and Youth Rebellion in America." *Journal of Popular Culture* 16 (1983): 123-33.

"Conservative Church Teens Sexually Active, Researchers Discover," *Grand Rapids Press,* 2 Feb. 1988, p. A-3.

Considine, David M. "The Cinema of Adolescence." *Journal of Popular Film & Television* 9 (1981): 123-36.

_____. "Movies and Minors." *Top of the News* 40 (Spring 1984): 253-65.

Cook, David A. *A History of Narrative Film.* 2nd ed. New York: W. W. Norton, 1990.

Cook, Jim, and Mike Lewington, eds. *Images of Alcoholism.* London: British Film Institute, 1979.

Cooper, B. Lee. *The Popular Music Handbook: A Resource Guide for Teachers, Librarians, and Media Specialists.* Littleton, Co.: Libraries Unlimited, Inc., 1984.

_____. "Social Concerns, Political Protest, and Popular Music." *Social Studies* 79 (Mar.-Apr. 1988): 53-60.

Corliss, Richard. "Did You Ever See a Dream Stalking?" *Time,* 5 Sept. 1988, pp. 66-67.

_____. "Magic Shadows from a Melting Pot." *Time,* 8 July 1985, p. 92.

_____. "The Medium Is the Message." *Film Comment* 19 (July-Aug. 1983): 34.

_____. "Turned On? Turn It Off: Switching Channels May Be One Cure for the Contagion of Porn." *Time: Special Issue, United States Constitution Bicentennial,* 6 July 1987, pp. 72-74.

_____. "Well, Hello Molly!" *Time,* 26 May 1986, pp. 67-69.

Cott, Nancy F. *The Bonds of Womanhood: "Woman's Sphere" in New England, 1790-1835.* New Haven: Yale University Press, 1977.

Cowie, Peter, ed. *A Concise History of the Cinema.* New York: Barnes, 1971.

_____, ed. *Eighty Years of Cinema.* New York: Barnes, 1977.

Cowing, Cedric B. "Sex and Preaching in the Great Awakening." *American Quarterly* 20 (1968): 624.

Cowley, Susan Cheever. "The Travolta Hustle." *Newsweek,* 29 May 1978, p. 97.

Cox, Harvey. "The Family: Between Myth and Promise." *American Baptist Quarterly* 3 (Mar. 1984): 31-41.

Cressey, Paul G. "The Motion Picture as Informal Education." *Journal of Educational Sociology* 7 (1934): 504-15.

Crichton, Sarah. "Off the Beach Blanket and into the Bedroom: What on Earth Is Going On in Teenage Movies?" *MS.,* June 1985, pp. 90-91.

Cripps, Thomas. *Black Film as Genre.* Bloomington: Indiana University Press, 1978.

Cross, Whitney R. *The Burned-Over District: The Social and Intellectual History of Enthusiastic Religion in Western New York, 1800-1850.* Ithaca, N.Y.: Cornell University Press, 1950.

Csikzentmihalyi, Mihaly, Reed Larson, and Suzanne Prescott. "The Ecology of Adolescent Activity and Experience." *Journal of Youth and Adolescence* 6 (Sept. 1977): 281-94.

Cunningham, Hugh. *Leisure in the Industrial Revolution.* New York: St. Martin's Press, 1980.

Czitrom, Daniel J. *Media and the American Mind: From Morse to McLuhan.* Chapel Hill, N.C.: University of North Carolina Press, 1982.

Darton, Robert. *The Great Cat Massacre and Other Episodes in French Cultural Theory.* New York: Vintage Books, 1985.

Davies, Philip, and Brian Neve, eds. *Cinema, Politics, and Society in America.* New York: St. Martin's Press, 1981.

Davis, Donald M. "Nihilism in Music Television." Paper presented to the Mass Communication Division of the Speech Communication Association at its annual meeting, Chicago, Nov. 1984.

De Curtis, Anthony. "The Year in Music." *Rolling Stone,* 15-29 Dec. 1988, pp. 13-140.

de Lauretis, Teresa. "Aesthetic and Feminist Theory: Rethinking Women's Cinema." In *Feminist Art Criticism: An Anthology,* ed. Arlene Raven et al., 133-52. Ann Arbor: UMI Research Press, 1988.

_____. *Alice Doesn't: Feminism, Semiotics, Cinema.* Bloomington: Indiana University Press, 1984.

Demo, Mary Penasack. "Adolescents: Your Children and Mine." *Communication Education* 30 (Jan. 1981): 71-77.

Demos, John. *A Little Commonwealth: Family Life in Plymouth Colony.* New York: Oxford University Press, 1970.

_____. *Past, Present, and Personal: The Family and Life Course in American History.* New York: Oxford University Press, 1986.

Demos, John, and Sarane S. Boocock, eds. *Turning Points: Historical and Sociological Essays on the Family.* Chicago: University of Chicago Press, 1978.

Dempsey, David. *Sing a Song of Social Significance.* 2nd ed. Bowling Green: Bowling Green State University Popular Press, 1983.

_____. " 'Teen Angel': Resistence, Rebellion and Death—Revisited." *Journal of Popular Culture* 16 (Spring 1983): 116-22.

_____. "Why the Girls Scream, Weep, Flip." *New York Times Magazine,* 23 Feb. 1964, p. 70.

Denisoff, R. Serge. *Inside MTV.* New Brunswick: Transaction Books, 1988.

Denisoff, R. Serge, and Mark Levine. "Generations and Counterculture: A Study in the Ideology of Music." *Youth & Society* 2 (Sept. 1970): 33-58.

_____. "The One Dimensional Approach to Popular Music: A Research Note." *Journal of Popular Culture* 4 (Spring 1971): 911-19.

Denisoff, R. Serge, with William L. Schurk. *Tarnished Gold: The Record Industry Revisited.* New Brunswick: Transaction Books, 1986.

Derry, Charles. *Dark Dreams: The Horror Film from Psycho to Jaws.* New York: Barnes, 1977.

_____. "More Dark Dreams: Some Notes on the Recent Horror Film." In *American Horrors: Essays on the Modern American Horror Film,* ed. Gregory A. Waller, 162-74. Urbana: University of Illinois Press, 1987.

Desmond, Roger Jon. "Adolescents and Music Lyrics: Implications of a Cognitive Perspective." *Communication Quarterly* 35 (Summer 1987): 276-84.

De Vries, Daniel. *The Films of Stanley Kubrick.* Grand Rapids: Eerdmans, 1973.

Dickstein, Morris. "It's a Wonderful Life, But . . ." *American Film* 5 (May 1980): 42-47.

Dika, Vera. "The Stalker Film, 1978-81." In *American Horrors: Essays on the Modern American Horror Film*, ed. Gregory A. Waller, 86-101. Urbana: University of Illinois Press, 1987.

Dillard, R. H. W. *Horror Films*. New York: Simon & Schuster, 1976.

_____. "Night of the Living Dead: It's Not Like Just a Wind That's Passing Through." In *American Horrors: Essays on the Modern American Horror Film*, ed. Gregory A. Waller, 14-29. Urbana: University of Illinois Press, 1987.

DiMaggio, Paul. "Classification in Art." *American Sociological Review* 52 (Aug. 1987): 440-45.

Disraeli, Benjamin. *Coningsby: Or, The New Generation*. London: Henry Colburn, 1844.

Doane, Mary Ann. *The Desire to Desire: The Woman's Film of the 1940s*. Bloomington: Indiana University Press, 1988.

Doherty, Thomas. "The Exploitation Film as History: Wild in the Streets." *Literature/Film Quarterly* 12 (1984): 186-94.

_____. "MTV and the Music Video: Promo and Product." *Southern Speech Communication Journal* 52 (Summer 1987): 349-61.

_____. *Teenagers and Teenpics: The Juvenilization of American Movies in the 1950s*. No. 3 in the Media and Popular Culture series. Boston: Unwin Hyman, 1988.

Donahue, Susan Mary. *American Film Distribution: The Changing Marketplace*. Ann Arbor: UMI Research Press, 1985.

Donleavy, J. P., and John Irving. Letters appearing in *The Paris Review*, Spring 1988, pp. 300-303.

Donnerstein, Edward I., and Daniel G. Linz. "The Question of Pornography: It Is Not Sex, But Violence, That Is an Obscenity in Our Society." *Psychology Today*, Dec. 1986, p. 56.

Dotter, Daniel. "Growing Up Is Hard to Do: Rock and Roll Performers as Cultural Heroes." *Sociological Spectrum* 7 (1987): 25-44.

Douglas, Ann. *The Feminization of American Culture*. New York: Alfred A. Knopf, 1978.

Dove, Charles P. *Labeling Rock Music: Editorial Commentary*. Washington: Government and Law Library Services Division, 30 Oct. 1985.

Drew, Donald J. *Images of Man: A Critique of the Contemporary Cinema*. Downers Grove, Ill.: InterVarsity Press, 1974.

Dubiel, Helmut. *Theory and Politics: Studies in the Development of Critical Theory*. Trans. Benjamin Gregg. Cambridge, Mass.: MIT Press, 1985.

Duckworth, Joseph B., and Peter K. Hoover-Suczek. "Reel to Reel: Teaching Adolescent Psychology through Film." *Phi Delta Kappa* 57 (May 1976): 595-97, 601.

Durgnat, Raymond. *The Crazy Mirror: Hollywood Comedy and the American Image*. New York: Delta, 1969.

_____. *The Strange Case of Alfred Hitchcock; or, The Plain Man's Hitchcock*. Cambridge, Mass.: MIT Press, 1974.

Dworkin, Martin S. "Movie Politics." *Dalhousie Review* 44 (1964): 75-82.

Eaton, Marcia Muelder. *Basic Issues in Aesthetics.* Belmont, Calif.: Wadsworth, 1988.

Ecker, Gisela, ed. *Feminist Aesthetics.* Trans. Harriet Anderson. Boston: Beacon Press, 1985.

Edmondson, Linda Harriet. *Feminism in Russia, 1900-17.* Stanford: Stanford University Press, 1984.

Egan, Jack. "Hollywood's Numbers Game." *U.S. News and World Report,* 2 Apr. 1990, pp. 39-42.

Ehrenreich, Barbara. *The Hearts of Men: American Dreams and the Flight from Commitment.* Garden City, N.Y.: Doubleday, 1983.

Eisen, Jonathan, ed. *The Age of Rock: Sounds of the American Cultural Revolution.* New York: Vintage Books, 1969.

Elder, Glen, Jr. "Adolescence in Historical Perspective." In *Growing Up in America: Historical Experiences,* ed. Harvey J. Graff. Detroit: Wayne State University Press, 1987.

"Electronic Potsherds: X-Rated Videomaterial in the Home." *America,* 4 Apr. 1981, p. 266.

Elkind, David. *All Grown Up and No Place to Go: Teenagers in Crisis.* Reading, Mass.: Addison-Wesley, 1984.

Ellis, Godfrey J. "Youth in the Electronic Environment: An Introduction." *Youth & Society* 15 (Sept. 1983): 3-12.

Ellul, Jacques. *Propaganda.* Trans. Konrad Kellen and Jean Lerner. New York: Alfred A. Knopf, 1965.

———. *The Technological Society.* Trans. John Wilkinson. Introduction by Robert K. Merton. New York: Alfred A. Knopf, 1964.

English, Deirdre. "The Politics of Porn: Can Feminists Walk the Line?" *Mother Jones,* Apr. 1980, pp. 20-28.

"An Entertainment Engine Takes Shape." *New York Times,* 6 Mar. 1989, p. 37.

Enzensberger, Hans Magnus. *The Consciousness Industry: On Literature, Politics and the Media.* New York: Seabury Press–Continuum Books, 1974.

Evans, Max. *Sam Peckinpah: Master of Violence.* Vermillion, S.D.: Dakota Press, 1972.

Evans, Walter. "The All-American Boys." *Journal of Popular Culture* 6 (Summer 1972): 104-21.

———. "Monster Movies and Rites of Initiation." *Journal of Popular Film* 4 (1975): 124-42.

Everson, William K. *The Detective in Film.* Secaucus, N.J.: Citadel, 1972.

Ewen, Stuart. *All Consuming Images: The Politics of Style in Contemporary Culture.* New York: Basic Books, 1988.

———. *Captains of Consciousness: Advertising and the Social Roots of the Consumer Culture.* New York: McGraw-Hill, 1976.

Ewen, Stuart, and Elizabeth Ewen. *Channels of Desire: Mass Images and the Shaping of American Consciousness.* New York: McGraw-Hill, 1982.

Faber, R. J., Jane E. Brown, and Jack M. McLeod. "Coming of Age in the Global Village: Television and Adolescents." In *Children Communicating,* vol. 7, *Sage Annual Reviews of Communication Research,* ed. Ellen Wartella, 215-47. Beverly Hills: Sage Publications, 1979.

Fabrikant, Geraldine. "Deal Is Expected for Sony to Buy Columbia Pictures." *New York Times,* 26 Sept. 1989, pp. 1, 40.

_____. "Let's Make a Deal: Entertainment Mergers Show Desire to Run Production and Distribution." *New York Times,* 5 Apr. 1989, p. 29.

_____. "Time-Warner Merger Raises Concerns on Power of a Giant." *New York Times,* 6 Mar. 1989, pp. 1, 37.

"Fan Wins Singer's House." *New York Times,* 31 Mar. 1989, p. B-3.

Farber, Stephen. *The Movie Rating Game.* Washington: Public Affairs, 1972.

Fass, Paula S. *The Damned and the Beautiful: American Youth in the 1920s.* New York: Oxford University Press, 1979.

Fein, Esther B. "Costly Pleasures." *New York Times Book Review,* 26 May 1985, p. 25.

Fell, John L. *Film and the Narrative Tradition.* Norman, Okla.: University of Oklahoma Press, 1974.

_____. *A History of Films.* New York: Holt, Rinehart & Winston, 1979.

Ferrarotti, Franco. *The End of Conversation: The Impact of Mass Media on Modern Society.* Contributions in Sociology, no. 71. New York: Greenwood Press, 1988.

Ferrer, Frank. "Exploitation Films." *Film Comment* 6 (Fall 1963): 31-33.

"Film 'Future': GI Baby Boom," *Variety,* 5 Mar. 1958, p. 1.

Firstenberg, Jean. "From Capra to Lappola." *American Film* 7 (June 1982): 79.

Fishbein, Leslie. "The Demise of the Cult of True Womanhood in Early American Film, 1900-1930: Two Modes of Subversion." *Journal of Popular Film and Television* 12 (1984): 66-72.

Fishburn, Katherine. *Women in Popular Culture: A Reference Guide.* Westport, Conn.: Greenwood Press, 1982.

Fishwick, Marshall. *Seven Pillars of Popular Culture.* Contributions to the Study of Popular Culture, no. 10. Westport, Conn.: Greenwood Press, 1985.

Fleischmann, Mark. "Chimes of Freedom." *Cable Choice,* Dec. 1988, p. 20.

Fliegelman, Jay. *Prodigals and Pilgrims: The American Revolution against Patriarchal Authority, 1750-1800.* New York: Cambridge University Press, 1982.

Foreman, Henry James. *Our Movie-Made Children.* New York: Macmillan, 1933.

Foster, Hal, ed. *The Anti-Aesthetic: Essays on Postmodern Culture.* Port Townsend, Wash.: Bay Press, 1983.

Foster, Harold M. "Film in the Classroom: Coping with 'Teenpics.' " *English Journal* 76 (Mar. 1987): 86-88.

Fotheringham, Allan. "The Prudes Are in Full Swing." *Maclean's,* 30 June 1986, p. 52.

Frank, Douglas. "Babes in Babylon: Growing Up Christian in a Society That Consumes Its Young." Calvin College *Dialogue* 20 (Mar. 1988): 10-23.

Freitag, Michael. "Judy McGrath: Television Executive." *New York Times,* 9 Apr. 1989, p. 38.

Friedenberg, Edgar Z. *The Vanishing Adolescent.* New York: Dell, 1959.

Friedman, Lester D. *Hollywood's Image of the Jew.* New York: Frederick Ungar, 1982.

Frith, Simon. *Music for Pleasure: Essays in the Sociology of Pop.* New York: Routledge, 1988.

_____. "Rock and Popular Culture." In *American Media and Mass Culture: Left Perspectives*, ed. Donald Lazere, 309-22. Berkeley: University of California Press, 1987.

_____. *Sound Effects: Youth, Leisure, and the Politics of Rock 'n' Roll*. New York: Pantheon Books, 1981.

Frith, Simon, and Angela McRobbie. "Rock and Sexuality." *Screen Education* 29 (Winter 1978-79): 3-19.

Frith, Simon, and Howard Horne. *Art into Pop*. London: Methuen, 1987.

Fry, Donald L., and Virginia H. Fry. "Some Structural Characterics of Music Television Video: A Montage Analysis." Paper presented at the annual meeting of the Speech Communication Association, Chicago, Nov. 1984.

Furhammar, Leif, and Folke Isaksson. *Politics and Film*. Trans. Kersti French. New York: Praeger, 1971.

Gallagher, Tag. *John Ford: The Man and His Work*. Berkeley: University of California Press, 1988.

Gallup, George, Jr. "Forecast for America." *Television and Families* 8 (Winter 1985): 11-17.

Gans, Douglas. "Art and Entertainment." *Perspectives of New Music* 24 (Fall-Winter 1985): 24-37.

Gans, Herbert J. *Popular Culture and High Culture: An Analysis and Evaluation of Taste*. New York: Basic Books, 1974.

Gantz, Walter, and Howard M. Gartenberg. "Pop Music and Adolescent Socialization: An Information Perspective." Paper presented at the annual meeting of the International Communication Association, Philadelphia, 1-5 May 1979.

Gantz, Walter, and James B. Weaver III. *Parent-Child Communication about Television: A View from the Parent's Perspective*. Paper presented to the Theory and Methodology Division of the Association for Education in Journalism and Mass Communication at their annual convention in Gainesville, Fla., Aug. 1984.

Geertz, Clifford. *The Interpretation of Cultures*. New York: Basic Books, 1973.

Gehr, Richard. "The MTV Aesthetic." *Film Comment* 19 (July-Aug. 1983): 37-40.

Gendron, Bernard. "Theodor Adorno Meets the Cadillacs." In *Studies in Entertainment*, ed. Tania Modleski, 18-36. Bloomington: Indiana University Press, 1986.

George, Nelson. *The Death of Rhythm and Blues*. New York: Pantheon Books, 1988.

Gerard, Jeremy. "An MTV for Grown-Ups Is Seeking Its Audience." *New York Times*, 7 Aug. 1989, p. Y-13.

Gianetti, Louis. *Understanding Movies*. 4th ed. Englewood Cliffs, N.J.: Prentice-Hall, 1987.

Gibbs, Nancy. "How America Has Run Out of Time." *Time*, 24 Apr. 1989, pp. 58-61.

Gibson, Arthur. *The Silence of God: Creative Response to the Films of Ingmar Bergman*. New York: Harper, 1969.

Gilbert, James. *A Cycle of Outrage: America's Reaction to the Juvenile Delinquent in the 1950s*. New York: Oxford University Press, 1986.

Gillet, Charlie. *The Sound of the City: The Rise of Rock and Roll.* Rev. ed. New York: Pantheon Books, 1970.

Gillis, John R. "Youth and History: Progress and Prospect." *Journal of Social History* 7 (Winter 1973): 201-7.

_____. *Youth and History: Tradition and Change in European Age Relations, 1770– Present.* New York: Academic Press, 1974.

Gilmore, Mikal. "Interview with Mick Jagger." *Rolling Stone,* 20th anniversary issue, 5 Nov. 1987, pp. 30-35.

Gitlin, Todd. *Inside Prime Time.* New York: Pantheon Books, 1983.

_____. *The Sixties: Years of Hope, Days of Rage.* New York: Bantam Books, 1987.

Glatzer, Richard, and John Raeburn, eds. *Frank Capra: The Man and His Films.* Ann Arbor: University of Michigan Press, 1975.

Glucksmann, André. "Report on Research on the Effect of Violent Scenes in Movies and Television on Youth." *Communications* 7 (1966): 74-119.

Gold, Richard. "No Bigness Like Show Bigness." *Variety,* 14-20 June 1989, pp. 1, 6-7.

Golding, Peter, and Graham Murdock. "Theories of Communication and Theories of Society." *Communication Research* 5 (July 1978): 339-56.

Goldman, Albert. *Freakshow: The Rocksoulbluesjazzsickjewblackhumorsexpoppsych Gig and Other Scenes from the Counter-Culture.* New York: Atheneum, 1971.

Goldman, Stuart. "That Old Devil Music." *National Review,* 24 Feb. 1989, pp. 28-31, 59.

Good, Howard. *Outcasts: The Image of Journalists in Contemporary Film.* Metuchen, N.J.: Scarecrow Press, 1989.

Gordon, Michael, ed. *The American Family in Social-Historical Perspective.* New York: St. Martin's Press, 1973.

Goudzwaard, Bob. *Capitalism and Progress: A Diagnosis of Western Society.* Trans. and ed. by Josina Van Nuis Zylstra. Grand Rapids: Eerdmans, 1979.

_____. *Idols of Our Time.* Trans. Mark Vander Vennen. Downers Grove, Ill.: InterVarsity Press, 1984.

Graff, Gerald, and Michael Warner, eds. *The Origins of Literary Studies in America: A Documentary Anthology.* New York: Routledge, 1989.

Graff, Harvey J. "Early Adolescence in Antebellum America: The Remaking of Growing Up." *Journal of Early Adolescence* 5 (1985): 411-27.

Graham, Lawrence, and Lawrence Hamdan. *Youthtrends: Capturing the $200 Billion Youth Market.* New York: St. Martin's Press, 1987.

Grant, Barry K., ed. *Film Genre: Theory and Criticism.* Metuchen, N.J.: Scarecrow Press, 1977.

Green, Garrett. *Imagining God: Theology and the Religious Imagination.* San Francisco: Harper & Row, 1989.

Greenberg, Bradley S., and Carrie Heeter. "Mass Media Orientations among Hispanic Youth." *Hispanic Journal of Behavioral Sciences* 5 (Sept. 1983): 305-23.

Greenberg, Clement. "Work and Leisure under Industrialism: The Plight of Our Culture: Part II." *Commentary* 16 (July 1953): 54-62.

Greenfield, Patricia Marks. *Mind and Media: The Effects of Television, Video Games, and Computers*. Cambridge, Mass.: Harvard University Press, 1984.

Greenhouse, Steven. "For Europe, U.S. May Spell TV." *New York Times*, 31 July 1989, pp. 19, 26.

Greenwald, John. "Shooting the Works." *Time*, 21 May 1990, pp. 64-66.

Greeson, Larry E., and Rose Ann Williams. "Social Implications of Music Videos for Youth: An Analysis of the Content and Effects of MTV." *Youth & Society* 18 (Dec. 1986): 177-89.

Greven, Philip J. *Four Generations: Population, Land, and Family in Colonial Andover, Massachusetts*. Ithaca, N.Y.: Cornell University Press, 1970.

_____. "Youth, Maturity, and Religious Conversion: A Note on the Ages of Converts in Andover, Massachusetts, 1711-1749." In *Growing Up in America: Historical Experiences*, ed. Harvey J. Graff, 144-55. Detroit: Wayne State University Press, 1987.

Gross, David. "Lowenthal, Adorno, Barthes: Three Perspectives on Popular Culture." *Telos* 45 (Fall 1980): 122-40.

Grossberg, Lawrence. "Interpreting the Crisis of Culture in Communication Theory." *Journal of Communication* 29 (Winter 1979): 56-68.

_____. "MTV: Swinging on the (Postmodern) Star." In *Cultural Politics in Contemporary America*, ed. Ian Angus and Sut Jhally, 254-68. New York: Routledge, 1989.

_____. "Rock and Roll in Search of an Audience." In *Popular Music and Communication*, ed. James Lull, 175-97. Newbury Park, Calif.: Sage Publications, 1987.

Grover, Robert. "Recent Trends in Children's Films." *Top of the News* 40 (Spring 1984): 285-89.

Groves, Don. "There's No Business Like Show Business, More Banks Say; Investments Lucrative." *Variety*, 14-20 June 1989, p. 16.

Gunter, B. G. "Youth, Leisure, and Post-Industrial Society: Implications for the Family." *Family Coordinator* 24 (Apr. 1975): 199-207.

Guralnick, Peter. *Sweet Soul Music: Rhythm and Blues and the Southern Dream of Freedom*. New York: Harper & Row, 1986.

Habermas, Jürgen. *Legitimation Crisis*. Trans. Thomas McCarthy. Boston: Beacon Press, 1975.

_____. *The Structural Transformation of the Public Sphere: An Inquiry into a Category of Bourgeois Society*. Trans. Thomas Burger. Cambridge, Mass.: MIT Press, 1989.

_____. *The Theory of Communicative Action*. 2 vols. Trans. Thomas McCarthy. Boston: Beacon Press, 1984, 1987.

Halberstam, David. *The Powers That Be*. New York: Alfred A. Knopf, 1979.

Hampton, Wayne. *Guerrilla Minstrels: John Lennon, Joe Hill, Woody Guthrie, Bob Dylan*. Knoxville: University of Tennessee Press, 1986.

Handlin, Oscar, and Mary F. Handlin. *Facing Life: Youth and the Family in American History*. Boston: Little, Brown, 1971.

Hanhardt, John G., ed. *Video Culture: A Critical Investigation*. Rochester, N.Y.:

Peregrine Smith Books in association with Visual Studies Workshop Press, 1986.

Harcourt, Peter. "Making the Scene: Some Speculations on the Values of Contemporary American Cinema." *Arts in Society* 10 (1973): 182-91.

Hareven, Tamara, and Andrejs Plakans. *Family History at the Crossroads: A Journal of Family History Reader.* Princeton: Princeton University Press, 1987.

Harmetz, Aljean. "Another 'Nightmare': A Studio's Sweet Dream." *New York Times,* 13 July 1989, pp. 11, 14.

_____. " 'Star Wars' Is 10, and Lucas Reflects." *New York Times,* 21 May 1987, p. 22.

_____. "U.S.C. Breaks Ground for a Film-TV School." *New York Times,* 25 Nov. 1981, p. C-16.

Harrington, John, ed. *Literature and/as Film.* Englewood Cliffs, N.J.: Prentice-Hall, 1977.

Harrington, Michael. *Decade of Decision: The Crisis of the American System.* New York: Simon & Schuster, 1980.

Haskell, Molly. *From Reverence to Rape: The Treatment of Women in the Movies.* New York: Holt, Rinehart & Winston, 1974.

Hatch, David, and Stephen Millward. *From Blues to Rock: An Analytical History of Pop Music.* Manchester, Eng.: Manchester University Press, 1987.

Hatch, Nathan O. *The Democratization of American Christianity.* New Haven: Yale University Press, 1989.

_____. "The Origins of Civil Millennialism in America: New England Clergymen, the War with France, and the Revolution." *William and Mary Quarterly* (third series) 31 (1974): 407-30.

Hauser, Arnold. *The Sociology of Art.* Trans. Kenneth J. Northcott. Chicago: University of Chicago Press, 1982.

Hawke, David Freeman. *Everyday Life in Early America.* New York: Harper & Row, 1988.

Hebdige, Dick. *Subculture: The Meaning of Style.* London: Methuen, 1979.

Hedegaard, Erik. "MTV's VH-1: Music Video for the Housewives." *Rolling Stone,* 17 Jan. 1985, p. 38.

Heller, Terry. *The Delights of Terror: An Aesthetics of the Tale of Terror.* Urbana: University of Illinois Press, 1987.

Hendrick, Harry. "The History of Childhood and Youth." *Social History* 9 (Jan. 1984): 87-96.

Hendry, Leo B., and Helen Patrick. "Adolescents and Television." *Journal of Youth & Adolescence* 6 (Dec. 1977): 325-36.

Henry, William A., III. "Another Kind of Ratings War: Campaign against TV Sex & Violence." *Time,* 6 July 1981, pp. 17-20.

Higham, John. "The Reorientation of American Culture in the 1890s." In *Writing American History: Essays on Modern Scholarship,* 73-102. Bloomington: Indiana University Press, 1970.

Hinds, Michael deCourcy. "Young Consumers: Perils and Power." *New York Times,* 11 Feb. 1989, p. 16.

Hiner, N. Ray. "Adolescence in 18th Century America." *History of Childhood Quarterly* 3 (1975): 253-80.

Hirsch, Paul. *The Structure of the Popular Music Industry.* Ann Arbor: University of Michigan Press, 1970.

Hitchens, Gordon. "The Truth, the Whole Truth and Nothing But the Truth about Exploitation Films." *Film Comment* 2 (Spring 1964): 1-13.

Hluchy, Patricia, and Gillian MacKay. "Spielberg's Magic Screen." *Maclean's*, 4 June 1984, pp. 38-44.

Holifield, E. Brooks. *A History of Pastoral Care in America.* Nashville: Abingdon Press, 1983.

Holloway, Ronald. *Beyond the Image: Approaches to the Religious Dimension in the Cinema.* Geneva, Switz.: World Council of Churches, 1977.

Holosko, M. J., G. M. Gould, and J. Baggaley. "Why Teenagers Watch Television: Implications for Educational Television." *Journal of Educational Television* 9 (1983): 57-62.

Horkheimer, Max. "Art and Mass Culture." *Studies in Philosophy and Social Science* 9 (1941): 290-304.

_____. *Critique of Instrumental Reason.* Trans. Matthew J. O'Connell et al. New York: Continuum, 1972.

Horkheimer, Max, and Theodor W. Adorno. *Dialectic of Enlightenment.* Trans. John Cumming. New York: Seabury Press, 1972.

Horowitz, Helen Lefkowitz. *Campus Life: Undergraduate Cultures from the End of the Eighteenth Century to the Present.* New York: Alfred A. Knopf, 1987.

Howitt, Dennis, and Guy Cumberbatch. "The Parameters of Attraction to Mass Media Figures." *Journal of Moral Education* 2 (June 1973): 269-81.

Huaco, George A. *The Sociology of Film Art.* New York: Basic Books, 1965.

Hudson, Kenneth. *The Language of the Teenage Revolution: The Dictionary Defeated.* London: Macmillan Press Ltd., 1983.

Hurley, Neil. *Theology through Film.* New York: Harper, 1970.

Huyssen, Andreas. *After the Great Divide: Modernism, Mass Culture and Postmodernism.* Bloomington: Indiana University Press, 1986.

_____. "The Cultural Politics of Pop: Reception and Critique of U.S. Pop Art in the Federal Republic of Germany." *New German Critique* 4 (Winter 1975): 77-97.

Inge, M. Thomas, ed. *Handbook of American Popular Culture.* 3 vols. Westport, Conn.: Greenwood Press, 1978-81.

Innis, Harold A. *The Bias of Communication.* Toronto: University of Toronto Press, 1964.

_____. *Empire and Communication.* Toronto: University of Toronto Press, 1972.

Jacobs, Diane. *Hollywood Renaissance.* Rev. ed. New York: Dell, 1980.

Jacobs, Lewis, ed. *The Emergence of Film Art: The Evolution and Development of the Motion Picture as an Art from 1900 to the Present.* New York: Hopkins & Blake, 1969.

Jacobs, Norman, ed. *Culture for the Millions? Mass Media in Modern Society.* Boston: Beacon Press, 1968.

Jameson, Fredric. "Cognitive Mapping." In *Marxism and the Interpretation of Culture,* ed. Cary Nelson and Lawrence Grossberg, 347-57. Urbana: University of Illinois Press, 1988.

_____. "Postmodernism, or the Cultural Logic of Late Capitalism." *New Left Review* 146 (July-Aug. 1984): 53-92.

_____. "Reification and Utopia in Mass Culture." *Social Text* 1 (Winter 1979): 130-48.

Jarvie, Ian. *Movies and Society.* New York: Basic Books, 1970.

_____. *Movies as Social Criticism: Aspects of Their Psychology.* Metuchen, N.J.: Scarecrow Press, 1978.

_____. *Philosophy of Film: Epistemology, Ontology, Aesthetics.* New York: Methuen, 1988.

Jay, Martin. *Adorno.* Cambridge, Mass.: Harvard University Press, 1984.

_____. *The Dialectical Imagination: A History of the Frankfurt School and the Institute of Social Research, 1923-1950.* Boston: Little, Brown, 1973.

Johnson, Brian. "The Boss." *Maclean's,* 2 Sept. 1985, p. 26.

Johnson, Hillary, Alison Humes, and Harriet F. Pilpel. "The Porn Debates: Does Pornography Cause Violence against Women?" *Vogue,* Sept. 1985, pp. 678-83.

Johnson, Lesley. "The Uses of the Media: An Interpretation of the Significance of the Mass Media in the Lives of Young People." *Discourse* 4 (Apr. 1984): 18-31.

Johnson, Mary Jane Earle. "Rock Music as a Reflector of Social Attitudes among Youth in America during the 1960's." Ph.D. diss., St. Louis University, 1978.

Johnson, Paul E. *A Shopkeeper's Millennium: Society and Revivals in Rochester, New York, 1815-1837.* New York: Hill & Wang, 1978.

Johnson, Robert K. *Francis Ford Coppola.* Boston: Twayne, 1977.

Johnstone, John W. "Social Integration and Mass Media Use among Adolescents: A Case Study." In *The Uses of Mass Communications: Current Perspectives on Gratification Research,* vol. 3 of Sage Annual Reviews of Communication Research, ed. Jay G. Blumler and Elihu Katz, 35-47. Beverly Hills: Sage Publications, 1974.

Jones, Landon Y. *Great Expectations: America and the Baby Boom Generation.* New York: Ballantine Books, 1980.

Jones, LeRoi. *Blues People: The Negro Experience in White America and the Music That Developed from It.* New York: William Morrow, 1963.

Kael, Pauline. "The Current Cinema: Rice Krispies." *New Yorker,* 1 Nov. 1982, p. 146.

_____. *State of the Art.* New York: New American Library, 1985.

Kagan, Norman. *The Cinema of Stanley Kubrick.* New York: Holt, Rinehart & Winston, 1972.

Kaminsky, Stuart M. *American Film Genres: Approaches to a Critical Theory of Popular Film.* New York: Dell, 1974.

_____. *John Huston.* Boston: Houghton Mifflin, 1978.

_____. "Kung Fu Film as Ghetto Myth." *Journal of Popular Film* 3 (1974): 129-38.

Kaplan, E. Ann. *Rocking around the Clock: Music Television, Postmodernism, and Consumer Culture.* New York: Methuen, 1987.

Kaplan, E. Ann, ed. *Women in Film Noir*. London: British Film Institute, 1980.

Kaplan, Carl. "Filthy Rich: Soft-Core Video Tapes." *Esquire,* Jan. 1985, p. 11.

Karimi, Amir Massoud. *Toward a Definition of the American Film Noir, 1941-1949*. New York: Arno, 1976.

Katz, Michael B. "Child Saving." *History of Education Quarterly* 26 (Fall 1986): 413-24.

Kaufmann, Donald L. "Woodstock: The Color of Sound." *Journal of Ethnic Studies* 2 (Fall 1974): 32-49.

Kaufmann, Stanley. "The Pornographers." *New Republic,* 15 June 1987, pp. 25-27.

Kealy, Edward R. "Conventions and the Production of the Popular Music Aesthetic." *Journal of Popular Culture* 16 (Fall 1982): 100-115.

Kellner, Douglas. "TV, Ideology, and Emancipatory Popular Culture." *Socialist Review* 45 (1979): 15-53.

Kellner, Douglas, ed. *Postmodernism/Jameson/Critique*. Washington: Maisonneuve Press, 1989.

Kelly, Sean. "Parting the Iron Curtain: MTV Europe in Talks with East German TV." *Electronic Media,* 15 May 1989, pp. 16, 33.

Keniston, Kenneth. "Youth: A 'New' Stage of Life." *American Scholar* 39 (Autumn 1970): 631-54.

Kessler, Shelley. "Teens Talk about Sexuality, Sex and Television." *Television & Children* 6 (Fall 1983): 37-39.

Kett, Joseph F. *Rites of Passage: Adolescence in America, 1790 to the Present*. New York: Basic Books, 1977.

Kildoy, Gregg. "Ninth Annual Grosses Gloss." *Film Comment,* Mar.-Apr. 1984, p. 63.

Kirn, Margaret J. "Disneyland and Walt Disney World: Traditional Values in Futuristic Form." *Journal of Popular Culture* 15 (Summer 1981): 116-40.

King, Paul, with Jackie Flaum. *Sex, Drugs, & Rock 'n' Roll: Healing for Today's Troubled Youth*. Bellevue, Wash.: Professional Counselor Books, 1988.

King, Wayne. "Fan Will Win Bon Jovi's Jersey Roots." *New York Times,* 28 Mar. 1989, p. B-2.

Klapper, Zina. "Sex, Porn and Art Actions: Praying Mantis Women's Brigade of Santa Cruz." *Mother Jones,* June 1981, pp. 6-11.

Knight, Arthur. *The Liveliest Art: A Panoramic History of the Movies*. New York: New American Library, 1957.

Koenig, Rhoda. "Review: *A Prayer for Owen Meany* by John Irving." *New York,* 20 Mar. 1989, pp. 82-83.

Kolakowski, Leszek. *The Presence of Myth*. Trans. Adam Czerniawski. Chicago: University of Chicago Press, 1972.

Kolker, Robert Phillip. *The Altering Eye: Contemporary International Cinema*. New York: Oxford University Press, 1984.

_____. *A Cinema of Loneliness: Penn, Kubrick, Scorsese, Spielberg, Altman*. 2nd ed. New York: Oxford University Press, 1988.

Koop, Everett. "Report of the Surgeon General's Workshop on Pornography and Public Health." *American Psychologist* 12 (Oct. 1987): 911-13.

Kotarba, Joseph A., ed. *Youth & Society* 18 (June 1987), special issue devoted to adolescents and rock and roll.

Kowalski, Rosemary Ribich. *Women and Film: A Bibliography.* Metuchen, N.J.: Scarecrow Press, 1976.

Kramer, Gary. "R. & R. a Teen-Age Must." *Billboard,* 10 Nov. 1956, p. 21.

Kuhn, Annette. *Women's Pictures: Feminism and Cinema.* London: Routledge & Kegan Paul, 1982.

Lafferty, William. "Film and Television." In *Film and the Arts in Symbiosis: A Resource Guide,* ed. Gary R. Edgerton, 273-309. New York: Greenwood Press, 1988.

Larkin, Jack. *The Reshaping of Everyday Life, 1790-1840.* New York: Harper & Row, 1988.

Larson, Reed, and Robert Kubey. "Television and Music: Contrasting Media in Adolescent Life." *Youth & Society* 15 (Sept. 1983): 13-31.

Lasch, Christopher. *The Culture of Narcissism.* New York: W. W. Norton, 1978.

_____. *Haven in a Heartless World: The Family Besieged.* New York: Basic Books, 1977.

_____. *The Minimal Self: Psychic Survival in Troubled Times.* New York: W. W. Norton, 1986.

Laslett, Peter. "Age at Menarche in Europe since the Seventeenth Century." In *The Family in History,* ed. T. K. Rabb and R. I. Rotberg, 28-47. New York: Harper & Row, 1973.

LaValley, Albert J., ed. *Focus on Hitchcock.* Englewood Cliffs, N.J.: Prentice-Hall, 1972.

Lawhead, Steve. *Rock of This Age: The Real and Imagined Dangers of Rock Music.* Rev. ed. Downers Grove, Ill.: InterVarsity Press, 1987.

Lawrence, Frances Cogle, et al. "Adolescents' Time Spent Viewing Television." *Adolescence* 21 (Summer 1986): 431-36.

Lazere, Donald, ed. *American Media and Mass Culture: Left Perspectives.* Berkeley: University of California Press, 1987.

Leab, Daniel J. *From Sambo to Superspade: The Black Experience in Motion Pictures.* Boston: Houghton Mifflin, 1975.

Leach, Michael. *I Know It When I See It: Pornography, Violence, and Public Sensitivity.* Philadelphia: Westminster Press, 1975.

Lears, Jackson. *No Place of Grace: Antimodernism and the Transformation of American Culture, 1880-1920.* New York: Pantheon Books, 1981.

Lee, Eui Bun, and Louis A. Browne. "Television Uses and Gratifications among Black Children, Teenagers, and Adults." *Journal of Broadcasting* 25 (Spring 1981): 203-8.

Lenihan, John H. *Showdown: Confronting Modern America in the Western Film.* Urbana: University of Illinois Press, 1980.

Lenz, Günter H., and Kurt L. Shell, eds. *The Crisis of Modernity: Recent Critical Theories of Culture and Society in the United States and West Germany.* Frankfurt am Main, West Germany: Campus Verlag, Forschung/Research, 1986.

Leppert, Richard, and Susan McClary, eds. *Music and Society: The Politics of*

Composition, Performance and Reception. Cambridge, Eng.: Cambridge University Press, 1987.

Levin, Harry. *Playboys and Killjoys: An Essay on the Theory and Practice of Comedy.* New York: Oxford University Press, 1987.

Levine, Lawrence W. *Highbrow/Lowbrow: The Emergence of Cultural Hierarchy in America.* Cambridge, Mass.: Harvard University Press, 1988.

Levine, Richard M. "Life after Flashdance." *Esquire,* Jan. 1984, p. 86.

Lévi-Strauss, Claude. "The Structural Study of Myth." In *Structural Anthropology,* trans. C. Jacobson and B. G. Schoepf, 206-31. New York: Basic Books, 1963.

Levy, Alan. "Peekaboo Sex, or How to Fill a Drive-in." *Life,* 16 July 1965, p. 82.

Levy, Steven. "AD Nauseam: How MTV Sells Out Rock & Roll." *Rolling Stone,* 8 Dec. 1982, pp. 30-34 et passim.

Lewis, George H. "Between Consciousness and Existence: Popular Culture and the Sociological Imagination." *Journal of Popular Culture* 15 (Spring 1982): 81-92.

_____. "The Sociology of Popular Culture." *Current Sociology* 26 (Winter 1978): 1-160.

_____. "Taste Cultures and Their Composition: Towards a New Theoretical Perspective." In *Mass Media and Social Change,* Sage Studies in International Sociology, no. 22, ed. Elihu Katz and Tamás Szeckso, 201-17. Beverly Hills: Sage Publications, 1981.

Lin, Carolyn A., and David J. Atkin. "Parental Mediation and Rulemaking for Adolescent Use of Television and VCRs." *Journal of Broadcasting & Electronic Media* 33 (Winter 1989): 53-57.

Linz, Daniel G., Edward Donnerstein, and Steven Penrod. "Effects of Long-term Exposure to Violent and Sexually Degrading Depictions of Women." *Journal of Personality and Social Psychology* 55 (Nov. 1988): 758-59.

_____. "The Findings and Recommendations of the Attorney General's Commission on Pornography: Do the Psychological 'Facts' Fit the Political Fury?" *The American Psychologist* 12 (Oct. 1987): 916-24.

Lipsitz, George. *Class and Culture in Cold War America: A Rainbow at Midnight.* New York: Praeger, 1981.

Littwin, Susan. "How TV Americanizes Immigrants . . . for Better or Worse." *TV Guide,* 9 Apr. 1988, p. 10.

_____. *The Postponed Generation: Why America's Grown-up Kids Are Growing Up Later.* New York: William Morrow, 1986.

Litwak, Mark. *Reel Power: The Struggle for Influence and Success in the New Hollywood.* New York: New American Library–Plume, 1987.

Lloyd, Ronald. *American Film Directors.* New York: Watts, 1976.

Loder, Kurt. "Bruce!" *Rolling Stone,* 28 Feb. 1985, p. 23.

Lodziak, Conrad. *The Power of Television: A Critical Appraisal.* New York: St. Martin's Press, 1986.

Lohr, Steve. "European TV's Vast Growth: Cultural Effect Stirs Concern." *New York Times,* 16 Mar. 1989, pp. 1, 39.

_____. "Murdoch's Big Bet on Sky Television." *New York Times,* 11 Sept. 1989, pp. 23, 32.

Lorch, Sue. "Metaphor, Metaphysics, and MTV." *Journal of Popular Culture* 22 (Winter 1988): 143-55.

Lowenthal, Leo. *Literature, Popular Culture and Society.* Palo Alto, Calif.: Pacific Books, 1961.

Lucanio, Patrick. *Them or Us: Archetypal Interpretations of Fifties Alien Invasion Films.* Bloomington: Indiana University Press, 1987.

Lull, James. "Family Communication Patterns and the Social Uses of Television." *Communication Research* 7 (July 1980): 319-34.

Lull, James, ed. *Popular Music & Communication.* Newbury Park, Calif.: Sage Publications, 1987.

Lunn, Eugene. *Marxism and Modernism: An Historical Study of Lukács, Brecht, Benjamin, and Adorno.* Berkeley: University of California Press, 1982.

McBride, Joseph, and Michael Wilmington. *John Ford.* New York: Da Capo, 1975.

MacCabe, Collin, ed. *High Theory/Low Culture: Analyzing Popular Television and Film.* New York: St. Martin's Press, 1986.

McCarthy, Thomas. *The Critical Theory of Jürgen Habermas.* Cambridge, Mass.: MIT Press, 1978.

McClelland, Doug. *The Unkindest Cuts: The Scissors and the Cinema.* New York: Barnes, 1972.

McConnell, Frank D. *The Spoken Seen: Film and the Romantic Imagination.* Baltimore: Johns Hopkins University Press, 1975.

McDannel, Colleen. *The Christian Home in Victorian America, 1840-1900.* Bloomington: Indiana University Press, 1986.

McDonald, Archie P., ed. *Shooting Stars: Heroes and Heroines of Western Film.* Bloomington: Indiana University Press, 1988.

McDonald, Bruce. "Semiology Goes to the Midnight Movie." *Et Cetera* 37 (Fall 1980): 216-23.

McDonald, Dwight. "Profiles: A Caste, a Culture, a Market-1." *New Yorker,* 22 Nov. 1958, pp. 58-94.

McDonough, Jimmy. "Sexposed: Adult Films Genre." *Film Comment* 22 (July-Aug. 1986): 53-61.

McDowell, Josh. "Teen Sex Survey in the Evangelical Church." Dallas: Josh McDowell Ministry, 1987.

McGee, Mark Thomas, and R. J. Robertson. *The J.D. Films: Juvenile Delinquency in the Movies.* Jefferson, N.C.: McFarland, 1982.

Macklin, William R. "MTV Revue Misses Key Elements." *Grand Rapids Press,* 31 July 1989, pp. D-7, D-8.

MacLeod, Anne S. *A Moral Tale: Children's Fiction and American Culture, 1820-1860.* Hamden, Conn.: Archon, 1975.

MacLeod, David I. *Building Character in the American Boy: The Boy Scouts, YMCA, and Their Forerunners, 1870-1920.* Madison: University of Wisconsin Press, 1983.

McLeod, Jack, and Jane Delano Brown. "The Family Environment and Adolescent Television Use." In *Children and Television*, ed. Ray Brown, 199-223. Beverly Hills: Sage Publications, 1976.

McLoughlin, William L. *Revivals, Awakening, and Reform*. Chicago: University of Chicago Press, 1978.

Madden, D. "The Necessity for an Aesthetics of Popular Culture." *Journal of Popular Culture* 7 (1973): 1-13.

Madsen, Axel. *The New Hollywood: American Movies in the Seventies*. New York: Crowell, 1975.

Magistrale, Anthony. "Protecting the Children: Huckleberry Finn, E.T. and the Politics of Censorship." *Childhood Education* 61 (Sept.-Oct. 1984): 9-12.

Malamuth, Neil M., and Edward Donnerstein, eds. *Pornography and Sexual Aggression*. Orlando: Harcourt Brace Jovanovich, 1984.

Malone, Bill C. "Elvis, Country Music, and the South." *Southern Quarterly* 18 (1979): 123-34.

Mandel, Ernest. *Late Capitalism*. Trans. Joris De Bres. Atlantic Highlands, N.J.: Humanities Press, 1975.

Mapp, Edward. *Blacks in American Films: Today and Yesterday*. Metuchen, N.J.: Scarecrow Press, 1972.

Marc, David. *Comic Visions: Television Comedy and American Culture*. Boston: Unwin Hyman, 1989.

Marcus, Greil. *Mystery Train: Images of America in Rock 'n' Roll Music*. Rev. ed. New York: E. P. Dutton, 1982.

Marcuse, Herbert. "The Affirmative Character of Culture." In *Negations: Essays in Critical Theory*, trans. Jeremy Shapiro, 88-133. London: Allen Lane, The Penguin Press, 1968.

_____. *One Dimensional Man: Studies in the Ideology of Advanced Industrial Society*. Boston: Beacon Press, 1964.

Marsden, Michael T., John G. Nachbar, and Sam L. Grogg, Jr. *Movies as Artifacts: Cultural Criticism of Popular Film*. Chicago: Nelson, 1982.

Marsh, Dave. *Glory Days: Bruce Springsteen in the 1980s*. New York: Pantheon Books, 1987.

Martin, Bernice. "The Socialization of Disorder: Symbolism in Rock Music." *Sociological Analysis* 40 (Summer 1979): 87-124.

_____. *A Sociology of Contemporary Cultural Change*. New York: St. Martin's Press, 1981.

Marx, Karl. *Capital: A Critique of Political Economy*, vol. 1: *The Process of Capitalist Production*. Trans. from the 3rd German edition by Samuel Moore and Edward Aveling, ed. Frederick Engels. New York: International Publishers, 1967.

Mast, Gerald. *The Comic Mind: Comedy and the Movies*. Indianapolis: Bobbs-Merrill, 1973.

_____. *Howard Hawks, Storyteller*. New York: Oxford University Press, 1982.

_____. *The Movies in Our Midst: Documents in the Cultural History of Film in America*. Chicago: University of Chicago Press, 1982.

_____. *A Short History of the Movies*. New York: Pegasus, 1976.

May, John R., and Michael Bird, eds. *Religion in Film*. Knoxville: University of Tennessee Press, 1982.

Maynard, Richard A. *The Black Man on Film: Racial Stereotyping*. Rochelle Park, N.J.: Hayden, 1974.

Mead, Margaret. *Age Discrepancies in the Understanding and Use of Modern Technology, Especially the Mass Media, or How Parents and Teachers Fail to Tune in on Children's Media Environment*. Washington: Academy for Educational Development, Inc., Office of Education (DHEW), Bureau of Research, 1970.

_____. *Culture and Commitment: A Study of the Generation Gap*. Garden City, N.Y.: Doubleday–Natural History Press, 1970.

_____. *And Keep Your Powder Dry*. New York: William Morrow, 1942.

_____. "Prefigurative Culture and Unknown Children." In *Youth: Divergent Perspectives*, ed. P. Manning, 193-206. New York: John Wiley, 1973.

Meltroff, Andrew N. "Imitation of Televised Models by Infants." *Child Development* 59 (Oct. 1988): 1221-29.

Merriam, Alan P. *The Anthropology of Music*. Evanston, Ill.: Northwestern University Press, 1964.

Meyers, Donna. "Film Literacy—A Door to Door Dialogue with Young Adults." *Top of the News* 40 (Spring 1984): 290-98.

Meyrowitz, Joshua. "The Adultlike Child and the Childlike Adult: Socialization in an Electronic Age." *Daedalus* 113 (1984): 19-48.

_____. *No Sense of Place: The Impact of Electronic Media on Social Behavior*. New York: Oxford University Press, 1985.

Miller, Debby. "Bruce Springsteen Gives the Little Guy Something to Cheer About." *Rolling Stone*, 19 July–2 Aug. 1984, p. 102.

Miller, Don. *B Movies*. New York: Ballantine Books, 1988.

Miller, Mark Crispin. *Boxed In: The Culture of TV*. Evanston, Ill.: Northwestern University Press, 1988.

Miller, Ned. "Sex Roles in Stereo." *Health*, June 1988, p. 24.

Miller, Percy. *The Life of the Mind in America: From the Revolution to the Civil War*. New York: Harcourt, Brace, 1965.

Mintz, Steven. *A Prison of Expectations: The Family in Victorian Culture*. New York: New York University Press, 1983.

Mintz, Steven, and Susan Kellogg. *Domestic Revolutions: A Social History of American Family Life*. New York: Free Press, 1988.

Modell, John. *Into One's Own: From Youth to Adulthood in the U.S., 1920-1975*. Berkeley: University of California Press, 1989.

Modleski, Tania, ed. *Studies in Entertainment: Critical Approaches to Mass Culture*. Bloomington: Indiana University Press, 1986.

_____. *The Women Who Know Too Much: Hitchcock and Feminist Film Theory*. New York: Routledge, 1988.

Monaco, James. *American Film Now*. New York: Oxford University Press, 1979.

_____. *How to Read a Film: The Art, Technology, Language, History and Theory of Film and Media*. Rev. ed. New York: Oxford University Press, 1981.

Morella, Joe, and Edward Z. Epstein. *Rebels: The Rebel Hero in Films.* New York: Citadel, 1971.

Morgan, Edmund S. *The Puritan Family: Religion and Domestic Relations in 17th-Century New England.* New York: Harper & Row, 1966.

Morgan, Michael, and Nancy Rothschild. "Impact of the New Television Technology: Cable TV, Peers, and Sex-Role Cultivation in the Electronic Environment." *Youth & Society* 15 (Sept. 1973): 33-50.

Morrow, James. "Dandelions and Seedpods: The Flowering of Fantasy Films." *Media and Methods* 15 (May-June 1979): 18-20 et passim.

"MTV Dance Show Going on Road." *Variety,* 14-20 June 1989, p. 71.

Murdock, Graham, and Robin McCron. "Television and Teenage Violence." *New Society* 46 (14 Dec. 1978): 632-33.

Murray, Edward. *The Cinematic Imagination: Writers and the Motion Picture.* New York: Frederick Ungar, 1972.

_____. *Ten Film Classics: A Re-Viewing.* New York: Frederick Ungar, 1978.

Nachbar, John G., ed. *Focus on the Western.* Englewood Cliffs, N.J.: Prentice-Hall, 1974.

_____. *Western Films: An Annotated Critical Bibliography.* New York: Garland, 1975.

Nasaw, David. *Children of the City: At Work and at Play.* Garden City, N.Y.: Doubleday–Anchor Press, 1985.

Nasko, Janet. *Movies and Money: Financing the American Film Industry.* Norwood, N.J.: Ablex, 1982.

"Naughty Photos: A Panel Links Porn to Violence." *Time,* 26 May 1986, p. 27.

Neier, Aryeh. "Memoirs of a Woman's Displeasure: Linda Lovelace's 'Ordeal.' " *The Nation* 16 (Aug. 1980): 137.

Nelson, John Wiley. *Your God Is Alive and Well and Appearing in Popular Culture.* Philadelphia: Westminster Press, 1976.

Neuman, R. P. "Masturbation, Madness, and the Modern Concepts of Childhood and Adolescence." *Journal of Social History* 8 (Spring 1975): 1-27.

Newman, Barbara M., and Philip R. Newman. *Development through Life: A Psychosocial Approach.* Homewood, Ill.: Dorsey Press, 1975.

Nochschild, Adam. "Culture Vultures: How the Elite Stole Art," review of *The Emergence of Cultural Hierarchy in America* by Lawrence W. Levine. *Mother Jones,* Dec. 1988, pp. 52-53.

Novak, Steven J. *The Rights of Youth: American Colleges and Student Revolt, 1798-1815.* Cambridge, Mass.: Harvard University Press, 1977.

Nye, Russell. *The Unembarrassed Muse: The Popular Arts in America.* New York: Dial Press, 1979.

O'Donovan, Oliver. *Resurrection and Moral Order.* Grand Rapids: Eerdmans, 1986.

Orth, Maureen. "From Sweathog to Disco King." *Newsweek,* 19 Dec. 1977, p. 63.

Palmer, Edward L. *Television and America's Children: A Crisis of Neglect.* New York: Oxford University Press, 1988.

Palmer, William J. *The Films of the Seventies: A Social History.* Metuchen, N.J.: Scarecrow Press, 1987.

Pareles, Jon. "Pop Record Business Shows Signs of Recovery." *New York Times*, 28 Nov. 1983, p. C-13.

Parish, James Robert, and Michael R. Pitts. *The Great Gangster Pictures*. Metuchen, N.J.: Scarecrow Press, 1976.

Peary, Gerald, and Roger Shatzkin, eds. *The Modern American Novel and the Movies*. New York: Frederick Ungar, 1978.

Pellauer, Mary. "Pornography: An Agenda for the Churches" (After the Revolution: The Church and Sexual Ethics, part 4). *Christian Century*, 29 July 1987, pp. 651-56.

Percy, Walker. *Lost in the Cosmos: The Last Self-Help Book*. New York: Farrar, Straus & Giroux, 1983.

Perrett, Geoffrey. *A Dream of Greatness: The American People, 1945-1963*. New York: Coward, McCann & Geoghegan, 1979.

Peters, David F., and Gary W. Peterson. "Adolescents' Construction of Social Reality: The Impact of Television and Peers." *Youth & Society* 15 (1983): 67-85.

Pettigrew, Jim. "MTV Network Strives to Broaden Video Base." *Electronic Media*, 22 May 1989 (Special Report), p. 12.

Place, J. A. *The Western Films of John Ford*. New York: Citadel, 1976.

Platt, Anthony E. *The Child Savers: The Invention of Delinquency*. Chicago: University of Chicago Press, 1969.

Pleasants, Henry. "Afro-American Epoch Emergence of a New Idiom." *Music Educators Journal* 57 (Sept. 1970): 33-37.

"Polka Rhythm Push Aimed at Teen-Ager." *Billboard*, 10 Nov. 1956, p. 19.

Polskin, Howard. "You Can Win a Pink House—Or a Camel Ride in Egypt with Tom Petty." *TV Guide*, 5 Dec. 1987, pp. 12-14.

Postman, Neil. "The Disappearance of Childhood." *Childhood Education* 61 (Mar.-Apr. 1985): 286-93.

Poulos, Rita Wicks, Eli A. Rubinstein, and Robert M. Liebert. "The Effects of Television on Children and Adolescents: A Symposium: Positive Social Learning." *Journal of Communication* 25 (Autumn 1975): 90-97.

Powdermaker, Hortense. *Hollywood: The Dream Factory*. Boston: Little, Brown, 1950.

Pratley, Gerald. *The Cinema of John Huston*. New York: Barnes, 1977.

Prawer, S. S. *Caligari's Children: The Film as Tale of Terror*. Oxford: Oxford University Press, 1980.

Prescott, Peter S. Review of *A Prayer for Owen Meany* by John Irving. *Newsweek*, 10 Apr. 1988, p. 64.

Radnoti, Sandor. "Mass Culture." *Telos* 48 (Summer 1981): 27-47.

Raffa, Jean Benedict. "Television and Values: Implications for Education." *Educational Forum* 49 (Winter 1985): 189-98.

Ravitch, Diane, and Chester E. Finn, Jr. *What Do Our 17-Year-Olds Know?: A Report on the First National Assessment of History and Literature*. New York: Harper & Row, 1987.

"Record Labeling." Hearing before the Committee on Commerce, Science, and

Transportation, U.S. Senate, 99th Congress, First Session on Contents of Music and the Lyrics of Records, 19 Sept. 1985.

Reno, Jamie. "Ridgemont Redux." *Premiere*, 25 Sept. 1989, p. 24.

Rhode, Eric. *A History of the Cinema from Its Origins to 1970.* New York: Hill & Wang, 1976.

Rich, Frank. "The Year of John Travolta." *Seventeen*, Nov. 1978, p. 113.

Richardson, Robert. *Literature and Film.* Bloomington: Indiana University Press, 1969.

Richter, Hans. *The Struggle for the Film: Towards a Socially Responsible Cinema.* Trans. Ben Brewster, ed. Jurgen Romhild. New York: St. Martin's Press, 1986.

Ridless, Robin. *Ideology and Art: Theories of Mass Culture from Walter Benjamin to Umberto Eco.* New York: P. Lang, 1984.

Riesman, David, with Nathan Glazer and Reuel Denney. *The Lonely Crowd: A Study of the Changing American Character.* Garden City, N.Y.: Doubleday, 1954.

Roberts, Elizabeth. "Teens, Sexuality and Sex: Our Mixed Messages." *Television and Children* 6 (Fall 1983): 9-12.

Roberts, Robert C. Review of *Pornography: A Christian Critique* by John H. Court. *Christianity Today*, 29 May 1981, pp. 51-52.

Robins, J. Max. "Into the Groove." *Channels*, May 1989, pp. 22-29.

Robins, Wayne. "Video Woes: A Midlife Crisis for Music Television?" *Grand Rapids Press*, 23 Feb. 1987, p. C-14.

Robinson, Rhonda S. "Learning to See: Developing Visual Literacy through Film." *Top of the News* 40 (Spring 1984): 267-75.

"Rock Video: Any End in Sight?" *Grand Rapids Press*, 18 June 1983, pp. B-1, B-2.

Roffman, Peter, and Jim Purdy. *The Hollywood Social Problem Film: Madness, Despair, and Politics from the Depression to the Fifties.* Bloomington: Indiana University Press, 1981.

Rohrbaugh, John, and Richard Jessor. "Religiosity in Youth: A Personal Control against Deviant Behavior." *Journal of Personality* 43 (1975): 136-55.

Rollins, Peter C., ed. *Hollywood as the Historian: American Film in a Cultural Context.* Lexington: University Press of Kentucky, 1983.

Rollins, Peter C. "The Vietnam War: Perceptions through Literature, Film, and Television." *American Quarterly* 36 (1984): 419-32.

Rosen, Marjorie. *Popcorn Venus: Women, Movies, and the American Dream.* New York: Coward, 1973.

Rosenberg, Bernard, and David Manning White, eds. *Mass Culture: The Popular Arts in America.* Glencoe, Ill.: Free Press, 1957.

_____, eds. *Mass Culture Revisited.* New York: Van Nostrand Reinhold, 1971.

Rosenblatt, Paul C., and Michael R. Cunningham. "Television Watching and Family Tensions." *Journal of Marriage & the Family* 38 (Feb. 1976): 105-11.

Rosenstone, Robert A. " 'The Times They are A-Changin': The Music of Protest." *American Academy of Political & Social Science Annals* 382 (Mar. 1969): 131-44.

Rosow, Eugene. *Born to Lose: The Gangster Film in America.* New York: Oxford University Press, 1978.

Ross, Dorothy. *G. Stanley Hall: The Psychologist as Prophet.* Chicago: University of Chicago Press, 1972.

Rubin, Alan M. "Television Usage, Attitudes and Viewing Behaviors of Children and Adolescents." *Journal of Broadcasting* 21 (Summer 1977): 355-69.

_____. "Television Use by Children and Adolescents." *Human Communication Research* 5 (Winter 1979): 109-20.

_____. "Uses of Daytime Television Soap Operas by College Students." *Journal of Broadcasting & Electronic Media* 29 (Summer 1985): 241-58.

Rubin, Stephen Jay. *Combat Films: American Realism, 1945-1970.* Jefferson, N.C.: McFarland, 1981.

Ryan, Mary P. *Cradle of the Middle Class: The Family in Oneida County, New York, 1790-1865.* New York: Cambridge University Press, 1981.

Ryken, Leland, ed. *The Christian Imagination: Essays on Literature and the Arts.* Grand Rapids: Baker Book House, 1981.

_____. *Work and Leisure in Christian Perspective.* Portland, Ore.: Multnomah Press, 1987.

Salzman, Jack, ed. *American Studies: An Annotated Bibliography.* 3 vols. New York: Cambridge University Press, 1986.

Sarris, Andrew. "Bravo Beatles!" *Village Voice,* 27 Aug. 1964, p. 13.

_____. *Confessions of a Cultist: On the Cinema, 1955-1969.* New York: Simon & Schuster, 1970.

_____. *The Primal Screen: Essays on Film and Related Subjects.* New York: Simon & Schuster, 1973.

Sayre, Nora. *Running Time: Films of the Cold War.* New York: Dial Press, 1982.

Schatz, Thomas. *Hollywood Genres: Formulas, Filmmaking, and the Studio System.* Philadelphia: Temple University Press, 1981.

Scherman, Robert. "What Are Our Kids Buying?" *Journal of Popular Culture* 3 (Fall 1969): 274-80.

Schickel, Richard. *The Men Who Made the Movies: Interviews with Frank Capra, George Cukor, Howard Hawks, Alfred Hitchcock, Vincente Minnelli, King Vidor, Raoul Walsh, and William A. Wellman.* New York: Atheneum, 1975.

Schlegel, Alice. "Issues in the Study of Adolescence and Youth." *Youth & Society* 8 (June 1977): 417-28.

Schrader, Paul. *Transcendental Style in Film: Ozu, Bresson, Dreyer.* Berkeley: University of California Press, 1972.

Schuth, H. Wayne. *Mike Nichols.* Boston: Twayne, 1978.

Seerveld, Calvin G. *Rainbows for the Fallen World: Aesthetic Life and Artistic Task.* Toronto: Tuppence Press, 1980.

Seigel, Janet. "From Page to Screen: Where the Author Fits In." *Top of the News* (Spring 1984): 277-83.

Sennett, Richard. *The Fall of the Public Man.* New York: Alfred A. Knopf, 1977.

"Sex and Violence." *Science News,* 13 Sept. 1980, pp. 166-68.

Shadoian, Jack. *Dreams and Dead Ends: The American Gangster/Crime Film.* Cambridge, Mass.: MIT Press, 1977.

Shales, Tom. "The ReDecade." *Esquire*, Mar. 1986, pp. 67-72.

Shames, Laurence. *The Hunger for More: Searching for Values in an Age of Greed.* New York: Time Books, 1989.

Shaw, Arnold. *Black Popular Music in America*. New York: Macmillan–Schirmer Books, 1986.

Sheppard, R. Z. Review of *A Prayer for Owen Meany* by John Irving. *Time*, 3 Apr. 1989, p. 80.

Sherman, Barry L., and Joseph R. Dominick. "Guns, Sex and Rock and Roll: A Content Analysis of Music Television." Paper presented at the annual meeting of the Speech Communication Association, Chicago, Nov. 1984.

Shils, Edward. "Daydreams and Nightmares: Reflections on the Criticism of Mass Culture." *Sewanee Review* 65 (Autumn 1957): 587-608.

Shindler, Colin. *Hollywood Goes to War: Films and American Society, 1939-1952.* Boston: Routledge, 1979.

Shore, Michael. *The Rolling Stone Book of Rock Video*. New York: Rolling Stone Press, 1984.

Simon, John. *Private Screenings*. New York: Macmillan, 1967.

Sinclair, Andrew. *John Ford*. New York: Dial Press, 1979.

Sklar, Kathryn Kish. *Catharine Beecher: A Study in American Domesticity.* New Haven: Yale University Press, 1973.

Sklar, Rick. *Rocking America: An Insider's Story*. New York: St. Martin's Press, 1984.

Sklar, Robert. *Movie-Made America: A Social History of American Movies.* New York: Random House, 1975.

Smith, Barbara Hernstein. *Contingencies of Value: Alternative Perspectives for Critical Theory.* Cambridge, Mass.: Harvard University Press, 1988.

Smith, Daniel Scott. "Parental Power and Marriage Patterns: An Analysis of Historical Trends in Hingham, Massachusetts." In *Growing Up in America: Historical Experiences*, ed. Harvey J. Graff, 156-69. Detroit: Wayne State University Press, 1987.

Smith, Daniel Scott, and Michael Hindus. "Premarital Pregnancy in America, 1640-1971: An Overview and an Interpretation." *Journal of Interdisciplinary History* 5 (Spring 1975): 537-70.

Smith, David M. "The Concept of Youth Culture: A Reevaluation." *Youth & Society* 7 (June 1976): 347-66.

Smith, Jane. "Pluck Little Ladies and Stout-Hearted Chums: Serial Novels for Girls, 1900-1920." *Prospects* 3 (1977): 155-74.

Smith, Julian. *Looking Away: Hollywood and Vietnam*. New York: Scribner's, 1975.

Smith, Timothy L. "Righteousness and Hope: Christian Holiness and the Millennial Vision in America, 1800-1900." *American Quarterly* 31 (Spring 1979): 21-45.

Smith-Rosenberg, Carroll. *Disorderly Conduct: Visions of Gender in Victorian America.* New York: Alfred A. Knopf, 1985.

Smythe, Dallas W. "Communications: Blindspot of Western Marxism." *Canadian Journal of Political and Social Theory* 1 (Fall-Autumn 1977): 1-27.

Snow, Robert P. "Youth, Rock 'n' Roll, and Electronic Media." *Youth & Society* 18 (June 1987): 326-43.

Sobchack, Vivian. "Bringing It All Back Home: Family Economy and Generic Exchange." In *American Horrors: Essays on the Modern American Horror Film*, ed. Gregory A. Waller, 175-94. Urbana: University of Illinois Press, 1987.

Soggin, J. Alberto. *Old Testament and Oriental Studies*. Rome: Biblical Institute Press, 1975.

Sölle, Dorothee. " 'Thou Shalt Have No Other Jeans Before Me.' " In *Observations on "The Spiritual Situation of the Age": Contemporary German Perspectives*, ed. Jürgen Habermas, trans. Andrew Buchwalter, 157-68. Cambridge, Mass.: MIT Press, 1984.

Solomon, Stanley J. *Beyond Formula: American Film Genres*. New York: Harcourt Brace Jovanovich, 1976.

Solomon, Stanley J., ed. *The Classic Cinema: Essays in Criticism*. New York: Harcourt Brace Jovanovich, 1973.

Sommerville, C. John. "Bibliographical Note: Toward a History of Childhood and Youth." *Journal of Interdisciplinary History* 3 (Autumn 1972): 439-47.

Sonenfield, Irwin. "The Mystical Rite of Youth Culture: Search and Celebration in Popular Music." *Music Educators Journal* 59 (Feb. 1973): 26-31.

Sorel, Nancy. "A New Look at 'Noble Suffering' [Childbirth]." *New York Times Book Review*, 26 Jan. 1986, p. 3-1.

Soren, David. *The Rise and Fall of the Horror Film: An Art Historical Approach to Fantasy Cinema*. Columbia, Mo.: Lucas, 1977.

Spatz, Jonas. *Hollywood in Fiction: Some Versions of the American Myth*. The Hague, Netherlands: Mouton, 1969.

Spring, Joel H. "Mass Culture and School Sports." *History of Education Quarterly* 14 (Winter 1974): 483-98.

Starr, Jerold M. "American Youth in the 1980s." *Youth & Society* 17 (June 1986): 323-45.

Stevenson, Richard W. "TV Boom in Europe Aids U.S. Producers." *New York Times*, 28 Dec. 1987, pp. 21, 23.

Stilson, Janet. "Latest VH-1 Promotion Puts Pedal to the Metal." *Electronic Media*, 5 June 1989, p. 29.

Stoddard, Karen M. *Saints and Shrews: Women and Aging in American Popular Film*. Westport, Conn.: Greenwood Press, 1978.

Stone, Vernon A., and Steven Chaffee. "Family Communication Patterns and Source-Message Orientation." *Journalism Quarterly* 47 (Summer 1979): 239-46.

Stout, Harry S. "Religion, Communications, and the Ideological Origins of the American Revolution." *William and Mary Quarterly* (third series) 34 (Oct. 1977): 519-41.

Street, John. *Rebel Rock: The Politics of Popular Music*. Oxford: Basil Blackwell, 1986.

Strenski, Ivan. *Four Theories of Myth in Twentieth-Century History: Cassirer, Eliade, Lévi-Strauss, and Malinowski*. Iowa City: University of Iowa Press, 1988.

Sun, Se-Wen, and James Lull. "The Adolescent Audience for Music Videos and Why They Watch." *Journal of Communication* 36 (Winter 1986): 115-25.

Surlin, Stuart H., and Joseph R. Dominick. "Television's Function as a 'Third Parent' for Black and White Teen-Agers." *Journal of Broadcasting* 15 (Winter 70-71): 55-64.

Susman, Warren. *Culture as History.* New York: Pantheon Books, 1984.

Sutherland, Daniel E. *The Expansion of Everyday Life, 1860-1876.* New York: Harper & Row, 1989.

Swomley, John M. "Wrongheaded Pornography Campaign." *Christian Century,* 9 Mar. 1988, pp. 251-53.

Tangney, June Price. "Aspects of the Family and Children's Television Viewing Content Preferences." *Child Development* 59 (Aug. 1988): 1070-79.

Tanner, J. M. "Sequence, Tempo, and Individual Variation in the Growth and Development of Boys and Girls Aged Twelve to Sixteen." *Daedalus* 100 (Fall 1971): 907-30.

Taylor, Charles. *Hegel and Modern Society.* Cambridge, Eng.: Cambridge University Press, 1979.

Teachout, Terry. "The Pornography Report That Never Was." *Commentary* 81 (Aug. 1987): 51-58.

"Teenage Biz vs. Repair Bills." *Variety,* 19 Dec. 1956, p. 20.

Thompson, David. *America in the Dark: Hollywood and the Gift of Unreality.* New York: William Morrow, 1977.

Tierney, Joan D. "Parents, Adolescents and Television: Culture, Learning, Influence: A Report to the Public." Summary of the findings of a report prepared for Canadian Radio-Television, May 1978.

_____. "Parents, Adolescents and Television, Part I: Adolescents and Television Heroes: The Perception of Social Values in Favorite Television Series." Report based on a paper presented at the annual meeting of the International Sociological Association, Uppsala, Sweden, 17 Aug. 1978.

_____. "Parents, Adolescents and Television, Part II: Adolescents and Television Heroes: Conceptual and Methodological Considerations of Analysis of Responses and Information Processing Strategies." Report based on a paper presented at the annual meeting of the International Association for Mass Communication Research, Warsaw, Poland, 7 Sept. 1978.

_____. "Parents, Adolescents and Television, Part III: Defining Ethnicity through Measurement Constructs: A Cultural Perspective According to Harold B. Innis." Research report prepared for Canadian Radio-Television Commission, Ottawa, Ontario, 1979.

Timson, Judith. Review of *A Prayer for Owen Meany* by John Irving. *Maclean's,* 3 Apr. 1989, p. 63.

"Today's Teenagers." *Time,* 29 Jan. 1965, p. 57.

Toffler, Alvin. *The Culture Consumers: A Study of Art and Affluence in America.* New York: St. Martin's Press, 1964.

Travis, Leroy D., and Claudio Violato. "Mass Media Use, Credulity and Beliefs about Youth: A Survey of Canadian Education Students." *Journal of Educational Research* 27 (Mar. 1981): 16-34.

Treusky, Anne T. "The Saintly Child in American Fiction." *Prospects* 1 (1975): 389-413.

Trilling, Diana. "*Easy Rider* and Its Critics." In *Mass Culture Revisited*, ed. Bernard Rosenberg and David Manning White, 233-48. New York: Van Nostrand, 1971.

Truffaut, François. *Hitchcock*. New York: Simon & Schuster, 1976.

Tucker, Larry A. "Television's Role regarding Alcohol Use among Teenagers." *Adolescence* 20 (Fall 1985): 593-98.

Tuska, Jon. *The American West in Film: Critical Approaches to the Western*. Westport, Conn.: Greenwood Press, 1985.

_____. *Dark Cinema: American Film Noir in Cultural Perspective*. Westport, Conn.: Greenwood Press, 1984.

Twitchell, James B. *Dreadful Pleasures: An Anatomy of Modern Horror*. New York: Oxford University Press, 1985.

Tyler, Parker. *The Hollywood Imagination*. New York: Creative Age, 1944.

_____. *Magic and Myth of the Movies*. New York: Holt, 1947.

_____. *Sex, Psyche, Etcetera in the Film*. New York: Horizon, 1969.

"The Under-25 Generation." *Time*, 6 Jan. 1987, p. 18.

Updike, John. "Introduction to *Soundings in Satanism*." In *Picked-Up Pieces*, 87-91. New York: Alfred A. Knopf, 1976.

U.S. Senate. Committee on Commerce, Science, and Transportation. *Contents of Music and the Lyrics of Records*. 99th Cong., 1st Sess., 19 Sept. 1985.

Van Hoose, John J. "The Impact of Television Usage on Emerging Adolescents." *High School Journal* 63 (Mar. 1980): 239-43.

Varnado, S. L. *Haunted Presence: The Numinous in Gothic Fiction*. Tuscaloosa: University of Alabama Press, 1987.

Vaughn, Susan. "Monster Movies?" *School Library Journal*, Oct. 1971, pp. 83-85.

Veblen, Thorstein. *The Theory of the Leisure Class: An Economic Study of Institutions*. New York: New American Library–Mentor Books, 1953.

Vogel, Amos. *Film as a Subversive Art*. New York: Random House, 1974.

Wagner, Geoffrey. *The Novel and the Cinema*. Rutherford, N.J.: Fairleigh Dickinson University Press, 1975.

Walker, Alexander. *Stanley Kubrick Directs*. New York: Harcourt Brace Jovanovich, 1971.

Wall, James M. "Art Speaks to Us of the Unity of Life" (editorial). *Christian Century*, 18-25 June 1986, pp. 571-72.

_____. *Church and Cinema: A Way of Viewing Film*. Grand Rapids: Eerdmans, 1971.

_____. "Owen Meany and the Presence of God" (editorial). *Christian Century*, 22 Mar. 1989, pp. 299-300.

_____. "Tracing the Yuppie from Adam 'til Now" (editorial). *Christian Century*, 2 Oct. 1985, pp. 851-52.

Waller, Gregory A., ed. *American Horrors: Essays on the Modern American Horror Film*. Urbana: University of Illinois Press, 1988.

Walters, Barry. "Like It or Not MTV Lives!" *Village Voice*, 2 June 1987, pp. 39-40.

Walters, Ronald G. *American Reformers, 1815-1860*. New York: Hill & Wang, 1978.

Ward, Bernie. "Music Video Grows Up." *Sky*, Apr. 1985, pp. 80-91.

Warnock, Mary. "A Fall from Grace," review of *Pornography and Sexual Violence: Evidence of the Links*, ed. Gary McCuen, and *The Question of Pornography:*

Research Findings and Policy Implications by Edward Donnerstein, Daniel Linz, and Steven Penrod. *Times Literary Supplement,* 12 Feb. 1988, p. 157.

Watkins, Bruce. "Television Viewing as a Dominant Activity of Childhood: A Developmental Theory of Television Effects." *Critical Studies in Mass Communication* 2 (Dec. 1985): 323-37.

Weintraub, Neil T. "Some Meanings Radio Has for Teenagers." *Journal of Broadcasting* 15 (Spring 1971): 147-52.

Wellmer, Albrecht. "Art and Industrial Production." *Telos* 57 (Fall 1983): 53-62.

_____. "On the Dialectic of Modernism and Postmodernism." *Praxis International* 4 (Jan. 1985): 337-62.

Welter, Barbara. "The Cult of True Womanhood, 1820-1860." *American Quarterly* 18 (1966): 151-74.

White, Armond. "Kidpix." *Film Comment* 21 (July-Aug. 1985): 9-15.

White, David Manning, and Richard Averson. *The Celluloid Weapon: Social Comment in the American Film.* Boston: Beacon Press, 1972.

Will, George. "Scary to Consider Horror Fixation." *Grand Rapids Press,* 12 Dec. 1989, p. A-17.

Williams, Christian. "MTV Is Rock around the Clock." *Philadelphia Inquirer,* 3 Nov. 1982, pp. D-1, D-4.

Williams, Don. *Bob Dylan: The Man, the Music, the Message.* Old Tappan, N.J.: Fleming H. Revell, 1985.

Williams, Raymond. *Television: Technology and Cultural Form.* New York: Schocken Books, 1975.

Williamson, Judith. *Consuming Passions: The Dynamics of Popular Culture.* New York: Marion Boyars, 1986.

Willis, Donald C. *The Films of Frank Capra.* Metuchen, N.J.: Scarecrow Press, 1974.

Wilson, John F., and Thomas P. Slavens. *Research Guide to Religious Studies.* Chicago: American Library Association, 1982.

Wisehart, Bob. "MTV Is Growing Up and Changing Format as Audience Matures." *Grand Rapids Press,* 23 July 1989, pp. H-1, H-6.

Wolff, Janet. *The Social Production of Art.* New York: St. Martin's Press, 1981.

Wolterstorff, Nicholas. *Art in Action: Toward a Christian Aesthetic.* Grand Rapids: Eerdmans, 1980.

Wood, Robin. *Arthur Penn.* New York: Praeger, 1969.

_____. *Hitchcock's Films.* New York: Castle, 1965.

Wright, Will. *Sixguns and Society: A Structural Study of the Western.* Berkeley: University of California Press, 1975.

Wyatt, Justin, and R. L. Rutsky. "High Concept: Abstracting the Postmodern." *Wide Angle* 10 (Fall 1988): 42-49.

"Z as in Zzz, or Zowie." *Newsweek,* 5 May 1967, p. 61.

Zappa, Frank. "The Oracle Has It All Psyched Out." *Life,* 28 June 1968, p. 85.

Zuidervaart, Lambert. "Realism, Modernism, and the Empty Chair." In *Postmodernism/Jameson/Critique,* ed. Douglas Kellner, 203-27. Washington: Maisonneuve Press, 1989.

_____. "The Social Significance of Autonomous Art: Adorno and Bürger." *Journal of Aesthetics and Art Criticism* 48 (Winter 1990): 61-77.

Index

ABC, 93
ABC–Paramount Records, 93
Abdul, Paula, 293
Abyss, The, 244
Adams, Henry, 262
Adorno, Theodor W., 114-18
Age of Indifference, The, 201
Alien, 243-44
Aliens, 244
All in the Family, 106-7
Almost Grown, 175
Alther, Lisa, 80
American Bandstand, 49, 68, 81, 180, 186, 286
American Express Corporation, 183
American Gigolo, 97
American Graffiti, 81, 108-9, 147, 220
American International Pictures (AIP), 91-92, 217-19, 222, 246
American Medical Association, 98
American Television and Communications, 133, 134
America's Most Wanted, 253
Ammirati & Puris Advertising Agency, 143
. . . *And Justice for All,* 172
Animal House, 223, 246, 252
Anka, Paul, 93
Apocalypse Now, 147, 220
Arkoff, Samuel, 217-18
Arnold, Matthew, 262
As Nasty As They Wanna Be, 280
Atlantic Records, 133
Aufderheide, Pat, 191, 193, 199
Avalon, Frankie, 92, 147

Bach, Johann S., 267
Back to the Future, 299
Baker, Anita, 133
Baker, Susan, 279
Ball, Lucille, 96

Band-Aid, 172
Bandwagon, The, 215
"Banned in the U.S.A.," 280
Barthes, Roland, 127
Batman, 95, 117, 125, 133, 138, 147, 213, 290, 296
"Be True to Your School," 150
Beach Boys, 150, 165-66, 168, 193
Beach Party, 219
Beatles, 93, 103-4, 147, 152, 153, 179, 292, 300
Bee Gees, 105
Beethoven, Ludwig van, 267
Bell, Clive, 286
Ben Hur, 216
Berry, Chuck, 90, 155, 170, 173, 175
Beverly Hillbillies, The, 105
BHC Inc., 133
Big Chill, The, 147
Bikini Beach, 219
Blackboard Jungle, 87, 91, 92, 216
Blades, Ruben, 153
Bon Jovi, Jon, 193, 197
Bonnie and Clyde, 94, 219
Boone, Pat, 60
Boorstin, Daniel, 48
Born in the U.S.A., 100-102
Born on the Fourth of July, 137
Boy Scouts, 34, 36, 56
Brando, Marlon, 216
Breakfast Club, The, 147, 229, 232
Broadcast News, 257
Bronson, Charles, 240
Brueggemann, Walter, 276
Buggles, 178-79
Bunker, Archie, 107
Burke, Kenneth, 99
Burns, George, 65
Buscaglia, Leo, 257
Bushnell, Horace, 29
Byrds, 294

Capitol record company, 89
Capital Cities/ABC, 136
Carson, Johnny, 65
"Catch a Wave," 165
CBS Inc., 136
CBS Records, 135
CBS Television Network, 105-6, 138
Chapman, Tracy, 133, 171
Chess Records, 90
Chess/MCA Records, 175
Christian Endeavor, 36
Cimino, Michael, 220
Cinemax, 133
Clark, Dick, 49, 63, 68, 81, 180, 286
Clean and Sober, 225
Close Encounters of the Third Kind, 220, 244
Cockburn, Bruce, 303-5
Cocks, Jay, 190
Cocoon, 244
Columbia Records, 89, 103
Columbia Pictures, 123
Columbia Pictures Entertainment, 135
Concert for Bangladesh, 172
Consumer Reports, 209
Copland, Aaron, 267
Coppola, Francis Ford, 125, 220
Corliss, Richard, 205, 207, 229-30
Cosby Show, The, 136
Creedence Clearwater Revival, 152
Crockett, Davy (almanacs), 27, 28
Crowe, Cameron, 227-28, 296
Cruise, Tom, 226, 246, 247, 248, 284
"Crumblin' Down," 172
Curtis, James, 51

Dallas, 133
"Dancing in the Dark," 101-2
"Darlington County," 101
Darnton, Robert, 274
Darwin, Charles, 262
Davenport, James, 19
Dean, James, 216, 218
Decca Records, 89
Deer Hunter, The, 220
Denisoff, R. Serge, 181, 207
"Diamonds Are a Girl's Best Friend," 96
Dickens, Charles, 267
Dickstein, Morris, 150, 234
Dick Van Dyke Show, The, 106
Dillard, R. H. W., 244
Dirty Dancing, 129, 147, 187, 222
"Dixie Fried," 166
Do the Right Thing, 117
Donnerstein, Edward, 236
"Downbound Train," 102
Dracula, 243

Driving Miss Daisy, 293
Duran Duran, 186
Dwight, Timothy, 24
Dylan, Bob, 151, 153, 175, 294
Dynasty, 125

Eagles, 151, 294
Eastwood, Clint, 231, 240
Easy Rider, 94, 219
"Eat Me Alive," 280
Ebert, Roger, 234
Edwards, Jonathan, 19, 24
Eisenhower, Dwight, 116, 150, 156, 157
Eisenstein, Sergei, 267
"Eleanor Rigby," 292
Elektra Entertainment, 133
Elkind, David, 257
Ellington, Duke, 151
Ellul, Jacques, 204
Emerson, Ralph Waldo, 26
Empire Strikes Back, The, 109
Enlighten Thy Daughter, 215
Epworth League, 36
E.T.: The Extra-Terrestrial, 220, 243-44, 270
Ewen, Stuart, 126
Exorcist, The (series), 244

Fabrikant, Geraldine, 134
Falcon Crest, 133
Farm Aid, 172
Fast Times at Ridgemont High, 227-29, 296
Fatal Attraction, 98
Ferris Bueller's Day Off, 86, 147, 158, 223, 230-31
Finney, Charles, 25-26, 29
Fitzgerald, F. Scott, 258, 267
Flashdance, 95, 147, 187, 206, 221
"Flashdance (What a Feeling)," 95
Fleetwood Mac, 153, 179
Flock of Seagulls, 186
Flynn, Errol, 108
"Fool on the Hill, The," 292
Footloose, 95, 147, 221-22
Fox Television Network, 253
Frankenstein, 243
Franklin, Benjamin, 16, 267
Freed, Alan, 90-91, 153
Fricke, David, 175
Friday the 13th, 233, 236, 242
Frith, Simon, 126, 162
Full Metal Jacket, 300
"Fun, Fun, Fun," 165-66
Funicello, Annette, 92, 147

Galbraith, John Kenneth, 116
Gallup, George, Jr., 59

Gans, Herbert, 281
Garbo, Greta, 85
Geertz, Clifford, 244, 269, 274
Gehr, Richard, 188, 207
General Electric, 136
General Motors, 124, 128
Ghostbusters II, 296
Gilbert, Eugene, 80
Gilbert, John, 85
Gitlin, Todd, 106-7
Glen Campbell Goodtime Hour, The, 105-6
Glory, 137, 293
"Glory Days," 101
Godfather, The, 220
Gold, Richard, 135, 136
Goldman, Alfred, 158
Good Morning, Vietnam, 147, 158-59
Goodman, Benny, 150
Gore, Tipper, 278-79, 287, 288, 302
Gortikov, Stanley, 279
Goudzwaard, Bob, 140, 302
Graduate, The, 94, 219-20, 257
Graham, Sylvester, 26-27
Grateful Dead, 151, 152
Grease, 94, 129, 147, 179, 220, 221, 252
Great Gatsby, The, 258
Green Acres, 105
Gremlins, 222, 235
Gremlins II, 222
Griffith, D. W., 267
Grossberg, Lawrence, 189, 190, 203
Gunsmoke, 105

"HA" TV Comedy Network, 183
Habermas, Jürgen, 123
Haley, Bill, 92, 159
Hall, G. Stanley, 34-35
Halloween, 222, 233
Hampton, Wayne, 157-58
Happy Days, 86, 129
Hard Day's Night, A, 147, 219
Harmetz, Aljean, 128
HBO Video, 133
Heaven's Gate, 220
Heckerling, Amy, 228
Hee Haw, 105
Help!, 147, 219
High Noon, 215
Hill Street Blues, 107
Hitchcock, Alfred, 267
Hoffman, Abbie, 172
Holly, Buddy, 153
Home Box Office, 133, 134, 212
"Hotel California," 294
Hughes, John, 86-87, 221, 223, 224, 229-32, 247, 248

Hurried Child, The, 257

"I Can't Get No Satisfaction," 150
"I Want to Hold Your Hand," 103
I Was a Teenage Werewolf, 91
"In God We Trust," 287-89
Indiana Jones and the Temple of Doom, 230, 238
Indiana Jones and the Last Crusade, 230, 296

Jackson, Janet, 293
Jackson, Michael, 95, 148, 186, 292
Jagger, Mick, 170, 171, 303
Jaws, 220
Jefferson Airplane, 152
Jeffersons, The, 107
Jones, Landon, 163, 220
Joplin, Janis, 96
Judas Priest, 280

Kanew, Jeff, 227
Kaplan, E. Ann, 169, 189, 203, 204
Katzman, Alan, 217
Katzman, Sam, 91
Keaton, Michael, 225
Kett, Joseph, 83-84
Kinflicks, 80
Knot's Landing, 133

L.A. Law, 107, 137
Lasch, Christopher, 105
Last Temptation of Christ, The, 266
Lauper, Cyndi, 96, 153
Led Zeppelin, 152
Lee, Spike, 248
Lennon, John, 157-58
Less than Zero, 225
Lester, Richard, 219
Lewis, Huey, 151
Licensing Company of America, 133
Lincoln, Abraham, 265
"Little Deuce Coupe," 150
Little Richard, 150
Live Aid, 172
Lodziak, Conrad, 57, 67
Londoner, David, 134-35
Looking Out for Number One, 257
Lorch, Sue, 202-3, 207-8
Los Lobos, 153
Lou Grant, 107
Love Me Tender, 216
Lowe, Rob, 224
Lucanio, Patrick, 241
Lucas, George, 108-10, 127-29, 212, 220, 273
Lucasfilm, 128

M*A*S*H, 106-7
MCA/UA Communications Company, 135
MGM, 215
MTM Enterprises, 107
Madonna, 96, 133, 148, 153, 224, 284
Man in the Gray Flannel Suit, The, 257
Mandel, Ernest, 119, 122
"Maniac," 95
Married . . . with Children, 123, 253
Mary Tyler Moore Show, The, 106-7
Marx, Karl, 45
Maude, 107
Mayberry R.F.D., 105
McCartney, Paul, 104
McLuhan, Marshall, 202
Mead, Margaret, 55-56, 62
Mellencamp, John (Cougar), 169, 172
Melville, Herman, 267
Merriwell, Frank, 34
Metallica, 172
Miami Vice, 125, 206
"Michelle," 292
Miller, Mark Crispin, 137
Milli Vanilli, 293
Mischief, 227
Mitchell, Elvis, 175
Monroe, Marilyn, 96
"Moondog's Rock and Roll Party," 91, 153
Morgan, Michael, 70
Morse, Samuel, 16
Motion Picture Association of America (MPAA), 91, 216, 222
Motion Picture Production Association, 220
Moviegoer, The, 262
"Mr. Tambourine Man," 294
Mulcahy, Russell, 205-6
Murdoch, Rupert, 121
Murphy, Eddie, 240
"My Hometown," 102
My Tutor, 227

NBC Television Network, 106, 136
National Coalition on Television Violence, 236
National Council of Churches, 233
National Family Association, 233
National PTA, 279
Nebraska, 100
Network, 257
New Line Cinema, 212
Nicholson, Jack (actor), 125, 213
Nicholson, Jack (AIP), 217-18
Nick at Nite, 182, 198
Nickelodeon, 182, 198

Night of the Living Dead, The, 242
Nightmare on Elm Street, 212, 222, 233, 235-36
9 1/2 Weeks, 206
"No Particular Place to Go," 155
"No Surrender," 101

Odysseus, 265
Odyssey, 116
Omen, The (series), 244
Ono, Yoko, 158
Otto, Rudolf, 243
Our Gang, 215
Ozzie and Harriet, 150

Palestrina, Giovanni da, 175
Paramount Pictures, 139, 223
Pareles, Jon, 189, 293
Parents' Music Resource Center (PMRC), 161-62, 278-79
Peale, Norman Vincent, 257
Percy, Walker, 262
Perkins, Carl, 166
Petticoat Junction, 105
Phyllis, 107
Pittman, Bob, 189-90, 192
Plato, 286
Platoon, 147
Polka Time Show, 93
Polskin, Howard, 192-93
Porky's, 212, 222, 223, 225, 227, 246, 247
Porky's II: The Next Day, 227, 247
Porky's Revenge, 227, 247
Predator, 221
Presley, Elvis, 49, 60, 90, 93, 147, 150, 153, 156-57, 159, 179, 216
Pretty in Pink, 229
Prince, 148, 161
Private Lessons, 227, 246
Private School, 227

Qintex Group, 135

Radecki, Thomas, 236-37
Raging Bull, 97
Raiders of the Lost Ark, 220, 230
Rambo (character), 248, 265
Rambo (film), 238, 299
Rambo: First Blood II, 221, 240, 247
Rambo III, 299
RCA, 89
Rebel without a Cause, 87, 91, 216
Recording Industry Association of America, 279
Red Skelton Hour, The, 105
Reed, Lou, 171

Reiss, Craig, 193
Return of the Jedi, 109
Revenge of the Nerds, The, 222, 227
Rhoda, 107
Ringer, Robert, 257
Ringwald, Molly, 229
Risky Business, 147, 226, 246, 247, 252
Robocop, 221
Robocop II, 221
"Rock around the Clock" (song), 92
Rock around the Clock (film), 217
"Rock Circus," 160
Rocky (character), 220, 248
Rocky (film), 220
Rogers, Fred, 235
"Roll over, Beethoven," 173
Rolling Stone, 54, 189
Rolling Stones, 93, 150, 152, 159, 170-71,
    172, 257, 303
Ronstadt, Linda, 153
Rooney, Mickey, 215
Rosemary's Baby, 244
Rothschild, Nancy, 70
Rumours, 179
Run DMC, 303
Running Man, 221
Rutsky, R. L., 207

Sarris, Andrew, 219
Saturday Night Fever, 94, 103, 104-5, 147,
    179, 220, 221
Say Anything, 296
"School Days," 155
Schrader, Paul, 97-98
Schwarzenegger, Arnold, 221, 231
Seerveld, Calvin, 287
Sgt. Pepper's Lonely Hearts Club Band, 103-4,
    300
Shales, Tom, 95, 96
Shakespeare, William, 174
Shames, Laurence, 139, 140
Shane, 215
Shocked, Michelle, 171
Showtime, 212
Singin' in the Rain, 215
Single European Act, 50
Siskel, Gene, 234
Sixteen Candles, 224, 229, 232
Sky Television, 121
Skyywalker Records, 280
Snider, Dee, 287, 288
Snow, Robert, 54, 166
Sölle, Dorothee, 141
Some Kind of Wonderful, 221
Sony, 123, 135
Sound of Music, The, 219

Spielberg, Steven, 97, 108, 220, 230, 235
Spring Break, 227
Springsteen, Bruce, 100-103, 110, 148, 155-
    56, 169, 196, 280
St. Elsewhere, 107
Stallone, Sylvester, 96, 220, 221, 231, 240
Star Wars, 108-9, 127-29, 212, 220, 221, 247,
    270
Stewart, Jimmy, 224
Storz, Todd, 89
"Strawberry Fields," 292
Stray Cats, 186
Stryper, 287, 289
Sun Records, 90
Superman, 244
"Surf City," 150
"Surfer Girl," 165
"Surfin' U.S.A.," 165
"Sweet Little Sixteen," 155

Tarratt, Margaret, 241
Taxi Driver, 97
Ten Commandments, The, 216
Tennent, Gilbert, 19
Texas Chainsaw Massacre, The, 242
thirtysomething, 137
Thriller (album), 95
"Thriller" (video), 95, 186
Tierney, Joan, 60, 68
Tiffany, 153
Tiger Beat, 54
Time Inc., 133
Time Warner Inc., 133-34, 136, 138
Top Gun, 147, 159, 187, 248
Total Recall, 221
Townshend, Pete, 172
Travolta, John, 104-5, 220
Trip, The, 219
Trudeau, Gary, 173
True North, 304
Tucker, 125
Twain, Mark, 148
Twentieth Century-Fox, 108, 121, 212, 216
21 Jump Street, 253
"Twist and Shout," 158
Twisted Sister, 287-89
Twitchell, James, 241-42
2 Live Crew, 280
2001: A Space Odyssey, 219

U2, 133, 148
"Under Cover of Night," 172
"Under the Blade," 287, 288-89
United Artists, 219, 220, 227, 228
Un-American Activities Committee, 214
Updike, John, 244, 245

Valens, Richie, 153
Variety, 80
Varnado, S. L., 243
Vega, Suzanne, 171
Viacom, Inc., 182, 183
Video Hits-1 (VH-1), 183, 193, 198
"Video Killed the Radio Star," 178
"Violence and Sexual Violence in Film,
    Television, Cable and Home Video"
    (National Council of Churches Report),
    233

Waiting for a Miracle (album), 304-5
"Waiting for a Miracle" (single), 304-5
Wall Street, 257
Warner-Annex Satellite Entertainment
    Company, 178
Warner Brothers Film Company, 133, 134
Warner Brothers Television, 133
Warner Cable Communications, 133, 134
Warner/Chappell Music, 133
Warner Communications Inc., 133, 135
Warner Home Video, 133
Warner Records, 94, 133
Wayne, John, 96, 108, 224
WEA Corporation, 133
Weld, Theodore, 27

Welk, Lawrence, 93
West Side Story, 252
Wexler, Norman, 104
What Price Innocence?, 215
Whitefield, George, 19, 21, 22
Who, the, 152, 172
Widmer, Kinsley, 52-53
Wild Angels, The, 219
Wild One, The, 91, 216, 252
Wilder, Thornton, 265
Wildmon, Donald, 233
Will, George, 234, 238
Williamson, Judith, 140
Wilson, Sloan, 257
Winning through Intimidation, 257
Wizard of Oz, The, 109
Wolfman Jack, 63
Wood, Robert D., 105-6, 108
Woodstock, 94, 172
Wyatt, Justin, 207

YMCA, 34, 36
"Yesterday," 292

Zappa, Frank, 92, 162, 278-79, 302
Zapped!, 227

Acknowledgments

The authors and publisher gratefully acknowledge permission to quote from the following musical compositions:

Excerpt from "Dancing in the Dark" by Bruce Springsteen. Used with permission of Bruce Springsteen. Copyright © 1984 by ASCAP.

Excerpt from "Dixie Fried" by Howard Griffin and Carl Lee Perkins. Copyright © 1956 by Hi Lo Music, Carl Perkins Music, Inc., and Unichappell Music, Inc.

Excerpt from "The Heart of Rock and Roll" by Huey Lewis and Johnny Colla. Copyright © 1984 by Hulex Music (ASCAP). All rights reserved.

Excerpt from "Kids" from the musical Bye-Bye Birdie. Copyright © 1960 (renewed 1988) by Lee Adams and Charles Straus-Strada Music.

Excerpt from "Mr. Tambourine Man" by Bob Dylan, copyright © 1965 by Warner Bros. Inc. All rights reserved. Used by permission.

Excerpt from "No Particular Place to Go" by Chuck Berry. Copyright © 1964 by Arc Music Corporation. Reprinted by permission. All rights reserved.

"Under the Blade" by Dee Snider. Copyright © 1985 by Snidest Music Co. Inc. Used with permission of Zomba Enterprises. All rights reserved.

"Waiting for a Miracle" from the album entitled Waiting for a Miracle. Words and music by Bruce Cockburn. Copyright © 1986 by Golden Mountain Music Corporation. Used by permission.